INTRODUCTION TO
Microsoft Office 2016

by

Kathleen M. Austin

Lorraine N. Bergkvist

Publisher
The Goodheart-Willcox Company, Inc.
Tinley Park, Illinois
www.g-w.com

PREFACE

In today's competitive job market, well-developed employability skills are required—especially those associated with computer and technology usage. The ability to use Microsoft Office is a necessary job-specific skill for the 21st-century workplace. By studying *Introduction to Microsoft Office 2016*, you will master basic skills needed to be successful in using Microsoft Office, as well as learn key principles and concepts about information technology.

Introduction to Microsoft Office 2016 will prepare you for Microsoft Office Specialist (MOS) certification in Word, Excel, PowerPoint, and Access as well as the Key Applications exam for IC3 Digital Literacy Certification. Earning industry-recognized certification proves that you have the skills needed on the job, and this distinction can put you in a competitive situation in the workplace.

This text is presented in a logical, conceptual progression. You begin by learning about the basics of information technology and then progress to Microsoft Office applications. Each chapter is designed in a matter that is easy to read, follow, and understand. Figures, photos, and illustrations help provide clarity, understanding, and comprehension. Hands-On Examples featured in the chapters enable you to practice the skills presented in an easy and intuitive manner.

On completing this book, you will be able to:

- describe how technology has evolved from early computers through modern-era cloud computing;
- identify malicious forms of software and develop strategies for staying safe online;
- understand how files and folders interact with each other in a Windows operating system;
- identify common elements and features of Microsoft Office software;
- use Microsoft Word to create formal and informal documents, some of which may include references such as footnotes, endnotes, and bibliographies;
- create effective Microsoft PowerPoint presentations that include animations, transitions, and media;
- build user-friendly spreadsheets with Microsoft Excel;
- perform mathematical and logical functions in Microsoft Excel; and
- create and maintain a Microsoft Access database by entering data manually and importing data.

ABOUT THE AUTHORS

Kathleen M. Austin was a senior lecturer in the School of Information Arts and Technologies at the University of Baltimore. She has participated in the development of many educational multimedia projects. She has authored, coauthored, or contributed to several textbooks, including Consumer Mathematics and Mathematics of the World of Work. She holds a Master of Science degree in Computer Science from Johns Hopkins University and a Doctor of Communications Design from the University of Baltimore as well as IC3 certification.

Lorraine N. Bergkvist was an Adjunct Professor at the University of Baltimore providing instruction in Visual Basic programming, database implementation, and web-page creation. She is also the owner of Kingsville Résumé Center, which provides professional résumé-writing services as well as consulting and editing in the information technology field. She developed the curriculum and taught the Introduction to Technology course at the University of Baltimore and the College of Notre Dame of Maryland. She holds a Bachelor of Science degree from Trinity University, a Master of Education degree from Towson University, and IC3 certification. She has received several scholarships and grants in the technology field.

STUDENT RESOURCES

Student Text

Introduction to Microsoft Office 2016 is a technology-driven resource that introduces students to information technology basics and provides in-depth coverage of Microsoft Office applications. It aligns to the objectives for Microsoft Office Specialist and IC3 Digital Literacy Key Applications certification exams. By studying *Introduction to Microsoft Office 2016*, students can jump-start their careers and better position themselves as desirable employment candidates.

G-W Online Textbook

The G-W Online Textbook platform gives students instant access to the textbook and resources with browser-based devices including iPads, notebooks, PCs, and Mac computers. Textbook pages look exactly the same as the printed text, and all materials are located on a convenient online bookshelf and accessible at home, at school, or on the go. A linked table of contents provides quick access to each chapter. A search tool enables users to locate a specific topic or word within the text. Students can enlarge or compress a page or print individual pages for off-line reading.

G-W Learning Companion Website

The G-W Learning companion website is a study reference that contains e-flash cards, vocabulary exercises, interactive quizzes, and more! Accessible from any digital device, the G-W Learning companion website complements the textbook and is available at no charge. Visit www.g-wlearning.com/informationtechnology/.

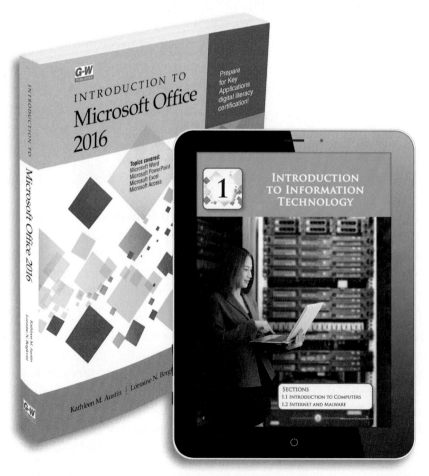

Instructor's Resource CD

One resource provides instructors with time-saving preparation tools such as answer keys, lesson plans, correlation charts to standards, and other teaching aids.

Online Instructor Resources

Online Instructor Resources provide all the support needed to make preparation and classroom instruction easier than ever. Available in one accessible location, support materials include answer keys, lesson plans, solution files for projects, and more! Online Instructor Resources are available as a subscription and can be accessed at school or at home.

LMS Integration

Integrate Goodheart-Willcox content within your Learning Management System for a seamless user experience for both you and your students. LMS-ready content in Common Cartridge format facilitates single sign-on integration and gives you control of student enrollment and data. With a Common Cartridge integration, you can access the LMS features and tools you are accustomed to using and G-W course resources in one convenient location—your LMS.

In order to provide a complete learning package for you and your students, Common Cartridge by G-W includes the Online Textbook and Online Instructor Resources. When you incorporate G-W content into your courses via Common Cartridge, you have the flexibility to customize and structure the content to meet the educational needs of your students. You may also choose to add your own content to the course.

PREPARE FOR THE FUTURE

Almost every aspect of life is affected by information technology in some way: video games, television shows, banking and financial processes, and even research papers and reports. Possessing basic skills in information technology, including the ability to use Microsoft Office applications, is an important key to success. *Introduction to Microsoft Office 2016* prepares students for a competitive work environment through the development of technology skills.

Certification Preparation

This text prepares students for Microsoft Office Specialist (MOS) certification as well as the Key Applications exam for IC3 Digital Literacy Certification. Earning industry-recognized certification is important because it affirms that the certificate holder has met the standards for performance in a specific skill area. **Certification objectives** are listed at the beginning of each chapter to engage students and highlight important points presented in the content, and they are noted within the chapter where the material is covered.

Learning Goals

At the beginning of each chapter, a list of learning goals guides students as they read the material presented. Each goal is aligned with content headings, as well as with the summary at the end of the chapter. This alignment provides a logical flow through each page of the material so that students may build on individual knowledge as they progress through the chapters.

Review

It is important that students assess what they learn as they progress through the textbook. Multiple *formative assessment* opportunities are provided to confirm learning:

- A section review includes **Check Your Understanding** questions and **Build Your Vocabulary** activities to provide an opportunity for students to review content presented in each major section of the textbook. By completing these activities, students will be able to demonstrate their understanding of computing-related terminology.

- Each chapter opens with a **pretest** and concludes with a **posttest**. The pretest will help students evaluate their prior knowledge of the chapter content. The posttest will help them evaluate what they have learned after studying the chapter.

- A **Chapter Test** of 15 review questions highlights basic concepts presented in the chapter and provides a comprehensive self-assessment opportunity for students to evaluate their understanding of material presented.

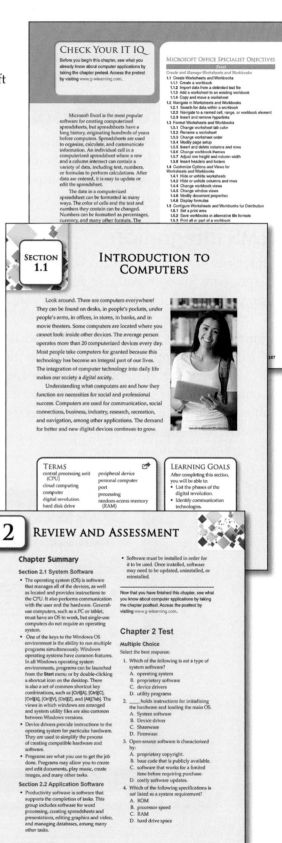

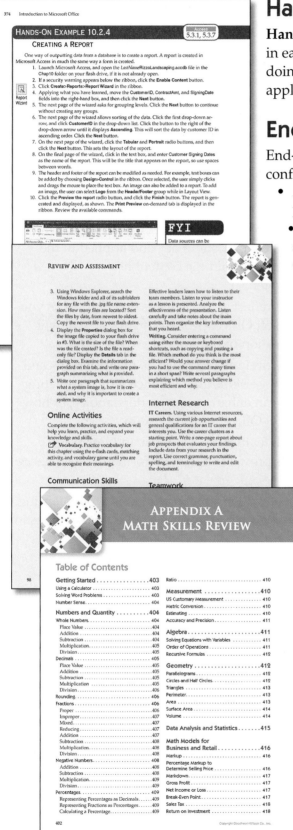

Hands-On Examples

Hands-On Examples guide students through concepts covered in each section so they can learn skills by reading and by doing. These activities provide an opportunity for independent application of the skills at the point of introduction of content.

End-of-Chapter

End-of-chapter materials provide opportunities for review, confirmation of learning, and applications of concepts.

- A concise **Summary** reiterates the chapter learning goals and provides a brief review of the content for student reference.
- **Application and Extension of Knowledge** activities challenge students to self-reflect what they learned in the chapter while drawing from their own ideas, experiences, and projects.
  - **Online Vocabulary Activities** provide an opportunity for students to identify important vocabulary.
  - **Teamwork** activities provide opportunities for collaboration and cooperative learning. This experience will help students learn how to interact with others in a productive manner.
  - **Internet Research** challenges students to put their Internet and research skills to work. Focusing on a specific topic to extract and analyze information helps students develop employability skills.
  - **Communication Skills** provide opportunities for students to demonstrate the literacy and career skills they have mastered. Students need good reading, writing, speaking, and listening skills in today's workplace.
  - The **Capstone Project** at the conclusion of each chapter guides students through creating a comprehensive, spiraling project based on a selected career path. Data files are available on the G-W Learning companion website that may be downloaded and completed as part of the capstone project. The website is located at www.g-wlearning.com/informationtechnology/.

Appendices

Two appendices are included at the end of the text. Appendix A, Math Skills Review, provides an overview of number sense, algebra, geometry, and statistics, as well as examples for each. Capitalization, Punctuation, and Number Expression are covered in Appendix B, which provides instruction for appropriate usage of capital letters, internal and external punctuation parks, and usage of numbers as text and figures. These appendices can serve as reference as students complete assignments in the chapters.

HOW TO USE THIS TEXT

The *Introduction to Microsoft Office 2016* textbook will help you learn, understand, and master Microsoft Office. The text approaches each program individually to focus learning on important aspects and uses for Word, PowerPoint, Excel, and Access.

Introduction to Microsoft Office 2016 is divided into 10 chapters. The text begins with general concepts about the information technology industry, such as the digital revolution and the evolution of computers. This is followed by an introduction to system and application software, file management, and common features found in Microsoft Office programs. The remaining chapters are dedicated to the instruction of Microsoft Word, PowerPoint, Excel, and Access to prepare you for the Microsoft Office Specialist certification exam, as well as the Key Applications exam for IC3 Digital Literacy Certification.

As you progress through the chapters, try to relate each topic to how it applies to developing your personal skill level. By following these suggestions, you can make the most of your Microsoft Office learning experience.

- Read the outcomes listed in the chapter opener. Each outcome is tied directly to the headings within the content. In addition, they are repeated in the chapter summary and applied in the end-of-chapter activities. The connection of outcomes throughout the content helps you focus and apply important information as you read each chapter.

- Pay attention to the figures. The images in the chapters reflect actual screens you will see as you begin using the Windows operating system and Microsoft Office. By studying these, you will extend your learning and improve retention and application of the content.

- Complete the Hands-On Examples. These activities are designed to replicate relevant skills and are located in close proximity to the content in which those skills are referenced. By completing these examples as you encounter them in the text, you can enhance your understanding of how to perform necessary functions covered on the Microsoft Office Specialist exam.

- Note the special features throughout the chapters. Each feature adds realism and interest to enhance learning. Ethics, Green Tech, and Career Skills provide valuable information to enhance your career preparation.

- Complete the end-of-chapter activities. By doing so, you will be able to self-assess your learning. This self-reflection is important to helping you determine your knowledge, skills, and abilities in Microsoft Office.

REVIEWERS

Goodheart-Willcox Publisher would like to thank the following teachers and administrators who reviewed selected chapters and contributed valuable input to this edition of *Introduction to Microsoft Office 2016*.

Lorie S. Atkinson
Technology Teacher
Elgin High School
Elgin, TX

Deborah Boone
Medical Office Administration & Office
   Administration Department Chair, School of
   Business
Halifax Community College
Weldon, NC

Cory Cooksey
Computer Science & Information System
   Department Chair
North Central Missouri College
Trenton, MO

Dr. Tristan Davison
Associate Professor, College of Business,
   Engineering and Technology
Daytona State College
Daytona Beach, FL

Kevin J. Grump
CTE Teacher
Oceanside High School
Oceanside, CA

Sandra Jaworski
Business Department Chair
Jeffersontown High School
Louisville, KY

Michael (Mike) Kane
Senior Lecturer
Rochester Institute of Technology
Rochester, NY

Brenda Siebold
Computer Applications Instructor
Military Academic Services
Barton Community College
Fort Riley, KS

Dr. Michelle Taylor
Project Manager
Mississippi State University
Starkville, MS

Michael E. Valdez
Supervisor Vocational Instruction
CA Department of Corrections and
   Rehabilitation
Office of Correctional Education
Sacramento, CA

Colleen L.B. Webb
Adjunct Faculty
Baker College Clinton Township/Port Huron
Clinton Township, MI

Elisha C. Wohleb
Associate Clinical Professor
Auburn University
Auburn, AL

BRIEF CONTENTS

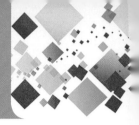

CONTENTS

HANDS-ON EXAMPLES

Chapter 8
Spreadsheet Software

Chapter 9
Advanced Spreadsheet Uses

Chapter 10
Database Software

1 INTRODUCTION TO INFORMATION TECHNOLOGY

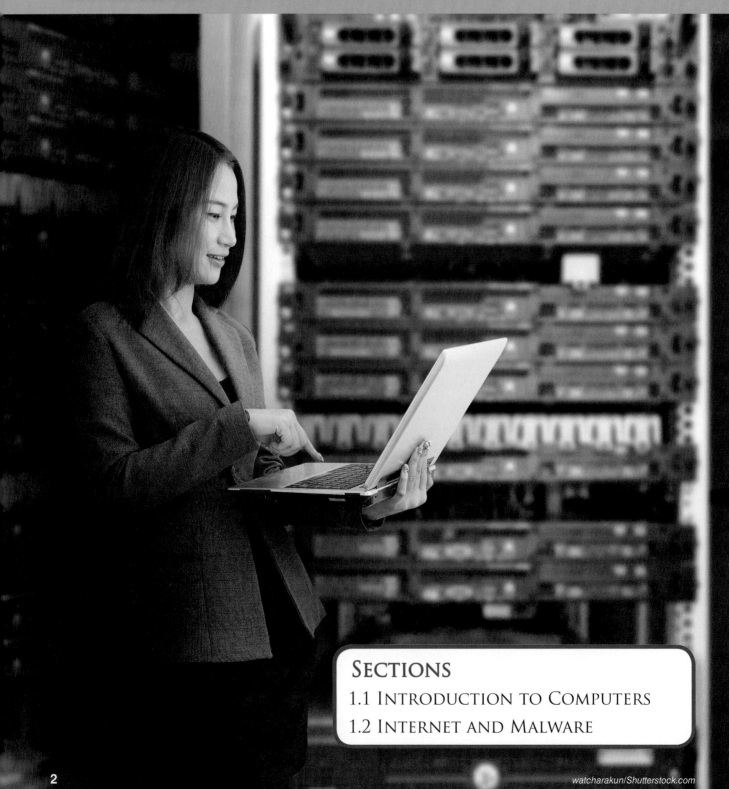

SECTIONS

1.1 INTRODUCTION TO COMPUTERS

1.2 INTERNET AND MALWARE

Most young adults have been using computers since they could read and write or, in many cases, even before then. Computers are used to complete school assignments, conduct business, and—most of all—communicate. Most people are computer *users*; they know how to *operate* these devices. However, to be computer *literate* you must understand the details of how computers work and the impact computers have on your life and career. Knowing how to use Microsoft Office applications is only a small part of being computer literate.

This chapter provides an overview of important topics in the field of information technology (IT). You may already know some of the facts, but some facts may be new to you. You will learn about computers, their historical time line, and the various ways in which they can be categorized. Additionally, information is included about the Internet and problems, such as malware, faced by information technology professionals and society as a whole.

INTRODUCTION TO COMPUTERS

Look around. There are computers everywhere! They can be found on desks, in people's pockets, under people's arms, in offices, in stores, in banks, and in movie theaters. Some computers are located where you cannot look: inside other devices. The average person operates more than 20 computerized devices every day. Most people take computers for granted because this technology has become an integral part of our lives. The integration of computer technology into daily life makes our society a *digital society*.

Understanding what computers are and how they function are necessities for social and professional success. Computers are used for communication, social connections, business, industry, research, recreation, and navigation, among other applications. The demand for better and new digital devices continues to grow.

wavebreakmedia/Shutterstock

TERMS

central processing unit (CPU)
cloud computing
computer
digital revolution
hard disk drive
hardware
input
mainframe computer
motherboard
output

peripheral device
personal computer
port
processing
random-access memory (RAM)
read-only memory (ROM)
server
supercomputer
volume label

LEARNING GOALS

After completing this section, you will be able to:

- List the phases of the digital revolution.
- Identify communication technologies.
- List the categories of computers.
- Identify the basic parts and functions of a computer.

Digital Revolution

The field of information technology (IT) includes all of the work done with computers, from the design and installation of hardware and software to the maintenance of these systems. The state of the art of computing today is ever changing with new and innovative additions, such as shown in Figure 1-1. These changes are part of the digital revolution. The **digital revolution** is the ever-expanding progression of technical, economic, and cultural changes brought about by computers. It has gone through four phases:

- giant computers
- personal computers
- networked computers
- cloud computing

A **computer** is a device that handles input, processes data, stores data, and produces usable output according to sets of stored instructions.

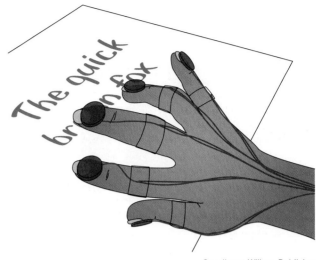

Goodheart-Willcox Publisher

Figure 1-1. An innovative method for data input to a computer uses sensors on the fingers to determine input.

Giant Computers

The first phase of the digital revolution occurred from the 1940s through the 1960s and is characterized by the use of giant computing machines. These machines were physically so large that they had to be located in special facilities, as shown in Figure 1-2. The computers required highly skilled technicians to run even simple reports. Programs had to be small and extremely efficient.

Personal Computers

The second phase of the digital revolution began with the advent of personal computers (PCs) in the 1970s and lasted through the early 1990s. PCs were small and inexpensive enough to be used in households and businesses. They were complete computers that could run programs all by themselves. The first PCs were only capable of displaying one color on the monitor screen against a black background.

Networked Computers

The popularity of personal computers only gradually increased until the mid-1990s. It was at this time when software became what most of the population could consider user-friendly. Also at this time, computer networks became interconnected through a large system of network

> # FYI
>
> *Data processing* was the term used from the 1940s to the 1970s to describe the computer operations. Today, this is known as *information management*.

US Army Photo

Figure 1-2. Programmers Elizabeth (Betty) Jean Jennings and Frances (Fran) Bilas preparing for the public unveiling of ENIAC. ENIAC was the first electronic digital computer.

Arjuna Kodisinghe/Shutterstock.com

Figure 1-3. Computer networks can be very large and may contain many servers to manage data.

hubs and switches, as shown in Figure 1-3. This marks the beginning of the third phase of the digital revolution, which would last through the early 2000s.

Internet

The Internet began as a project in the 1960s called ARPANET. The network was known as the wide area network (WAN). It was connected to the National Science Foundation network (NSFNET) in 1990, and in 1995 the last restrictions on its commercial use were eliminated. The Internet will be discussed in further detail later in this chapter.

World Wide Web

The World Wide Web (WWW), or the web, is a part of the Internet. The web *uses* the Internet, but the Internet and the web are not the same thing. The World Wide Web was launched in 1991. The World Wide Web was conceived and developed by Sir Tim Berners-Lee. The World Wide Web will be discussed in further detail later in this chapter.

Mobile Computers

Mobile devices are commonplace today. These are small, typically handheld digital devices that rely on satellite, microwave, and cellular transmissions for data transfer. Examples of mobile devices are cellular telephones and smartphones, tablet computers, e-book readers, and global positioning system (GPS) devices.

Cloud Computing

The fourth and current phase of the digital revolution began in the early 2000s when cloud computing appeared. **Cloud computing** involves storing and retrieving data from Internet-based spaces. Collectively, these spaces are called *the cloud*. The cloud is useful for backing up and sharing data, but it also made possible running a program that was not installed on the local computer. The cloud involves shared resources among computers.

Communication Technologies

Computer technology has made it possible for those with access to digital communication devices to stay in touch with others 24 hours a day. As a result, communication methods are changing at a rapid pace.

Speed

In the past, a person had to wait days for the post office to carry written communication in the form of a letter. The Internet has reduced waiting time for written communication to nanoseconds. Even spoken communication is carried over the Internet in real-time. *Bandwidth* is

FYI

The concept of cloud computing dates to the 1950s. Functional precursors to the cloud began appearing in the 1990s.

a measure of the amount of data that can travel on a communication system. Just as a large artery can carry more blood cells than a small capillary, a high-bandwidth Internet connection can carry more data at one time than a low-bandwidth connection.

Reach

Communication programs that share video, voice, and data are accessible to anyone with a computer or smartphone and an Internet connection. In developing countries, people who may have never owned a radio or television now often have smartphones. These devices allow global communication, which opens a wide view of world culture.

Advantages

The amount, intimacy, and power of computer-based communication have been enormously affected by social media through innovations such as Facebook, Twitter, Tumblr, and LinkedIn, as shown in Figure 1-4. Participation in Facebook has been described as an ongoing virtual reality show where the users are the entertainers as well as the audience.

Disadvantages

Internet-based communication has led to an epidemic of crime, including fraud, and unethical behavior, such as cyberbullying. In many cases, cyberbullying can be a crime, but it is always unethical behavior. E-mail scams such as phishing seek to steal a person's identity and use

Architect
An architect uses information technology in every phase of design and presentation. The use of 3D modeling software to design and develop structures, as well as the use of databases to identify the proper materials for strength and stability, is an ongoing process for architects. Architects often use word processing software to create documents that will serve as communication with the clients and the building contractors. They may also communicate using e-mail, the Internet, and by smartphones.

Pieter Beens/Shutterstock.com

Figure 1-4. Smartphones have been a key part of the growth of social media, which itself greatly affected computer-based communication.

FYI

There are many ways to classify computers. Other classifications or applications include the SETI project, ROCKS clusters and cluster computing, and the DWave quantum computer.

it to commit fraud, which is a form of theft. Computer viruses and other malware can also be transmitted by Internet-based communication.

Categories of Computers

Historically, computers were grouped in one of three categories based on size: mainframes, minicomputers, or microcomputers. A mainframe is a very large high-processing computer that is used for big computing needs. A minicomputer is a computer of midrange size and performance between a microcomputer and a mainframe. A microcomputer is a computer based on a microchip for the CPU.

The distinctions between the historical categories have become blurred so much that the term minicomputer is rarely used today. This is because the capability of microcomputers, smallest of the three, has significantly expanded. Today, computers are usually categorized based on usage and cost as well as size:

- supercomputers
- mainframes
- servers
- personal computers and mobile devices

Note that these are the categories of computers, which should not be confused with the four phases of the digital revolution.

Supercomputers

Supercomputers have processing power that can handle complex jobs beyond the scope of other computer systems. Supercomputers are the fastest computers. Examples of projects undertaken by supercomputers include breaking codes, molecular modeling, atmospheric modeling, and climate predicting. The tasks analyze enormous amounts of data. Supercomputers can be used to simulate global weather patterns, results from earthquakes, and consequences from nuclear explosions. Scientists and engineers are the primary users of supercomputers.

The speed of supercomputers is usually measured in floating point operations per second (FLOPS). *Floating point* means numbers containing decimal point fractions. Figure 1-5 shows the constantly increased capability of supercomputers over the years.

Mainframes

Mainframe computers provide centralized storage, processing, and overall management of large amounts of data. While supercomputers are used for crunching data and numbers, mainframes are used to process and store business transactions. The speed of mainframes is measured in millions of instructions per second (MIPS).

Servers

A server is a special type of computer found on a network. A **server** stores data and responds when requested by other computers in the network. It allows other computers on the network to share programs and

Ethics

Computer Ethics

While you are at work or school, it is important to be respectful in your use of computer equipment. The computer is available for your use as a tool for research or to accomplish a task. It is unethical to use the computer to download copyrighted material or harass others.

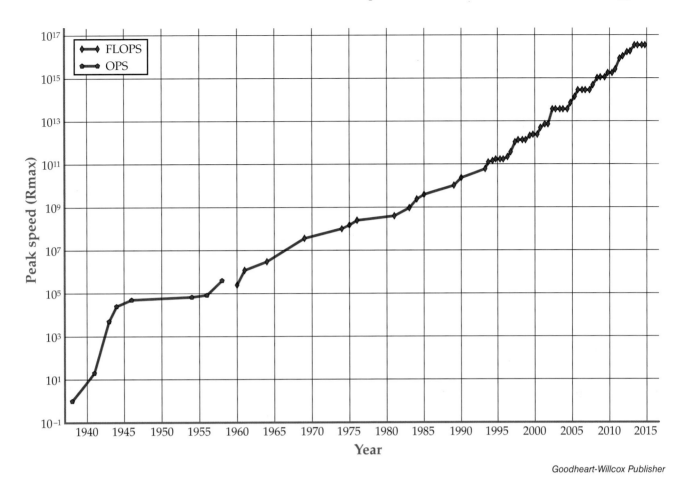

Goodheart-Willcox Publisher

Figure 1-5. The capability of supercomputers has constantly increased over the years.

data. Sharing data makes it possible for many users on the network to see and access each other's information. A server generally handles backing up the stored data for all users so that data can be retrieved if a part of the system malfunctions.

Personal Computers and Mobile Devices

A **personal computer** is a processing device designed to meet the needs of an individual user, whether in the home, a business, or a school. It has a screen, a mouse, and a keyboard, as shown in Figure 1-6, and is generally connected to the Internet. Personal computers vary in their speed, size, and portability. They come in the forms of desktop models, laptops and related models, and mobile devices.

Basic Parts and Functions of a Computer

No matter the size or use for a computer, all computers contain the same basic types of components. **Hardware** is the physical components

Venus Angel/Shutterstock.com

Figure 1-6. A personal computer has a screen, mouse, and keyboard in addition to the CPU unit.

of the computer. Generally speaking, there are four main hardware components to a computer:

- input device
- memory
- processor
- output device

This is the minimum hardware for a computer. If a device does not have all four components, it is not a computer.

All computers are also basically the same in terms of functions, which are parallel to the basic hardware. A computer is defined by these four basic capabilities or functions:

- accept data input
- store data
- process data
- produce output

This is the minimum functional definition of a computer. If a device does not have all four functions, it is not a computer. A computer with its attached devices is called a computer system.

Attached devices that are not critical to computer operation are called **peripheral devices**, or *peripherals.*

Input

The **input** function translates data from the human world into computer data. Input can be described as data that are entered, scanned, or otherwise sent to a computer system. The data can originate from a person, the environment, or another computer. Examples of input are:

- adding words and numbers into documents;
- setting the temperature in a thermostat containing an embedded computer;
- activating a sensor in a computerized house alarm system;
- scanning a photograph;
- recording video with a camcorder;
- loading an MP3 file; and
- sending an e-mail or tweet.

An input device provides the computer with data on which it can act, as shown in Figure 1-7. The input device is the basis of interaction with a computer. Data can be entered from a keyboard, key pad, touch pad, mouse, scanner, camera, microphone, or game controller.

Shetsoff Women Girls/Shutterstock.com

Figure 1-7. This musician is using several input devices, including a mouse, computer keyboard, and MIDI music keyboard.

Storage

Storage is where data are kept by the computer so the information can be viewed, played, or otherwise used. The most familiar storage locations are the computer system's memory and hard disk drive, but flash drives and other forms of external storage devices are also common.

Storage devices are usually automatically named by the operating system. The device drive name is a letter followed by a colon. For example, C: is the primary hard drive, and it is referred to as the "C drive." Additionally, the name of the device itself is called the **volume label** or *volume name*.

Memory is the part of the computer that stores information for immediate processing. It stores the code for the computer programs, data used for the programs, results from executing the programs, and much more. Some memory is *involatile*, which means it is kept even when the computer is turned off. The basic startup program in a computer is stored in persistent memory. Other memory is *volatile*, which means it is erased when the power is off. There are two types of memory:

- random-access memory
- read-only memory

Random-Access Memory

Random-access memory (RAM) is memory that can be changed. This hardware holds instructions that the processor can immediately use. RAM is what most users think of when the word *memory* is mentioned.

As various programs are used, the constantly changing instructions are loaded into RAM. When the computer is turned off, all data and instructions that were stored in RAM are erased. Therefore, RAM is volatile memory. It is just a temporary holding area for data and instructions.

The physical chips that hold RAM look like small black rectangles with many pairs of metal feet, as shown in Figure 1-8.

Radu Bercan/Shutterstock.com

Figure 1-8. The green board is a RAM unit, which holds many RAM chips. The RAM chips are black in this example. The metal feet are hidden because the chips are surface mounted.

Read-Only Memory

Read-only memory (ROM) is memory that cannot be changed. ROM contains static information the computer will always need to operate and that cannot be subject to variation. ROM holds its information even if the computer is turned off, which means it is involatile memory.

Measuring Memory

The capacity of memory is measured in how many bytes it can hold. One byte holds enough information for one character. Figure 1-9 describes the prefixes for various quantities of bytes and the approximate data storage capacity.

Storage Media

Magnetic media are made of iron oxide-coated disks that can be selectively magnetized to store on-off signals. The computer's internal hard disk drive is the most common example of a magnetic medium. A **hard disk drive**, or *hard drive*, is a sealed unit that contains a stack of individual disks, or platters, which are magnetic media that rotate at a very high speed, as shown in Figure 1-10. Solid-state storage media, such as flash drives, is based on circuitry rather than magnetic media.

Metric Symbols	Number of Bytes*	Equivalent Sizes
byte	1	One character.
kilobyte (KB)	1 thousand bytes	One short letter or memo.
megabyte (MB)	1 million bytes	A typical high-resolution photo is about 2.5MB. The information in 40 paperback books (a stack about three feet high) is about 50MB.
gigabyte (GB)	1 billion bytes	One hour of a feature film is about 1.5GB. The information in 800 paperback books (a stack about 650 feet high) is about 20GB.
terabyte (TB)	1 trillion bytes	The information in 800,000 paperback books (a stack about 10 miles high) is about 1TB. Library of Congress archives contain 160TB.
petabyte (PB)	1,000 terabytes	Seventy-seven million CDs each containing 700MB is 50PB.
exabyte (EB)	1,000 petabytes	All words ever spoken by human beings are about 5EB.
zettabyte (ZB)	1,000 exabytes	The information in 174 newspapers received daily by every person on Earth is about 4ZB.

*Note: there are actually 1,024 bytes in a kilobyte, so these values are rounded.

Goodheart-Willcox Publisher

Figure 1-9. Quantities of bytes and approximate storage capacity.

Platters

Read head

Hellen Sergeyeva/Shutterstock.com

Figure 1-10. A hard disk drive consists of multiple platters. The unit is enclosed, but the cover has been removed in this photo.

HANDS-ON EXAMPLE 1.1.1

STORAGE DEVICE NAMES AND VOLUME LABELS

The device drive name for installed storage devices can be easily identified using Windows Explorer. Rewritable storage media, such as a flash drive, can have its volume label changed.

1. Open Windows Explorer. This can be done by double-clicking the **Computer** icon on the desktop or by right-clicking on the **Start** menu button and clicking **Open Windows Explorer** in the shortcut menu.
2. Locate the left-hand pane in Windows Explorer. This contains a tree that shows the devices, folders, and files accessible to the computer, as shown.

Folder tree ⟶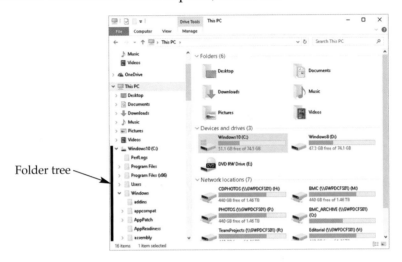

3. In the left-hand pane, locate the primary hard disk drive. What letter is assigned to this storage device?
4. Are there any other storage devices attached to the computer? Notice the icon in the tree for each attached device represents the type of device. What are the letters assigned to other storage devices?
5. Insert your flash drive into one of the USB ports on the computer.
6. In Windows 10, click the slide-in alert that indicates to choose what happens with removable drives. The autoplay dialog box is displayed. In Windows 8 and Windows 7, the autoplay dialog box should automatically appear. Make note of the drive letter for the flash drive shown in the dialog box.
7. Click **Open folder to view files** in the autoplay dialog box. Windows Explorer is launched.
8. Locate the flash drive in the left-hand pane. It will have the same drive letter that was displayed in the autoplay dialog box.
9. Right-click on the flash drive in Windows Explorer, and click **Rename** in the shortcut menu. The volume label for the drive becomes editable. Notice the current name is highlighted in blue. This means the text is selected.
10. Using the keyboard, enter the name MS-OFFICE.
11. Press the [Enter] key to rename the volume label. This flash drive will hold your notes from this course.

Processing

Processing of the data takes place between the input and the output. **Processing** is the transformation of input data and acting on those data.

In principle, processing is very simple: additions and decisions. These two instructions are used to load programs and data, to follow instructions, and to produce output. More complex actions are developed using these two basic functions. The result is called the *instruction set* for a central processing unit. The basic instruction set is different for each central processing unit.

RomboStudio/Shutterstock.com

Figure 1-11. A CPU being inserted into a socket on the motherboard.

Central Processing Unit

The **central processing unit (CPU)** is the device that fetches coded instructions, decodes them, and then runs or executes them. The CPU is also called a *microprocessor* or *chip*. Although it is about the size of a thumbnail, the CPU contains billions of circuits. See Figure 1-11. Due to their constant execution of actions, CPUs generate a lot of heat. To help prevent the CPU from overheating, fans are often mounted directly above them to help circulate air. Many computers contain multiple CPUs.

The CPU controls all jobs performed by the computer's other parts. The user runs a program, and its instructions set the CPU's list of jobs. The CPU has two primary components: the arithmetic/logic unit and the control unit.

Motherboard

The CPU and memory are both mounted on a larger printed circuit board called the motherboard or the *system board*. The **motherboard** connects all of the hardware in the computer. It provides the electrical connections through which all data are transferred between hardware devices. The three main components on the motherboard are the processor, memory, and expansion ports/slots.

A **port** is a point of interface between the motherboard and external devices. *Universal serial bus (USB)* is an industry standard for communication between devices and the computer.

Output

Output is data provided to the user. An output device produces an action based on the instructions from the CPU. The most common output device is a computer monitor. This device formats the 1s and 0s the CPU uses into human-readable material. Speakers output audio based on the 1s and 0s generated by the CPU.

FYI

Many stand-alone monitors contain USB ports on the side so peripherals can be attached without needing to reach the computer box.

HANDS-ON EXAMPLE 1.1.2

COMPONENT IDENTIFICATION

Using the image shown, identify the computer hardware components labeled by number.

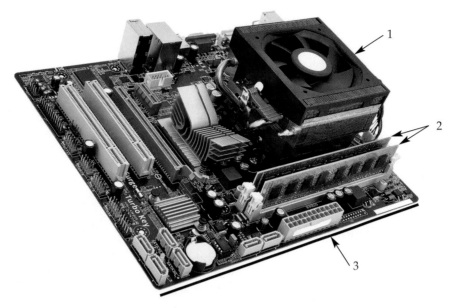

vetkit/Shutterstock.com

1. Object number 1 is called a(n) _____.
2. Objects number 2 are _____.
3. Assembly number 3 is called a(n) _____.

1.1   SECTION REVIEW

CHECK YOUR UNDERSTANDING

1. List the four phases of the digital revolution.
2. A measure of the amount of data that can travel on a communication system is called _____.
3. What are four main categories of computers?
4. What are the four functions of a computer?
5. What does an input device provide to the computer?

BUILD YOUR VOCABULARY

As you progress through this course, develop a personal IT glossary. This will help you build your vocabulary and prepare you for a career. Write a definition for each of the following terms and add it to your IT glossary.

central processing unit (CPU)
cloud computing
computer
digital revolution
hard disk drive
hardware
input
mainframe computer
motherboard
output

peripheral device
personal computer
port
processing
random-access memory (RAM)
read-only memory (ROM)
server
supercomputer
volume label

INTERNET AND MALWARE

The Internet is an interconnected network of networks used for communication. File transfers, electronic mail, messaging, news feeds, and the web are all made possible by the Internet. There are several parts to the Internet. These parts include computers, communication hardware, software, and standards. The World Wide Web is a collection of programs, called web servers, running on Internet networks all over the world. On these servers are over 50 billion hypertext pages, each one with its own uniform resource locator (URL) or web address. Searching through this information is supported by software called a search engine. Learning how to use the Internet is important, but so is maintaining one's safety while doing so.

Protection of digital data requires a combination of technologically advanced hardware, frequently updated software programs, and safe practices and procedures. Not only do you need to have the equipment, applications, and cyber-protection programs, you need to know how to properly use these items. Ultimately, it is the individual computer user who is responsible for cybersecurity.

Monkey Business Images/Shutterstock.com

TERMS

antivirus software
Boolean operator
browser
censorship
cookie
data vandalism
hacking
hypertext markup language (HTML)
malware
packet
phishing
search engine

LEARNING GOALS

After completing this section, you will be able to:
- Describe the operation of the Internet.
- Use a search engine to locate information.
- Identify types of computer threats.

Internet

The Internet is a worldwide communication network that connects individual computer networks. Messages are exchanged between these networks, and then the destination network must deliver the message to the correct computer in its network. It sounds complicated, but the process is very simple to understand.

The routing mechanism is based on small file fragments called **packets**. The transmission control protocol (TCP) identifies a file to be sent and breaks it into packets, each of which is given a header. The packet *header* contains the:

- file's source computer's *Internet protocol (IP) address*, which uniquely identifies each computer on a network;
- destination computer's IP address;
- packet number; and
- total number of packets in the entire file.

These packets are sent though the network of networked computers, possibly not on the same path, as shown in Figure 1-12.

World Wide Web

The *World Wide Web (WWW)* is a subset of the Internet that consists of a collection of documents connected by uniform resource locator (URL) codes and hypertext protocol, as illustrated in Figure 1-13.

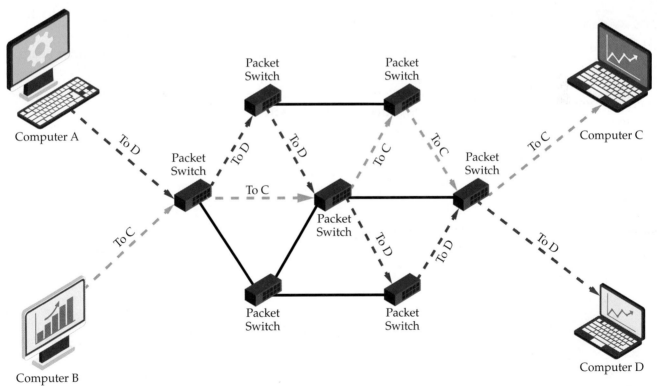

Goodheart-Willcox Publisher; Macrovector/Shutterstock.com

Figure 1-12. The TCP breaks a file into packets, which are then sent through the network.

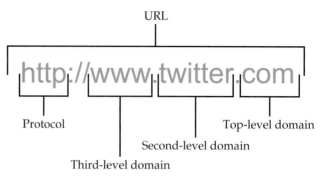

Goodheart-Willcox Publisher

Figure 1-13. A URL consists of several subparts. The second-level domain is what most people think of when talking about a website.

Servers connected to the Internet have a WWW folder at the root of the computer. Within this folder and its subfolders are all of the accessible documents for the web for the server. Figure 1-14 illustrates how the web works. These are the basic steps:

1. The user either enters a location in the navigation bar of a web browser or clicks a link on a web page, which issues the URL for a document to the browser.
2. The web browser transmits that to its WWW program on the host server.
3. HTTP locates the document specified by the URL and, if it does not reside on the same server, requests its delivery to the host.
4. If necessary, the document is delivered via TCP/IP packets to the host.
5. The host delivers the document to the requesting computer using HTTP.
6. The web browser determines how the document should be formatted and displays it.

Browsers

Browsers are the user's interface to the World Wide Web. A **browser** is a computer program that retrieves hypertext documents via HTTP and displays them on the computer monitor. The name is derived from the activity of browsing, or surfing, the web to locate files. While these

FYI

If you need help learning the functions of a new browser or version, hover the cursor over each icon to view the tooltip. If more information is required, use the help feature to search for the content of the tooltip.

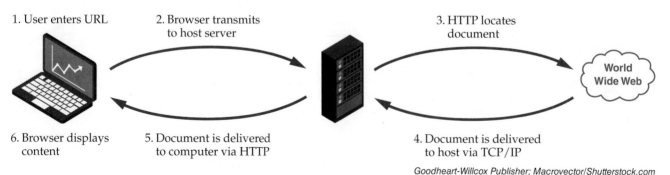

Goodheart-Willcox Publisher; Macrovector/Shutterstock.com

Figure 1-14. The operation of the web is really just a series of simple steps.

programs are also known as *web browsers,* browsers now offer many abilities beyond surfing the World Wide Web.

Examples of browsers are Chrome, Internet Explorer, Safari, and Firefox, among others. Figure 1-15 illustrates the main features of the Microsoft Edge browser.

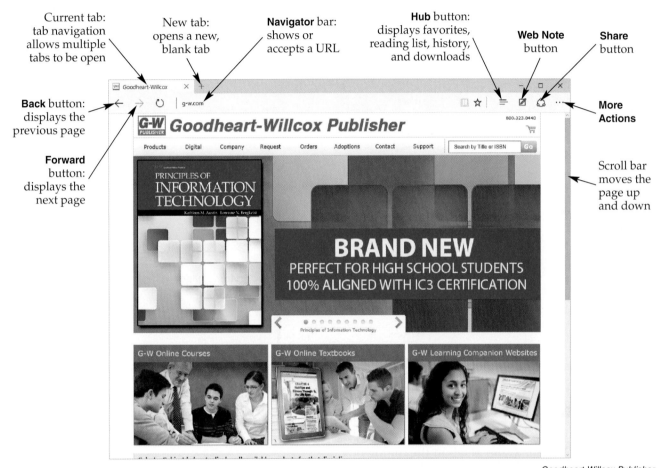

Goodheart-Willcox Publisher

Figure 1-15. The basic layout of the Microsoft Edge screen.

——— TITANS OF TECHNOLOGY ———

While computing has been a human need for thousands of years, electronic digital computers have existed for less than a century. Starting in 1945 with the development of the Electronic Numerical Integrator and Computer (ENIAC), the digital age was born. The leaders of the design team for the first programmable digital computer were J. Presper Eckert and John Mauchley at the University of Pennsylvania. They conceived the idea for using vacuum tubes to represent the on-off digital values. The calculations required 36 vacuum tubes to represent a single digit. Once the ENIAC was completed and tested, it was used at Aberdeen Proving Ground in Maryland to perform ballistics calculations. The first programmers were Kay McNulty, Betty Jennings, Betty Snyder, Marlyn Wescoff, Fran Bilas, and Ruth Lichterman.

HANDS-ON EXAMPLE 1.2.1

SETTING THE BROWSER HOME PAGE

When launched, a browser displays what has been set as the home page. Changing the home page is easy in Microsoft Edge.

1. Launch Microsoft Edge.
2. Click the **Tools** menu, and click **Internet Options** in the menu. The **Internet Options** dialog box is displayed, as shown.

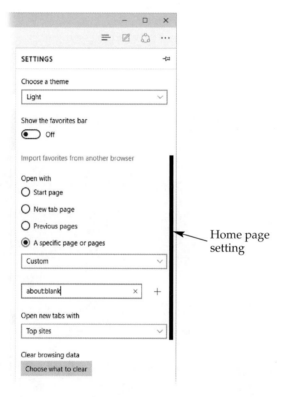

Home page setting

3. Click the **General** tab in the dialog box.
4. In the **Startup** area of the tab, click the **Start with home page** radio button.
5. Click in the text box at the top of the tab, and enter the URL of the web page to use as the home page. To have no home page, enter about:blank.
6. Click the **OK** button to apply the change.
7. Click the **Home** button on the navigation bar or press the [Alt][Home] key combination. Verify that the intended page has loaded.
8. Applying what you have learned, set the home page of Microsoft Edge to a search engine web page, such as Google.

HTML

Hypertext markup language (HTML) is a language used to create documents that tell browsers how to assemble text, images, and other content to display as a web page. The basis of HTML is tags, which are codes that let the browser know how to display a document. Figure 1-16 shows a basic web page and the HTML used to create it.

HTML provides for basic formatting for a document. A *cascading style sheet (CSS)* provides definitions that control the formatting of HTML documents and other markup documents. It has become the standard for how to control the appearance of a website.

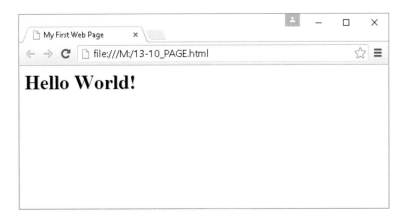

Web Page

```
<! DOCTYPE html>

<html>

        <title>
                My First Web Page
        </title>

        <body>
                <h1>
                        Hello World!
                </h1>
        </body>

</html>
```

Code

Goodheart-Willcox Publisher

Figure 1-16. Very little code is needed to create a simple web page.

FYI

Users can create HTML pages directly in Microsoft Word by resaving the file as a web page file type. This file type will open in the user's default web browser. Once saved, the user can view the plain text version of the file without HTML markup by right-clicking the file and choosing **Open with>Notepad**.

GS5

Key Applications

1.2

GS5
Key Applications
4.2

Green Tech

Power Strips

Computer workstations should be set up so all of the computer equipment is plugged into a power strip. Doing this allows the employee to have control of the power to an entire workstation. Power strips are now available with several different features. "Smart" power strips make it easy and convenient to save power each day.

Using Search Engines

A **search engine** is a software program that looks through massive databases of links and information to try to identify the best matches for the search request. Most modern search engines have natural language processing that makes searching very easy. For example, a question such as what is the boiling point of water can be entered as the search "term."

A technology named Boolean logic can be used to construct very precise search strings. **Boolean operators**, or logical operators, define the relationship between words in the search string. The Boolean operators AND, OR, and NOT can be used to create precise search strings. Also available are proximity operators such as NEAR or FOLLOWED BY. Figure 1-17 shows how the Boolean operators can be applied to a search string.

Computer Threats

There are many types of threats to computer systems and computer users. Malware most frequently finds its way into a computer as executable code hidden in another program. Often, the computer user does not find out about the infection until long after a successful attack. Other threats come from cookies, phishing, data vandalism, and computer hacking.

Malware

Malware is software that intentionally performs actions to disrupt the operation of a computer system, collect private information, or otherwise harm the computer or user. The word *malware* comes from "malicious software," meaning software that intends to harm. Malware is a broad category of harmful software. Some threats falling under malware are:

- computer viruses;
- computer worms;

Boolean Operator	Example	Effect
AND	space launches AND Pluto	Locate information in both phrases on the same page
OR	space launches OR Pluto	Locate information on either phrase
NOT	space launches NOT Pluto	Locate information on the first phrase, exclude information on the second phrase
NEAR	space launches NEAR Pluto	Locate information where both phrases are used in close proximity on the same page
FOLLOWED BY	space launches FOLLOWED BY Pluto	The first phrase comes before the second phrase on the page

Goodheart-Willcox Publisher

Figure 1-17. Boolean operators and proximity operators can be used to improve searches.

- Trojan horses;
- spyware;
- adware;
- scareware; and
- ransomware.

Cookies

Cookies are small text files that websites put on the computer hard disk drive when a user visits the websites. These are used to identify users. Cookies are often used to prepare customized web pages for the user. On many e-commerce sites, cookies are required to keep track of items in the shopping cart. Many password-protected websites also require cookies to keep the user logged in.

Phishing

Phishing is an attempt to get sensitive information by appearing as a harmless request. For example, a user may be told he or she has won a special prize or qualified for a no-cost introductory offer. Some information about a person that phishing scams commonly try to get includes:

- full name;
- employer's name;
- address;
- phone number;
- year of birth;
- credit card number; and
- Social Security number.

Once this information is in the hands of the phishers, it may be used to steal the person's identity or otherwise commit fraud.

Data Vandalism

Data vandalism is the manipulation or destruction of data found in cyberspace. It is unethical and can be illegal, as shown in Figure 1-18. For example, a hacker may break into a school computer database and alter grades.

Computer Hacking

Hacking is an activity by computer programmers to break into the e-mails, websites, computer systems, and files of other computer users. Hacking is often an unethical and illegal activity. However, there are legitimate hackers as well. Many companies hire hackers to find faults in their own computer systems. In this way, the faults can be fixed before they are exploited.

FYI

A malware attack may occur when the user downloads seemingly harmless data from the Internet or transfers files from a shared flash drive.

FYI

Visit the consumer information section of the US Federal Trade Commission website (www.consumer.ftc.gov), and search for "phone scams" to find more information.

Goodheart-Willcox Publisher

Figure 1-18. The Department of Justice maintains a website for reporting computer crimes, including hacking and data vandalism.

HANDS-ON EXAMPLE 1.2.2

CYBERSECURITY THREATS

The federal government and the White House have undertaken many cybersecurity policy initiatives. The White House website contains information about cybersecurity threats.

1. Launch a browser, and navigate to www.whitehouse.gov.
2. Using the website's search function, search for foreign policy cybersecurity.
3. Locate an article on foreign policy related to cybersecurity. Alternatively, directly navigate to the page www.whitehouse.gov/issues/foreign-policy/cybersecurity.
4. Read the article, and summarize the government's objectives.

Censorship

Many schools, companies, and organizations restrict the information that their members can access. **Censorship** is the act of limiting access to information or removing information to prevent the information from being seen. There must be a balance between providing a safe computing environment and allowing free access to information.

Defending Against Cyber Attacks

In the rapidly changing world of cyber attacks, it is a very good idea to run cyber-defense software. Cyber-defense software, usually called **antivirus software**, detects and removes malicious software from a computer. Most also actively prevent infections. Many companies offer cyber-defense software. Some are for-purchase and some are offered as freeware or open-source software.

Some antivirus software always monitors for viruses, which is known as *real-time protection.* With some software, however, a scan must be manually started. If the antivirus software detects a virus, it should be removed as quickly as possible. Most antivirus software will remove the virus as soon as it is detected. In some cases, however, the user must manually tell the software to remove any virus that is found. This added step has the advantage of being able to tell the software that a particular file or program is safe, but this should be done only if you are certain the file is not infected. A file that antivirus software thinks is infected when, in fact, it is not is called a *false positive.*

If for any reason a virus cannot be removed, it will be quarantined. This means the virus is isolated from the rest of the files on a computer. Once in quarantine, the virus cannot infect anything else. This is especially helpful if a critical file, such as a registry file, is infected.

Cyber threats rapidly evolve. Therefore, the software must be regularly updated. In most cases, the software will check for updates at a set interval, such as once a day or once a week. In this way, the software can quickly respond to new threats.

> ## FYI
>
> Cyber-defense software may be called antivirus, antimalware, or antispyware software. It may be known by other names as well.

1.2   SECTION REVIEW

 ### CHECK YOUR UNDERSTANDING

1. How does the World Wide Web relate to the Internet?
2. What serves as the user's interface to the World Wide Web?
3. List the three Boolean operators that can be used in a search string.
4. How is phishing different from malware?
5. When is hacking legitimate?

 ### BUILD YOUR VOCABULARY

As you progress through this course, develop a personal IT glossary. This will help you build your vocabulary and prepare you for a career. Write a definition for each of the following terms and add it to your IT glossary.

antivirus software	hypertext markup
Boolean operator	language (HTML)
browser	malware
censorship	packet
cookie	phishing
data vandalism	search engine
hacking	

1 REVIEW AND ASSESSMENT

Chapter Summary

Section 1.1 Introduction to Computers

- The digital revolution is the ever-expanding progression of technical, economic, and cultural changes brought about by computers. It has gone through four phases: giant computers, personal computers, networked computers, and cloud computing.

- Computer technology has made it possible for those with access to digital communication devices to stay in touch with others 24 hours a day. Advances in this technology have increased the speed of communication and the breadth of geographic reach, but there are advantages and disadvantages to the technology.

- Historically, computers were grouped in one of three categories based on size: mainframes, minicomputers, or microcomputers. Computers today are usually categorized based on usage and cost as well as size: supercomputers, mainframes, servers, and personal computers and mobile devices.

- All computers contain the same basic types of components: input device, memory, processor, and output device. If a device does not have all four components, it is not a computer.

Section 1.2 Internet and Malware

- Information on the Internet and World Wide Web is transmitted in packets. The Internet protocol address uniquely identifies each computer on a network and is used to correctly route packets.

- A search engine examines massive databases trying to identify the best matches to the search phrases. Boolean operators can be used to fine-tune searches.

- Malware is software that intentionally performs actions to disrupt the operation of a computer system, collect private information, or otherwise harm the computer or user. Other computer threats come from phishing, data vandalism, cookies, and computer hacking.

Now that you have finished this chapter, see what you know about computer applications by taking the chapter posttest. Access the posttest by visiting www.g-wlearning.com.

Chapter 1 Test

Multiple Choice

Select the best response.

1. Which event is *not* a major phase of the digital revolution?
   A. Giant computers.
   B. The Industrial Revolution.
   C. Cloud computing.
   D. Personal computers.

2. The Internet began as:
   A. the World Wide Web
   B. NSFNET
   C. ARPANET
   D. WWW

3. Which of the following is *not* one of the basic capabilities of a computer?
   A. produce output
   B. store data
   C. process data
   D. operate peripherals

4. What is the client software program that retrieves web documents and displays them to the user?
   A. preprocessor
   B. server
   C. host
   D. browser

5. Which of the following is *not* a major computer threat?
   A. hackers
   B. scareware
   C. malware
   D. ARPANET

Completion

Complete the following sentences with the correct word(s).

6. Collectively, Internet-based spaces used to store and retrieve data are called _____.

7. _____ have processing power that can handle complex jobs beyond the scope of other computer systems.

8. _____ memory is kept even when the computer is turned off, while _____ memory is erased when the power is off.

9. A(n) _____ uniquely identifies a computer on a network.

10. The act of limiting access to information or removing information to prevent it from being seen is called _____.

Matching

Match the correct term with its definition.
   A. hard disk drive
   B. bandwidth
   C. phishing
   D. random-access memory (RAM)
   E. malware

11. Measure of the amount of data that can travel on a communication system.

12. Holds instructions that the processor can immediately use.

13. Sealed unit that contains a stack of individual disks, or platters, which are magnetic media that rotate at a very high speed.

14. Software that intentionally performs actions to disrupt the operation of a computer system, collect private information, or otherwise harm the computer or user.

15. Attempt to get sensitive information by appearing as a harmless request.

Application and Extension of Knowledge

1. Write a one-page paper describing why you feel an information technology worker must keep his or her skills up to date.

2. Look at your home computer or a computer in the school's computer lab. Make a list of all peripherals attached to the computer. Write one sentence for each device explaining why you think it is a peripheral. Be prepared to discuss this list with the rest of the class.

3. Conduct an audit of the hardware in your school's computer lab. What items are common to all computers? What items are found on only some computers? Explain why you think these discrepancies exist.

4. Go to the World Wide Web Consortium (W3C) website (www.w3.org). Use the site's search function, and search for a little history of the World Wide Web. In the search results, look for a similarly named article. Read the W3C article, and write a one-page summary of the key game-changing events. Be sure to cite the information source.

5. Conduct a search online for laws that relate to Internet security. Note when they were created and what purpose they serve. Next, research laws regulating hacking and browser hijacking. Summarize what you learned about Internet security and ethical conduct in a two-page essay.

Online Activities

Complete the following activities, which will help you learn, practice, and expand your knowledge and skills.

 **Vocabulary.** Practice vocabulary for this chapter using the e-flash cards, matching activity, and vocabulary game until you are able to recognize their meanings.

Communication Skills

Reading. Skimming means to quickly glance through an entire document. Skimming will give you a preview of the material to help comprehension when you read the chapter. You should notice headings, key words, phrases, and visual elements. The goal is to identify the main idea of the content. Skim this chapter. Provide an overview of what you read.

Writing. Rhetoric is the study of writing or speaking as a way of communicating information or persuading someone. Describe a rhetorical technique that a writer can use to provide information or persuade someone about a digital device. Write an example of the technique you chose.

Speaking. Most people in the United States act as responsible and contributing citizens. How can a person demonstrate social and ethical responsibility in a digital society?

Internet Research

Digital Citizenship. Using the Internet, research digital citizenship using various Internet resources. List and analyze specific elements of digital citizenship that users of technology should understand when using the Internet. What are the day-to-day effects of digital citizenship on society? Summarize your findings.

Teamwork

Working with your team, research antivirus or antimalware software. Make a chart showing at least five options, the system requirements, and the cost to purchase. One of the software options should be freeware, or software that can be used permanently without cost to the user. Write a memo to your supervisor or instructor listing the options and your recommendation of software.

Activity Files

Visit www.g-wlearning.com/informationtechnology/ to download the activity files for this chapter. These activities will expand your learning of the material presented in this chapter and allow you to practice what you have learned. Follow the instructions provided in each file to complete the activity.

Activity File 1-1 Bug Origins

Activity File 1-2 Malware

Activity File 1-3 ENIAC

Activity File 1-4 Search Engine Filtering

Activity File 1-5 Using Computers Appropriately

CAPSTONE PROJECT

The capstone project builds from one chapter to the next. It allows you to apply the skills you have learned to create a complete project in a desired career area. Select one of the four career areas listed below and follow the given instructions. You will work only in this career area for every subsequent chapter.

Agriculture, Food, and Natural Resources

In this activity, you will assume the role of a graduate looking for work in the agriculture, food, and natural resources industries. You will visit the Advance CTE website to research all the careers available in this cluster. Access the *Introduction to Microsoft Office 2016* companion website (www.g-wlearning.com/informationtechnology/) to view the instructions for this chapter's Agriculture, Food, and Natural Resources capstone project.

Business, Management, and Administration

In this activity, you will assume the role of a graduate looking for work in the business, management, and administration industries. You will visit the Advance CTE website to research all the careers available in this cluster. Access the *Introduction to Microsoft Office 2016* companion website (www.g-wlearning.com/informationtechnology/) to view the instructions for this chapter's Business, Management, and Administration capstone project.

Health Science

In this activity, you will assume the role of a graduate looking for work in the health science industries. You will visit the Advance CTE website to research all the careers available in this cluster. Access the *Introduction to Microsoft Office 2016* companion website (www.g-wlearning.com/informationtechnology/) to view the instructions for this chapter's Health Science capstone project.

Science, Technology, Engineering, and Mathematics

In this activity, you will assume the role of a graduate looking for work in the science, technology, engineering, and mathematics industries. You will visit the Advance CTE website to research all the careers available in this cluster. Access the *Introduction to Microsoft Office 2016* companion website (www.g-wlearning.com/informationtechnology/) to view the instructions for this chapter's Science, Technology, Engineering, and Mathematics capstone project.

2

INTRODUCTION TO SYSTEM AND APPLICATION SOFTWARE

SECTIONS

Software is what makes the hardware work. Without software, a computer waits for instructions. Although the user cannot see, hear, or feel it, the software contains all of the instructions to operate the hardware. A set of instructions that tells the computer what to do is called a software program. Programs tell a computer to do specific jobs. These jobs include, among others, creating a document, scanning a photo, editing a video, and connecting to the Internet.

There are two basic types of software: system software and application software. System software works to help the CPU find programs, assign memory, run the devices, and provide utility programs. Application software is the software that performs the user's work. Applications include Microsoft Office, video games, phone apps, and web browsers. Users have a wide choice of software. Program selection is limited by what type of hardware is connected to the computer. Other choices depend on what tasks the user wants to perform. This chapter investigates many types of software.

SYSTEM SOFTWARE

There are similar tasks common to most applications, such as saving data, retrieving documents, and printing. This is why operating systems were created. The operating system, or OS for short, sits between the hardware and the applications to handle all common tasks in one way. For a visual metaphor, think of a road as the hardware. The cars driving on the road are the applications. The drivers are the users, and the crossing guard is the operating system. It is the operating system that keeps all of the applications running smoothly and connected with the CPU and the peripherals.

System software contains the operating system, utilities, device drivers, and programs. Utilities help with housekeeping tasks. Programs are the applications that users run to complete the desired tasks. This section discusses operating systems, utilities, and programs.

lightwavemedia/Shutterstock.com

LEARNING GOALS

After completing this section, you will be able to:
- Define operating system.
- Describe Windows operating systems.
- Discuss programs.

TERMS

booting
firmware
operating system (OS)
system software
utility program

Operating Systems

System software includes four types of software: the operating system, utility programs, device drivers, and programs. All computers that run more than one program must have an operating system. General-use computers, such as a PC or tablet, must have an OS to work. Single-use computers, such as those in satellites and space probes, do not require an operating system. The **operating system (OS)** is software that manages all of the devices, as well as locates and provides instructions to the CPU. The OS works behind the scenes to perform communication with the user and the hardware. See Figure 2-1. Most of the time it is silently working in the background to monitor system activity and optimize its own efficiency.

The OS is specific to the type of the computer. See Figure 2-2. The various versions of Windows, Mac OS, and GNU/Linux are all examples of computer operating systems.

Before the operating system can run, the computer must go through boot procedures to get the basic functions started and the OS loaded. **Booting**, or *bootstrapping*, describes using a small program to get the computer running and the OS loaded. This program is stored in ROM on the motherboard. It contains circuitry and software, sometimes referred to as **firmware**, that hold instructions for initializing the hardware and loading the main OS. In PCs, firmware is generally used to remember how to boot the computer. On smartphones, the entire OS and bundled application suites are stored in firmware.

FYI

When people wore big, heavy boots, they had trouble pulling them on. Shoe manufacturers included a small strap across the heel so the wearer could pull on the boot without any help. This is the origin of the computer term *booting*.

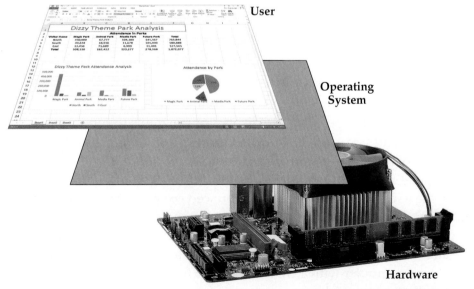

Goodheart-Willcox Publisher; Denis Dryashkin/Shutterstock.com

Figure 2-1. The operating system sits between the hardware and the software providing communication between them, facilitating the execution of the software programs, and managing the hardware resources.

Operating System	Platforms	Distinctions
Windows	PCs, Microsoft phones, and tablets Apple products in a Windows partition	Most widely used OS Multiple versions Proprietary
iOS	Apple mobile products, iPhone, iPad, iTouch, etc.	Proprietary Distribution of apps limited to Apple App Store
Mac OS	Macintosh computers	Proprietary
Unix	PCs, large mainframe computers, supercomputers, web servers	Open source Free to use Stable, less downtime than Windows Better security Greater processing power Generally found on networked systems
Linux	PCs, several mobile devices, large mainframe computers, web servers	Open source, based on Unix Free to use Low resource requirements High security level Generally found on networked systems
Android	Google mobile OS based on Linux	Open source Open distribution of apps via Internet

Goodheart-Willcox Publisher

Figure 2-2. Several operating systems are available. The platforms on which each is used vary by application.

Six events take place when a computer running one of the Windows operating systems boots up, starting with the power being turned on:

1. The power light comes on, the fan starts up, and electricity is sent throughout the hardware components.
2. The CPU follows the instructions set up in ROM.
3. The CPU performs tests on the computer's critical internal systems.
4. The CPU finds all connected peripheral devices, checks their settings, and alerts the user if there is a problem.
5. The CPU loads the OS from the hard drive into RAM.
6. The OS reads a file that contains configuration data to tell it what windows to open, icons to display, or programs to run.

When the main screen appears on the computer monitor, the system is ready to follow the user's directions.

Operating systems changed with the introduction of a graphical user interface (GUI), which is usually pronounced *goo-ey*. Users did not have to behave like programmers and enter commands. With a GUI, users could use a mouse to select options from menus. Personal computers then became very popular. The Apple Macintosh was the first commercially successful computer with a GUI OS. The OS for this computer was called System Software, which was eventually changed to Mac OS. GUI versions of Windows soon followed the introduction of the Macintosh computer.

HANDS-ON EXAMPLE 2.1.1

BASIC COMPUTER COMPONENTS

Locate a computer to use for this activity. Do not open the computer box unless directed to do so by your instructor.

1. Click the **Apps** button or the **Start** button.
2. In Windows 10, click **File Explorer**, and then click This PC in the tree on the left-hand side of File Explorer. In Windows 8, click **This PC** in the **Windows System** group of the **Apps** menu. In Windows 7, click **Computer** in the right-hand column of the **Start** menu. A list of hard drives and devices with removable storage is displayed, as shown. Name them.

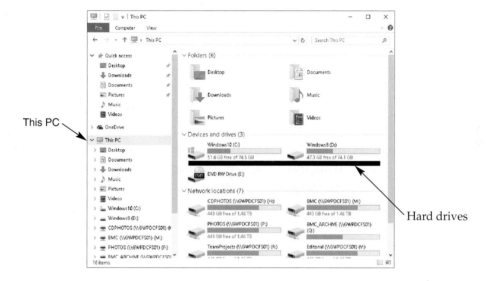

3. Click **System Properties** at the top of the window.
4. List the Windows version that the computer is using.
5. Identify the type of processor.
6. Identify the installed memory (RAM).

Windows Operating System Overview

The functions described here are specific to Windows, but most operating systems have similar settings. The Windows desktop is a virtual workspace for the operating system. Program icons and document files can be placed on the desktop for easy access. In Windows 10 and Windows 7, the desktop is automatically displayed when the OS starts up. In Windows 8, you are automatically switched to the desktop when a program is launched.

One of the keys to the Windows OS is the ability to have multiple programs running at the same time. The user sees each program in a box called a window. Each program window appears as a tab in the task bar. To switch between windows, either click the tab on the task bar or use the [Alt][Tab] key combination.

Starting Programs in Windows

There are several ways to start, or *launch,* a program in Microsoft Windows. The most common ways are to use an icon in the **Apps** or **Start** menu or a desktop icon. If the program appears as an icon on the desktop, double-click the icon to launch the program.

In Windows 10, click or tap the **Start** button on the taskbar at the bottom of the screen. Next, click **All apps** in the menu. An alphabetical listing of applications and programs is displayed, as shown in Figure 2-3. Scroll through the list to find the correct program, and click or tap it to launch the program.

Another way to launch a program is to double-click the icon for a document file, either on the desktop or in a file folder. Most documents are associated with a program based on the file extension of the document. Double-clicking on a document file will launch the associated program and load the document. If a document file extension is not associated with a program, Windows will ask you to select a program to use to open the file.

One more way to start a program is to click the **Start** or **Apps** button or press the Windows key on the keyboard. The search box at the bottom of the **Start** menu is automatically active, and you can begin entering the name of an application. In Windows 10, you can also click in the search box on the task bar.

FYI

In a Mac environment, the [Cmd] + spacebar key combination is used to search for a program.

Common Tasks Using Windows

There are several key combinations and mouse clicks that behave in the same manner no matter what program windows are open. There are

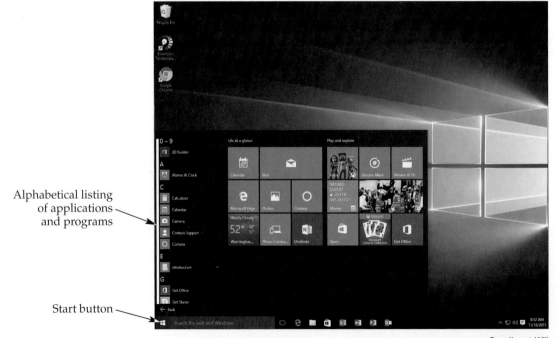

Alphabetical listing of applications and programs

Start button

Goodheart-Willcox Publisher

Figure 2-3. In Windows 10, clicking the **Start** button followed by **All apps** displays an alphabetical listing of all installed applications and programs.

clicking, double-clicking, dragging, and right-clicking. There are standard key combinations as well.

The [Ctrl][A] key combination is used to select all items in the current view, such as all words in a document or all files in a folder. The [Ctrl][C] key combination copies the current selection to the system clipboard. The [Ctrl][X] key combination removes, or cuts, the current selection and places it on the system clipboard. The [Ctrl][V] key combination pastes the contents of the system clipboard in the current location. The [Ctrl][Z] key combination reverses the last operation, which is called an *undo*.

The [Alt][Tab] key combination is used to navigate through open program windows. Holding down the [Alt] key while repeatedly pressing the [Tab] key selects which window will be made active, as shown in Figure 2-4. When the correct icon is highlighted, release the [Alt] key to make that window active. The desktop is treated as a window in this navigation.

All open windows can be arranged for better viewing and use. Right-click on the taskbar, but not on an icon, to display a shortcut menu. This menu contains choices to **Cascade windows**, **Show windows stacked**, and **Show windows side by side**. Cascading windows are displayed one on top of another, offset slightly so a small portion of each window underneath can be seen. Stacked windows are displayed the width of the desktop and top to bottom, but the windows do not overlap. Side-by-side windows are displayed the height of the desktop and side by side, but the windows do not overlap.

Career Skills

Computer Support Specialist
Computer Support Specialists provide a wide range of help for technology users. Often referred to as help desk technicians, these IT workers help users understand how to operate a wide range of software and hardware technologies. They also manage a user's access to the network. Their goal is to support the users of the network.

System Utility Programs

In terms of system software, **utility programs** assist in managing and optimizing a computer's performance. These programs can add extra protection against viruses and malware, assist in installing or removing software, find files, and speed up communication.

An example of a Windows system utility is the disk defragmenter. The disk defragmenter, or *defrag*, reorganizes the files stored on a disk so, as much as possible, files are not divided between storage locations. Each time the file is saved, a new piece of the file is stored. This new piece, or

Goodheart-Willcox Publisher

Figure 2-4. The [Alt][Tab] key combination is used to switch between windows.

segment, may not be stored next to all of the other segments of the file. Segments of the file are stored in free space throughout the hard drive. As a result, the file may not be one piece in a single location on the disk. As files are deleted, space is freed between files and segments. When segments are scattered, it takes the disk drive longer to read and use the files. This scattering is called fragmentation.

HANDS-ON EXAMPLE 2.1.2

WINDOWS SYSTEM UTILITIES

Many of the Windows system utilities are accessed via the Control Panel window. Other system utilities are accessed through the **Start** screen or menu.

1. In Windows 10, right-click the **Start** menu button. In Windows 8, click the **Apps** button at the bottom of the **Start** screen. In Windows 7, click the **Start** menu button.
2. Click **Control Panel** in the menu to display the Control Panel window.
3. Hover the cursor over a category. A tooltip will appear to identify what the utilities in that category can do. Help is available at every step to explain the process.
4. Click the **Uninstall a program** link below the **Programs** category. A list of the currently installed programs is displayed in the Control Panel window. Review the list to see what programs are installed. Do not uninstall any programs without permission.
5. Close the Control Panel window.
6. Display the **Start** screen or menu.
7. In Windows 10, click in the search box on the taskbar. In Windows 8, move the cursor to the upper-right corner and click **Search** when the menu appears. In Windows 7, the search box is located at the bottom of the **Start** menu.
8. Click in the search box, and enter cttune.exe.
9. In the search results, click the cttune.exe program file. The **ClearType Text Tuner** dialog box is displayed, as shown. This is a wizard to adjust the clarity of the text display.

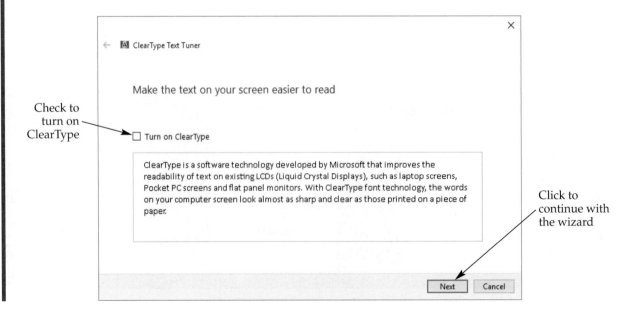

Check to turn on ClearType

Click to continue with the wizard

HANDS-ON EXAMPLE 2.1.2 (CONTINUED)

10. Check the **Turn on ClearType** check box, and click the **Next** button to move to next page of the wizard.

11. The next four pages of the wizard give you a choice of sample text. Click the sample text that appears the best to you, and click the **Next** button.

12. The final page of the wizard indicates it is finished. Close the program by clicking the **Finish** button.

2.1 | SECTION REVIEW

CHECK YOUR UNDERSTANDING

1. What is an operating system?

2. Define the process of using a small program to get the computer running and the OS loaded.

3. List the six events that take place when a Windows operating system boots up.

4. Which type of system software assists in managing and optimizing a computer's performance?

5. What does disk defragmenter do?

BUILD YOUR VOCABULARY

As you progress through this course, develop a personal IT glossary. This will help you build your vocabulary and prepare you for a career. Write a definition for each of the following terms and add it to your IT glossary.

booting   system software
firmware   utility program
operating system (OS)

APPLICATION SOFTWARE

Application software is what you use to make the computer work for you. This may mean creating a letter or editing a photograph. You may wish to play an MP3 file or watch a movie. All of these tasks are done with application software.

All software must be used in a legal manner. In order to do so, the user must understand the license assigned to the software. Additionally, it is important to keep track of different versions of software. When installing software, a user must know the system requirements of the software version and be able to determine if his or her computer system can run the software.

michaeljung/Shutterstock.com

TERMS

application software
end user license
    agreement (EULA)
file format
open-source software
podcasting
productivity software
proprietary software
system requirements
template

LEARNING GOALS

After completing this section, you will be able to:
- Describe productivity software.
- Install software.

Productivity Software

Application software allows the user to perform specific activities, such as writing term papers, sending e-mail, paying taxes, editing photos, playing games, and taking online courses. **Productivity software** is a type of application software that supports the completion of tasks. It is one of the most well-known software types. This group includes software for word processing, creating spreadsheets and presentations, editing graphics and video, and managing databases, among many other tasks. Productivity software often contains templates to help the user get started on a task or wizards to simplify complex tasks.

A *suite* is a group of programs, usually with similar interfaces, that provide complementary tasks. All of the individual programs function independently. When used together, data can be easily shared across the suite. The most common programs in an "office suite" are word processing, spreadsheet, presentation, and database management software. These programs are listed individually and alphabetically in the **Start** menu, as shown in Figure 2-5. Microsoft Office and Corel Office are examples of suites of integrated productivity software. The software in these two suites is proprietary. Open-source alternatives for office suites are OpenOffice and LibreOffice.

Proprietary software, or *closed software*, is owned by the creator and cannot be sold, copied, or modified by the user without permission

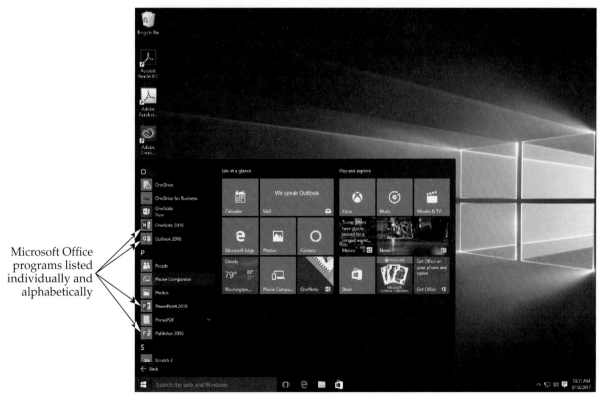

Microsoft Office programs listed individually and alphabetically

Goodheart-Willcox Publisher

Figure 2-5. The programs contained in the Microsoft Office suite are listed individually in the **Start** menu.

FYI

If open-source software is the basis for a new application, credit should be given to the original programmers even if it is not required.

from the creator. **Open-source software** is software that has no licensing restrictions. The base code is available for anyone to distribute, copy, and modify.

Before software can be used, however, a license must be obtained. Most software programs are governed by an end user license agreement. The **end user license agreement (EULA)** is a contract outlining the set of rules that every user must agree to before using the software. Some EULAs allow the software to be installed only once on one machine. Other agreements may allow the software to be installed multiple times on the same machine to allow for reinstallation after a hard drive failure.

Most application software can save information in various file formats. The **file format** indicates the manner in which the data it contains are stored on the disk. The primary file format for given software is said to be the software's *native format*. The purpose of the file format is to make it easy to reopen the file and arrange it on the screen. On a Windows system, the file extension indicates the file format.

Documents

When personal computers became popular, word processors were one of the first types of programs written for them. Word-processing software assists the user with composing, editing, designing, printing, and publishing documents. All modern word-processing software makes it possible to quickly enter text, complete insertions and deletions, correct mistakes, make revisions, check for spelling and grammar errors, combine documents, and add illustrations. Word processors are the most common type of application software.

When a word processor is launched, it will create a blank document or offer the option to select a template. A **template** has formatting and organizational suggestions that can help the user create a professional-looking document. For example, Microsoft Word offers templates for letters, flyers, faxes, meeting agendas, budgets, and many more.

Spreadsheets

Spreadsheet software is used to create, organize, and edit data in a table composed of rows and columns, as shown in Figure 2-6. The cells in the table can contain text, numbers, or mathematical equations. Each table or grid, which is the spreadsheet, is called a worksheet. Each spreadsheet document file may contain multiple worksheets.

Spreadsheet software is very popular with accountants, payroll administrators, and financial managers. It can perform complex calculations. It makes keeping a grade book, balancing a checkbook, or computing the monthly payment on a car loan easy. Spreadsheet software is also very useful in creating colorful graphs based on data entered in table format.

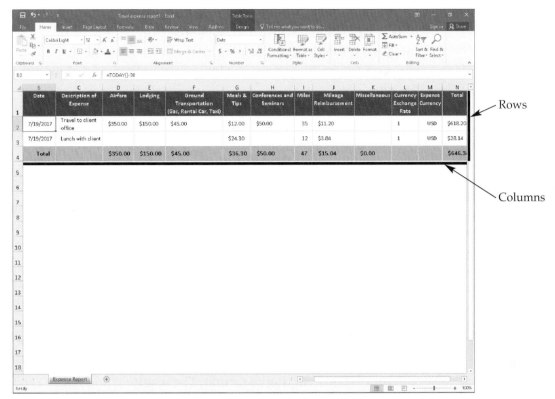

Rows

Columns

Goodheart-Willcox Publisher

Figure 2-6. A spreadsheet contains data arranged in rows and columns.

Data Management

A database is information stored in tables. Database software is used for tracking large amounts of data. It is useful because it can retrieve a small part of the data that the user requests.

Businesses use databases to monitor all of the information about clients. The benefit of a database is seen when the user asks, or *queries,* the database to show a specific piece of information. For example, the user could request just the information of clients in one particular location. Most businesses also use database software to track their employees and related data, such as address, job title, salary, and certifications. Schools use database software to track information about students, including courses, grades, and attendance.

Presentations

Presentation software provides tools to combine text, photographs, clip art, video, and graphs into a series of slides for playback. A presentation allows a speaker to visually enhance the topic of the speech. Enhancing the experience of the audience can make the event more memorable. Slide shows are used extensively in classroom lectures, business presentations, company meetings, sales events, and conferences.

Presentations, or slide shows, are normally projected onto a large screen for viewing by a group of people. Sometimes, presentations are intended for individual viewing on a computer screen. Often, a slide show presented to a group is later posted to the Internet for individual viewing.

Presentation software includes tools to add transitions between slides. The elements on each slide can be animated to add movement. Speaker notes can also be included to help the presenter.

Graphics

Graphics are pictures, drawings, photographs, and images used as decoration or to enhance or illustrate a topic. Generally, graphics can be called artwork. Graphics software is used to create, edit, print, and distribute the artwork. Professional artists use graphics software as a primary tool. However, there is graphics software designed for novice users as well. There are two types of graphics software: raster and vector.

Digital Audio

Digital-audio software is used to create and edit music, narration, and other sounds in digital format. The resulting audio files can be played on computers, portable music players, or entertainment centers or added to videos or web pages. Podcasting is another use for digital audio. **Podcasting** is the distribution of audio files, such as episodes of radio or music broadcasts, over the Internet via automated or subscribed downloads.

Two common audio file formats are waveform audio file (WAV) and MP3. The WAV format is the primary format used in Windows for uncompressed audio. The MP3 format is highly compressed. This allows the size of recordings to be reduced. For example, if a CD holds 10 uncompressed songs, it may be able to hold over 100 of those songs if they were compressed in the MP3 format.

Videos

Video software is used to create, edit, and publish digital video recordings. Using this software, titles, animation, audio, and effects can be added to video recordings. Additionally, the video itself can be trimmed and spliced to remove unwanted footage. Many video-editing programs use drag-and-drop techniques that make it possible to create professional-looking products with little training.

The equipment necessary to create digital video recordings is small, light, and portable. It uses built-in hard drives, flash drives, or DVDs to record many hours of video. Digital camcorders are available in a range of prices and features. Smartphones can also be used to record video, typically at a lower quality than what a digital camcorder can create.

Ethics

Code of Ethics

Most companies establish a set of ethics that employees must follow. The code of ethics outlines acceptable behavior when interacting with coworkers, suppliers, and customers. Some businesses even post their code of ethics on their websites. Employees must be familiar with the code in order to make correct decisions on behalf of the company, including those related to using the company's computers and other technology.

Apps

GS5
Key Applications
6.1, 6.2, 6.3

Apps are small self-contained programs used to enhance existing functionality in a simple, user-friendly way. Smartphones all come with powerful web browsers. However, inputting URLs or managing bookmarks on a mobile phone is cumbersome. Many online sites and services offer a standalone app as a way to access content. This gives the user better control, thereby making everything simpler and quicker to open and use.

For example, if the user signs in to a bank's website using the phone's browser, it will be difficult for text entry and resizing the display to see the text box for entering a PIN. A banking app simplifies the process, storing the login information for next time, and making the critical data more readable on a smaller display.

Examples of functions offered by other apps include calculating tips, keeping one's day organized, calculating fuel usage, and tracking when a car needs an oil change. However, there are also apps called "time killers." These include video game, crossword puzzle, and video streaming apps.

Many apps are free, while some are premium apps that must be purchased. Obtaining apps is easy. For iPhones, the only place to get apps is in the Apple App Store. For Android phones, apps are downloaded from the Google Play site. For different smartphones, conduct an Internet search with the brand of the phone followed by the word apps, such as Palm apps.

Make sure the app will run on your operating system and device before downloading it. Some apps will only run on a tablet or smartphone, some only on a desktop or laptop computer, and some on all platforms. Additionally, some apps are not downloads, but rather are browser-based and can run on all platforms and operating systems.

Users need data plans in order to download apps directly from the phone's mobile browser. Additionally, some apps, such as certain phone-tracking applications, require the user have a data plan. Any apps that upload information collected by the application to a web-based server will require that the phone have a data plan. A data plan is one way to pay for Internet connection when the user is not able to connect to the Internet via a Wi-Fi hotspot.

Green Tech

Green Team

There are many ways to go green in the workplace. Assembling an employee green team is a good place to start. Most green teams focus on addressing employee workplace habits, such as implementing a recycling program and purchasing software as downloads instead of as boxed CDs. Companies that work toward sustainability are socially responsible and create goodwill.

HANDS-ON EXAMPLE 2.2.1

OFFICE SUITE SOFTWARE

The programs in the Microsoft Office suite of software share a similar interface. It is common for the software in a suite to have similar functions in similar locations.

1. Close any open applications.
2. Open Microsoft Word, and start a blank document.

HANDS-ON EXAMPLE 2.2.1 CONTINUED

3. Open Microsoft Excel, and start a blank workbook.
4. Open Microsoft PowerPoint, and start a blank presentation.
5. Right-click on the Windows taskbar, and click **Show windows stacked** in the shortcut menu, as shown.

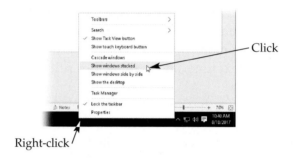

6. List the ribbon tabs that are in all three programs. For example, all three programs have a **Home** tab.
7. Click the **Home** tab in each program.
8. List the group names on the **Home** tab that are in all three programs. For example, all three programs have a **Clipboard** group on the **Home** tab.
9. Which one group on the **Home** tab contains the same tools in all three programs?

Goodheart-Willcox Publisher

Figure 2-7. Most programs have an installer that is used to properly set up the software on the computer.

Installing Software

When a user chooses what software to use, the software program must be placed on the system. This is called *installing* the software or *setup.* The process for installing software is created by the programmers who developed the software. Simple applications might just require copying the program files to the hard drive. More complex software generally requires an advanced procedure that modifies the operating system, as shown in Figure 2-7.

Before attempting to install software, the user should verify that the software and the computer are compatible. This means checking that the software is made for the installed operating system and that there is enough space to install the program files. Each software program should list the **system requirements**, which are specifications for the processor speed, RAM, hard drive space, and any additional hardware or software needed to run the software.

New Installation

For Windows-compatible products, a standard setup procedure is dictated by Microsoft. This procedure performs several steps:

- determine if the software already exists
- look for enough space to install
- copy the program files onto the disk
- set up data files and folders
- create shortcuts to the program in the **Apps** or **Start** menu and optionally on the taskbar or desktop
- enter a file association for each file type that is created by the new program

Some installation utilities offer options for the advanced user. For example, a software program may allow a full or partial installation. A full installation would consist of all files required for the program to work plus other files such as samples or a library. A partial installation consists of only the files required for the program to work. In some cases, a partial installation will allow the user to select some of the additional files to be installed.

If you are unsure of what features to install, it is generally safe to accept the default settings.

HANDS-ON EXAMPLE 2.2.2

SYSTEM REQUIREMENTS

Memory and storage specifications are two common system requirements. In Windows, it is easy to find out how much memory and storage exist on the system.

1. In Windows 10, click **File Explorer** in the **Start** menu, and then click This PC in the tree on the left-hand side of File Explorer. In Windows 8, click the **Apps** button, and click **This PC** in the **Windows System** group. In Windows 7, click the **Start** menu button, and click **Computer** in the right-hand pane. Windows Explorer is launched with the computer selected.
2. Scroll down until the local hard drive (C:) is visible in the right-hand pane. Write down the amount of free space reported. This is the amount of space available for software installation, although never allow a hard drive to be completely full.

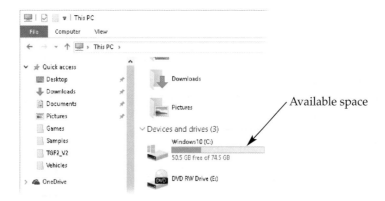

Available space

HANDS-ON EXAMPLE 2.2.2 CONTINUED

3. Click **System properties** in the ribbon or on the menu bar. Windows Explorer displays basic information about the computer in the right-hand pane, as shown.

Information about the computer

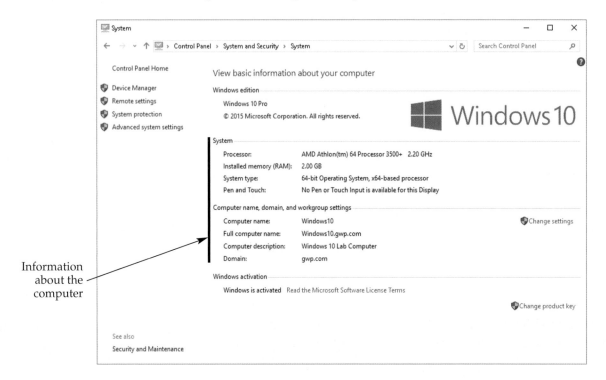

4. In the **Windows** section of the information, determine the operating system. Record this information.
5. In the **System** section of the information, determine the amount of memory installed. Record this information.
6. Go to a store, either online or a physical store, that sells software. Select a program that interests you. Determine if your computer system meets the operating system, memory, and storage system requirements of the software.

Updates

Updates, sometimes called *patches* or *service packs*, are fixes to the software to correct bugs, remove security issues, or otherwise improve a version of a software program. When a software update becomes available, it is a good idea to apply it.

Microsoft automatically handles updates on its operating systems. Part of the shutdown process involves connecting with the Microsoft website to see if any updates need to be loaded. If an update is available, the system will automatically download and install it. Microsoft will report to the user how many updates are being applied as well as the progress of the installation. In some cases, an update requires the system to be restarted to activate the upgrade.

TITANS OF TECHNOLOGY

Grace Murray Hopper made many key contributions to software development in the early stages of digital computers. Formerly an instructor at Vassar College, Hopper earned her PhD in mathematics from Yale University. She joined the Naval Reserve during World War II. Because of her high intelligence and innovative spirit, she was tapped to work on the Mark series of digital computers at Harvard. She rose to the rank of Rear Admiral in the US Navy, the first woman to reach that rank. Her programming career started by rearranging wires on circuit panels to provide instructions for the Mark I computer. After tiring of rewiring the same set of instructions and then having to move them to accommodate new instructions, Dr. Hopper invented relocatable code. This provided for her inventions of compilers and human-readable code. She wrote the first compiler, which was B-O for the Univac. It was created to accept human-readable code and translate it into computer code. Eventually, she coauthored the COBOL language, which is still used in some business applications to this day. Her most far-reaching contribution was the standardization of compilers. She directed teams at the Navy to develop procedures and eventually automated the process for validation of COBOL compilers. Often called the Grand Lady of Software, Dr. Hopper's impact on the field of software development is still felt today.

Some PCs are rarely turned off. In this case, Windows can be configured to automatically install updates without a shutdown. It is common in business and school settings for computers to remain on overnight so that updates can be installed without interrupting work.

Most software will have updates throughout the life of a version. If the software is registered, the developer will generally send a notification when a new update is available. Many software programs automatically check for updates whenever the computer is connected to the Internet.

FYI

The computer should not be turned off until the update procedure is complete.

Uninstallation

A software program should be removed when it is no longer needed or seems to be causing a problem on a system. The process of removing software is called *uninstallation*. Often, this is referred to as performing an *uninstall*.

When a program is installed, many files are copied to the hard drive, often in many locations. Many installations also alter the operating system. The proper way to remove software is to use the uninstall option that came with the software. Running this option will remove all of the files that were installed, reverse any alterations to the OS, and remove shortcuts to the program. If an uninstall feature is not included with the software, use the **Add or Remove Programs** function in the Windows Control Panel to remove the program, as shown in Figure 2-8.

Reinstallation

Reinstallation is the process of reloading a software program on the computer system, usually in the same location as an existing installation of that software. Reinstallation, often called performing a *reinstall*, is usually done to reset an installed program to its defaults or to fix the program if it has become corrupted.

To reinstall software, take the same steps as installing new software. Follow the installation program wizard. Many installation programs will detect if the software is already installed and give the user the option to repair or fully reinstall the software. In some cases, the software cannot be reinstalled unless the previous version has been removed. The installation wizard should step through whatever process is needed to reinstall or repair the software.

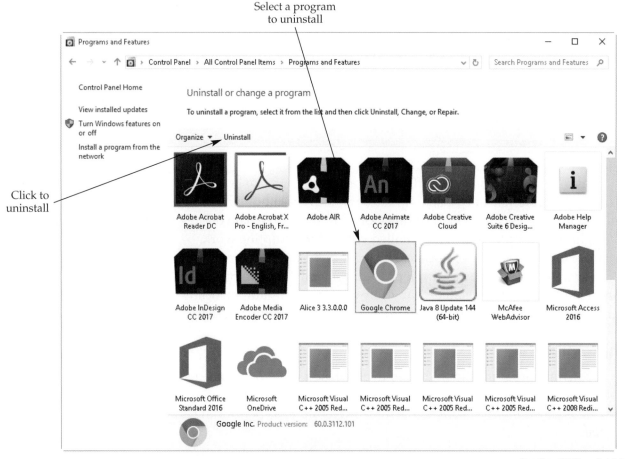

Figure 2-8. Windows contains a utility that is used to remove installed programs from the computer.

2.2 | SECTION REVIEW

CHECK YOUR UNDERSTANDING

1. Describe an end user license agreement.
2. What does a file format indicate?
3. What is *native format*?
4. What should be listed in the system requirements for software?
5. Describe the purpose of a patch or service pack.

BUILD YOUR VOCABULARY

As you progress through this course, develop a personal IT glossary. This will help you build your vocabulary and prepare you for a career. Write a definition for each of the following terms and add it to your IT glossary.

application software
end user license
  agreement (EULA)
file format
open-source software

podcasting
productivity software
proprietary software
system requirements
template

2 REVIEW AND ASSESSMENT

Chapter Summary

Section 2.1 System Software

- The operating system (OS) is software that manages all of the devices, as well as locates and provides instructions to the CPU. It also performs communication with the user and the hardware. General-use computers, such as a PC or tablet, must have an OS to work, but single-use computers do not require an operating system.

- One of the keys to the Windows OS environment is the ability to run multiple programs simultaneously. Windows operating systems have common features. In all Windows operating system environments, programs can be launched from the **Start** menu or by double-clicking a shortcut icon on the desktop. There is also a set of common shortcut key combinations, such as [Ctrl][A], [Ctrl][C], [Ctrl][X], [Ctrl][V], [Ctrl][Z], and [Alt][Tab]. The views in which windows are arranged and system utility files are also common between Windows versions.

- Programs are what you use to get the job done. Programs may allow you to create and edit documents, play music, create images, and many other tasks.

Section 2.2 Application Software

- Productivity software is software that supports the completion of tasks. This group includes software for word processing, creating spreadsheets and presentations, editing graphics and video, and managing databases, among many other tasks.

- Software must be installed in order for it to be used. Once installed, software may need to be updated, uninstalled, or reinstalled.

Now that you have finished this chapter, see what you know about computer applications by taking the chapter posttest. Access the posttest by visiting www.g-wlearning.com.

Chapter 2 Test

Multiple Choice
Select the best response.

1. Which of the following is *not* a type of system software?
   A. operating system
   B. proprietary software
   C. device drivers
   D. utility programs

2. _____ holds instructions for initializing the hardware and loading the main OS.
   A. System software
   B. Device driver
   C. Shareware
   D. Firmware

3. Open-source software is characterized by:
   A. proprietary copyright.
   B. base code that is publicly available.
   C. software that works for a limited time before requiring purchase.
   D. costly software updates.

4. Which of the following specifications is *not* listed as a system requirement?
   A. ROM
   B. processor speed
   C. RAM
   D. hard drive space

5. If an uninstall feature is not included with the software, use the _____ function in the Windows Control Panel to remove it.
   A. **Delete Software**
   B. **Uninstall**
   C. **Add or Remove Programs**
   D. **System Restore**

Completion

Complete the following sentences with the correct word(s).

6. Using a small program to get the computer running is called _____.

7. _____ assist in managing and optimizing a computer's performance.

8. _____ supports the completion of tasks, such as creating documents or spreadsheets.

9. A(n) _____, or service pack, is a fix to software to correct bugs, remove security issues, or improve a version of the program.

10. _____ is the process of reloading a software program on the computer system.

Matching

Match the correct term with its definition.

A. end user license agreement (EULA)

B. podcasting

C. file format

D. system software

E. operating system (OS)

11. Distribution of audio files over the Internet via automated or subscribed downloads.

12. Software that manages all of the devices.

13. Contract outlining the set of rules that every user must agree to before using the software.

14. Indicates the manner in which data is stored on the disk.

15. Includes four types of software: the operating system, utility programs, device drivers, and programs.

Application and Extension of Knowledge

1. Identify five examples of utility software. Classify each as a high- or low-importance utility. Prepare for a class discussion explaining why you classified each as you did.

2. Use the search function in the Windows **Start** screen or menu to search for resmon. This is the Resource Monitor utility. Launch it. Click the **Overview** tab in the Resource Monitor. Examine what information is displayed in the graphic on the right. Identify the percentage of CPU usage. Speculate how this utility can help examine the performance of a computer system.

3. Identify three application software programs on your computer. Compare and contrast their functions and why you use them. Prepare for a class-wide discussion on the importance of application software to your daily life.

4. Locate the end user license agreement (EULA) for a software program you use often. Read it. What did you learn regarding the usage of this program you did not previously know?

5. Locate the system requirements for a software program you currently want to buy. List the requirements. What kind of updates, if any, will you need to make to your computer to get the most out of this software?

Online Activities

Complete the following activities, which will help you learn, practice, and expand your knowledge and skills.

Vocabulary. Practice vocabulary for this chapter using the e-flash cards, matching activity, and vocabulary game until you are able to recognize their meanings.

Communication Skills

Writing. Generate your own ideas relevant to using digital technology in the appropriate manner. Use multiple authoritative print and digital sources and document each. Write several paragraphs about your findings to demonstrate your understanding of digital citizenship.

Listening. Passive listening is casually listening to someone speak. Passive listening is appropriate when you do not have to interact with the speaker. Listen to a classmate as he or she is having a conversation with you. Focus attention on the message. Ask for clarification for anything that you do not understand. Provide verbal and nonverbal feedback while the person is talking.

Speaking. Career-ready individuals understand that demonstrating leadership qualities is a way to make a positive contribution to a team. Identify leadership characteristics that you believe all members of a technology team should possess. Use a graphic organizer to record your ideas. Share with the class.

Internet Research

Hard Disk Drives. Research the evolution of the hard disk drive (HDD) using various Internet resources. Write several paragraphs that describe how HDDs have developed since their inception. Did the hard disk drive replace any technology when it was developed? Has new technology begun to replace the hard disk drive? Use correct grammar, punctuation, and terminology as you write.

Teamwork

With your team, create a list of long or complex words or phrases that might be used in technical writing related to information technology. List each of the words and phrases on a dry-erase board or flip chart. As a team, work together to think of simpler words or phrases to replace each list item. Use a thesaurus if one is available.

Activity Files

Visit www.g-wlearning.com/informationtechnology/ to download the activity files for this chapter. These activities will expand your learning of the material presented in this chapter and allow you to practice what you have learned. Follow the instructions provided in each file to complete the activity.

Activity File 2-1 Comparing Operating Systems

Activity File 2-2 Utility Software

Activity File 2-3 Application Software

Activity File 2-4 Accessibility Software

Activity File 2-5 Software Corruption

CAPSTONE PROJECT

The capstone project builds from one chapter to the next. It allows you to apply the skills you have learned to create a complete project in a desired career area. Read the instructions below for the career area you chose to work in for this course. Work in the same career area in each chapter.

Agriculture, Food, and Natural Resources

In this activity, you will assume the role of an employee tasked with selecting the appropriate version and delivery method of office-suite software. You will visit the Microsoft Office website to research all the available versions and make a decision about which is best for the given scenario. Access the *Introduction to Microsoft Office 2016* companion website (www.g-wlearning.com/informationtechnology/) to view the instructions for this chapter's Agriculture, Food, and Natural Resources capstone project.

Business, Management, and Administration

In this activity, you will assume the role of an employee tasked with selecting the appropriate version and delivery method of office-suite software. You will visit the Microsoft Office website to research all the available versions and make a decision about which is best for the given scenario. Access the *Introduction to Microsoft Office 2016* companion website (www.g-wlearning.com/informationtechnology/) to view the instructions for this chapter's Business, Management, and Administration capstone project.

Health Science

In this activity, you will assume the role of an employee tasked with selecting the appropriate version and delivery method of office-suite software. You will visit the Microsoft Office website to research all the available versions and make a decision about which is best for the given scenario. Access the *Introduction to Microsoft Office 2016* companion website (www.g-wlearning.com/informationtechnology/) to view the instructions for this chapter's Health Science capstone project.

Science, Technology, Engineering, and Mathematics

In this activity, you will assume the role of an employee tasked with selecting the appropriate version and delivery method of office-suite software. You will visit the Microsoft Office website to research all the available versions and make a decision about which is best for the given scenario. Access the *Introduction to Microsoft Office 2016* companion website (www.g-wlearning.com/informationtechnology/) to view the instructions for this chapter's Science, Technology, Engineering, and Mathematics capstone project.

Copyright Goodheart-Willcox Co., Inc.   Chapter 2 Introduction to System and Application Software   55

3

FILE MANAGEMENT

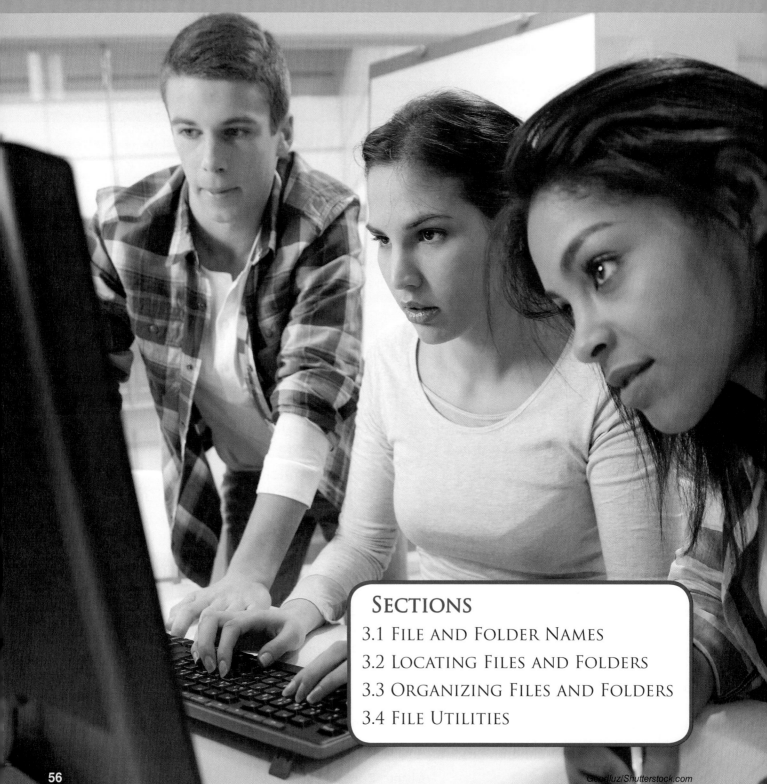

SECTIONS

3.1 FILE AND FOLDER NAMES

3.2 LOCATING FILES AND FOLDERS

3.3 ORGANIZING FILES AND FOLDERS

3.4 FILE UTILITIES

Check Your IT IQ

Before you begin this chapter, see what you already know about computer applications by taking the chapter pretest. Access the pretest by visiting www.g-wlearning.com.

Good file management means that the user knows how to organize information on a computer. Not only do files need to be named in a meaningful way, the user must be able to locate files when necessary. A sign of poor file management is file names that do not indicate what the file contains. Not keeping track of where files are saved is also a sign of poor file management.

Files can be lost for many reasons: accidental deletion, unintentional overwriting with another file, theft, misplaced removable media, hard disk failure, or loss of the computer. Part of good file management is keeping multiple copies of a file in case of a loss. Good file management also implies that the user has created a safe location for saving the files. In a networked environment, many opportunities are present for other users to accidentally or intentionally cause file losses.

Microsoft Office Specialist Objectives

Excel

Create Charts and Objects

5.3 Insert and Format Objects

5.3.3 Modify object properties

PowerPoint

Create and Manage Presentations

1.5 Change Presentation Options and Views

1.5.3 Set file properties

Word

Create and Manage Documents

1.4 Customize Options and Views for Documents

1.4.5 Add document properties

FILE AND FOLDER NAMES

A computer file is a collection of 1s and 0s that has meaning. This collection resides in computer memory or in a storage location. Software programs may create temporary files that are deleted when the software program no longer needs them. Other files contain information created by a user, and the software allows the user to save and open the file for further use. When a file is saved, it is given a file name so that the file can be located and used again. It is a good practice to assign meaningful and memorable file names so you or another person can recognize the files.

Windows uses a system of named folders to catalog and contain files. Notice that the names in Windows echo activities in an office or school setting. When students save paper files that belong together, they often use a manila folder. A Windows folder performs the same function for electronic files. Folders allow similar files or all files for a project to be organized together. This section discusses the naming of files and folders.

Goodluz/Shutterstock.com

TERMS

CamelCase	folder name
file association	library
file name	naming convention
file name extension	nested
file path	reserved symbols
file tree	subfolder
folder	

LEARNING GOALS

- Explain how to create meaningful, legal file names.
- Use Windows Explorer to rename files and folders.

Windows File and Folder Names

The **file name** is a label that identifies a unique file on a computer system. There are three parts to a file name in the Windows operating system:

- the file name
- a period (or "dot")
- the file name extension

For example, consider abcde.ext as the file name. In this example, abcde is the file name and ext is the file name extension. The period separates the file name and the file name extension. Notice that Windows uses the term *file name* for both the whole name and the part of the name before the period.

A **folder** is a container in which files are stored. A **subfolder** is a folder contained within another folder. A subfolder within a parent folder is referred to as a **nested** folder. There may be several levels of nesting, as a subfolder may itself contain a subfolder that in turn contains another subfolder, as shown in Figure 3-1. A **folder name** is a label that identifies a unique folder on a computer system. In the Windows operating system, a folder name consists of only a name. There is no extension, so there is no period, either.

> ## FYI
>
> The terms *folder* and *directory* are used interchangeably. They mean the same thing.

Legal Names

File names in Windows are limited by the number of characters in the folders and subfolders that hold the file. For example, C:\Program Files\abcde.ext indicates a file named abcde.ext that is located in

Goodheart-Willcox Publisher

Figure 3-1. A folder may contain many subfolders, each of which may contain additional subfolders.

Sustainability Training
Green companies lead by example and educate their employees on sustainable business practices. Through sustainability training, employees learn the importance of *going green* at work and the best practices to reduce waste and lower energy consumption. Training employees in simple green procedures can not only help save the environment, but save the company money, too.

the Program Files folder on the C: drive. This string is called the **file path**, which is the drive and folder location of a file plus its file name. The total number of characters in the file path cannot exceed 260 characters. Notice that the path includes the colon (:) for the drive letter and backslashes (\) to indicate where there is a change in folder.

The file path can be seen in the **Properties** dialog box. Right-click on a file, and click **Properties** in the shortcut menu. The file name is listed at the top of the **General** tab, and the path to the folder containing the file is shown in the **Location:** area, as shown in Figure 3-2. The full file path is the location plus the file name.

The limit of 260 characters provides ample space for writing a clear and unique name for each file and folder. Any character from the keyboard may be used in a name *except* for a few reserved symbols. **Reserved symbols** are characters that Windows uses for special meaning. The reserved symbols are shown in Figure 3-3.

Although Windows allows spaces in names, spaces cause problems in other software environments. Some software will stop reading the name at the first space. A URL or web address that contains a space will be misinterpreted. For example:

http://www.pages.com/my document.doc

will be read as:

http://www.pages.com/my

For this reason, it is best to not use spaces in file and folder names.

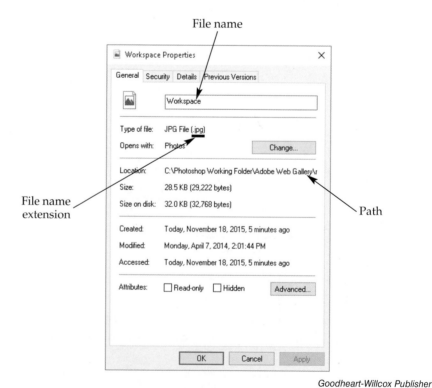

Goodheart-Willcox Publisher

Figure 3-2. The file name, file name extension, and file path are shown in the **Properties** dialog box.

Symbol	Description
<	Less than symbol or left chevron
>	Greater than symbol or right chevron
:	Colon
"	Double quote
/	Forward slash
\	Backslash
|	Vertical bar or pipe
?	Question mark
*	Asterisk

Goodheart-Willcox Publisher

Figure 3-3. Reserved symbols cannot be used in file or folder names.

All files and folders should have unique names. Although most operating systems will allow you to create many files with the same name as long as they are in different folders or drives, this is not a good idea. When looking for a specific file and several appear, the user will not know which one is correct.

Meaningful Names

The file name should clearly describe what is in the file. For example, suppose a student uses labReport to name a biology project. This may be satisfactory if there is only one lab report. However, if another lab report is created later, it would not be clear which file is for which report. Instead, more descriptive file names such as LabReportBio and LabReportDNA better describe the content of the files. A **naming convention** is a pattern that is followed whenever a file name is created.

Without spaces between words, long file names can be hard to read. For example, the name reportforlabexperiment is difficult to read. This name would be easy to read if there were an indication of the individual words. **CamelCase** is a naming convention in which the beginning of each word in the name is capitalized. This allows the file name to be read easily. For example, the name reportforlabexperiment becomes ReportForLabExperiment in CamelCase. The CamelCase naming convention got its name due to the apparent humps the capital letters make in the name, as shown in Figure 3-4.

Goodheart-Willcox Publisher; Teguh Mujiono/Shutterstock.com

Figure 3-4. CamelCase is using a capital letter for the first letter in each word in a file name.

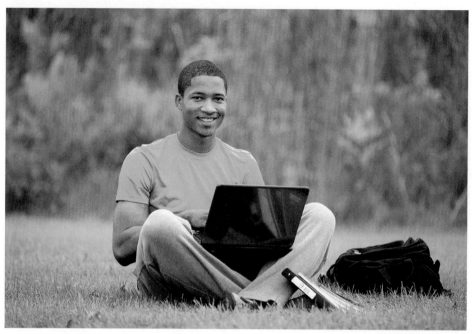

Flashon Studio/Shutterstock.com

Computer files for schoolwork can be arranged in folders to keep everything orderly.

GS5
Key Applications
2.10.1, 3.11, 5.1.2

FYI

Changing the file
name extension does
not change the format
of the file. To change
the format of the file,
it must be saved in a
different format.

File Name Extensions

The second part of the file name is the period. Although the first part of the file name may contain periods as well, the last period on the right is the one Windows uses to begin the file name extension.

The third part of the file name is the file name extension, which follows the last dot. The **file name extension**, or file extension, tells the Windows operating system which software to use to open the file. The file name extension *indicates* the format of the file, but does not control the format of the file. The software saving the file controls the format.

Generally, when saving a file, the user adds the file name and Windows adds the correct file name extension. For example, if the user saves a document from Microsoft Word, the software saves the file as a Word document and adds the extension of .docx. It is good practice to let Windows choose the file name extension. Windows determines the file name extension based on the software program used to create the file. When performing a "save as" in many programs, the user can select one of many different file types in which to save the file. For example, image editing software, such as Photoshop or GIMP, may have a native file format, but also allows saving in several other formats, such as TIFF or JPEG.

When a file icon is double-clicked, Windows will locate software to open the file, launch the software, and load the file. This is made possible by a feature called file association. **File association** is a process in which Windows links a file name extension to a software program. For example, if a file has an extension of .docx, double-clicking on the file icon causes Windows to launch Microsoft Word and load the file into Word.

Figure 3-5 shows a few common file name extensions and the Windows program commonly associated with the file type. In Windows,

Extension	File Type	Associated Application
.avi	Video	Windows Media Player
.css	Cascading style sheet	Default browser
.doc, .docx	Document	Microsoft Word
.exe	Executable application	Windows operating system
.htm, .html	Hypertext markup (web page)	Default browser
.jpg, .jpeg	Compressed image	Default image editor
.m4a	Audio-only MPEG4	Windows Media Player
.mp3	Music or sound	Windows Media Player
.pdf	Portable Document Format	Adobe Reader
.pps	Slide show	Microsoft PowerPoint
.ppt	Presentation	Microsoft PowerPoint
.rtf	Rich text format document	Default document editor
.swf	Flash format	Flash Player
.tif, .tiff	Compressed image file	Windows Photo Viewer
.txt	Text	Notepad
.wpd	Document	Corel WordPerfect
.xls, .xlsx	Spreadsheet	Microsoft Excel
.zip	Compressed archive	Windows Explorer

Figure 3-5. These are common file name extensions.

these associations may be changed using the **File Associations** dialog box. To access this, open the Control Panel window, click **Programs**, click **Default Programs**, and then click **Associate a file type or protocol with a program**.

Do not manually change a file name extension unless there is a very good reason to do so. Changing the extension removes the file association. Additionally, some software will not recognize or open a file using **File**>**Open** unless the file has the proper extension.

Naming a Group of Related Files

A project may contain several related files. Using a similar word pattern in the file names of these files reminds the user that the files are all related. For example, after completing a science experiment on determining the boiling points of different liquids, the students have been asked to record the following.

- hypothesis and methods in a text document
- data and charts in a spreadsheet
- experiment setup in a photograph
- photograph and results on a web page
- results in a presentation

A good way to organize similar files is to begin each file name with a common word. In this example, all documents relate to the boiling lab, so the word boiling can start each file name followed by the detail of each document:

- BoilingDescription.doc
- BoilingData.xls
- BoilingSetup.jpg
- BoilingResults.htm
- BoilingPresentation.ppt

Another naming convention is to include the creation date in the file name. The date a file was created or last updated is automatically recorded and can be displayed in Windows File Explorer. However, in some cases, adding a date to the file name is more useful because that will not change each time the file is saved. This is often done to maintain a date record or to help in sorting files. For example, the file name 160513LabResults.doc refers to the result of a lab test conducted in the year 2016 (16), in the month of May (05), and on the thirteenth day (13). Using this naming convention allows lab results from many different dates to be sorted by the year, then the month within a year, and finally by the day within a month regardless of when the content of the file had been updated.

Windows File Explorer

Windows File Explorer is a file-management utility with a graphical user interface that can be used to find anything in the computer's storage areas. The Windows File Explorer is part of the Windows operating system and controls parts of the GUI, including the desktop and the **Start** or **Apps** menu.

The first version of Windows contained MS-DOS Executive as the file utility. It also served as the graphical user interface instead of the **Start** or **Apps** menu and desktop found in later versions of Windows. MS-DOS Executive gave way to File Manager in Windows 3.0, at which time the program no longer served as the GUI and was strictly a file-management utility. Windows File Explorer and the **Start** menu first appeared in Windows 95. At this point, the program again became part of the GUI. The **Apps** menu is used in Windows 8.

Windows File Explorer contains the address bar and ribbon or toolbar at the top of the window, as shown in Figure 3-6. Along the left-hand side of the window is the navigation pane. This pane contains a list of the available drives and folders shown in a tree format. On the right-hand side of the window is the file list. This shows the files and folders contained within what is selected in the navigation pane. Above the file list is the search box. This is used to locate files and folders, as discussed in the next section.

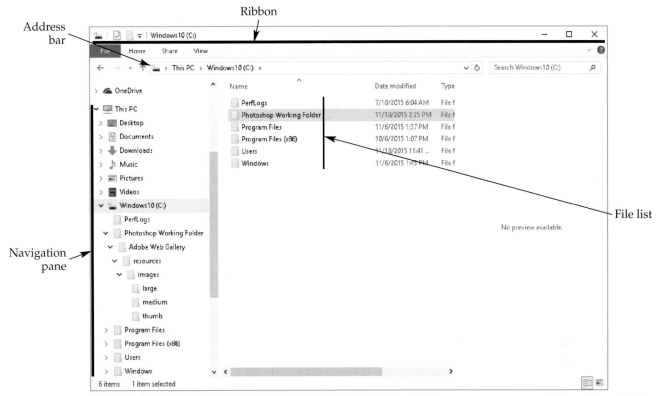

Goodheart-Willcox Publisher

Figure 3-6. Windows File Explorer is used to locate and manage files in the Windows operating system.

The list of available drives and folders shown in the navigation pane is a tree. A **file tree** can be expanded to display subfolders and the files contained within them, as shown in Figure 3-7. Each folder in the tree is called a branch. The last item in an expanded branch is called a leaf. To expand a branch in the file tree, move the mouse over the folder name until a triangle is displayed to the left of the folder icon. Then, click the triangle. If the folder contains subfolders, they will be displayed indented below the parent folder. To collapse a branch in the file tree, click the triangle next to an expanded branch.

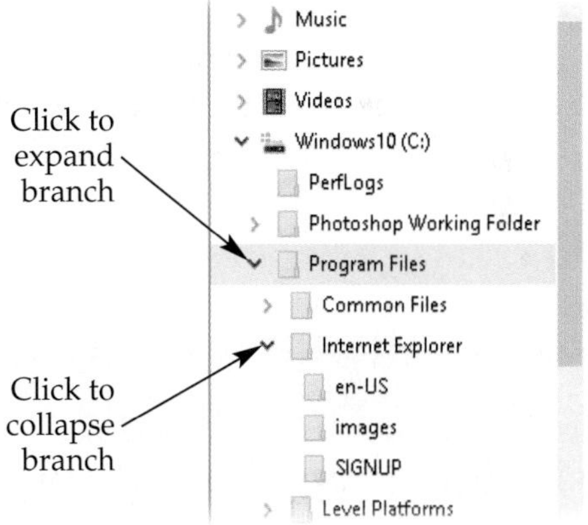

There are several folder views in which the content of a folder can be displayed. Some of these views include changing the size of the icons for files and folders, displaying the icons in a list, and displaying detailed information about the files and folders.

Goodheart-Willcox Publisher

Figure 3-7. The navigation pane displays the folder structure using a tree metaphor.

Folders

Folders provide an organizational tool that can be used to keep similar files together. Similar files may be related to the same event, of the same file type, or for any reason meaningful to the user. Double-clicking a folder on the desktop launches Windows File Explorer, which displays the content of the folder.

A general rule of thumb is to keep only as many files in a folder as can be displayed in Windows File Explorer without scrolling. If there are more files than that, it is likely the files can be organized into subfolders. For example, suppose a user creates a folder named SchoolWork within his or her Documents folder. Items in the Documents folder that are related to schoolwork can then be moved into the SchoolWork folder. This reduces the number of files located in the Documents folder.

A folder is simply a special type of file. Therefore, follow the same naming rules used for other files. However, as stated earlier, a folder name does not have a file name extension.

Libraries

In Windows File Explorer, a **library** is a collection of similar files and folders that are displayed together, but that may be stored in different locations. A library displays all of the common files available to all users and the current user's files in the same view. The library structure was introduced in Windows 7 to help multiple users run the same computer. Unlike a folder, there is no file or folder connected to a library. If a library is deleted, the files and folders displayed in the library are unaffected.

The idea behind a library is there may be several folders on the disk drive containing similar files that commonly need to be accessed at the same time. For example, the Pictures library, which appears in Windows File Explorer in the Libraries branch, displays the folders My Pictures and Public Pictures. These folders are not subfolders within a *folder* named Pictures, they are simply displayed in the *library* named Pictures for easy access. This is the concept of libraries.

Ethics

File Sharing

There are many types of computer files, from program files such as executables to document files such as songs, photographs, and e-books. However, almost all files are owned by someone. It is unethical and, in many cases, illegal to share files for which you are not the owner.

HANDS-ON EXAMPLE 3.1.1

WINDOWS FILE EXPLORER

The ability to effectively use Windows File Explorer is an essential skill for any computer user. Begin by learning the different elements of Windows File Explorer and how to navigate the folder and library structures. Note: libraries are disabled by default in Windows 8.1.

1. In Windows 10, right-click on the **Start** menu button, and click **File Explorer** in the shortcut menu. In Windows 8, launch File Explorer by clicking the **Apps** button and then clicking **File Explorer** in the **Windows System** group of the **Apps** menu. In Windows 7, right-click on the **Start** menu button, and click **Open Windows Explorer** in the shortcut menu.

HANDS-ON EXAMPLE 3.1.1 (CONTINUED)

2. In Windows 8, click the **View** tab, click the **Navigation Pane** button, and click **Show libraries** in the drop-down menu so it is checked. Leave it checked if already checked. This ensures libraries are visible.

3. Locate the elements of the Windows File Explorer window shown in Figure 3-6.

4. Single-click the Libraries branch in the navigation (left-hand) pane. The defined libraries are displayed in the file list in the right-hand pane. Note: in Windows 10, the libraries are not listed as subfolders within a Libraries branch.

5. Double-click the Pictures library in the file list. The Libraries branch is expanded in the navigation pane, the Pictures branch is highlighted, and the content of the Pictures library is displayed in the file list.

6. In Windows 7, double-click the Sample Pictures library in the file list. Note: Windows 10 and Windows 8 do not include any of the sample files and folders found in Windows 7.

7. In Windows 10 and Windows 8, click the **View** tab, and click **Medium Icons** in the **Layout** group. In Windows 7, click the **View** pull-down menu, and click **Medium Icons** in the menu.

8. Applying what you have learned, expand the tree in the navigation pane to show the folders on the local drive, the subfolders within the Windows folder, the subfolders within the Web subfolder, the subfolders within the Wallpaper subfolder, and the files within the Windows subfolder (C:\Windows\Web\Wallpaper\Windows). This nested folder should contain at least one image file.

9. Select an image file by single-clicking it. Notice the details pane updates with information about the file and the menu bar contains more options. The details pane is turned off by default in Windows 10 and Windows 8. To turn it on, click the **Details Pane** button in the **Panes** group on the **View** tab of the ribbon.

Displaying File Name Extensions

By default, the file name extensions are hidden by the operating system. This can lead to confusing situations if there are several files with the same name, but different file name extensions. Turning on the display of file name extensions can help the user tell one file from another file with the same name.

For example, it is a common practice to name image files by the content of the image. The files Jellyfish.jpg and Jellyfish.bmp are both image files. However, with the file name extensions hidden, the user will see both files as only Jellyfish when viewed in Windows File Explorer. It is only when the file name extensions are displayed that the difference between the files becomes clear, as shown in Figure 3-8.

FYI

The icon associated with a file helps indicate the file type, but many file types share the same icon or similar icons.

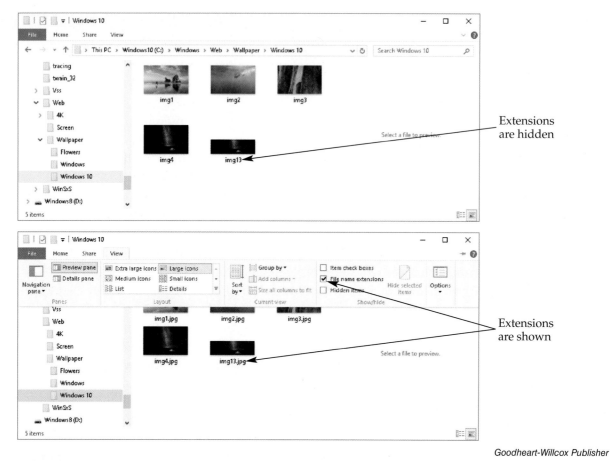

Goodheart-Willcox Publisher

Figure 3-8. File name extensions are hidden by default, but can be displayed.

TITANS OF TECHNOLOGY

David A. Huffman, a computer scientist and inventor, was an early pioneer in the development of computers. He won many awards. However, the one he earned in 1998 from the IEEE Information Theory Society made a big impact on data compression technologies. This award recognized his invention of the Huffman minimum-length lossless data-compression code. The compression code was the topic of a term paper he wrote while a graduate student at the Massachusetts Institute of Technology in 1952. Before his method was used, file compression tended to lose some or much of the fidelity of the original file. Huffman's idea defined a compression scheme whereby none of the data were lost. Decompression restored the file to its original fidelity. This data compression method has since been used to compress image files as well as the data stream for high-definition television (HDTV) broadcasts. The technology is also used in fax machines and modems. The compression method is known as Huffman encoding. Huffman was also very interested in origami, the ancient Japanese art of paper folding. He contributed to the branch of mathematics involved in the paper folding techniques.

HANDS-ON EXAMPLE 3.1.2

DISPLAYING FILE NAME EXTENSIONS

File name extensions are hidden by default. However, many users prefer to have file name extensions visible. This is a simple setting in Windows.

1. Launch Windows File Explorer.
2. Applying what you have learned, navigate to the C:\Windows\Web\Wallpaper\Windows folder.
3. In Windows 10 and Windows 8, click the **View** tab, and click the **Options** button (not the drop-down arrow below it). In Windows 7, click the **Organize** button on the toolbar, and click **Folder and search Options** in the drop-down menu that is displayed. The **Folder Options** dialog box is displayed.
4. Click the **View** tab in the dialog box. Notice all of the settings for how files are displayed.
5. Scroll down in the **Advanced Settings** list, and uncheck the **Hide extensions for known file types** check box, as shown.

6. Click the **Apply to Folders** button at the top of the tab so file name extensions will be displayed in *all* folders.
7. Click the **OK** button to apply the change and close the dialog box. Notice the file name extension is displayed for the file in the folder. In this case, the file in the folder is in the JPG format, which is a graphics file.
8. Double-click on the file to open it in the program associated with the .jpg file extension.

Renaming Files and Folders

FYI

Two single clicks must have enough time between them so the operating system will not interpret the clicks as a double-click.

Often, a file or folder must be renamed. This may be done to correct spelling, make the name more descriptive, or simply to change the name to suit the user. However, only the file name should be changed, not the file name extension. If the file name extension is changed, the file association may be broken. This may make the file unrecognizable by the associated software.

There are several ways to rename a file or folder in Windows File Explorer. One way is to right-click on the file or folder and click **Rename** in the shortcut menu. Another way is to single-click twice on the file or folder in the file list. A third way is to select the file or folder in the file list, and then in Windows 10 and Windows 8, click **Home>Organize>Rename**. In Windows 7, click **File>Rename**. With any of these methods, the file name is replaced with an edit box, and the current file name is highlighted and ready for editing. Once the file name is highlighted, edit the name, and press the [Enter] key once to complete the process.

HANDS-ON EXAMPLE 3.1.3

NAMING FOLDERS

Removable media, such as flash drives, are commonly used by students to maintain schoolwork. In Chapter 1, you began setting up a flash drive for use in this class. Now you will add folders to this device for a class named Physical Science.

1. Insert the flash drive set up in Chapter 1 into the computer. If the **AutoPlay** dialog box appears, cancel it.
2. Launch Windows File Explorer.
3. In the navigation pane on the left, highlight the MS-OFFICE flash drive.
4. Click the arrow to the left of the drive icon for the flash drive to expand the folder tree for the drive. Currently, the drive contains no folders (unless folders have previously been added), so there is nothing to expand.
5. Make sure the flash drive is highlighted in the navigation pane. When creating a folder, it will be placed in whatever location is currently highlighted in the navigation pane.
6. In Windows 10 and Windows 8, click **Home>New>New Folder**. In Windows 7, click the **New Folder** button on the toolbar. A new folder is added to the file list, and the default name of New Folder is highlighted for editing. The folder tree for the flash drive also is automatically expanded in the navigation pane.

HANDS-ON EXAMPLE 3.1.3 (CONTINUED)

7. Change the default name to SciencePhysical, and press the [Enter] key to finish creating the folder.
8. Highlight the SciencePhysical folder in the navigation pane.
9. Applying what you have learned, add a subfolder named BoilingLab in the SciencePhysical folder.
10. Click the arrow to the left of the SciencePhysical folder in the navigation pane to expand the folder tree. The BoilingLab folder is displayed below the SciencePhysical folder in the tree, which indicates it is a subfolder.
11. Right-click on the SciencePhysical folder in the navigation pane, and click **Rename** in the shortcut menu.
12. Change the name of the folder to PhysicalScience, and press the [Enter] key. Notice how the BoilingLab subfolder remains in the parent folder even after the parent is renamed, as shown.

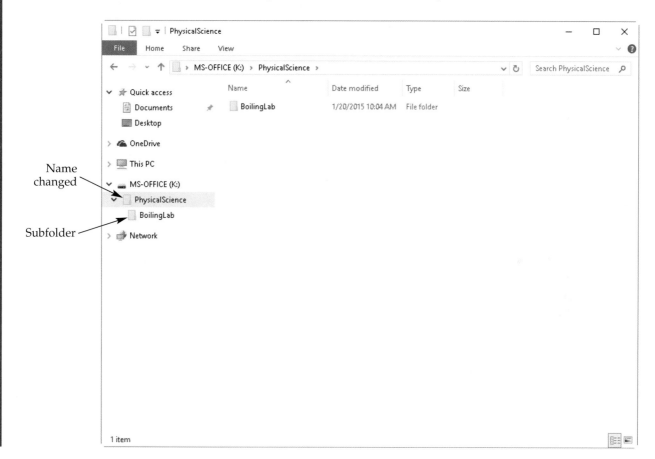

3.1 | SECTION REVIEW

 ## CHECK YOUR UNDERSTANDING

1. What are the three parts of a file name?
2. What are the two parts of the file path?
3. Write this file name in CamelCase: My Picture of Venice.jpg.
4. What is a library in Windows Explorer?
5. Why would you turn on the display of file name extensions?

 ## BUILD YOUR VOCABULARY

As you progress through this course, develop a personal IT glossary. This will help you build your vocabulary and prepare you for a career. Write a definition for each of the following terms and add it to your IT glossary.

CamelCase	folder name
file association	library
file name	naming convention
file name extension	nested
file path	reserved symbols
file tree	subfolder
folder	

LOCATING FILES AND FOLDERS

bikeriderlondon/Shutterstock.com

It is not unusual to hear novice computer users say that they cannot find files they created. This may be explained by the fact that disk drives may have gigabytes or terabytes of storage space and contain hundreds or thousands of folders. However, being unable to locate a file often means the user did not have a plan for saving and locating files.

Windows provides an organizational plan for collecting files of a similar type in one location. This organizational scheme includes folders for My Documents, My Music, My Pictures, and My Videos. However, many users create custom folders to group files according to their own ways of working. Some choose to group files by creation dates, while others group files around a certain topic, such as vacations or school courses. Each person should choose a scheme that makes sense for him or her and that will support rapid retrieval of each file. A good guide is the English proverb, "A place for everything and everything in its place."

TERMS
file management
root
sorting
wildcard

LEARNING GOALS
- Locate files and folders on a computer system.
- Sort the list of files in a folder.
- Discuss sharing files online.

Locating Files and Folders

File management is working with files on the hard disk or other storage medium. Good management involves organizing files in logical locations. Doing so makes it easier for users to recall where a file is saved.

All files are stored in a hierarchy that begins at the top folder of the drive. This top folder is called the **root**. For example, some folders that exist at the root of the primary hard drive in the Windows operating system include Program Files, Users, and Windows. The file path begins at the drive root.

Media Reader Devices

A media reader device uses digital files in standard formats to recreate the original content. The media may be video, photos, audio, or text such as an e-book. To locate the files, open the corresponding app. For example, to locate e-book files, open the e-book–reader app. To locate image files, open the photograph-viewer app.

Files may be stored on the device or in the cloud. E-book readers support a file management tool called the *library*. Users can view titles and add or delete e-book files using this tool. Music readers may use CDs, DVDs, SD cards, or direct download to access songs. Often connecting a reader device to a PC provides additional file-management capability. Songs can be swapped from the reader to the PC in order to conserve storage space on the reader device.

Image Files on Mobile Devices

Most mobile devices include a camera for taking photos and videos. These files are saved on the mobile device. Newer devices create images with high resolution, resulting in very large files. Because the files are digital, it is easy to take many shots of a subject until a satisfying image is created. It is possible to run out of storage space on mobile devices. To regain storage space, delete all photos of lesser quality or that are unneeded.

The files can be sorted into folders by date or topic. These folders are called *albums*. Create an album, and then drag photos into it. It is also possible to copy these photos to a computer. The synchronization, or syncing, process makes a copy of every photo on the device. When the mobile device is connected to the computer, it becomes a device on that computer. Navigate to the location of the photos, select the photos to copy, and copy them to the desired folder on the computer. It is important to monitor the number of photos on the device so that new photos are not missed due to insufficient storage, or time is not lost deleting photos on the fly.

Searching for Files

The search box in Windows File Explorer is used to locate files and folders. To conduct a search, first highlight the drive, folder, or subfolder to search in the navigation pane. The default text in the search box reflects what is selected. For example, if the Desktop branch is selected in the navigation pane, the default text in the search box is Search Desktop.

Next, click in the search box and enter the name of the file or folder for which to look. If the entire name is not known, a partial name can be entered. When the [Enter] key is pressed, the search begins. A green bar slides across the address bar to indicate the search progress. Every file found matching the search criteria will be displayed in the file list. Scroll through the list to locate the correct file or folder.

Sometimes the list of files found is longer than a user wants to sift through. Suppose a user was hunting for a picture file and simply entered pictures in the search box. Many unwanted files would be suggested. Narrowing the search criteria will speed up locating the file. **Wildcards** can be used in the search box to represent unknown characters. An asterisk (*) represents one or more characters in a file name. A question mark (?) represents just one character.

For example, to find all of the boiling lab files, enter boiling*. To find the boiling lab files that end in 1, enter boilinglab?1. This will return the files boilinglab01 and boilinglab11. However, the file boilinglab111 will not be returned because there is an extra character and the ? wildcard allows for one character.

It is possible to search for only files of a certain type by entering the asterisk wildcard and the file name extension. For example, to locate all JPEG images, enter *.jpg. This method can be combined with part of the file name to limit the search by file type. For example, to locate all boiling lab files that are in Excel format, enter boiling*.xlsx or boilinglab*.xlsx.

Searching Inside Files

By default, Windows File Explorer searches inside certain file types. During a search, Windows not only looks for file and folder names that meet the search criteria, but also looks at the content of these files. For example, the DOC and DOCx file types are by default set to have the content of the file searched. If a search is conducted with the phrase boiling, the results would include not only the files BoilingLab01.xlsx and BoilingLab02.xlsx, but also the file Results.docx if the word *boiling* is contained in that document.

Windows can be told to search the content of *all* file types. This may be useful, but it may also increase the amount of time it takes to conduct a search. In Windows 10 and Windows 8, click the **Options** button on the right-hand side of the **View** tab in the ribbon of File Explorer. In Windows 7, click **Folder options...** in the **Tools** pull-down menu of Windows Explorer. In the **Folder Options** dialog box that is displayed, click the **Search** tab, as shown in Figure 3-10. In Windows 10 and Windows 8, check the **Always search file names and contents** check box. In Windows 7, click **Always search file names and contents** radio button. Click the **OK** button to apply the setting and close the dialog box.

> **FYI**
>
> A file search will take less time if the search is the content of a specific folder rather than an entire drive.

> **FYI**
>
> Instead of setting Windows to search the content of all file types, it is possible to add specific file types to the list of files whose content will be searched using the **Indexing Options** link in the Control Panel window.

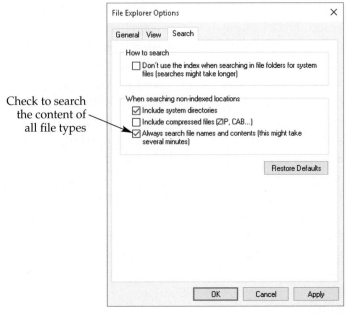

Check to search the content of all file types

Figure 3-10. By default, Windows searches the content of certain file types, but it can be set to search the content of all file types.

HANDS-ON EXAMPLE 3.2.1

SEARCHING FOR FILES AND FOLDERS

The ability to search for files is critical to becoming a successful computer user. It is not uncommon for a computer user to work with hundreds if not thousands of files over the course of a year. Even the best computer users will need to search for files and folders.

1. Launch Windows File Explorer.
2. Expand the folder tree for the primary hard drive (C:) in the navigation pane on the left, and highlight the Windows folder. The search box should display Search Windows.
3. Click in the search box. The default text is replaced with a vertical bar cursor. For a few seconds, a list of recent search phrases is also displayed.
4. Enter *.jpg in the search box. When the [Enter] key is pressed, the search begins.
5. A green bar appears in the address bar to indicate the progress of the search. When the green bar reaches the right-hand side of the address bar and disappears, the search is complete. The file list displays the files found in the Windows folder, as well as all of its subfolders, that are of the JPG type.

Sorting Files

Sorting is arranging a list by a certain criterion, such as alphabetically, by date, or by size. This can help locate the file or folder. By default, Windows File Explorer shows files sorted alphabetically by name, from A to Z. Sorting files by date is also useful to show which files have been saved more recently than others. Sorting by date is especially useful if multiple versions of the same file exist in different locations.

To sort files, display the details view. In Windows 10 and Windows 8, click **View>Layout>Details**. In Windows 7, click the **View>Details**. In the details view, headers are displayed in the file list, as shown in Figure 3-11. Clicking the Name header toggles between sorting the files alphabetically from A to Z and from Z to A. Clicking the Date header toggles between sorting the files from oldest to newest and newest to oldest. A small triangle pointing either up or down in one of the headers in the file list indicates which header is used as the sort criterion. The direction the triangle is pointing indicates if the sort is *ascending* (A to Z, for example) or *descending* (Z to A, for example).

Click the drop-down arrow in the header in the file list to show additional sorting options.

Headers

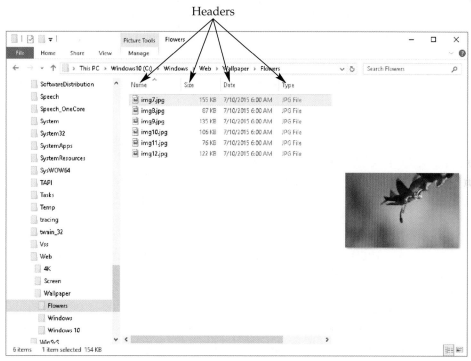

Goodheart-Willcox Publisher

Figure 3-11. The details view displays headers, which can be used to sort files.

HANDS-ON EXAMPLE 3.2.2

SORTING FILES

Sorting files is useful when a search returns a long list of files. However, sorting can be useful anytime the content of a folder is displayed.

1. Launch Windows File Explorer.
2. Highlight the Windows folder in the navigation pane on the left.
3. In Windows 10 and Windows 8, click **View>Layout>Details**. In Windows 7, click **View>Details**.
4. Scroll through the list of files and folders. When sorted in ascending alphabetical order, all folders are listed before the files.
5. Click the Date modified header so the triangle points down. Notice that the file list displays the files at the top in ascending order of when they were last modified. In ascending order of date, the most recent file is at the top. The folders are at the bottom of the list after the files and are also sorted in ascending order by date.
6. Click the Date modified header to toggle the sort to descending order. Now the folders appear first in the list with the oldest one at the top. The files appear after the list, also sorted in descending order.
7. Click the Name header so the triangle points up. All of the files and folders are now in ascending alphabetical order with the folders at the top of the list and the files after the folders.

Sharing Files Online

New technologies provide storage not on a local computer that also support sharing files. Some of these technologies, such as Dropbox (www.dropbox.com) and Google Cloud (www.google.com/cloud), are free to use. In some cases, there is a maximum of free capacity that can be expanded by purchasing a subscription.

Each user creates an account on these file sharing sites. Personal files may be uploaded or downloaded. Only a user's e-mail address is required to share files or a link to a file or folder with another user. To share with the public, a file is selected and the option to share publicly is clicked. Options include how much access to the file is permitted. Choices are full edit capability that includes ability to delete the file, or read access that allows only being able to read the content of the file.

Caution must be taken to protect the files on these cloud technologies. A publicly shared file can be seen by anyone. You may be able to restrict what can be done to the file, but if it is public, anyone can see it. A privately shared file can be seen only by those who have been given access to the file.

3.2 | SECTION REVIEW

 CHECK YOUR UNDERSTANDING

1. What is the top folder of the file tree called?
2. In which utility is the file search option found in Windows?
3. Which wildcard represents a single unknown character?
4. What should be entered to search for all image files with the .jpg file name extension?
5. How are files sorted by date in Windows Explorer?

 BUILD YOUR VOCABULARY

As you progress through this course, develop a personal IT glossary. This will help you build your vocabulary and prepare you for a career. Write a definition for each of the following terms and add it to your IT glossary.

file management
root
sorting
wildcard

ORGANIZING FILES AND FOLDERS

Operating systems allow users to create their own folders and subfolders. Organizing personal storage locations helps the user to save and retrieve data. Using Windows File Explorer, the user can easily view and create new folders. When using an external drive, it is a good idea to create the same folder hierarchy that is used on the internal drive. Having the same organizational scheme across devices will provide a more efficient transfer of files and folders from one device to another. Locating files on the external drive will be easier, too.

When files or folders are transferred from one device to another, they can be either copied or moved. There is a big difference between copying a file or folder and moving it. There is an even bigger difference when files or folders are copied or moved across devices. This section explains how to copy and move files and folders.

Ermolaev Alexander/Shutterstock.com

LEARNING GOALS
- Explain the difference between copying files and moving files.
- Delete files and folders from a computer system.

TERMS
copy
destination
drag-and-drop
move
recycle bin
shortcut menu
source

Copying and Moving Files and Folders

Proper file management is a key to being an efficient computer user. Proper *file-management techniques* include tasks such as creating files and folders; naming and renaming files and folders; copying and moving files between folders; copying and moving folders; and deleting files and folders. Files and folders can be easily moved around any storage drive or between devices. The **source** is the folder where the file or folder being transferred is originally located. The **destination** is the folder to where the file or folder is being transferred. The transfer can be move or copy.

There are often several methods to accomplish a task in Windows. Copying and moving files and folders are examples of where there is more than one way to do something. Particularly useful is the shortcut menu. The **shortcut menu** is a point-of-use menu displayed by right-clicking. Many software programs, including the Windows OS, have various shortcut menus. A shortcut menu is context-sensitive and anticipates common actions that a user may take. *Context-sensitive* means what is displayed in the menu is based on what was right-clicked. For example, to copy a file from one drive to another, right-click on that file and click **Copy** in the shortcut menu, as shown in Figure 3-12.

Selecting Files and Folders

To select, or highlight, a single file or folder, simply single-click it in Windows File Explorer. However, there are a couple of ways to select multiple files or folders. Once a selection is made, whether it consists of a single file or folder or multiple ones, it can be copied, moved, or deleted.

One way to select multiple files or folders is to drag a selection window around them in Windows File Explorer. Click in a blank area above the first file or folder name to select, hold down the left mouse button, and drag to the last file or folder to select. As you drag, a box

FYI

Most standard open and save dialog boxes in Windows can be used to perform some file management, such as copying, moving, renaming, and deleting files or folders.

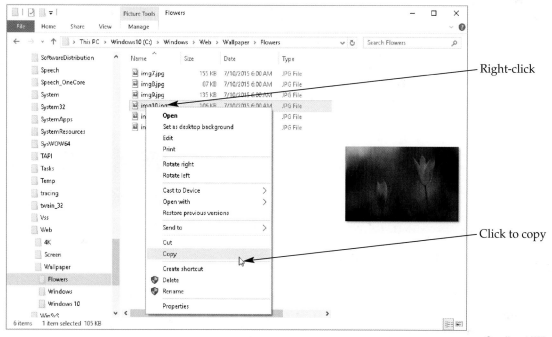

Goodheart-Willcox Publisher

Figure 3-12. The shortcut menu can be used to copy or move a file.

called a selection window is drawn. Any files or folders within the selection window will be selected, as shown in Figure 3-13. When the files and folders to select are highlighted by the selection window, release the left mouse button. This method only works to select files or folders in sequence.

Another way to select files or folders in sequence is to use the [Shift] key. This is often easier than trying to drag a selection window. To use this method, click the first file or folder to select it. Then, hold down the [Shift] key, and click the last file or folder in sequence. The first and last file or folder and all files or folders between them are selected.

To select individual files or folders that are not in sequence, the [Ctrl] key must be used. Hold down the [Ctrl] key, and then click the files and folders to select. The files and folders do not need to be in sequence, but they must be in the same parent folder.

Copying Files and Folders

A **copy** of a file or folder is an exact duplicate of the original at the time the copy was made. When a file or folder is copied from one folder to another, there are two versions of the file. One version exists in the source folder and one version exists in the destination folder. To copy a file or folder using the shortcut menu:

1. Right-click on the file in the source folder. This selects the file and displays the shortcut menu.
2. Click **Copy** in the shortcut menu. A copy of the file is placed on the system clipboard.

Files to be selected

Drag a window

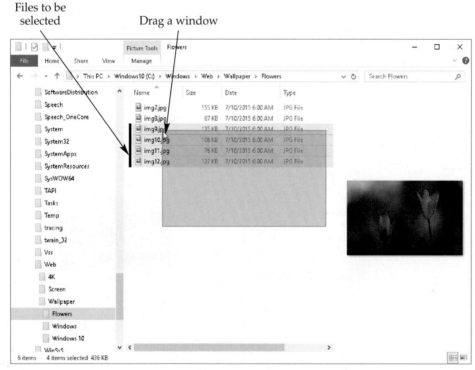

Figure 3-13. Multiple files can be selected by dragging a window around them.

3. Select the destination folder in the navigation pane.

4. Right-click in a blank area of the file list, and click **Paste** in the shortcut menu. A copy of the original file is created from the content on the system clipboard and placed in the destination folder.

On occasion, a file of the same name may be in the destination folder. Windows will prompt the user to choose what to do, as shown in Figure 3-14. There are three options:

- **Copy and Replace**
- **Don't copy**
- **Copy, but keep both files**

The **Copy and Replace** option overwrites the file or folder of the same name in the destination folder. This means the original file in the destination folder will be gone. It is important to be sure that it is appropriate to overwrite the file or folder in the destination folder before choosing this option.

The **Don't copy** option cancels the action. The file or folder remains in the source folder. The file or folder of the same name in the destination folder is also unaffected. Choosing this option provides an opportunity to go to the destination folder, determine whether or not the file or folder with the same name may be deleted, and then restart the copy procedure, if appropriate.

The **Copy, but keep both files** option preserves the file in the destination folder. The copy being created is placed in the destination folder with the original name appended with a number. Choosing this method provides an opportunity to examine both files.

FYI

If the source and destination folders are the same, the copy is automatically renamed to end with – Copy to avoid conflicting file names.

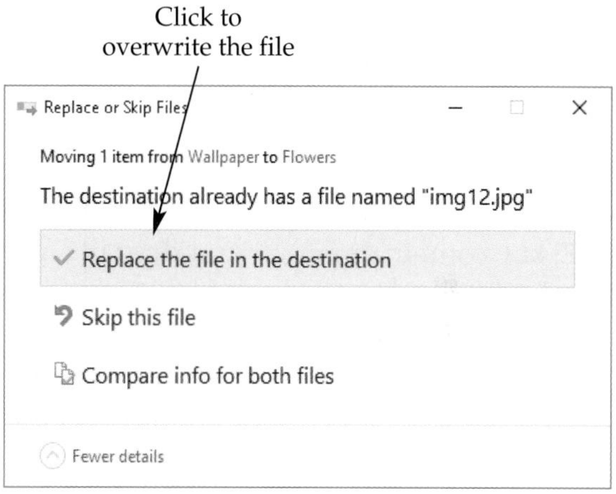

Click to overwrite the file

Goodheart-Willcox Publisher

Figure 3-14. If a file of the same name exists in the destination folder, you are asked what to do.

Moving Folders and Files

To **move** a file or folder means to remove it from the source folder and place it in the destination folder. When a file or folder is moved, there is only one version of it. After the action, the file or folder appears only in the destination folder. To move a file or folder using the shortcut menu:

1. Right-click on the file in the source folder. This selects the file and displays the shortcut menu.

2. Click **Cut** in the shortcut menu. The original file is removed from the source folder and placed on the system clipboard.

3. Select the destination folder in the navigation pane.

4. Right-click in a blank area of the file list, and click **Paste** in the shortcut menu. The original file is placed in the destination folder. It also remains on the system clipboard.

The only difference between the procedures for copying and moving using the shortcut menu is the file or folder is *cut* instead of *copied*. Cutting removes the original from the source folder and places it in the destination folder. In effect, the file or folder is moved to the destination folder. If the destination folder contains a file or folder with the same name as the original, the user is prompted to choose what to do, just as with copying a file.

Other Methods to Copy and Move

GS5
Key Applications
1.8

FYI

The keyboard shortcuts for copy, cut, and paste can be used in many software programs to edit content. The [Ctrl][Z] key combination is standard for reversing an action.

There are keyboard shortcuts that can be used to copy and move files and folders. To copy a file or folder, first select the item. Then, press the [Ctrl][C] key combination. This copies the file or folder to the system clipboard. To move a file or folder, select the item, and press the [Ctrl][X] key combination to cut the item. To complete either operation, select the destination folder in the navigation pane, and press the [Ctrl][V] key combination to paste the content of the system clipboard. To undo an operation, press the [Ctrl][Z] key combination. Note that the keys [Z], [X], [C], and [V] are next to each other on the keypad, which makes it easy to complete these common tasks with the left hand.

Another alternate method to copy or move a file or folder is to drag-and-drop it. **Drag-and-drop** is a procedure in which an item is selected in one location, moved with the mouse, and placed in another location. To drag, click the item in the source location, hold down the left mouse button, and move the mouse to the destination location. To drop, release the mouse button. To cancel a drag-and-drop, press the [Esc] key before dropping the item. When drag-and-drop is used between two drives, the operation is *copy*. When drag-and-drop is used between locations on the same drive, the operation is *move*. It is important to remember this default behavior.

The default drag-and-drop behavior can be modified with the [Ctrl] and [Shift] keys. To copy a file or folder, regardless of whether the operation is between drives or on the same drive, hold down the [Ctrl] key, then drag-and-drop the item into the destination location. To move a file or folder, hold down the [Shift] key, then drag-and-drop the item into the destination location.

Another way to modify the default drag-and-drop behavior is to right-click instead of left-click. Right-click on the item to copy or move, hold down the right mouse button, and drop the item in the destination location. When the item is dropped, a shortcut menu is displayed that contains options to copy or move the item or cancel the operation.

HANDS-ON EXAMPLE 3.3.1

COPYING FILES

The ability to apply proper file-management techniques, such as copying and moving files and folders, is a critical skill for a successful computer user. Copying and moving files and folders are easy tasks. Many users prefer to drag-and-drop files instead of using the keyboard.

1. Insert your MS-OFFICE flash drive into the computer.
2. Launch Windows File Explorer.

HANDS-ON EXAMPLE 3.3.1 (CONTINUED)

3. Applying what you have learned, search the Windows folder for any file with the .jpg file extension.

4. Select any one image file in the file list by left-clicking on it once.

5. Hold down the [Ctrl] key, and click any two other image files to select them. Because the [Ctrl] key is held down, the files do not need to be sequential to the first file.

6. Press the [Ctrl][C] key combination to copy the selected image files.

7. Select the MS-OFFICE flash drive in the navigation pane.

8. Applying what you have learned, create a folder on the flash drive named Images.

9. Select the new folder in the navigation pane.

10. Press the [Ctrl][V] key combination to paste the copied image files into the Images folder.

11. Applying what you have learned, search the Windows folder for any file with the .jpg file extension.

12. Click and hold any image file in the file list, drag the file to the Images folder on the flash drive, and drop the file. If the file tree for the flash drive is not expanded, hold the file over the flash drive icon for a couple of seconds until the tree is automatically expanded. Then, drop the file into the Images folder. Because this operation is across drives, not within the same drive, it is a copy operation, not a move operation.

Deleting Files and Folders

In order to effectively manage files, you need to be able to remove files and folders that are no longer useful. In Windows, deleting a file or folder is a simple process. Restoring a deleted file or folder is also a simple process.

Deleting

To delete a file or folder, select it and press the [Delete] key or right-click on it and click **Delete** in the shortcut menu. In Windows 10 and Windows 8, you can also click **Home>Organize>Delete** in the ribbon in File Explorer. In Windows 7, you can also click the **Organize** button on the Windows Explorer toolbar and then click **Delete** in the drop-down menu. No matter which method is used, a dialog box appears asking to confirm the deletion. Click the **Yes** button to delete the selected file or folder. Click the **No** button to cancel the operation.

FYI

Select a group of files or folders to delete the entire group in one step.

Restoring

When asked to confirm a deletion, the dialog box asks Are you sure you want to move this folder to the Recycle Bin? Windows uses the concept of a recycle bin as an *undelete* function for deleted files and folders. The **recycle bin** is a special folder used as a collection point for all files and folders that have been deleted. It can hold a certain volume of deleted material, and the maximum size can be changed. As long as a deleted file or folder is stored in the recycle bin, it can be restored or undeleted.

Career Skills

Graphic Artist

Graphic artists are often called on to determine which file format to use for an online production. They must learn to balance the image quality with the file size. Their aim is to produce the finest quality image while ensuring the smallest file size for fast transmission, all without violating the integrity of the original image.

To restore a file or folder, display the content of the recycle bin. This can be done by double-clicking the **Recycle Bin** icon on the desktop or, in Windows 7, by selecting the Recycle Bin branch in the navigation pane in Windows Explorer. With the content of the recycle bin displayed, right-click on the file or folder to restore, and click **Restore** in the shortcut menu. In Windows 10 and Windows 8, you can also select the file or folder, and click the **Manage>Restore>Restore the selected items**. In Windows 7, you can also select the file or folder, and click the **Restore this item** button on the toolbar. Once restored, the item is removed from the recycle bin and placed in the location from where it was deleted.

The recycle bin is a folder, and its content takes up storage space. To free this storage space, the recycle bin can be emptied. However, doing so permanently removes the deleted files and folders, and they cannot be restored. To empty the recycle bin, display its contents. Then, in Windows 8, click **Manage>Manage>Empty Recycle Bin**. In Windows 7, click the **Empty Recycle Bin** button on the toolbar. A message appears asking to confirm removing the items from the recycle bin. Click the **Yes** button to remove the items or the **No** button to cancel the operation.

3.3   SECTION REVIEW

CHECK YOUR UNDERSTANDING

1. The _____ is a point-of-use menu displayed by right-clicking.
2. How do you select a file or folder in Windows Explorer?
3. When applying file-management techniques, what is the difference between copying a file and moving it?
4. Which key combination is used to apply the file-management technique of cutting a file instead of copying it?
5. To manage files that have been deleted, what utility does Windows use as a storage location to allow a deleted file to be restored?

BUILD YOUR VOCABULARY

As you progress through this course, develop a personal IT glossary. This will help you build your vocabulary and prepare you for a career. Write a definition for each of the following terms and add it to your IT glossary.

copy
destination
drag-and-drop
move

recycle bin
shortcut menu
source

FILE UTILITIES

Windows Explorer is an example of a file utility. File utilities perform common functions such as backing up and restoring files as well as displaying and editing a file's properties. These programs are called utilities because they help the user perform useful, repetitive tasks. One of the most important file-management tasks is to back up files in the event that the original files are lost, deleted, or corrupted. Utilities also assist in determining the most recent version of a file.

Sending large files as attachments to an e-mail message or copying large files to a flash drive may be a problem. Large files take more time to copy or move through the e-mail network. A file utility that can make files smaller is an advantage here. Utility programs can be accessed through the Control Panel window and through the Accessories folder in the **Apps** or **Start** menu.

TERMS
backup
extracting
file attribute
file compression
file properties
help
system image

LEARNING GOALS
- Use the Windows help system.
- Explain the properties associated with a file.
- Describe the process of backing up files and folders.
- Discuss file compression methods.

Windows Help

Help is a resource to assist the user in learning how to use a feature of the program. It is a knowledge database of topics related to the software. Help is provided by almost all software programs, including the Windows operating system.

The help feature for Windows File Explorer can be launched by clicking the **Help** button (question mark) in the upper-right corner of the window. The **Windows Help and Support** dialog box is displayed. Because help was accessed from within Windows File Explorer, the initial content displayed is related to file management. However, the **Windows Help and Support** dialog box is the interface for the entire Windows help feature.

At the top of the **Windows Help and Support** dialog box is a search box. Enter a word or phrase related to the topic you wish to view, and click the **Search** button (magnifying glass). A list of related topics is displayed. The name of each topic is a hyperlink. Clicking the hyperlink displays the full article. For example, if the phrase folder management is entered in the search box, a list of topics related to managing files, folders, and other items is displayed.

Windows will try to rank topics in an order most likely to match the search phrase, but do not assume the first topic will contain the information you seek. Carefully read the name of each topic. Evaluate how closely the words in the title match the search phrase. Once you have determined which topic is most likely to contain the information you seek, click the hyperlink. Then, scan the article to see if it appears to contain the information. If not, click the **Back** button and evaluate other topics. Otherwise, read the details of the article.

File Properties

The **file properties** are all information about the file, but not the data contained within the file. Properties include, among other things, the creation date, date of the last save, current permission setting, and whether or not it is hidden. The file properties are displayed in the **Properties** dialog box. To open this dialog box, right-click on a file, and then click **Properties** in the shortcut menu.

In most cases, there are three tabs in the **Properties** dialog box, as shown in Figure 3-15: **General**, **Security**, and **Details**. In Windows 7, there is usually a fourth tab named **Previous Versions**. In some cases, depending on the file type and system configuration, there may be more tabs. Under each tab are options and settings that may be displayed or edited.

General Tab

The **General** tab of the **Properties** dialog box lists information such as the file type, the size of the data contained and the size of the file on the disk, and the path to the folder where the file is located. The file name is displayed in a text box at the top of the tab and may be renamed there. Also listed are three dates and times.

FYI

The help feature for Windows can also be accessed through the **Apps** or **Start** menu. When accessed in this way, the initial topics are for Windows in general.

Excel

5.3.3

PowerPoint

1.5.3

Word

1.4.5

- Created is the date and time when the file was created.
- Modified is the date and time when the file was last changed.
- Accessed is the date and time when the file was last opened, but not saved.

The software program associated with the file type is indicated in the **Opens with:** area. This is the software that will be launched when the file icon is double-clicked in Windows File Explorer. To change the associated software, click the **Change...** button. In the **Open with** dialog box that is displayed, a different software program can be selected. The association is applied to all files of the file type.

A **file attribute** is a characteristic of a file about the display, archiving, and save status of files. There are two file attributes that can be set on the **General** tab:

- read-only
- hidden

Read-only permits no editing, saving, or deleting. Check the **Read-only** check box to guard against accidental overwriting. Users may view it, but may not overwrite it. Hidden keeps the file from being listed in

Tabs

File information

Goodheart-Willcox Publisher

Figure 3-15. The **Properties** dialog box contains information about the file.

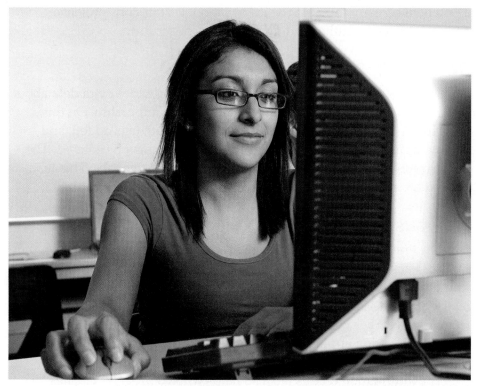

bikeriderlondon/Shutterstock.com

Good file management is a key to successful computing.

Windows File Explorer. Many system files have the **Hidden** check box checked. Clicking the **Advanced** button opens a dialog box in which other settings regarding the save process for a file can be made.

Security Tab

The **Security** tab of the **Properties** dialog box permits the author to modify the permissions for sharing a file with other users on a network. Windows lets users form a workgroup when PCs are connected to a network. In addition, multiple users on a Windows PC may share files with one another. Some users only require need-to-know access to a file's contents. Permissions allow restricted access to a file. Permissions are an extension of the **Read-only** attribute available on the **General** tab.

For example, people may be working on developing a certain project as a group. Instead of carrying the common files around on a flash drive, Windows allows users in a group to see each other's files on their own computers. This means they can allow other users to modify the file or simply read it. One user may create a file and give permission to other users to view the file content, but not change it. For example, it may be a final version that has been adopted in some manner and no one should be able to change it unless authorized. These permissions are settings in the file properties.

Permissions are important to an organization for several reasons. The information of a company must be secured. Workers who need to read a document may not be authorized to make changes to it. In addition, organizations can monitor who has attempted to access files for which they have no permission via log files. This monitoring can identify a potential security threat to the information. Permissions protect a document from unauthorized modifications or scrutiny.

Details Tab

The **Details** tab of the **Properties** dialog box provides extra data about the creation of the file and information related to authorship. On this tab, the file can be assigned a title and subject, rated, tags added, and comments added. It is here that the author's name may be entered. The tab also summarizes all of the selections on the first two tabs. This tab is context-sensitive and differs by file format.

Previous Versions Tab

The **Previous Versions** tab of the **Properties** dialog box lists when the file was backed up and supports restoring an earlier version of the file. This is very helpful if changes have been made and the file saved, thereby overwriting the earlier version. If the user decides not to make those changes, an earlier version of the file can be retrieved from the backup files. This function applies only to files that have been backed up with Windows Backup and Restore, which is discussed later.

The information on this tab also helps when a program crashes, or unexpectedly stops working. When Windows crashes, it is expected to try to restore the user's work from previous saved versions. The information on this tab provides details to step through the restore operation.

HANDS-ON EXAMPLE 3.4.1

FILE ASSOCIATION

By default, in Windows the JPG file type is associated with an image viewer, such as Photos or Windows Photo Viewer. However, it may be more efficient to have the image file opened in an editor, such as Microsoft Paint.

1. Launch Windows File Explorer.
2. Applying what you have learned, search the Windows folder for any file with the .jpg file extension.
3. Right-click on any image file, and click **Properties** in the shortcut menu.
4. Click the **General** tab in the dialog box.
5. Look at the program listed in the **Opens with:** area. The default program is Windows Photo Viewer.
6. Click the **Change...** button. In Windows 10 and Windows 8, click the **More apps** or **More Options** link in the dialog box, and then the **Look for another app on this PC** link. The **Open with** dialog box is displayed, as shown.

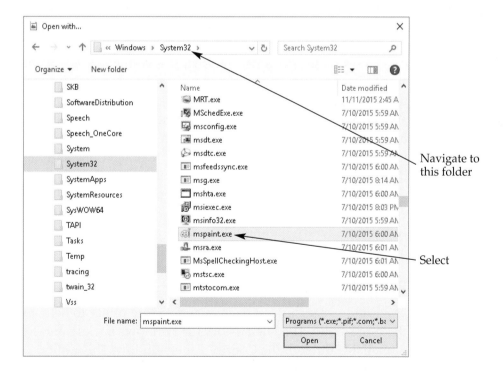

7. Navigate to the Windows\System32 folder, and select the mspaint.exe file. Click the **Open** button. The association for the JPG file type is changed to Microsoft Paint. The **Properties** dialog box is updated to reflect this.
8. Click the **OK** button to close the **Properties** dialog box.
9. Double-click on any JPG file in Windows File Explorer. Microsoft Paint is launched, and the image file is loaded into Paint.

File Backups

A **backup** is a copy of a file that can be safely retrieved if anything unfortunate happens to the most recent version of the file. Mishaps are common in file management. Files can be accidentally deleted, overwritten, modified, or corrupted. A file becomes corrupted when something happens to affect the storage location of the file. Users create backups to ensure that all is not lost if something happens to a file.

Saving Copies of Files

The simplest way to back up a file is to save it on a different storage device. If the user is saving data files on a course flash drive, the files should also be saved on another flash drive, a server, or in the cloud. An advantage of using the cloud is that the file is offsite. The cloud service being used also has backup measures to protect the file. When creating a backup on a different device, the user must remember where the copy is and to keep it current.

Saving Versions of Files

Another backup scheme is to save versions of the file. This method allows restoring one of many earlier states of a file, thus reversing changes. Most software programs offer a **Save As** function for saving a file under a different name. This function can be used to easily create versions.

For example, suppose a student is working on a file named TermPaper.docx. It is easy to save a newer version as TermPaperV1.docx, then TermPaperV2.docx, and so on. The student edits the newest version and saves it as the next version number after enough changes have been made that he or she wants to keep intact. After the final version is complete and the earlier versions are no longer needed, they may be deleted to clean up the folder.

When working on a team, it is important to establish the naming convention for creating versions. All members of the team must understand which file should be in use at any given time. The read-only attribute is useful in locking all files that should not be edited.

Windows Backup and Restore

Windows includes a backup and restore utility to help automate these processes. The File History (or Windows Backup and Restore) utility is available through the Control Panel window. This utility compresses all data files and saves them to another disk volume. A *disk volume* acts like a separate physical drive, but is really contained on the same drive. The utility prompts the user through restoring one of the files to the disk. This utility can also be used to create a system image, as shown in Figure 3-16.

A **system image** is a backup that is an exact duplicate of all data on the drive, including the drives required for Windows to run, your system settings, programs, and document files. A system image allows you to

---

FYI

Always back up a file before a significant amount of work is to be done and after that work has been completed.

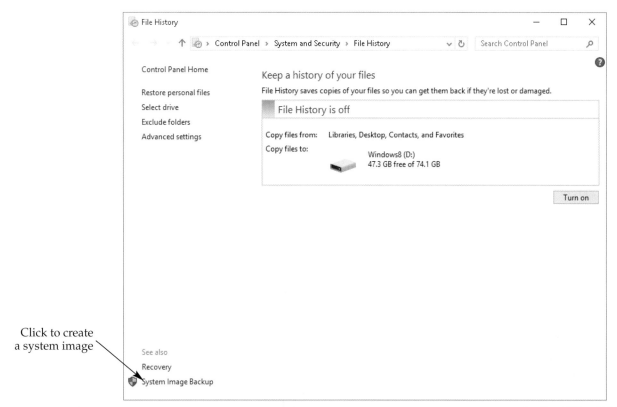

Click to create
a system image

Figure 3-16. The Windows Backup and Restore utility is used to back up files and create a system image.

completely restore all data to a previous point that was working. This is usually done to correct a serious problem that causes the system to stop working.

There are many third-party backup utilities available. Some are freeware and some are for-purchase software. Most backup programs can be scheduled to automatically run at periodic intervals established by the user. It is common to set a backup utility to run overnight when there is no user activity on the system.

File Compression

The amount of space a file takes up on the disk is not as great of a concern today as it was when disk drives were very limited in size. However, when sharing files, file size is a concern. Large files take longer to move across a network than small files. Many e-mail services limit the size of a file that can be attached to a message. Large files take up more space on an external drive and may quickly fill up the device. The solution is file compression. **File compression** is a process of compacting the data in a file or group of files to reduce the overall size.

When a file is created by a software program, it is generally formatted so that reloading the file is quick and efficient. As a result, the file may be larger than it needs to be. Some file-compression technologies eliminate repeated patterns in a file to reduce the overall size. There are other steps to take to compress a file, but the result is the same. The original content of the file is preserved, but the file is smaller.

FYI

Some compressed file types, such as JPG, may be "lossy," which means some of the original bits may be removed during compression.

Many image file types are automatically compressed. The JPG or JPEG file type is a compressed image file. Trying to compress this file type or any of the other compressed file types will not yield much reduction in file size.

FYI

The ZIP file type is just one of many for compressing files and folders. Other common file types include 7Z, RAR, SIT, and TAR.

Compress Files Using Windows File Explorer

Windows File Explorer provides a utility that compresses one file or a group of files at the same time. To do this, first select the file, group of files, or a folder. Next, right-click on the selection, and click **Send to>Compressed (zipped) folder** in the shortcut menu. All of the files selected are compressed into a single file, which in Windows is considered a folder. The default name of the ZIP file is the same name as the first file or folder selected based on the current sort. The ZIP file is placed in the same location as the original selection. The original selection is unaltered.

FYI

Some software can open a file directly from within a compressed file without the need to extract the file.

Extract Files Using Windows File Explorer

Extracting is what Windows calls the process of taking a file out of a ZIP file. Other software may call this process *unzipping*, *unpacking*, or *unstuffing*. Because the files have been compressed, the original software for the file association no longer recognizes the file as a type it can read. The file must be uncompressed.

Double-click on a ZIP file to begin the extraction process. The content of the file is displayed in Windows File Explorer, as shown in Figure 3-17. Notice the **Extract all** button on the ribbon or toolbar. Clicking this button will copy all files and folders in the ZIP file to their uncompressed formats. The user specifies the location to where the files will be extracted. Files and folders can also be extracted using the drag-and-drop file management method.

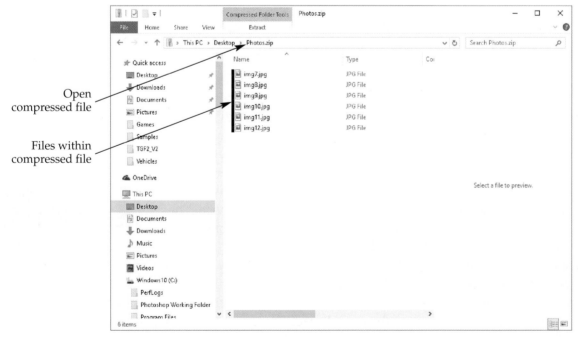

Goodheart-Willcox Publisher

Figure 3-17. Double-clicking on a ZIP file displays its contents in Windows File Explorer.

HANDS-ON EXAMPLE 3.4.2

COMPRESSING FILES

It is a common practice to compress multiple files into a single ZIP file in order to e-mail them. This not only reduces the overall size, it allows the recipient to save a single ZIP file from the e-mail instead of having to save multiple files.

1. Launch Windows File Explorer.
2. Applying what you have learned, search the Windows folder for any file with the .jpg file extension.
3. Applying what you have learned, select three or four image files.
4. Right-click on the selection, and click **Send to>Compressed (zipped) folder** in the shortcut menu. Because Windows cannot create a ZIP file in the search results, a message appears asking if you would like to create the ZIP file on the desktop. Click the **Yes** button.
5. Display the Windows desktop. The easiest way to do this is to use the [Alt][Tab] key combination to navigate through open windows. When the desktop is displayed, release the [Alt] key.
6. Locate the new ZIP file on the desktop. The icon for the file looks like a folder with a zipper on it. The name of the ZIP file will be the same as the first file you selected in the file list.
7. Double-click the ZIP file to display its contents in Windows File Explorer. Notice that the image files you selected are contained in the ZIP file.

3.4 | SECTION REVIEW

 ### CHECK YOUR UNDERSTANDING

1. How is help launched for Windows Explorer?
2. What are file properties?
3. Read-only and hidden are examples of file _____.
4. List three ways to back up your work.
5. How do you compress a group of files selected in Windows Explorer?

 ### BUILD YOUR VOCABULARY

As you progress through this course, develop a personal IT glossary. This will help you build your vocabulary and prepare you for a career. Write a definition for each of the following terms and add it to your IT glossary.

backup   file properties
extracting   help
file attribute   system image
file compression

3 REVIEW AND ASSESSMENT

Chapter Summary

Section 3.1
File and Folder Names

- The file name is a label that identifies a unique file on a computer system. A folder is a container in which files are stored.
- Windows File Explorer is a file-management utility with a graphical user interface that can be used to find anything in the computer's storage areas. The list of available drives and folders shown in the navigation pane is a file tree.

Section 3.2
Locating Files and Folders

- Good file management involves organizing files in logical locations. The ability to locate files is a key skill in good computer use.
- Files and folders can be arranged by a certain criterion, such as alphabetically, by date, or by size. This can help locate a file or folder.
- Files can be shared online, either publicly or privately. When shared publicly, anyone can view the file. A privately shared file can be seen only by those given access to it.

Section 3.3
Organizing Files and Folders

- Files and folders can be easily copied or moved about any storage drive or between devices. The source is the original location, while the destination is the new location.
- Deleting files and folders is an important part of good file management. A deleted file or folder can be restored if needed.

Section 3.4
File Utilities

- Help is a resource to assist the user in learning how to use a feature of the program. Help is provided by almost all software programs, including the Windows operating system.
- The file properties are all information about the file, but not the data contained within the file. The file properties are displayed in the **Properties** dialog box.
- A backup is a copy of a file that can be safely retrieved if anything unfortunate happens to the most recent version of the file. A backup can be created on a different device or versions of the file can be created.
- File compression is a process of compacting the data in a file or group of files to reduce the overall size. File compression can be done to save disk space or to reduce the file size for e-mail transmission.

Now that you have finished this chapter, see what you know about computer applications by taking the chapter posttest. Access the posttest by visiting www.g-wlearning.com. ↗

Chapter 3 Test

Multiple Choice
Select the best response.

1. Using capital letters to show where new words start in a file name is called _____.
   A. CamelCase
   B. title case
   C. uppercase
   D. lowercase

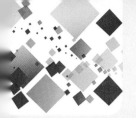

2. Which of the following is not a good file-management practice?
   - A. Create descriptive names for folders and files.
   - B. Store all of the data files at the top level of the drive to make them easier to find.
   - C. Remove folders and files when they are no longer needed.
   - D. Make enough subfolders so that the files in any one folder are readily visible.

3. What are used in the search box to represent unknown characters?
   - A. digits
   - B. characters
   - C. blanks
   - D. wildcards

4. Which key combination is used to copy a file?
   - A. [Ctrl][X]
   - B. [Ctrl][C]
   - C. [Ctrl][V]
   - D. [Ctrl][Z]

5. Where are deleted files and folders stored in Windows?
   - A. In the recycle bin.
   - B. In the root folder of the drive.
   - C. In the original folder.
   - D. They are not retained.

Completion

Complete the following sentences with the correct word(s).

6. The three parts of a file path in Windows are the _____.

7. A(n) _____ is a pattern that is followed whenever a file name is created.

8. The asterisk (*) and question mark (?) are _____ to use in names when searching for files or folders.

9. _____ is a procedure in which an item is selected in one location, moved with the mouse, and placed in another location.

10. File properties are displayed in the _____ dialog box.

Matching

Match the correct term with its definition.

- A. Subfolder
- B. Rename
- C. Sort
- D. Copy
- E. Backup

11. Make copies of files in case of loss.

12. Put a file in a new location while keeping the original file in its place.

13. Nested within the parent folder.

14. Arrange files based on their properties.

15. Single-click twice on the file or folder in the file list.

Application and Extension of Knowledge

1. You and your team must create a display of these ecosystems: desert, rainforest, deciduous forest, tundra, and marine. The display will include images of the ecosystems and the animals, trees, and flowers found in them. There will also be documents for annual rainfall, manufacturing, human habitation, and traffic. Plan a folder structure so that each team member can locate the proper place to store relevant files. Create a naming convention that will make it clear what each file contains.

2. Using the naming convention created in #1, set up the folder structure. Where will the project folder be located? Will each team member have access to this folder?

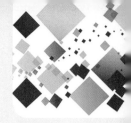

3. Using Windows Explorer, search the Windows folder and all of its subfolders for any file with the .jpg file name extension. How many files are located? Sort the files by date, from newest to oldest. Copy the newest file to your flash drive.

4. Display the **Properties** dialog box for the image file copied to your flash drive in #3. What is the size of the file? When was the file created? Is the file a read-only file? Display the **Details** tab in the dialog box. Examine the information provided on this tab, and write one paragraph summarizing what is provided.

5. Write one paragraph that summarizes what a system image is, how it is created, and why it is important to create a system image.

Online Activities

Complete the following activities, which will help you learn, practice, and expand your knowledge and skills.

Vocabulary. Practice vocabulary for this chapter using the e-flash cards, matching activity, and vocabulary game until you are able to recognize their meanings.

Communication Skills

Speaking. All careers require that individuals be able to participate and contribute to one-on-one discussions. Developing intrapersonal communication skills is one way to achieve career opportunities. As your instructor lectures on this chapter, contribute thoughtful comments when participation is invited.

Listening. Hearing is a physical process. Listening combines hearing with evaluation.

Effective leaders learn how to listen to their team members. Listen to your instructor as a lesson is presented. Analyze the effectiveness of the presentation. Listen carefully and take notes about the main points. Then organize the key information that you heard.

Writing. Consider entering a command using either the mouse or keyboard shortcuts, such as copying and pasting a file. Which method do you think is the most efficient? Would your answer change if you had to use the command many times in a short span? Write several paragraphs explaining which method you believe is most efficient and why.

Internet Research

IT Careers. Using various Internet resources, research the current job opportunities and general qualifications for an IT career that interests you. Use the career clusters as a starting point. Write a one-page report about job prospects that evaluates your findings. Include data from your research in the report. Use correct grammar, punctuation, spelling, and terminology to write and edit the document.

Teamwork

Work with your team to develop a list of questions that could be used to gather information about what electronics are purchased or used by young adults. Next, create a focus group for the research. Appoint a mediator who will ask the questions and a recorder who will record the answers. As a team, interpret the results of the focus group.

Activity Files

Visit www.g-wlearning.com/informationtechnology/ to download the activity files for this chapter. These activities will expand your learning of the material presented in this chapter and allow you to practice what you have learned. Follow the instructions provided in each file to complete the activity.

Activity File 3-1 CamelCase

Activity File 3-2 Wildcards

Activity File 3-3 Deleting and Restoring Files

Activity File 3-4 Naming Conventions

Activity File 3-5 File Compression

CAPSTONE PROJECT

The capstone project builds from one chapter to the next. It allows you to apply the skills you have learned to create a complete project in a desired career area. Read the instructions below for the career area you chose to work in for this course. Work in the same career area in each chapter.

Agriculture, Food, and Natural Resources

In this activity, you will build a folder hierarchy that you will use for the remainder of the capstone activities. You will create a root folder with subfolders and nested folders in which to store your completed files. Access the *Introduction to Microsoft Office 2016* companion website (www.g-wlearning.com/informationtechnology/) to view the instructions for this chapter's Agriculture, Food, and Natural Resources capstone project.

Business, Management, and Administration

In this activity, you will build a folder hierarchy that you will use for the remainder of the capstone activities. You will create a root folder with subfolders and nested folders in which to store your completed files. Access the *Introduction to Microsoft Office 2016* companion website (www.g-wlearning.com/informationtechnology/) to view the instructions for this chapter's Business, Management, and Administration capstone project.

Health Science

In this activity, you will build a folder hierarchy that you will use for the remainder of the capstone activities. You will create a root folder with subfolders and nested folders in which to store your completed files. Access the *Introduction to Microsoft Office 2016* companion website (www.g-wlearning.com/informationtechnology/) to view the instructions for this chapter's Health Science capstone project.

Science, Technology, Engineering, and Mathematics

In this activity, you will build a folder hierarchy that you will use for the remainder of the capstone activities. You will create a root folder with subfolders and nested folders in which to store your completed files. Access the *Introduction to Microsoft Office 2016* companion website (www.g-wlearning.com/informationtechnology/) to view the instructions for this chapter's Science, Technology, Engineering, and Mathematics capstone project.

4

COMMON OFFICE APPLICATION FEATURES

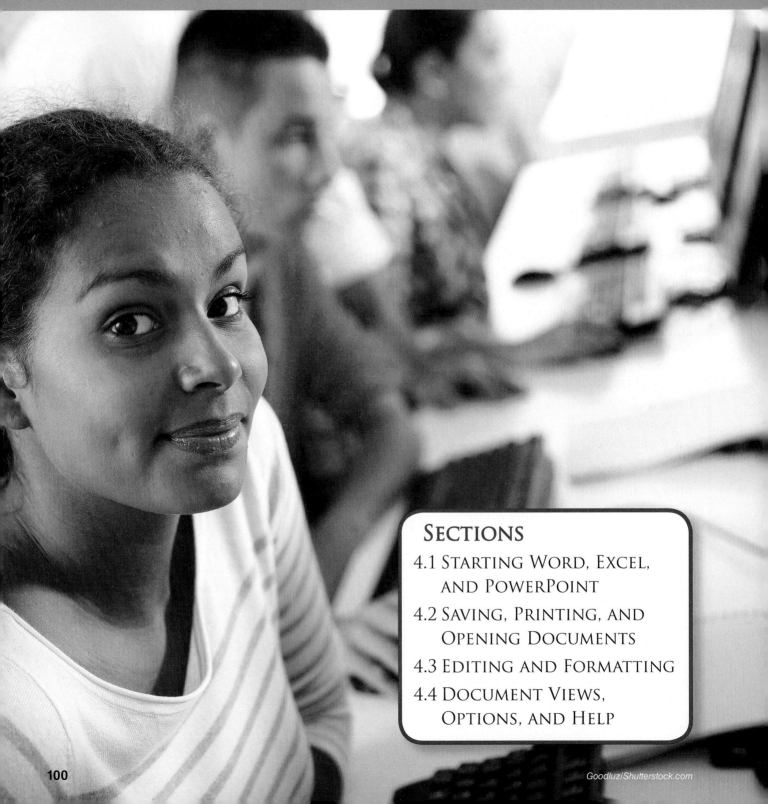

SECTIONS

An office suite is used to create and share personal and business documents. The most common software in an office suite includes word-processing, spreadsheet, presentation, and database programs. An advantage of purchasing an office suite is that the basic functions work similarly in all of the software. For example, once a user learns how to save a file in one of the applications, or modules, he or she can do the same thing in other modules because the procedure is the same in all of the applications. Because the user has a basic set of directions common to all applications in the suite, it is easy to switch from one application to another.

Microsoft Office 2016 is the most popular office suite and what is demonstrated in this text. The programs included in the Microsoft Office suite are Word, Excel, PowerPoint, Access, and others.

MICROSOFT OFFICE SPECIALIST OBJECTIVES

Access

Create and Manage a Database

1.5 Print and Export Data
   1.5.2 Print records
   1.5.3 Save a database as a template

2.3 Manage Records in Tables
   2.3.5 Find and replace data

Create Forms

4.3 Format a Form
   4.3.2 Configure Print settings
   4.3.8 Insert images

Excel

Create and Manage Worksheets and Workbooks

1.4 Customize Options and Views for Worksheets and Workbooks
   1.4.3 Customize the Quick Access toolbar
   1.4.7 Change magnification by using zoom tools

1.5 Configure Worksheets and Workbooks for Distribution
   1.5.2 Save workbooks in alternative file formats

   1.5.6 Inspect a workbook for hidden properties or personal information
   1.5.7 Inspect a workbook for accessibility issue
   1.5.8 Inspect a workbook for compatibility issues

Manage Data Cells and Ranges

2.1 Insert Data in Cells and Ranges
   2.1.3 Paste data by using special paste options

2.2 Format Cells and Ranges
   2.2.3 Format cells by using Format Painter

Create Charts and Objects

5.3 Insert and Format Objects
   5.3.1 Insert text boxes and shapes

   5.3.2 Insert images
   5.3.4 Add alternative text to objects for accessibility

PowerPoint

Create and Manage Presentations

1.5 Change Presentation Options and Views
   1.5.2 Change views of a presentation

Insert and Format Text, Shapes, and Images

2.1 Insert and Format Text
   2.1.2 Apply formatting and styles to text
   2.1.3 Apply WordArt styles to text
   2.1.5 Create bulleted and numbered lists

2.2 Insert and Format Shapes and Text Boxes
   2.2.2 Insert text boxes
   2.2.3 Resize shapes and text boxes
   2.2.4 Format shapes and text boxes

2.3 Insert and Format Images
   2.3.3 Apply styles and effects

2.4 Order and Group Objects
   2.4.1 Order objects
   2.4.2 Align objects
   2.4.3 Group objects
   2.4.4 Display alignment tools

Insert Tables, Charts, SmartArt, and Media

3.3 Insert and Format SmartArt Graphics
   3.3.1 Create SmartArt graphics
   3.3.2 Convert lists to SmartArt graphics
   3.3.3 Add shapes to SmartArt graphics
   3.3.4 Reorder shapes in SmartArt graphics
   3.3.5 Change the color of SmartArt graphics

Manage Multiple Presentations

5.1 Merge Content from Multiple Presentations
   5.1.3 Insert comments
   5.1.4 Review comments

5.2 Finalize Presentations
   5.2.1 Protect a presentation
   5.2.2 Inspect a presentation
   5.2.3 Proof a presentation
   5.2.4 Preserve presentation content

Word

Create and Manage Documents

1.1 Create a Document
   1.1.2 Create a blank document using a template

1.2 Navigate Through a Document
   1.2.1 Search for text
   1.2.4 Move to a specific location or object in a document

1.4 Customize Options and Views for Documents
   1.4.1 Change document views
   1.4.2 Customize views by using zoom settings
   1.4.3 Customize the Quick Access toolbar
   1.4.4 Split the window
   1.4.6 Show or hide formatting symbols

1.5 Print and Save Documents
   1.5.1 Modify print settings
   1.5.2 Save documents in alternative file formats
   1.5.3 Print all or part of a document
   1.5.4 Inspect a document for hidden properties or personal information
   1.5.5 Inspect a document for accessibility issues
   1.5.6 Inspect a document for compatibility issues

Format Text, Paragraphs, and Sections

2.1 Insert Text and Paragraphs
   2.1.1 Find and replace text
   2.1.2 Cut, copy, and paste text
   2.1.3 Replace text by using AutoCorrect

2.2 Format Text and Paragraphs
   2.2.1 Apply font formatting
   2.2.2 Apply formatting by using Format Painter

   2.2.4 Clear formatting
   2.2.7 Change text to WordArt

Create Tables and Lists

3.2 Modify a Table
   3.2.1 Sort table data

3.3 Create and Modify a List
   3.3.1 Create a numbered or bulleted list
   3.3.2 Change bullet characters or number formats for a list level
   3.3.3 Define a custom bullet character or number format
   3.3.4 Increase or decrease list levels
   3.3.5 Restart or continue list numbering
   3.3.6 Set starting number value

Insert and Format Graphic Elements

5.1 Insert Graphic Elements
   5.1.1 Insert shapes
   5.1.2 Insert pictures
   5.1.3 Insert a screen shot of screen clipping
   5.1.4 Insert text boxes

5.2 Format Graphic Elements
   5.2.1 Apply artistic effects
   5.2.2 Apply picture effects
   5.2.3 Remove picture backgrounds
   5.2.4 Format objects
   5.2.5 Apply a picture style
   5.2.6 Wrap text around objects
   5.2.7 Position objects
   5.2.8 Add alternative text to objects for accessibility

5.3 Insert and Format SmartArt Graphics
   5.3.1 Create a SmartArt graphic
   5.3.2 Format a SmartArt graphic
   5.3.3 Modify SmartArt graphic content

STARTING WORD, EXCEL, AND POWERPOINT

Microsoft Office is a software suite designed for home users, large and small businesses, and students. Methods of creating, retrieving, and saving files are consistent throughout the suite. Entering, editing, and formatting text have standard procedures. Steps for printing are also the same throughout the application. The help files built into the applications provide essential assistance.

Opening the application of an office suite is standard throughout the suite. Whenever the user starts one of these applications, templates for a new blank document, spreadsheet, or presentation appear. Another advantage of Microsoft Office is the ability to open more than one application at a time. Then the user can view them on the same screen. Also, the user can have more than one document (spreadsheet or presentation) visible at a time to compare or edit.

michaeljung/Shutterstock.com

TERMS

access key
active window
cell
dialog box launcher
document template
insertion point
key tip badge
maximized

minimized
on-demand tab
presentation
restoring
ribbon
spreadsheet
windowed

LEARNING GOALS

After completing this section, you will be able to:

- Launch a Microsoft Office application.
- Describe features common to Microsoft Office applications.
- Explain the process of displaying multiple windows.

Launching Applications

Like all applications in Windows, the Microsoft Office suite is accessed via the **Start** or **Apps** menu. In Windows 10, click the **Start** menu button, click **All apps**, and scroll to and expand the **Microsoft Office** group, as shown in Figure 4-1. In Windows 8, click the **Apps** menu button to display the **Apps** menu. Then, scroll to the **Microsoft Office** group. In Windows 7, click the **Start** menu button to display the **Start** menu. Then, click **All Programs** followed by the **Microsoft Office** folder.

Launching Microsoft Word

To launch Microsoft Word, click the **Word 2016** icon in the **Start** or **Apps** menu. Wait for the program to load and display the startup screen. Word 2016 begins by presenting the user with the choice to open a document, begin a new blank document, or begin a document based on a template.

A blank document contains no text and has a minimum number of standard formatting styles. A **document template** is a document preformatted for a specific use and may contain placeholder text or images the user replaces with actual content. Word contains many templates. Templates are also found in Microsoft Excel and Microsoft PowerPoint.

Microsoft Word is able to save documents in a variety of file formats. For example, a document created in Microsoft Word 2016 can be saved

GS5
Key Applications

2.4

FYI

Versions of Microsoft Word previous to Word 2013 automatically open a blank document when launched.

Word

1.1.2

GS5
Key Applications

2.10.1

Microsoft Office applications

Goodheart-Willcox Publisher

Figure 4-1. The applications in the Microsoft Office suite are accessed in the Windows 10 **Start** menu.

in a format that can be read by earlier versions of Microsoft Word. In addition, Microsoft Word documents can be saved in other formats. A popular format is portable document format (PDF). Documents saved in PDF format have all text and graphics intact, but cannot be edited by the PDF-reader software. Files can also be saved as Extensible Markup Language (XML) documents, which are used for web pages. It is also possible to save Word files into a format that can be read by OpenOffice, an open-source word-processing program. Also, Word files can be saved as plain text with the .txt extension. This is the most portable format since any other software that can read text can read this format.

Launching Microsoft Excel

GS5
Key Applications
3.12

To launch Microsoft Excel, click the **Excel 2016** icon in the **Start** or **Apps** menu. Wait for the program to load and display the startup screen. Excel 2016 begins by presenting the user with the choice to open a spreadsheet, begin a new blank spreadsheet, or begin a spreadsheet based on a template.

A **spreadsheet** is a special type of document in which data are organized in columns and rows. The individual box where a row and column intersect is called a **cell**. When a cell is selected, its border is thicker than normal. This is called the *active cell*. Text or numbers that are entered are placed in the active cell.

GS5
Key Applications
3.11

Microsoft Excel is able to save spreadsheets in a variety of file formats. As with Microsoft Word, Microsoft Excel can save spreadsheets in a format for earlier versions of the software. Microsoft Excel can also save files in PDF, XML, and text formats. Microsoft Excel files can be saved for the OpenOffice spreadsheet function as well. Another popular format is called comma-separated values (CSV). It is the most portable format for copying spreadsheet data into other applications.

Launching Microsoft PowerPoint

To launch Microsoft PowerPoint, click the **PowerPoint 2016** icon in the **Start** or **Apps** menu. Wait for the program to load and display the startup screen. PowerPoint 2016 begins by presenting the user with the choice to open a presentation, begin a new blank presentation, or begin a presentation based on a template.

A **presentation** contains individual slides used to communicate information to an audience. Each slide may contain text, images, sounds, tables, or other information. The presentation is played back as a slide show.

GS5
Key Applications
5.1.2

Microsoft PowerPoint is able to save spreadsheets in a variety of file formats. Files can be saved in a format for earlier versions of the software. Files can also be saved as PowerPoint Show (PPS) files, which allows sharing with others who do not have Microsoft PowerPoint. Less-popular formats for presentations include PDF, XML, and text files. Files can also be saved in the OpenOffice format.

Common Features and Functions

The interface of each application in a suite is similar. This is to allow a user to learn basic commands and features once instead of individually for each program. For example, each program in the Microsoft Office suite contains the **Quick Access** toolbar. It contains the **Save**, **Undo**, and **Redo** or **Repeat** buttons in each program of the suite. The **Quick Access** toolbar is always displayed above the ribbon in the Microsoft Office suite and can be customized by right-clicking the toolbar and selecting **Customize the Quick Access Toolbar** from the shortcut menu.

Basic Option Settings

Microsoft Office applications have common basic option settings that the user can adjust. These options are found in the backstage view, which is displayed by clicking the **File** tab in the ribbon. Click **Options** on the left-hand side of the backstage view to open the **Options** dialog box.

In the **Options** dialog box, click **General** on the left-hand side. General options include choosing interface, personalization, and startup options. For example, the mini toolbar that is normally displayed when text is selected can be disabled. Also, you can enter your name and initials so tracked changes will be recorded as made by you.

Click **Proofing** on the left-hand side of the dialog box. There are several check boxes on this screen that allow you to set what is checked or ignored during a spelling and grammar check. The **AutoCorrect Options…** button opens the **AutoCorrect** dialog box for making settings on automatic spelling corrections.

Click **Save** on the left-hand side of the dialog box. The options on this screen allow you to select how often the file is automatically saved, where it is saved, and in which format. To change the default file format, click the **Save files in this format:** drop-down list. To change the location of auto recover files, enter the path in the **AutoRecover file location:** text box.

Insertion Point

The **insertion point** is the location where text or images will be placed within the document. It appears as a vertical line within the document. To avoid errors, it is important to be aware of the location of the insertion point before adding text or images. The insertion point appears the same in all Microsoft Office suite applications.

Ribbon Interface

The **ribbon** is the main command interface for the Microsoft Office suite of software. It consists of tabs, each containing commands arranged in groups, as shown in Figure 4-2. The name of each ribbon indicates the type of commands it contains. The groups on each tab contain similar or related commands. To activate a command on the ribbon, click the command button using the mouse.

In Microsoft Office 2016, each application contains the **File**, **Home**, **Insert**, and **Review** tabs in the ribbon. Other tabs will be present,

Excel
1.4.3

Word
1.4.3

GS5
Computing Fundamentals
3.4

Career Skills

Agriculture and Food Science Technician
Agricultural and food science technicians often work in laboratories assisting agriculture and food scientists. They perform duties such as measuring and analyzing food quality. They use word processing, spreadsheets, and databases to analyze and report on the research results. On occasion, they prepare presentations for the scientists as well.

Figure 4-2. The ribbon is the main command interface in the Microsoft Office suite of software.

depending on the application. Additionally, one or more on-demand tabs may be present. An **on-demand tab** is displayed depending on what is selected in the program document.

In the lower-right corner of most groups on the ribbon is a small arrow. This is called a **dialog box launcher**. Clicking the arrow opens a dialog box related to the commands in the group.

Keyboard Navigation

The ribbon is designed for using a mouse to select commands. However, the keyboard can also be used to navigate the ribbon and select commands. This allows the user to quickly complete tasks without removing his or her hands from the keyboard to use the mouse. Access keys are used to navigate the ribbon with the keyboard. An **access key** is the keyboard key or key combination used instead of the mouse to activate a command. These are often called *keyboard shortcuts*.

Access keys are displayed by pressing the [Alt] key on the keyboard. Little boxes called **key tip badges** appear over each command in the **Quick Access** toolbar and the ribbon tabs, as shown in Figure 4-3. To activate a command on the **Quick Access** toolbar, press the key or key combination shown in the key tip badge corresponding to the command. To access a command on the ribbon, first press the access key for the tab, even if the tab is currently visible, and then press the key or key combination shown for the command.

> **FYI**
>
> Many computer users find navigating the ribbon using the keyboard to be significantly faster and more efficient than using the mouse.

Key tip badges

Figure 4-3. Key tip badges are displayed on the ribbon when the [Alt] key is pressed.

HANDS-ON EXAMPLE 4.1.1

KEYBOARD NAVIGATION OF THE RIBBON

Learning to navigate the ribbon and activate commands using the keyboard can improve your efficiency using the software. Once learned, a keyboard shortcut is usually a much faster way to activate a command than using the mouse.

1. Launch Microsoft Word, and click Blank Document in the startup screen to begin a new document.
2. Press and release the [Alt] key. Key tip badges are displayed on the **Quick Access** toolbar and the ribbon.
3. Press the [W] key to activate the **View** tab in the ribbon. Make note of the access keys for commands on this tab.
4. Press the [1] key (number one) to display a full-page view of the document.
5. Applying what you have learned, use the keyboard to display the key tip badges on the **View** tab.
6. Press the [I] key (letter i) to display the document at a zoom level in which the width of the document fills the width of the window.

Toggle Buttons

Many command buttons on the ribbon are toggles. If a toggle button is clicked, the command is either activated or deactivated. Clicking the button toggles the command on and off. The **Show/Hide** button in Word (**Home>Paragraph>Show/Hide**) is an example of a toggle button. It displays nonprinting characters found on the page. For example, when this button is clicked, a paragraph symbol, called a *pilcrow*, is shown at the end of each paragraph. Clicking the button again hides the paragraph symbols along with all other nonprinting characters.

Other toggle buttons in Word include the **Bold**, **Italic**, and **Underline** buttons (**Home>Font**). These buttons are used to change the formatting of text, such as to emphasize it. The **Bold** button makes the lines composing the individual text characters thicker. For example, this text is bold: **bold**. The **Italic** button makes the characters slanted. For example, this text is italicized: *italic*. The **Underline** button adds a rule under the selected word or characters. For example, this text is underlined: underline. Clicking any of these buttons a second time toggles off the corresponding formatting for the selected word or characters.

Word

1.4.6

HANDS-ON EXAMPLE 4.1.2

TOGGLE BUTTONS

Many command buttons in the Microsoft Office suite of software are toggles. The concept of toggle buttons is important to understand.

¶

Show/
Hide

B

Bold

I

Italic

U

Underline

I

Italic

1. Launch Microsoft Word, and click Blank Document in the startup screen to begin a new document.
2. Click the **Show/Hide** toggle button so it is on.
3. Add your first and last names to the document. Notice that the insertion point and paragraph symbol move to the right as characters are entered.
4. Select your first name by double-clicking it. Selected text is highlighted.
5. Click **Home**>**Font**>**Bold** in the ribbon. The button is toggled on, and the text is bolded.
6. Applying what you have learned, select only your last name.
7. Click **Home**>**Font**>**Italic** in the ribbon. The button is toggled on, and the text is italicized.
8. Select both names by clicking at the beginning of your first name, holding down the left mouse button, and dragging to the end of your last name. Then release the left mouse button. Both names should now be highlighted.
9. Click **Home**>**Font**>**Underline** in the ribbon. The button is toggled on, and the text is underlined. Note: the underline may not be visible if Word thinks your names are misspelled words and places a red squiggly line under them to indicate this.
10. Applying what you have learned, select only your last name.
11. Click **Home**>**Font**>**Italic** in the ribbon. The button is toggled off, and your last name is no longer italicized, but it remains underlined.
12. Close Word by clicking the **Close** button (X) in the upper-right corner of the window. When asked to save the file, click the **No** button.

Displaying Multiple Windows

Each application in the Microsoft Office suite is opened in its own window. Additionally, by default, each document that is open in a Microsoft Office application appears in its own window. The current window, which is called the **active window**, is where any command that is entered will be applied.

When a window fills the entire screen, it is **maximized**. Other applications may be running in other windows, but those windows will not be visible except as buttons on the taskbar. To see more than one window, a maximized window must be resized smaller. A window that is visible, but does not fill the entire screen, is **windowed**. This is done by clicking the resizing button in the upper-right corner of the window. It is to the left of the **Close** button (X), and the button icon looks like two windows, one behind the other, as shown in Figure 4-4. Once the button is clicked, the window is resized smaller. The button also changes to the maximize button.

FYI

A window that is in the windowed state may be referred to as *restored down*.

A window can be resized once it is no longer maximized. Resizing a window is easy. Move the cursor over an edge of the window until it changes to a standard resizing cursor. A resizing cursor looks like two arrows pointing in the directions the window can be resized. When the cursor is over a left or right edge, the arrows will point horizontally. When the cursor is over a top or bottom edge, the arrows will point vertically. When the cursor is over a corner, the arrows will point diagonally. Once the resizing cursor is displayed, click, hold, and drag to resize the window.

Moving a window is easy. Click and hold on the window's title bar, and drag the window to a new location. If the window is dragged to the top of the screen, it will be maximized. If the window is dragged to the left side of the screen, the window will be resized to fill the left half of the screen. If the window is dragged to the right side of the screen, the window will be resized to fill the right half of the screen. If the title bar of a maximized window is grabbed and dragged, the window will be placed in a windowed state.

Multiple open windows also can be automatically arranged next to each other or one above the other. To do so, right-click on a blank area of the taskbar at the bottom of the screen to display a shortcut menu, as shown in Figure 4-5. The choices to arrange window positions include **Cascade windows**, **Show windows stacked**, and **Show windows side-by-side**.

A window can be removed from the desktop area without closing the window. A window in this state is called minimized. A **minimized** window is still running, but hidden from view except for the button on the taskbar corresponding to the application. To minimize a window, click the minimize button in the upper-right corner of the window. This button is to the left of the resize button, and its icon looks like a dash or hyphen, as shown in Figure 4-4. To display a minimized window, which is called **restoring** the window, click the application's button in the taskbar. The window is restored to its previous state, either maximized or windowed.

Goodheart-Willcox Publisher

Figure 4-4. The resizing button is used to window the application. The standard Windows **Close** button is used to close the application.

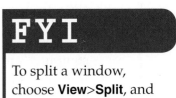

To split a window, choose **View>Split**, and adjust the divider bar as desired.

Word
1.4.4

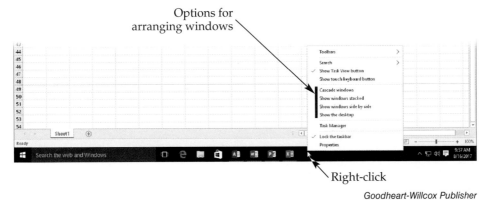

Goodheart-Willcox Publisher

Figure 4-5. Open windows can be arranged in one of several different ways.

If multiple documents are open for an application, after clicking the application button on the taskbar, click which document to restore. A window can also be restored using the [Alt][Tab] key combination to cycle through open application windows.

HANDS-ON EXAMPLE 4.1.3

MANAGING OPEN WINDOWS

It is quite common to have multiple application windows open at any given time. An essential skill for any computer user is managing open windows.

1. Launch Microsoft Word, and click Blank Document in the startup screen to begin a new document.
2. Launch Microsoft Excel, and click Blank Workbook in the startup screen to begin a new spreadsheet.
3. Launch Microsoft PowerPoint, and click Blank Presentation in the startup screen to begin a new slide show. There should be a button on the taskbar for Word, Excel, and PowerPoint because all three applications are running.
4. With PowerPoint the active window, click the standard close button (X) in the upper-right corner of the window to close the program. Since there were no entries or changes made, it will close immediately. The button on the taskbar corresponding to PowerPoint disappears.
5. If Word is not the active window, make it active by clicking the button on the taskbar corresponding to Word.
6. Add this line of text to the document: Introduction to Microsoft Office.
7. Minimize the Word window by pressing the minimize button in the upper-right corner of the window. Although the window is no longer visible, Word is still loaded in the computer's memory. The button corresponding to Word is still displayed on the taskbar.
8. If the Excel window is not active, make it active by clicking the button on the taskbar corresponding to Excel.
9. Click cell A1, which is the upper-left cell, so that it is active (surrounded by a thick border).
10. Enter your first name in cell A1.
11. Press the [Tab] key to fix the content of cell A1 and make cell B1 the active cell.
12. Enter your last name in cell B1. Do not be concerned if part of the first name is overwritten.
13. Press the [Enter] to fix the content of cell B1 and make cell A2 active.
14. Enter this formula in cell A2: =TODAY().
15. Press the [Enter] key to fix the content. Today's date appears in cell A2.
16. Right-click on an empty space on the taskbar to display a shortcut menu.

HANDS-ON EXAMPLE 4.1.3 (CONTINUED)

17. Click **Show windows side by side** in the shortcut menu. The Word and Excel windows are resized and positioned to be side by side, as shown. To make either window active, click anywhere within that window.

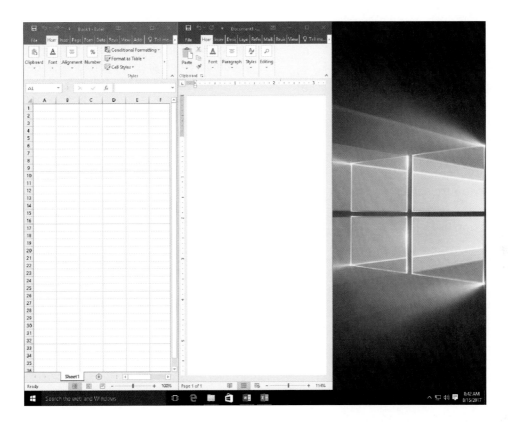

18. Applying what you have learned, use the shortcut menu to display the windows stacked and then cascading.
19. Applying what you have learned, minimize each window so the desktop is visible.

4.1 | SECTION REVIEW

 CHECK YOUR UNDERSTANDING

1. What is the location where text or images will be placed within the document?
2. What is the name of the command interface that appears at the top of all Microsoft Office applications?
3. Which command tabs are present in all Microsoft Office 2016 applications?
4. What happens if a toggle button is clicked?
5. What is the window called if it is running, but hidden from view except for a button on the taskbar?

 BUILD YOUR VOCABULARY

As you progress through this course, develop a personal IT glossary. This will help you build your vocabulary and prepare you for a career. Write a definition for each of the following terms and add it to your IT glossary.

access key
active window
cell
dialog box launcher
document template
insertion point
key tip badge
maximized

minimized
on-demand tab
presentation
restoring
ribbon
spreadsheet
windowed

Documents, spreadsheets, and presentations are created to be viewed again or printed on hard copy. While creating a document, spreadsheet, or presentation in Word, Excel, or PowerPoint, the information is stored in the computer's RAM. RAM is temporary and will hold the information as long as the computer is on and the application is open. That information has to be moved to a permanent storage location.

Microsoft Office can save and recover files if something causes the system to crash. This protects the user from lost data. The state of the program is also remembered. For example, Microsoft Office will remember how many windows were open and what applications were being displayed.

wavebreakmedia/Shutterstock.com

TERMS

backstage view
closing
collate
landscape
opening
portrait
print preview
printing
virtual printer

LEARNING GOALS

After completing this section, you will be able to:
- Describe the process for saving files.
- Explain how to print files.
- Close files and applications.
- Discuss opening of files.

Access

1.5.3

Excel

1.5.2

GS5

Key Applications

2.4

FYI

If the file has not yet been saved, clicking the **Save** button on the **Quick Access** toolbar will begin the "save as" function.

Word

1.5.2

Saving Files

The procedure for saving files is standard. Files can be saved on the computer's local hard disk drive, a network drive, a removable drive, or the cloud. When the user saves a file on the local hard drive or a portable flash drive, that same computer or flash drive must be used to retrieve the file. When the file is saved on a network, it is stored on a hard drive that can be reached from any computer on the network. If the user saves the file in the cloud, the file can be accessed from any location by means of an Internet connection.

Saving Files for the First Time

The first time a file is saved, it must be given a name. Click the **File** tab in the ribbon. The view that is displayed is called the **backstage view**, as shown in Figure 4-6. Click either **Save** or **Save As** in the backstage view. Since the file has not been saved, either command begins the "save as" function, which is used to name the file. To complete the save, select a location in the **Recent Folders** list or click the **Browse** button to navigate to a folder. A standard Windows **Save As** dialog box is displayed. Finally, enter a name for the file in the **File name:** text box in the **Save As** dialog box, and click the **Save** button. Be sure the correct location is current in the **Save As** dialog box before clicking the **Save** button.

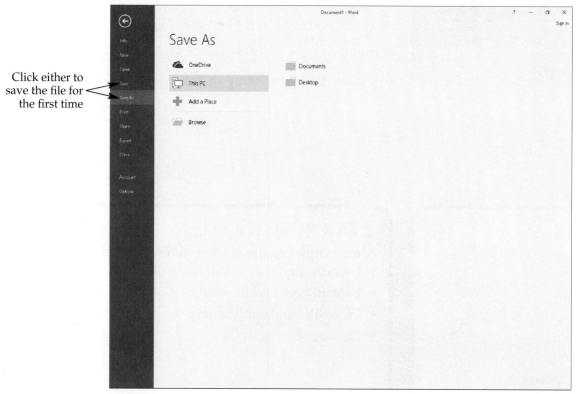

Click either to save the file for the first time

Goodheart-Willcox Publisher

Figure 4-6. Clicking the **File** tab displays the backstage view. What is shown in the backstage view depends on which category is clicked on the left-hand side.

After the initial save when file is named, the **Save** command can be used to save the file quickly. The **Save** command is found in the backstage view of the **File** tab or on the **Quick Access** toolbar. If the **Save As** command is used after the file has been saved at least once, a copy of the file is created under a different name or in a different location. The original document is no longer open.

HANDS-ON EXAMPLE 4.2.1

SAVING AN OFFICE DOCUMENT

Saving a document is one of the most basic skills a computer user must have. Until a document is saved the first time, it exists only in the computer's volatile memory. If the power is shut off, the document is lost unless it has been saved.

1. Insert your MS-OFFICE flash drive into the computer.
2. Applying what you have learned, create a folder on the flash drive named Chap04.
3. Applying what you have learned, maximize Microsoft Word if it is open, or launch Word and begin a new blank document.
4. If not already in the document, add this line of text: Introduction to Microsoft Office.
5. Click the **Save** button on the **Quick Access** toolbar. Since the document has not yet been saved, the **Save As** function is started.
6. Click the **Browse** button and navigate to the Chap04 folder on your flash drive.
7. Click in the **File name:** text box in the **Save As** dialog box, and enter your last name, as shown.

Save

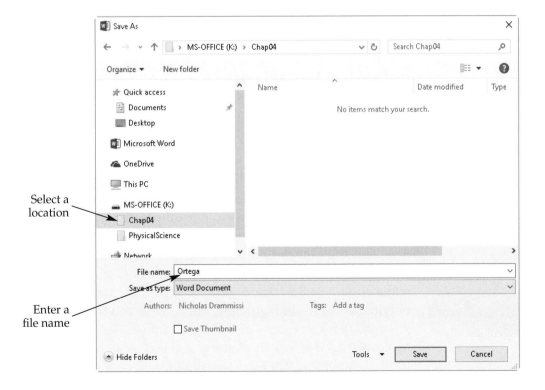

HANDS-ON EXAMPLE 4.2.1 (CONTINUED)

8. Click the **Save** button in the **Save As** dialog box. The document is saved to the flash drive with your last name as the file name. The .docx file name extension is automatically added to the file name. The file name becomes the name of the document, which is displayed in the title bar of the Word window.

9. Applying what you have learned, maximize Microsoft Excel if it is open, or launch Excel and begin a new blank document.

10. If not already in the spreadsheet, add this formula to cell A2: =TODAY().

11. Click the **Save** button on the **Quick Access** toolbar. Because the spreadsheet has not yet been saved, the **Save As** function is started.

12. Applying what you have learned, navigate to the Chap04 folder on your flash drive.

13. Click in the **File name:** text box in the **Save As** dialog box, and enter your first name.

14. Click the **Save** button in the **Save As** dialog box. The document is saved to the flash drive with your first name as the file name. The .xlsx file name extension is automatically added to the file name. The file name becomes the name of the document, which is displayed in the title bar of the Excel window.

15. Launch Windows Explorer, and display the content of the Chap04 folder on the flash drive. Verify that the DOCx and XLSx files you just saved are in the folder.

Access
1.5.2

Word
1.5.1, 1.5.3

GS5
Key Applications
2.6, 2.7

Updating Files

Once a file has been saved, updating it is a quick process. Clicking the **Save** button on the **Quick Access** toolbar or clicking **File>Save** immediately saves the current state of the file under the same file name. The original file is overwritten with current changes.

To create a copy of a file, first save the file to update it. Then, use the **Save As** command to save a copy under a different name or location. It is important to remember that after the **Save As** command, the active document is the copy with the new name, not the original file.

Printing Files

Printing is outputting the content of a file, usually as a hardcopy on paper. Before printing a document or spreadsheet, Microsoft Office offers the user a print preview screen. A **print preview** shows the document exactly how it will look when printed. If the document has more than one page, the user can click through the pages one by one. Most software also allows many options to be set when printing a file. Microsoft Office applications use the backstage view to preview the printing and set options, as shown in Figure 4-7. This is accessed by clicking **File>Print**.

By default, one copy of the document will be printed. If additional copies are needed, use the **Copies:** text box to set how many will be printed. A number can be entered in the text box, or the directional arrows can be used to set the number.

A computer may have more than one printer installed. Some computers have access to printers over a network. In addition, some virtual printers may be installed, such as the Microsoft XPS Document

Click
to print

Make settings
as needed

Click →

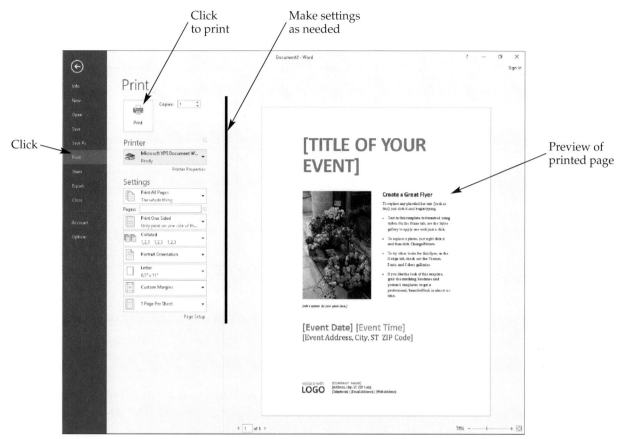

Preview of
printed page

Figure 4-7. The backstage view is used to preview the document before it is printed.

Writer. A **virtual printer** outputs a file instead of a physical hardcopy. Select the appropriate printer using the **Printer** drop-down list.

Options are selected under **Settings**. The specific options available may differ by application, but most Microsoft Office applications have similar options.

The first option allows the user to choose how much of the document to print. Depending on which application is printing, settings may include printing the entire document; printing specific pages, slides, or workbooks; or printing only what is selected in the document.

To **collate** is arranging multiple copies of a document so all pages are in the correct order. For example, if two copies of a five-page document are printed, collating prints pages one through five and then one through five again instead of printing two copies of page one, two copies of page two, and so on. There is an option to print collated or not collated.

The page layout is how the document will be placed on the sheet. The layout can be portrait or landscape, as shown in Figure 4-8. **Portrait** layout or orientation is when the long edge of the paper is on the sides. **Landscape** layout or orientation is when the long edge is on the top and bottom. When a layout option is selected, the preview is updated to reflect it.

The paper size should be set to the size of paper that is loaded in the printer. In some cases, such as with Excel, the document can be scaled down (reduced in size) to fit better on the selected paper size. The

Access
4.3.2

Ethics

Bias-Free Language
As you go to work or school each day, you may encounter others who categorize people using biased words and comments. Using age, gender, race, disability, or ethnicity as a way to describe others is unethical and sometimes illegal. Use bias-free language in all of your communication to show respect for others.

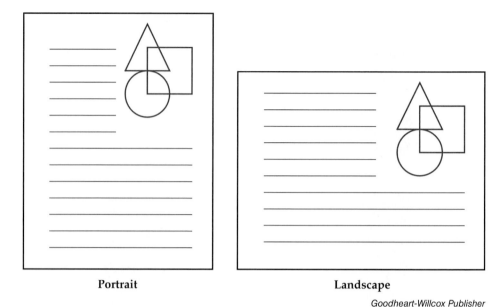

Portrait   Landscape

Goodheart-Willcox Publisher

Figure 4-8. The page layout can be either portrait or landscape.

Fit Sheet on One Page option in Excel is handy if the spreadsheet is larger than one page.

In some applications, such as Word and PowerPoint, the number of pages printed on each sheet of paper can be set. The default is one page per sheet. Printing more than one page per sheet decreases the size of each page. How it will appear is not reflected in the preview. Printing more than one page per sheet is useful for creating handouts, but can make the individual pages hard to read.

HANDS-ON EXAMPLE 4.2.2

PRINTING AN OFFICE DOCUMENT

It is common to print a document, whether on paper or to a file via a virtual printer. It is important to understand how to make settings when printing a document.

1. Applying what you have learned, maximize Microsoft Excel if it is open, or launch Excel and begin a new blank document.
2. If not already in the spreadsheet, add this formula to cell A2: =TODAY().
3. Click the **File** tab to display the backstage view.
4. Click **Print** in the backstage view to display the print preview and the options.
5. Select the printer specified by your instructor.
6. In the **Settings** area, click the bottom drop-down list, and click **Fit Sheet on One Page**. This option forces the spreadsheet to print on a single page, although in this case the content of the spreadsheet would fit on a single page without using this option.
7. Click the **Print** button at the top of the backstage view.

Closing Files and Applications

Closing means removing a file or application from RAM. When a file is not going to be used for a period of time, it should be closed. The same is true of a software application. This is a good practice because closing files and applications frees up space in memory for other applications.

To close a file in a Microsoft Office application, click the **File** tab, and then click **Close**. If the file has no unsaved changes, it is immediately closed, and the application remains open. If there are unsaved changes, the user is prompted to save the file before closing it.

An easy way to close an application is to click the standard Windows close button (X). This method can be used to close any Microsoft Office application or any other application.

Opening Files

Just as knowing how to save a file is a basic computer skill, knowing how to open a file is a basic skill. **Opening** a file is placing its content into RAM so the content can be used. Opening a file is a simple process: activate the **Open** command, navigate to the file location, and select the file.

In Microsoft Office, click **File>Open**. Then, click **Computer** in the backstage view, followed by the **Browse** button, as shown in Figure 4-9. A standard Windows **Open** dialog box is displayed. Navigate to the location where the file is saved, select the file, and click the **Open** button. The file contents are loaded into RAM and displayed in the application window.

The [Ctrl][O] key combination is a common shortcut for opening a file in an application.

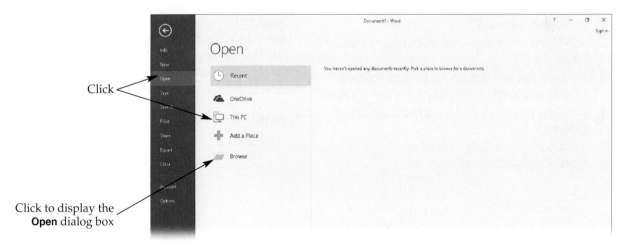

Click

Click to display the
Open dialog box

Goodheart-Willcox Publisher

Figure 4-9. Opening a document in a Microsoft Office application.

HANDS-ON EXAMPLE 4.2.3

OPENING AN OFFICE DOCUMENT

One of the most basic skills a computer user must have is the ability to open a file. It is important to understand where documents are stored and to select the correct document for opening.

1. Insert your MS-OFFICE flash drive into the computer.
2. If any Microsoft Office application is open, close it by clicking the standard Windows close button (X).
3. Launch Microsoft Word, and click **Open Other Documents** in the startup screen.
4. In the **Open** dialog box, navigate to the Chap04 folder on your flash drive.
5. Select the file named with your last name. By default, only Word files are displayed in the dialog box, but the file type can be changed if needed.
6. Click the **Open** button. The file is opened and displayed in the Word application window. Notice that the file content is the same as when it was last saved.

4.2 | SECTION REVIEW

 ## CHECK YOUR UNDERSTANDING

1. What does the **Save** command do if the file has not yet been saved?
2. How is the backstage view displayed in Microsoft Office?
3. What are the two options for how the printed page is arranged or laid out on a sheet of paper?
4. What are two ways to close a Microsoft Office application?
5. What is placing a file's content into RAM so the content can be used called?

 ## BUILD YOUR VOCABULARY

As you progress through this course, develop a personal IT glossary. This will help you build your vocabulary and prepare you for a career. Write a definition for each of the following terms and add it to your IT glossary.

backstage view	portrait
closing	print preview
collate	printing
landscape	virtual printer
opening	

EDITING AND FORMATTING

wavebreakmedia/Shutterstock.com

The applications in the Microsoft Office suite use the same techniques for editing and formatting text. To edit text means inserting, deleting, replacing, formatting, and copying and pasting text. Revising text is an important feature in all applications, not just Microsoft Word. One of the most valuable aspects of using Office is that you can quickly revise data. Editing and formatting skills form the foundation of all text-based activities throughout the suite.

The insertion point is where changes will take place. To set the insertion point, click at the location. Then the arrow keys on the keyboard can also be used to move the insertion point around the document. Keyboard navigation is often quicker than using the mouse.

LEARNING GOALS

After completing this section, you will be able to:

- Describe basic ways in which to edit text.
- Manipulate inserted media files.
- Reverse errors in a document.
- Discuss finding and replacing text.
- Explain how to move, copy, cut, and paste text and images.
- Apply formatting to text.

TERMS

ascending order	handles
bulleted list	inserting
character style	move
copy	numbered list
crop	paragraph style
cut	paste
descending order	sorting
drag-and-drop	style
editing	system clipboard
format painter	typeface
formatting	

Editing Text

Editing a document is making changes to the text, format, layout, or other aspects of the content. The insertion point is where changes will take place. To set the insertion point, click at the location. The arrow keys on the keyboard can also be used to move the insertion point around the document.

Deleting Text

The [Delete] key erases one character at a time to the right of the insertion point. The [Backspace] key erases one character at a time to the left of the insertion point. If a word, sentence, or paragraph is selected, either key erases the selection. If text is added, the selection is erased and replaced with the new text.

Selecting Text

To select an entire word, double-click the word. To select an entire line of text, move the cursor to the left of the line until it changes to an arrow. Then, click once. This selects a line of text, not a sentence, as shown in Figure 4-10. To select a sentence, hold down the [Ctrl] key, and then click anywhere in the sentence. This only works if there is not currently a selection. To select a paragraph, move the cursor to the left of the paragraph until it changes to an arrow, and then double-click. To select the entire document, move the cursor to the left of any paragraph, and then either triple-click or hold down the [Ctrl] key and click once. You can also press the [Ctrl][A] key combination to select the entire document.

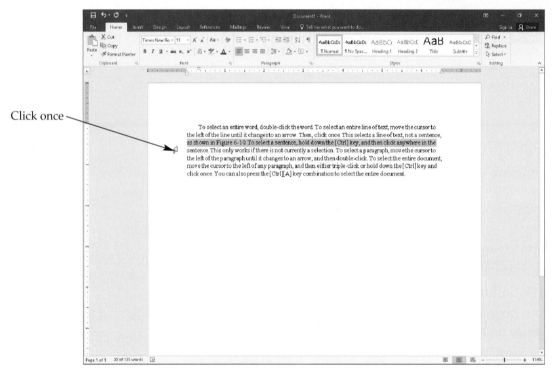

Click once

Goodheart-Willcox Publisher

Figure 4-10. When the cursor changes to an arrow, click once to select a line of text.

Selecting Nonadjacent Items

Sometimes it is necessary to select words, sentences, lines, or paragraphs that are not adjacent, or next to each other. Scrolling over the words will not work. Instead, select the first item, and then press and hold the [Ctrl] key. With the [Ctrl] key held down, additional items can be selected that are not adjacent to the first item. This selection method is useful if several nonadjacent items in a list, for example, need to be formatted the same.

Creating and Working with Lists

Lists are short lines or paragraphs of information, each typically only a few words in length, of related data. For example, a list may be the names of members in a class or the steps in the procedure for filling a car with gasoline. Lists are useful for displaying several small pieces of data in a format that is easy to read.

In a text or slide show document, there are two types of lists: bulleted and numbered. A **bulleted list**, also called an *unordered list*, consists of separate lines of text with a small graphic, such as a dot, in front of the line, as shown in Figure 4-11. A **numbered list**, also called an *ordered list*, consists of separate lines of text with numbers in sequential order in front of the text.

Creating a List

To create a bulleted list in Microsoft Word or Microsoft PowerPoint, select the lines that will compose the list. Then, click **Home>Paragraph> Bullets** in the ribbon. The selected paragraphs are converted to an automatic bulleted list. Each item in the list is indented on the left and a bullet is added to the beginning of each paragraph. You can also click the button, and then enter text. If you need to increase or decrease the list level of a specific bullet point, click **Home>Paragraph>Increase Indent** or **Decrease Indent**.

To create a numbered list in Microsoft Word or Microsoft PowerPoint, select the lines that will compose the list. Then, click **Home>Paragraph> Numbering** in the the ribbon. The selected paragraphs are converted to an automatic numbered list. Each item in the list is indented on the left and a number is added to the beginning of each paragraph. By default,

Bulleted List	**Numbered List**
• Describe basic ways to edit text.	1. Buckle your seatbelt.
• Manipulate inserted media files.	2. Put your foot on the brake.
• Reverse errors in a document.	3. Start the car.
• Discuss finding and replacing text.	4. Check for traffic and pedestrians.

Goodheart-Willcox Publisher

Figure 4-11. A bulleted list is in no particular order. A numbered list presents information in a specific order.

PowerPoint
2.1.5

Word
3.3.1

FYI

Due to the nature of Microsoft PowerPoint, most of the slide templates are set up to create automatic bulleted lists whenever text is added.

Word
3.3.4

FYI

To change bullet characters or number format, click **Home>Paragraph** and select the respective button. To create a custom bullet character, select **Define New Bullet**.

Word
3.3.2, 3.3.3

Blend Images/Shutterstock.com

Anytime you are working with lists, you may find the need to sort the items.

Word

3.2.1

FYI

A spreadsheet is basically a series of lists. Each column can be thought of as a vertical list consisting of rows.

FYI

To set a starting number in a list, right-click the desired text and select **Set Numbering Value** from the shortcut menu. A user can also **Restart at 1** or **Continue Numbering** from the shortcut menu.

Word

3.3.5, 3.3.6

the first number is 1, and each item in the list is sequentially numbered from there.

If the [Enter] key is pressed at the end of any paragraph in the list, the following line is automatically formatted as part of the bulleted or numbered list. To cancel the automatic bulleting or numbering on this new line, either press the [Enter] key a second time or click **Home**>**Paragraph**>**Bullets** in the ribbon.

Sorting a List

Sometimes, it is not enough just to create a list, but the items in the list must be placed in a certain order. **Sorting** is arranging a list in either ascending or descending order. **Ascending order** is when the lowest value, such as A or 1, is at the top of the list. This is often called *A to Z order*. **Descending order** is when the highest value, such as Z or 10, is at the top of the list. This is often called *Z to A order*.

Sorting can be used on a series of single words or numbers, numbered lists, and bulleted lists. The items to be sorted must be adjacent. Sorting is particularly useful when working with tables. The first character in each cell in the table is read and the table sorted accordingly. Microsoft Word and Microsoft Excel can sort lists.

To sort a list in Microsoft Word, first select all items to be sorted. Then, click **Home**>**Paragraph**>**Sort** in the ribbon. The **Sort Text** dialog box is displayed, as shown in Figure 4-12. Select whether to sort in ascending or descending order, and click the **OK** button to sort the list. Any empty lines, rows, or paragraphs will be placed either at the top or bottom of the list.

To sort a list in Microsoft Excel, first select all items to be sorted. This may be an entire column, selected adjacent cells within a column, or

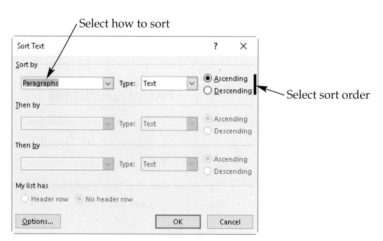

Goodheart-Willcox Publisher

Figure 4-12. Sorting text in Microsoft Word.

multiple columns. Then, click **Home**>**Editing**>**Sort & Filter** in the ribbon, as shown in Figure 4-13. In the drop-down list that is displayed, click **Sort smallest to largest** to sort in ascending order or **Sort largest to smallest** to sort in descending order.

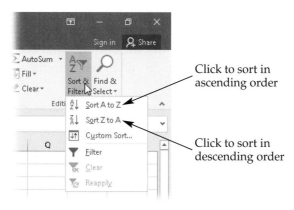

Goodheart-Willcox Publisher

Figure 4-13. Sorting data in Microsoft Excel. Note that ascending order is **Sort A to Z** and descending order is **Sort Z to A**.

HANDS-ON EXAMPLE 4.3.1

CREATING AND SORTING A LIST

Creating lists is a basic skill to have for creating documents. Many documents contain lists, such as sales data, addresses, names, or many other items.

1. Launch Microsoft Word, and begin a new blank document.
2. Enter the last names of five of your friends, each on a separate line (paragraph).
3. Move the cursor to the left of the first name in the list until it changes to an arrow, click and hold, and drag down to the last line in the list. When the entire list is highlighted, release the mouse button. The list is selected.

Bullets

4. Click **Home**>**Paragraph**>**Bullets** in the ribbon. The list is converted to an automatic bulleted list.
5. Click **Home**>**Paragraph**>**Sort** in the ribbon. The **Sort Text** dialog box is displayed.

Sort

6. In the **Sort by** area of the dialog box, click the left-hand drop-down arrow, and click **Paragraphs** in the list. This tells Word that the breaks between items are indicated by returns (paragraphs).
7. Click the right-hand drop-down arrow, and click **Text** in the list. This tells Word to sort letters.
8. Click the **Ascending** radio button. This tells Word to sort the list in A to Z order.
9. Click the **OK** button to sort the list.
10. Double-click the first name in the list to select it.
11. Hold down the [Ctrl] key, and double-click the third name in the list.
12. Hold down the [Ctrl] key, and double-click the last name in the list. The first, third, and fifth names should be highlighted to indicate they are selected, but the second and fourth names should not be selected.

GS5
Key Applications
7.1
Access
4.3.8
Excel
5.3.2
Word
5.1.1, 5.1.2, 5.1.3

FYI

Text boxes can be inserted to most Microsoft Office programs by clicking **Insert>Text>Text Box**. Shapes can be inserted by clicking **Insert>Shapes**. Both text boxes and shapes are created by clicking and dragging the cursor to the desired size.

Excel
5.3.1
PowerPoint
2.2
Word
5.1.4
Word
5.2.7

FYI

Photographs and images should always be resized proportionally.

Inserting Media Files

It is possible to insert various media files, such as images, into documents using office suite software and then manipulate them. In Microsoft Office, the ribbon interface includes on-demand tabs. For example, when an image is selected, the **Format** on-demand tab is available in the ribbon. This tab contains commands related to working with images, such as changing the border, wrapping text around the image, adding shadow effects, aligning the image on the page, and changing the size of the image.

Inserting a Media File

Adding a media file to a document is called **inserting** or *attaching*. Depending on which Microsoft Office application is being used, images, videos, and sounds can be inserted. For example, to insert an image into Microsoft Word, Microsoft PowerPoint, or Microsoft Excel, click the **Insert>Illustrations>Pictures** in the ribbon. A standard open dialog box is displayed. Navigate to the location where the image file is saved, select the file, and click the **Insert** button. The image is added to the document at the current insertion point.

Image Location and Size

When an image is selected, small squares or dots, called handles, are displayed in the middle of each edge and at the corners, as shown in Figure 4-14. **Handles** are used to change the size of the image. The corner handles are used to resize the image proportionally. This means the ratio of height to width remains the same. The handles on the top, bottom, and sides are used to resize the image nonproportionally. The ratio of height to width will change when these handles are used.

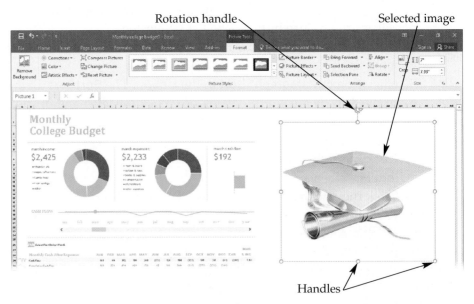

Rotation handle   Selected image

Handles

Goodheart-Willcox Publisher

Figure 4-14. When an image is selected, handles are displayed that can be used to resize the image.

The location of an image can be adjusted by dragging the frame. Click on the outer edge of the selected image, not on a handle, and drag the image to a new location. Note: depending on how the image was inserted, its position may be locked.

After an image has been placed and sized accordingly, it may need to be reordered. Consider a document or file in which multiple images are stacked on top of one another with some overlap. There is an order associated with that set of images. If images need to be reordered, it can be done by selecting the image and clicking **Format>Drawing Tools>Arrange**. There are two main ordering options: **Bring Forward**, which moves the selected object one level up in the stack, and **Send Backward**, which moves the object one level down in the stack. Within those two buttons, users can **Bring to Front**, which moves an object to the front of the stack, or **Send to Back**, which moves an object to the back of the stack.

Once the objects have been properly ordered, they can be further grouped and aligned. Grouping objects allows any edits or relocations to be done to all objects in the group rather than individually. To group objects, press and hold the [Ctrl] key while selecting the objects with the mouse. Then, click **Format>Drawing Tools** or **Picture Tools>Arrange>Group**. In the drop-down menu, select **Group**. Aligning objects ensures that they are distributed to the left, center, right, top, middle, or bottom of a slide. This is done by clicking **Format>Drawing Tools** or **Picture Tools>Arrange>Align**.

Cropping an Image

In some cases, only part of the image is needed. For example, a photograph may show a group of people, but only one person needs to be shown. It is possible to cut away the rest of the photograph. To **crop** an image is to trim the outer portion.

To crop an image in Microsoft Office, first select it. Then, click **Format>Size>Crop** in the ribbon. New handles are displayed on the image. Click one of the handles and drag inward to specify the area to keep. The portion that will be cropped is grayed out. The size of the image will be reduced without changing the proportions by removing the portion of the image that is grayed out. To complete the operation, click anywhere outside of the image.

Rotating an Image

In Microsoft Office, an image can be rotated on an imaginary axis projecting out of the screen. It can be rotated in 90-degree increments either clockwise or counterclockwise or manually rotated to any angle. An image can also be flipped horizontally or vertically.

To rotate an image to any angle, first select the image to display the handles. There is a special handle displayed at the top-middle of the image that looks like a circular arrow. Click this handle and drag to rotate the image. Holding down the [Shift] key while dragging limits the rotation to 15-degree increments.

PowerPoint
2.4.1, 2.4.2, 2.4.3

FYI

SmartArt can be inserted into most Microsoft Office programs by selecting **Insert>Illustrations>SmartArt**. One placed, SmartArt can be further customized in the **SmartArt Tools** on-demand tab.

PowerPoint
3.3

Word
5.3.1, 5.3.2, 5.3.3

GS5
Key Applications
7.2

FYI

Alignment tools such as guidelines and grids can help when placing images and media files. To toggle alignment tools on or off, select the desired tool from the **View** tab. The **Guides** button will show horizontal and vertical center lines; the **Gridlines** button will show additional gridlines.

PowerPoint
2.4.4

Effects can be added to an image by selecting the image and clicking **Format>Adjust>Artistic Effects**.

Word
5.2.1, 5.2.2

FYI

Users can remove the background of an image by selecting the image and clicking **Format>Adjust>Remove Background**.

Word
5.2.3

The ribbon can also be used to rotate an image. Select the image, and then click **Format>Arrange>Rotate Objects** in the ribbon to display a drop-down menu, as shown in Figure 4-15. Options in this menu allow the image to be rotated 90 degrees clockwise or counterclockwise or to be flipped horizontally or vertically.

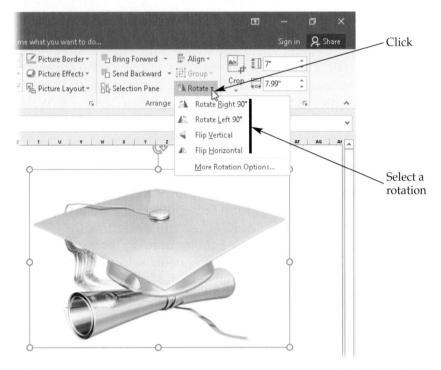

Goodheart-Willcox Publisher

Figure 4-15. Using commands in the ribbon to rotate an image.

HANDS-ON EXAMPLE 4.3.2 📑

Word
5.2.4, 5.2.5, 5.2.6, 5.2.8

MANIPULATING A MEDIA FILE

Photographs come in many different sizes. Once a photograph is inserted into a document, its size and location can be adjusted to fit the document. Additionally, the photograph itself can be manipulated, such as adding a border.

1. Insert your MS-OFFICE flash drive into the computer.
2. Navigate to the student companion website at www.g-wlearning.com, download the data files for this chapter, and save them in the Chap04 folder on your flash drive.
3. Applying what you have learned, open the Baltimore1 document file from the Chap04 folder on your flash drive.
4. Click at the end of the first paragraph. The insertion point is placed at that location.
5. Click **Insert>Illustrations>Pictures** in the ribbon. A standard open dialog box is displayed.

Pictures
6. Navigate to the Chap04 folder on your flash drive, select the FortMcHenry.jpg image file, and click the **Insert** button. This photograph is inserted, but notice that it is very large in relation to the document.
7. If the image is not already selected, click it to select it.

HANDS-ON EXAMPLE 4.3.2 (CONTINUED)

8. Click the handle at the lower-right corner of the photograph, and drag it toward the middle of the image.

9. Resize the image so it is about 2″ × 3″. The size of the image is displayed in the **Height:** and **Width:** text boxes (**Format>Size**) in the ribbon.

10. With the photo selected, click **Format>Arrange>Wrap Text** in the ribbon to display a drop-down menu.

Wrap Text

11. Click the **Square** option in the drop-down menu. The text is shifted up to fill the space to the right of the photo.

12. With the photo selected, click **Format>Picture Styles>Picture Border** in the ribbon to display a color palette.

Picture Border

13. Click a blue color swatch in the palette. A blue border appears around the photo, as shown.

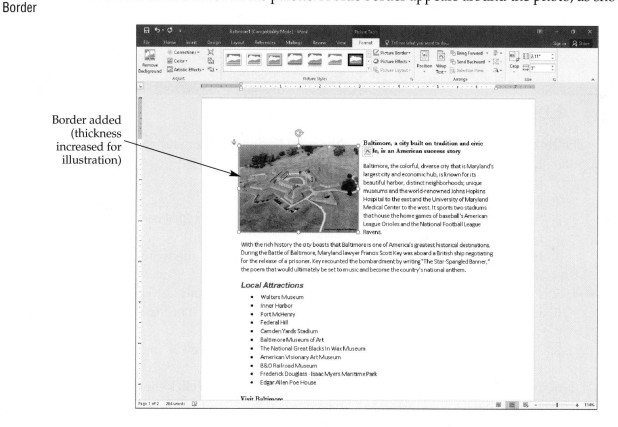

Border added (thickness increased for illustration)

Excel
5.3.4

Word
5.2.8

14. Alternative text, or *alt text*, is text that appears when the cursor is placed above an image or media file. This is done for accessibility purposes. To add alternative text to the image you just placed, right-click the image and select **Format Picture** from the shortcut menu. In the **Format Picture** panel, select **Layout & Properties** and choose **Alt Text**. In the **Description** field, enter the phrase Fort McHenry, Baltimore, MD and select **OK**.

15. Applying what you have learned, save the file as *LastName*Baltimore1 in the Chap04 folder on your flash drive, where *LastName* is your last name.

Reversing Errors

GS5

Key Applications

1.7

Most actions in software can be reversed, or undone. If an action cannot be undone, software will usually warn the user the action about to be taken is permanent. However, actions such as deleting, formatting, and moving text, as well as many other actions, can be quickly reversed with the **Undo** command. It is also possible to redo an action that was reversed with the **Undo** command. The **Redo** command restores the last action undone.

In Microsoft Office, the **Undo** and **Redo** commands are located on the **Quick Access** toolbar. Clicking the **Undo** button reverses the last action. The [Ctrl][Z] key combination is the shortcut for undo. Clicking the drop-down arrow next to the **Undo** button displays a list of actions that can be undone. This list allows the user to select multiple actions to undo in one step, but actions must be undone in order. You cannot pick and choose which actions to undo. Clicking the **Redo** button restores the last undone action. The [Ctrl][Y] keyboard combination is the shortcut for redo. Only one action can be redone at a time.

FYI

The **Repeat** command can be used to duplicate the last action.

HANDS-ON EXAMPLE 4.3.3

EDITING A DOCUMENT

The ability to edit a document is one of the most basic computer skills to have. Another basic computer skill is to be able to undo and redo changes.

1. Insert your MS-OFFICE flash drive into the computer.
2. Launch Microsoft Word.
3. Applying what you have learned, open the file *LastName*Baltimore1 from the Chap04 folder on your flash drive.
4. In the first line of text, click to the right of the letter g in the word bustling to place the insertion point at that location.
5. Press the [Backspace] key nine times to erase the word and one space.
6. Use the arrow keys to move the insertion point to the left of the letter q in the word quirky in the second paragraph.
7. Press the [Delete] key eight times to erase the word as well as the comma and space that follow it.
8. In the first line of the list under the paragraphs, double-click the word Area to select it. Notice that a mini toolbar is displayed when the cursor is over the selection.
9. Add the text Local. As soon as the first letter is added, the selection is replaced by the character.
10. Move the cursor to the left of the line in the list containing the text Federal Hill. When the cursor changes to an arrow, click once to select the entire line.
11. Press the [Delete] key to erase the line. In this case, the entire paragraph is deleted because the line was a single paragraph.
12. Click the **Undo** button on the **Quick Access** toolbar. The paragraph containing the text Federal Hill is restored as deleting it was the last change made to the document.

Undo

13. Applying what you have learned, move the insertion point to the end of the last line, which begins with the text Frederick Douglass.
14. Press the [Enter] key to add a new paragraph.
15. On the new line (paragraph), add the text Edgar Allen Poe House.
16. Save the file.

Searching for Text

Locating specific text within a document is very easy. This is accomplished with the **Find** and **Replace** commands. The ability to locate text is particularly valuable for long documents. If many instances of text appear in a document and must be changed, replacing the text is more efficient than editing each individual instance. Formatting and special characters can also be located and, if needed, replaced.

Finding Text

To locate specific text in Microsoft Office, click **Home>Editing>Find** in the ribbon or press the [Ctrl][F] key combination. In Microsoft Excel, the **Find and Replace** dialog box is displayed (or the **Find** dialog box in Microsoft PowerPoint). In Microsoft Word, the **Navigation** pane is displayed on the left side of the window. To display the **Find and Replace** dialog box in Word, click the arrow next to the search box in the **Navigation** pane, and click **Advanced Find...** in the drop-down list.

To use the **Navigation** pane in Word, click in the search box, and enter the word or phrase to locate. All instances of the search word are listed in the **Navigation** pane and highlighted throughout the document, as shown in Figure 4-16. Clicking an entry in the list automatically jumps the view of the document to that location and selects the word.

GS5
Key Applications
1.5

Access
2.3.5

Word
1.2.1, 2.1.1

FYI

The [Ctrl][F] key combination is a shortcut common to most software for activating the **Find** command.

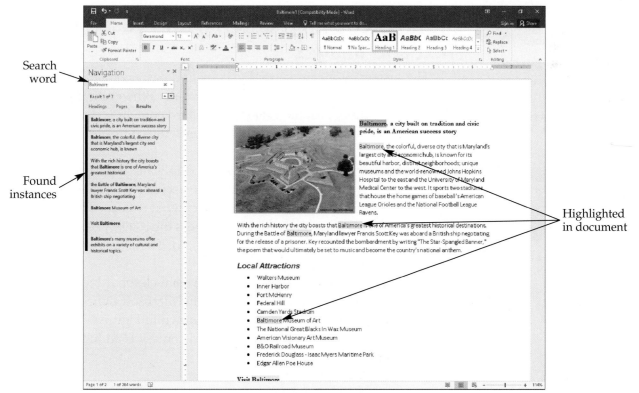

Search word

Found instances

Highlighted in document

Goodheart-Willcox Publisher

Figure 4-16. Using the **Navigation** pane in Microsoft Word to locate text in the document.

To use the **Find and Replace** dialog box to locate text, click the **Find** tab in the dialog box (this is not in PowerPoint). Then, click in the **Find what:** text box, enter the word to locate, and click the **Find Next** button. The view of the document is automatically centered on the first instance of the word, and the word is selected. By default, the search is conducted from the insertion point downward. To find the next instance of the word, click the **Find Next** button again. Once the dialog box is closed after conducting a search, the [Ctrl][Page Down] and [Ctrl][Page Up] key combinations can be used to quickly find the next or previous instance of the last search word.

Replacing Text

To replace specific text in Microsoft Office, click **Home>Editing>Replace** in the ribbon or press the [Ctrl][H] key combination. The **Find and Replace** dialog box is displayed (or the **Replace** dialog box in Microsoft PowerPoint). Click in the **Find what:** text box, and enter the word to locate. Next, click in the **Replace with:** text box, and enter the word to substitute. Click the **Find Next** button. The view of the document is automatically centered on the first instance of the word, and the word is selected. To replace that instance, click the **Replace** button, and the next instance is automatically located. To leave the located instance the way it is, click the **Find Next** button. To replace all instances in the document, click the **Replace All** button. The **Replace All** option should be used carefully as you will not have the opportunity to confirm each replacement.

Moving, Copying, Cutting, and Pasting Text and Images

The system clipboard is used to copy and paste content. The **system clipboard** is a virtual container for storing data. When new data are placed on the clipboard, the existing clipboard content is deleted. The current content of the clipboard remains until the computer is turned off or restarted.

A copy of text or an image is an exact duplicate of the original at the time the **copy** was made. The content exists in two locations. To copy content in Microsoft Office, first select what to copy. Then, click **Home>Clipboard>Copy** in the ribbon or press the [Ctrl][C] key combination. The content is placed on the system clipboard. Then, the content can be pasted elsewhere to create the copy.

To **paste** is to add the content of the system clipboard to the document at the insertion point. To paste in Microsoft Office, click **Home>Clipboard>Paste** in the ribbon, as shown in Figure 4-17, or press the [Ctrl][V] key combination. The clipboard content is added at the insertion point.

FYI

The shortcut menu can be used to copy, cut, and paste content.

GS5
Key Applications
1.1

Word
1.2.4, 2.1.2

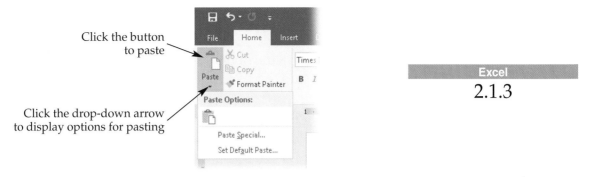

Click the button to paste

Click the drop-down arrow to display options for pasting

Excel
2.1.3

Figure 4-17. The ribbon can be used to paste content or the [Ctrl][V] key combination can be used.

To **cut** content means to remove it from the document and place it on the system clipboard. To cut content in Microsoft Office, first select what to cut. Then, click **Home>Clipboard>Cut** in the ribbon or press the [Ctrl][X] key combination. The content is removed from the document and placed on the system clipboard. By cutting and pasting, the content is, in effect, *moved* from one location to another.

To **move** content means to remove it from the source location and place it in the destination location. Cutting and pasting moves content, but the mouse can also be used to move content. First, select what is to be moved. Then, by clicking and holding down the left mouse button, the content can be *dragged* to the new location. Releasing the mouse button causes the content to be *dropped* into the new location. Therefore, this operation is called **drag-and-drop.** The system clipboard is not involved in this procedure.

HANDS-ON EXAMPLE 4.3.4

COPYING CONTENT BETWEEN DOCUMENTS

It is a common task to copy text from one document to another. An even more common task is to move text from one point in a document to another location in the same document.

1. Be sure the data files for this chapter have been downloaded to the Chap04 folder on your flash drive.
2. Launch Microsoft Word, and open the file *LastName*Baltimore1 from the Chap04 folder on your flash drive, if it is not already open.
3. Open the file Baltimore2 from the Chap04 folder on your flash drive.
4. Select all text in the Baltimore2 document by pressing the [Ctrl][A] key combination.

HANDS-ON EXAMPLE 4.3.4 (CONTINUED)

Copy

5. Click **Home>Clipboard>Copy** in the ribbon, as shown. All text in the document is placed on the system clipboard.

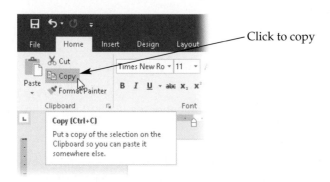

6. Close the Baltimore2 file without saving it.
7. In the *LastName*Baltimore1 file, place the insertion point at the end of the document.
8. Applying what you have learned, create a new line (paragraph).
9. Click **Home>Clipboard>Paste** in the ribbon. The content of the system clipboard, which is the text from the other document, is placed at the insertion point.

Paste

10. Applying what you have learned, select the line at the end of the document with the text Matisse's Marguerite: Model Daughter.
11. Click on the selection, hold, and drag the text to the beginning of the line above it. As you drag, a small rectangle appears next to the cursor.
12. Release the mouse button. The selected text is moved to the new location.
13. Save the file.

Word

2.2.1

FYI

The mini toolbar displayed when text is selected is intended for making formatting changes.

Formatting Text

Formatting text means changing the appearance of the characters. Bold, italic, and underline are examples of text formatting. Other examples include making the characters larger or smaller, striking a line through them, and changing their color. Formatting changes are applied to selected text or the text where the insertion point is located.

Fonts

A **typeface** is a design of characters. In common usage, the term *font* is used to mean typeface, although technically these are not the same thing. Common typefaces are Arial, Times New Roman, and Courier. Dozens of typefaces are installed with Windows and Microsoft Office. In Microsoft Office, the typeface is selected in the **Font** group on the **Home** tab of the ribbon. Click the **Font** drop-down arrow to see a list of installed fonts. The name of a font appears in a preview of the typeface. To change the typeface of the selection, click the font name in the list.

The size of the selected text can be changed using the **Font Size** text box or drop-down list in the **Font** group on the **Home** tab of the ribbon.

The size of text is measured in points. There are 72 points per inch, so an uppercase letter set in 11 point type is about 5/32″ tall, as shown in Figure 4-18.

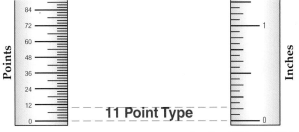

Goodheart-Willcox Publisher

Figure 4-18. Type is measured in points. There are 72 points per inch. Note: the measurement includes an allotment for the part of some letters that descends below the line.

Other text formatting options that can be set in the **Font** group on the **Home** tab of the ribbon include bold, italic, underline, strikethrough, subscript, superscript, and color. Bold, italic, and underline are discussed earlier in this chapter. Strikethrough is a horizontal line through the middle of characters. Click the **Strikethrough** button to format the selected text as strikethrough. Superscript is formatting that sets the character smaller than normal and raised, such as the 2 in X^2. Click the **Superscript** button to make the selected text superscript. Subscript is formatting that sets the character smaller than normal and lowered, such as the 1 in Y_1. Click the **Subscript** button to make the selected text subscript. To change the color of the selected text, click the drop-down arrow next to the **Font Color** button, and select a new color in the palette that is displayed.

Styles

A more efficient and complete method of formatting text is using styles. A **style** is a group of formatting settings that can be applied in one step. The look of text can be quickly changed by picking a new style. It immediately changes the typeface and paragraph properties of the text.

For text documents, there are two basic types of styles: paragraph and character. A **paragraph style** defines the formatting for a paragraph, including the text formatting. A **character style** defines the text formatting for individual characters. Paragraph-related formatting, such as margins and indents, are not part of a character style.

To see a list of the available styles in Microsoft Word, click the **More** button in the gallery in the **Styles** group on the **Home** tab of the ribbon, as shown in Figure 4-19. Clicking a style name in the gallery immediately applies the formatting defined in the style to the selected text.

PowerPoint
2.1.2, 2.3.3

FYI

To clear formatting, select the desired text and click **Home>Font>Clear Formatting**.

Word
2.2.4

Default styles

Goodheart-Willcox Publisher

Figure 4-19. The gallery in the **Styles** group contains the default Microsoft Word styles.

Be careful when applying styles. In Microsoft Word, if a character or word is selected, the style may be applied as a character style. Many of the built-in styles can be either paragraph or character styles. However, a new style can be defined to be only a paragraph or a character style. This helps avoid accidentally applying the wrong type of style.

Microsoft Word 2016 also contains collections of styles called style sets. A style set is a group of styles that have been designed to work together visually. To see the available style sets, click the **More** button in the gallery in the **Document Formatting** group in the **Design** tab of the ribbon. Clicking a style set name in the gallery makes all of the styles within the set available for use in the document.

HANDS-ON EXAMPLE 4.3.5

FORMATTING TEXT

To create professional documents, you must be able to change color, size, font, style, and paragraph formatting. The use of styles allows consistent formatting within a document.

1. Launch Microsoft Word, and open the file *LastName*Baltimore1 from the Chap04 folder on your flash drive, if it is not already open.
2. Place the insertion point anywhere in the first line at the top of the document.
3. Click the Heading1 style in the gallery in the **Styles** group on the **Home** tab of the ribbon. Since no text is highlighted, the style is applied to the entire paragraph instead of as a character style.
4. Applying what you have learned, apply the Heading2 style as a paragraph style to the line Local Attractions, as shown.

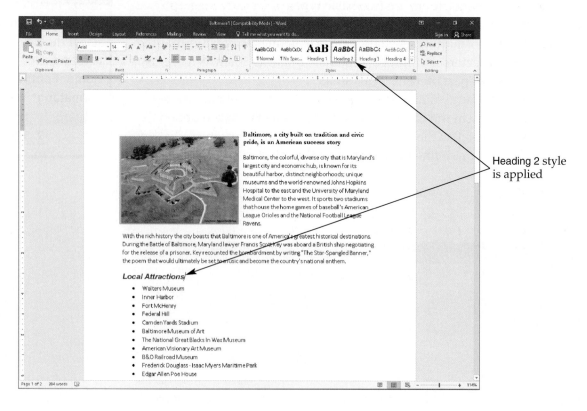

Heading 2 style is applied

HANDS-ON EXAMPLE 4.3.5 (CONTINUED)

5. Applying what you have learned, select the entire first paragraph (the one in Heading1 style).
6. Enter 20 in the **Font Size** text box (**Home>Font>Font Size**). This sets the point size to 20 points.
7. Select all lines of text in the list under Local Attractions, from Walters Museum to Edgar Allen Poe House.
8. Applying what you have learned, convert the lines of text to an automatic bulleted list.
9. Select the lines of text in the second list, from Divided Voices to Passages through Fire.
10. Applying what you have learned, convert the lines of text to an automatic bulleted list.
11. Save the file.

Format Painter

Word
2.2.2

A useful tool for formatting text is the format painter. The **format painter** copies the formatting applied to selected text and then applies that formatting to a second text selection. To use the format painter, select the text with the formatting to copy. Then, click **Home>Clipboard>Format Painter** in the ribbon. Finally, click the text to which the formatting is to be applied.

HANDS-ON EXAMPLE 4.3.6

Excel
2.2.3

FORMAT PAINTER

There are times when formatting must be applied many times. For example, suppose a document has important words in red and this must be changed to purple throughout. After reformatting the first instance, the format painter can be used to apply the new formatting to the other important words.

1. Launch Microsoft Word, and open the file *LastName*Baltimore1 from the Chap04 folder on your flash drive, if it is not already open.
2. Applying what you have learned, select the first paragraph (the one in Heading1 style).
3. Applying what you have learned, change the size of the text to 12 points.
4. With the text selected, click the **Font** drop-down arrow in the **Font** group on the **Home** tab of the ribbon, and click **Garamond** in the drop-down list. If Garamond is not available, select a different typeface.

Format Painter

5. With the text selected, click the **Format Painter** button in the **Clipboard** group on the **Home** tab of the ribbon. The cursor changes to a paintbrush.
6. Select the line of text that states Visit Baltimore. The text assumes all of the formatting applied to the first paragraph, including the style setting.
7. Save the file.

TITANS OF TECHNOLOGY

Jakob Nielsen, a cofounder of the Nielsen Norman Group, is a consultant on the usability of the World Wide Web and holds a PhD. in human-computer interaction. He studies user interactions and proposes quick and easy ways to implement software functions that increase user productivity. Early in his career, Dr. Nielsen worked mostly on large-scale software applications. However, while at Sun Microsystems in the 1990s, he switched to studying the usability of what was then the emerging technology of the World Wide Web. While his focus has been on the Internet, his advice to keep common actions performed in the same way is a key concept in the design of user interfaces. Dr. Nielsen has published many books and articles. His 1989 text *Coordinating User Interfaces for Consistency* is considered a standard in how to design a consistent look and feel for software. It is still in demand and frequently cited.

4.3 SECTION REVIEW

CHECK YOUR UNDERSTANDING

1. What key combination is used to select all text in a document?
2. What is trimming the outer portion of an image called?
3. Which command or function is used to locate specific text and substitute other text for it?
4. When text is cut, where is it placed?
5. What is the difference between a paragraph style and a character style?

BUILD YOUR VOCABULARY

As you progress through this course, develop a personal IT glossary. This will help you build your vocabulary and prepare you for a career. Write a definition for each of the following terms and add it to your IT glossary.

ascending order	handles
bulleted list	inserting
character style	move
copy	numbered list
crop	paragraph style
cut	paste
descending order	sorting
drag-and-drop	style
editing	system clipboard
format painter	typeface
formatting	

Document Views, Options, and Help

michaeljung/Shutterstock.com

To make software easier to learn and use, developers have included shortcuts, dialog boxes, ability to manipulate views, options, and help functions. This makes it possible to modify the program and decrease the time it takes to produce a document, spreadsheet, or presentation. Views of the file being worked on are easily adjusted for size.

The user can create many personalized settings, including general activities, saving, proofing, and customizing the ribbon. The help function of Microsoft Office is all-encompassing and always up-to-date. It replaces the printed user manuals that in the past were supplied with software. The help function is accessed in the same fashion from all Office applications.

Terms

metadata
protected view
read-only
zooming

Learning Goals

After completing this section, you will be able to:
- Explain how to change the view of a document.
- Discuss options that can be set in the Microsoft Office suite.
- Describe how to use the help function.

Document Views

There are many ways to view a document in Microsoft Office. The way a user views a document is largely a personal preference. For example, some users like to see a text document on a simulated page. Other users would rather not see the page, only the text. The view of the document does not affect how the document is constructed. Microsoft Word, Microsoft Excel, and Microsoft PowerPoint have various views for displaying the document. These views can be categorized as overall or protected.

Overall Views

Microsoft Word has five overall views: reading mode view, print layout view, web layout view, outline view, and draft view. Microsoft PowerPoint has eight overall views. Slide views include normal view, outline view, slide sorter view, notes page view, and reading view; master views include slide master view, handout master view, and notes master view. Microsoft Excel has three overall views: normal view, page break view, and page layout view, along with an option to create custom views. All views are set using the **View** tab of the ribbon, as shown in Figure 4-20. The five overall views in Microsoft Word are described here.

Word Overall Views

The print layout is the default view. In the print layout view, a simulated page is displayed so the margins can be seen. To display this view, click the **Print Layout** button in the **Views** group on the **View** tab of the ribbon.

The draft view is useful when the margins and the edges of the page do not need to be seen. In this view, the style area can also be displayed along the left edge, as shown in Figure 4-21. The style area is a quick reference for which styles are applied to the text. Many experienced users prefer to use the draft view. To display this view, click **View>Views>Draft View** in the ribbon.

The outline view is ideal for organizing the content of a document. In this view, the levels of heads can be displayed with the body copy hidden, just as if you were creating an outline on paper. The heads can be rearranged in this view, and the associated body copy will be moved as well. To display the outline view, click **View>Views>Outline View** in the ribbon.

The web layout view displays the document as it will appear as a web page. The simulated page and the vertical ruler are not displayed. When using Word to create a web page, it is important to use this view to check for display issues. To display this view, click **View>Views>Web Layout** in the ribbon.

Views

Goodheart-Willcox Publisher

Figure 4-20. The document view can be set using the **View** tab in the ribbon.

Draft view is displayed

Applied styles are listed

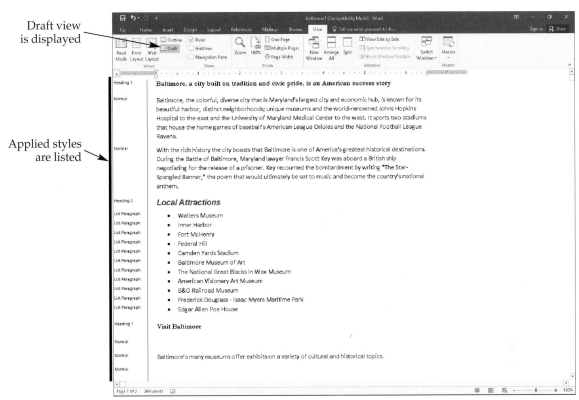

Figure 4-21. When the document is displayed in the draft view, the style names can be displayed along the left side of the document.

The reading mode view displays the document similar to how an e-book reader displays content. The document is displayed in spreads. A spread is a left- and right-hand page displayed side by side. The user can easily move from spread to spread using the controls in the view. However, the ribbon is not displayed. This is the only overall view in Word in which the document cannot be edited. To display the reading mode view, click **View>Views>Read Mode** in the ribbon.

Zooming

Zooming is changing the magnification of the view. There are several commands in the **Zoom** group on the **View** tab of the ribbon that can be used to change the magnification level. Clicking the **Zoom** button displays the **Zoom** dialog box in which a magnification level can be selected. Clicking the **100%** button sets the magnification level to actual size. The magnification level can also be adjusted using the slider at the lower-right corner of the application window. Depending on the Office application, there are also options for displaying one or two full pages, setting the magnification to the width of the document page, zooming to the selection, and fitting the document in the window.

Protected Views

A **protected view** is one in which most or all of the editing functions have been locked. If a document is going to be sent to others, it can be

GS5
Key Applications
1.11

Word
1.4.2

Excel
1.4.7

FYI

Holding down the [Ctrl] key and using the mouse wheel is a quick way to zoom in or out.

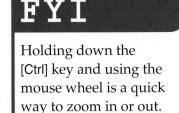

GS5
Key Applications
1.9, 1.10

PowerPoint
5.2.1, 5.2.4

saved as read-only. **Read-only** means the file can be opened and viewed, but cannot be changed. Making a document read-only prevents changes to the file, but does not prevent someone from saving a copy under a different name. The original file will remain intact, but the copy can be edited.

To save a Microsoft Word document as read-only, click **Review>Protect>Restrict Editing** in the ribbon. The **Restrict Editing** pane is displayed on the right-hand side of the screen, as shown in Figure 4-22. In the **Editing restrictions** area of the panel, check the **Allow only this type of editing in the document:** check box, and click **No change (Read-only)** in the drop-down list. Finally, click the **Yes, Start Enforcing Protection** button in the **Start enforcement** area of the pane. A Microsoft Excel spreadsheet can be similarly set as read-only, but there are different options.

File Metadata

Metadata are details about a file that describe or identify it. Metadata are also known as document properties. Metadata include features such as the document author's name, subject, file size, date the file was created or updated, and any keywords set up by the user. When a file is selected in Windows File Explorer, the metadata from that file may be displayed at the bottom of the window. Metadata are also used by databases, such as a Microsoft Access database. In this application, metadata are details about a database entry.

To view the metadata in any Microsoft Office file, click the **File** tab in the ribbon and then **Info**. The metadata will be displayed on the right-hand side of the backstage view.

Removing metadata is easy in Microsoft Office. Click the **Check for Issues** button in the **Info** backstage view, and then click **Inspect Document** in the drop-down menu. The **Document Inspector** dialog box is displayed in which you can choose which metadata to look for in the document. If any of the selected metadata are found, you are given the opportunity to remove the metadata. When the file is saved again, these properties will no longer be included in the file.

GS5
Key Applications
4.4

Excel
1.5.6

PowerPoint
5.2.2

Word
1.5.4

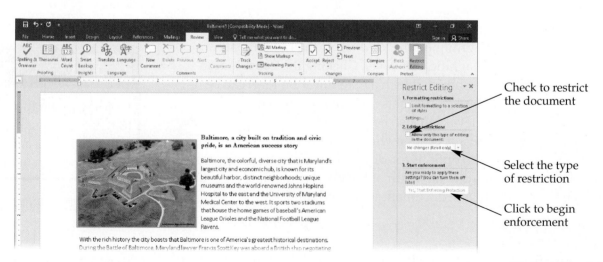

Goodheart-Willcox Publisher

Figure 4-22. A document can be restricted so no changes can be made to it.

In addition to inspecting a document for the purposes of removing metadata, document properties can be inspected for accessibility issues. Performing this inspection will differ depending on whether the user is operating with Office 365 or standard Microsoft Office. If using the cloud-based Office 365, click **Review>Check Accessibility**. If using standard Microsoft Office software suite, open the **Document Inspector** dialog box as previously described for metadata removal, but select **Check Accessibility** instead of **Inspect Document**. This same process can be used to check for compatibility issues by selecting **Check Compatibility**.

Office Options

Each Microsoft Office application has various options that can be set to match more closely how a user prefers to work. For example, the number of recent documents displayed on the opening screen can be changed. To change options, click **Options** in the **File** tab to open the **Options** dialog box. Settings made in the **Options** dialog box affect the entire Office application, not just the document that is open. The commonly changed settings are found in the **General**, **Proofing**, **Save**, and, in Microsoft Word, **Display** categories. To display the settings in a category, click the category name on the left side of the **Options** dialog box.

General

The **General** category contains choices the user can make related to the user interface, personalizing the application, and startup options. This includes the display of the mini toolbar when text is selected, showing a live preview when text is edited, permitting the display of screen tips, and entering a name for the user.

To display the mini toolbar or show a live preview, check the corresponding check box. There are three choices for how screen tips are displayed. The user name and initials can be entered in the corresponding text boxes. These are used as the document's author name and for marking changes.

Proofing

The **Proofing** category contains options for how the software helps the user correct mistakes. Clicking the **AutoCorrect Options...** button displays a dialog box for entering items to automatically change, as shown in Figure 4-23. When the user enters something that matches an item in this dialog box, the specified correction is automatically made. For example, a default entry is "teh." When the user enters this, it will be automatically changed to "the."

In addition, this category allows the user to decide how to handle certain spelling errors. The user can choose to have the application flag repeated words, ignore uppercase words, or ignore words with numbers. Many other proofing settings are available in this category. Proofing is discussed in more detail in Chapter 5.

Excel
1.5.7, 1.5.8

Word
1.5.5, 1.5.6

Green Tech

Cleaning Products
Products used to clean buildings and workstations can impact the environment. Toxic chemicals in many traditional cleaning products can pollute water sources and other business assets. They are also hazardous for employees to use. Conversely, green cleaning products are safe to use on almost any surface and are also safer for the employee using them.

PowerPoint
5.2.3

Word
2.1.3

FYI

Comments can be added to and reviewed in many Office applications by selecting **Review>New Comment** from the ribbon.

PowerPoint
5.1.3, 5.1.4

When the user enters this

Word substitutes this

Figure 4-23. The autocorrect feature can be used to automatically correct common misspellings.

Save

The **Save** category contains options related to how files are saved. One of the most important options is how often the auto recover information for files is automatically saved. The user can also specify where the auto recover information will be saved. The auto recover feature is used to restore the file if the application or system crashes. Set the save time to as much work as you are willing to redo. If you are willing to redo 30 minutes of work, this can be the time interval.

This category also provides options for the default file format and the default location of files. The location of files is the folder that will be displayed when opening or saving a file for the first time when the application is launched. It is common to set this to a project folder.

Display

The **Display** category is unique to Microsoft Word. The options in this category set how the document will be shown on the screen and when printed. There are options for showing white space and how hidden characters should appear. For example, the user can decide to show hard returns (paragraph marks), tabs, and text anchors. Options for printing include printing drawings, background colors, properties, and hidden text.

Resetting Defaults

If changes are made to the default option settings, each can be reversed by simply changing the setting back to the default. This must be done one at a time. However, if the ribbon has been customized, all changes can be reversed in one step. To help reduce the complexity of the ribbon, the user can customize it. Tabs that the user does not need can be removed. If, however, at a future time, the user wishes to have the ribbon appear with the original choices, it can be reset with one command.

To customize the ribbon, click the **Customize Ribbon** category in the **Options** dialog box. Then, add or remove buttons, groups, and tabs as needed, as shown in Figure 4-24. To return the ribbon to its default state, click the **Reset** button. Then, in the drop-down menu that is displayed, choose to reset only the selected tab or the entire ribbon.

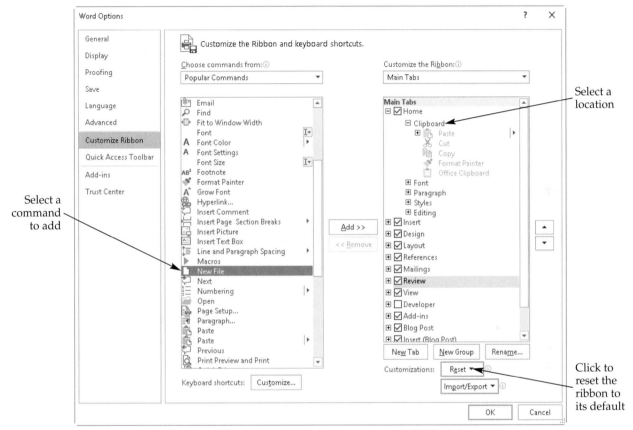

Goodheart-Willcox Publisher

Figure 4-24. The ribbon can be customized in the **Options** dialog box. It can also be reset to the default.

HANDS-ON EXAMPLE 4.4.1

OFFICE OPTIONS

The Microsoft Office applications have default settings that will be acceptable to the greatest number of users. However, many users prefer to customize option settings once they discover how they are most comfortable working with the software.

1. Launch Microsoft Word, Microsoft PowerPoint, or Microsoft Excel.
2. Click **File>Options**. The **Options** dialog box is displayed with the **General** category active.
3. Locate the **Personalize your copy of Microsoft Office** area on the right-hand side of the dialog box.
4. Click in the **User name:** text box, and enter your first and last name. This will be assigned as the creator of any new documents you save.

HANDS-ON EXAMPLE 4.4.1 (CONTINUED)

5. Click in the **Initials:** text box, and enter your initials. These will be used to indicate which comments or tracked changes you added to the document.
6. Click the **Proofing** on the left-hand side of the dialog box to display the options in that category on the right-hand side.
7. In the **When correcting spelling in Microsoft Office programs:** area, uncheck the **Ignore words in UPPERCASE** check box. This tells the software to spell-check any words that are set in all uppercase characters.
8. Click the **Save** category on the left-hand side of the dialog box to display the options in that category on the right-hand side.
9. In the **Save** documents area, make sure the **Save AutoRecover information every** check box is checked, and then click in the corresponding text box and enter 5. This tells the software to save a backup copy of the file every five minutes.
10. Click the **Customize Ribbon** category on the left-hand side of the dialog box to display the options in that category on the right-hand side.
11. Click the **Reset** button on the right-hand side of the dialog box. Then, click **Reset all customizations** in the drop-down list that is displayed. The ribbon and the **Quick Access** toolbar are restored to their default states. All customizations that have been made are removed.

Office Help

There are many ways to get help when using an office suite. When office suites were first created, the software came with large printed manuals. Now, all instructions, tips, and troubleshooting advice are available online and easily accessible through the software's help system. One of the greatest advantages of online help over a printed manual is the ability to search based on keywords. The help database consists of many articles of varying lengths. Because the articles are online, they are easily updated by the developers.

The initial help screen can be displayed in Microsoft Office by pressing the [F1] key or by entering text into the **Tell me what you want to do...** help bar, as shown in Figure 4-25. The software tries to make it easy to find solutions to common problems. The most popular topics that users ask about are listed on the initial screen of the online help.

For example, suppose a user is looking for keyboard shortcuts. Press the [F1] key to launch help, enter keyboard shortcuts in the search box, and click the **Search** button. The help system returns a list with many articles that it thinks are related to keyboard shortcuts. Evaluate the title of each article to locate one that best matches the information being sought, and click the title to display the article.

Using the software's online help is the fastest way to answer questions related to the application. However, there may be other ways to get help. Additional online help is available by contacting the software vendor. If a company has many computer users, it will usually have a dedicated IT staff that assists employees through a help desk. It is also possible that a coworker will know the answer to a software question. For many types of software, users have formed online forums or groups where questions can be posted and answered by other users.

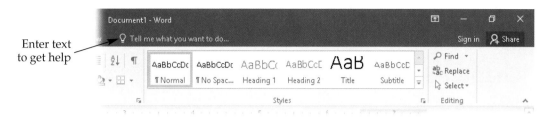

Enter text to get help

Goodheart-Willcox Publisher

Figure 4-25. The help function can be accessed by pressing the [F1] key or by entering text into the **Tell me what you want to do...** help bar.

HANDS-ON EXAMPLE 4.4.2

OFFICE HELP

Being able to use the online help system in an application is essential to learning how to use the software. Even after becoming proficient with the software, there will be times when help must be consulted.

1. Launch Microsoft Word.
2. Add your first and last name to the document.
3. Press the [F1] key to launch the online help system.
4. Click in the search text box, enter WordArt, and click the **Search** button. WordArt is a method of applying decorative effects to text.
5. Locate an article that discusses how to insert WordArt, click the title to display the article, and read it.
6. Use the [Alt][Tab] key combination to switch to the document window.
7. Using the information in the help article, change your name into WordArt. As needed, use the [Alt][Tab] key combination to switch between the document window and the help article.
8. Applying what you have learned, save the file as *LastName*WordArt in the Chap04 folder on your MS-OFFICE flash drive.

FYI

WordArt can be applied in most Microsoft Office programs by selecting **Insert>Text>WordArt**. Once created, WordArt can be customized, resized, and reformatted just as any other image, shape, text box, or graphic.

PowerPoint
2.1.3

Word
2.2.7

4.4 SECTION REVIEW

CHECK YOUR UNDERSTANDING

1. What are the two categories of views in Microsoft Office?
2. What is zooming?
3. What can be done in a read-only file?
4. How do you undo any customizations made to the ribbon?
5. Which key is used to access the help function?

BUILD YOUR VOCABULARY

As you progress through this course, develop a personal IT glossary. This will help you build your vocabulary and prepare you for a career. Write a definition for each of the following terms and add it to your IT glossary.

metadata
protected view

read-only
zooming

4 REVIEW AND ASSESSMENT

Chapter Summary

Section 4.1
Starting Word, Excel, and PowerPoint

- The Microsoft Office suite is accessed via the **Apps** or **Start** menu.
- The ribbon is the main command interface for the Microsoft Office suite of software and consists of tabs, each containing commands arranged in groups.
- The active window is where any command that is entered will be applied.

Section 4.2
Saving, Printing, and Opening Documents

- The first time a file is saved, it must be given a name. After the initial save when the file is named, the **Save** command can be used to quickly save the file.
- Printing is outputting the content of a file. This is usually done as a hardcopy.
- Closing means removing a file or application from RAM.
- Opening a file is placing its content into RAM so the content can be used.

Section 4.3
Editing and Formatting

- Editing a document is to make changes to the text, format, layout, or other aspects of the content.
- Media files, such as images, can be inserted into documents.
- Most actions in software can be reversed using the **Undo** command. The **Redo** command restores the last action undone.
- The **Find** command is used to locate specific text within a document. The **Replace** command not only locates specific text, it substitutes it for text the user enters.
- The system clipboard is a virtual container for storing data. It is used to copy or cut content and paste it elsewhere.

- Formatting text means changing the appearance of the characters. A style is a group of formatting settings that can be applied in one step.

Section 4.4
Document Views, Options, and Help

- There are many ways to view a document in Microsoft Office, such as appearing on a simulated page or only the text.
- Each Microsoft Office application has various options that can be set to more closely match how a user prefers to work.
- The help function provides information on how to use the software.

Now that you have finished this chapter, see what you know about computer applications by taking the chapter posttest. Access the posttest by visiting www.g-wlearning.com. ↗

Chapter 4 Test

Multiple Choice
Select the best response.

1. What is the vertical line called that shows where text will be inserted?
   A. clipboard
   B. pilcrow
   C. cell reference
   D. insertion point

2. Which type of button turns a feature on and off?
   A. screen tip
   B. mini toolbar
   C. live view
   D. toggle

3. Which option shows exactly how the document will look when printed?
   A. virtual printer
   B. print preview
   C. **Print** tab
   D. **Options** dialog box

4. What is another name for an unordered list?
   - A. numbered list
   - B. free-structure list
   - C. bulleted list
   - D. paragraph list

5. Changes to the ribbon can be made in which dialog box?
   - A. **Options**
   - B. **File**
   - C. **Ribbon**
   - D. **Print**

Completion

Complete the following sentences with the correct word(s).

6. _____ is displaying a minimized window.

7. _____ means removing a file or application from RAM.

8. _____ is a sort in which the lowest value appears at the top of the list.

9. Formatting applied to one section of text can be copied to another section of text using the _____.

10. To access the Microsoft Office help system, press the _____ key.

Matching

Match the correct term with its definition.

A. ribbon

B. backstage view

C. typeface

D. [Ctrl] key

E. read-only

11. Displayed by clicking the **File** tab.

12. A mode in which a file is open, but changes cannot be saved.

13. A design of characters.

14. Used to select nonadjacent items.

15. The main command interface in Microsoft Office.

Application and Extension of Knowledge

1. Launch Microsoft PowerPoint. List the tabs available in the ribbon. Do the same for Microsoft Excel and Microsoft Word. Can you identify any patterns in which tabs are available and the order in which they appear? Write a one-page paper explaining the interface of Microsoft Office. Discuss similarities and differences between the applications.

2. Launch Microsoft Excel, begin a blank spreadsheet, and save it as *LastName*Invoice in the Chap04 folder on your flash drive. Enter the data shown below to create an invoice. Apply the formatting as shown.

Invoice number:	**42111**
Service	**Fee**
Professional résumé	$ 325.00
Down payment	$ (100.00)
Student discount	$ (25.00)
Total due	$ 200.00

3. Open the *LastName*Invoice Excel file created in #2. Display the print preview by clicking **Print** in the **File** tab. List what settings can be made in the print preview. Write one or two sentences about what each setting does.

4. Launch Microsoft Word, begin a new blank document, and save it as *LastName*Resume in the Chap04 folder on your MS-OFFICE flash drive. You will be creating the beginning of a résumé. Enter the following contact information on separate lines: your first and last name, your street address, your city and state, your e-mail address. Enter the text shown below as the introduction to the résumé. Change your name to bold and 20 points in the typeface of your choice. Center your contact information.

Italicize the word Objective. Save the file, and then use the "save as" function to save it as a PDF file. Open the PDF and try to make changes; can you?

Objective

Challenging position in operations management where over twenty years of experience in top-level administration, financial management, budgeting, logistics, compliance, and information technology can be combined with skills in negotiation, leadership, communication, analysis, team building, problem solving, and attention to detail to maximize the success of a nonprofit organization.

---

5. Launch Microsoft PowerPoint, and begin a new blank document. Launch the help function, and search for help on adding a motion path. How many results are returned? Evaluate the returned results for relevance, and click the article that appears most relevant. Read the article, and write a one-page paper summarizing your findings.

Online Activities

Complete the following activities, which will help you learn, practice, and expand your knowledge and skills.

Vocabulary. Practice vocabulary for this chapter using the e-flash cards, matching activity, and vocabulary game until you are able to recognize their meanings.

Communication Skills

Reading. Read a magazine, newspaper, or online article about an IT company. Analyze the article and distinguish the facts from the author's point of view on the subject. Write a report in which you draw conclusions about the importance of information technology.

Use visual support, such as graphs, to share specific evidence from the article with your class to support your understanding of the topic.

Speaking. Select three of your classmates to participate in a cooperative learning situation such as a discussion panel. Acting as the team leader, name each person to a specific task such as timekeeper, recorder, etc. Discuss the topic of buying an electronic store franchise or a local electronics business that is available for sale. What are the advantages and disadvantages of not starting a business from scratch? Keep the panel on task and promote democratic discussion.

Writing. Making small improvements in the way things are done can bring about great benefits. Choose three entrepreneurs in the information technology field, and explain how they used innovation to start a new company or improve an existing product.

Internet Research

Typeface Anatomy. Research typeface anatomy using various Internet resources. What does the term mean? Create a list of some of the common terms used to describe a typeface. Illustrate your examples.

Teamwork

Working with your team, make a list of good listening skills versus bad listening skills. After you have completed the list, prepare a short skit that demonstrates both types of listening skills in an IT help desk setting. Incorporate both verbal and nonverbal communication tools to show active listening, such as body language, asking questions, or note-taking. Perform your skit in front of the class. Afterward, ask the audience to give feedback on the information you provided them.

Activity Files

Visit www.g-wlearning.com/informationtechnology/ to download the activity files for this chapter. These activities will expand your learning of the material presented in this chapter and allow you to practice what you have learned. Follow the instructions provided in each file to complete the activity.

Activity File 4-1 Keystroke Commands

Activity File 4-2 Opening and Printing a Microsoft Office File

Activity File 4-3 Creating and Sorting a List

Activity File 4-4 Adding Styles

Activity File 4-5 Adding Metadata

CAPSTONE PROJECT

The capstone project builds from one chapter to the next. It allows you to apply the skills you have learned to create a complete project in a desired career area. Read the instructions below for the career area you chose to work in for this course. Work in the same career area in each chapter.

Agriculture, Food, and Natural Resources

In this activity, you will explore careers in the agriculture, food, and natural resources industries. These industries offer opportunities for rewarding careers. Understanding common features and functions in Microsoft Office programs can help you while you assemble your career-research documents. Access the *Introduction to Microsoft Office 2016* companion website (www.g-wlearning.com/informationtechnology/) to view the instructions for this chapter's Agriculture, Food, and Natural Resources capstone project.

Business, Management, and Administration

In this activity, you will assume the role of an administrator in a small, growing, widget-development company. You will create the first of many files that will complete your capstone project. You will plan, establish goals for the project, and create and maintain a glossary that you will use during the project. Access the *Introduction to Microsoft Office 2016* companion website (www.g-wlearning.com/informationtechnology/) to view the instructions for this chapter's Business, Management, and Administration capstone project.

Health Science

In this activity, you will explore careers in the health science industries. These industries offer a number of career paths, as you will encounter in the activity. You will learn how Microsoft Office contributes to a career in health science through the application of common, basic functions of the office-suite programs. Access the *Introduction to Microsoft Office 2016* companion website (www.g-wlearning.com/informationtechnology/) to view the instructions for this chapter's Health Science capstone project.

Science, Technology, Engineering, and Mathematics

In this activity, you will assume the role of a NASA communications team member for the Near-Earth Object Project. You will begin by creating a document outlining your capstone plan. Then you will set goals for the project, and you will develop a glossary of career-related terms. Access the *Introduction to Microsoft Office 2016* companion website (www.g-wlearning.com/informationtechnology/) to view the instructions for this chapter's Science, Technology, Engineering, and Mathematics capstone project.

5

WORD-PROCESSING SOFTWARE

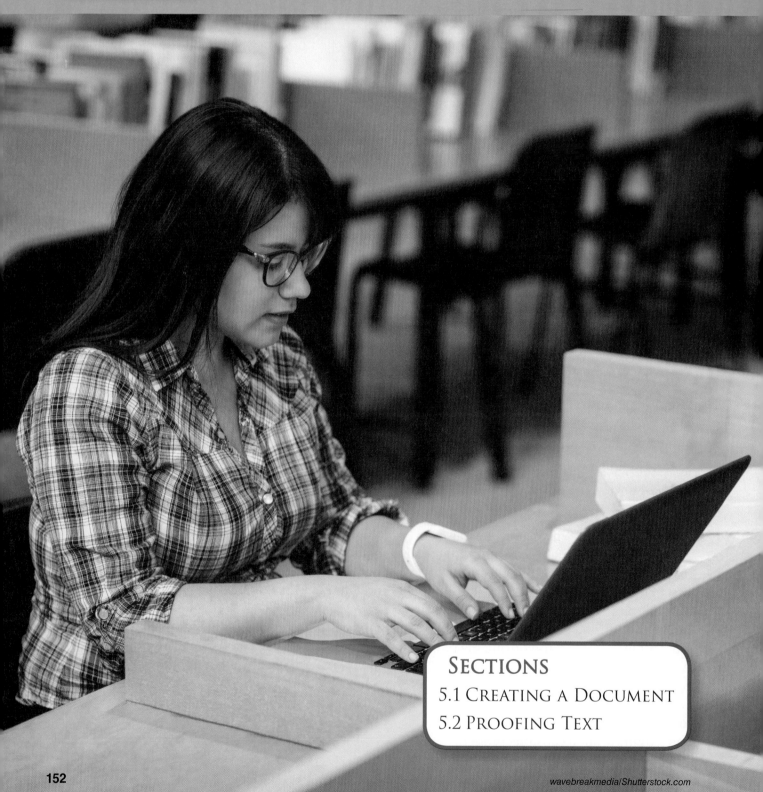

SECTIONS

Word-processing software is the most popular productivity software. Microsoft Word has an estimated half billion users around the world. Word-processing software helps users with the writing of all kinds of documents, from a five-page term paper to a brochure for a home-based business or a personal résumé. It allows the user to let ideas flow. The user can enter his or her thoughts without worrying about how the text will look or where the margins are. These elements are automatically applied, but can be modified to alter the appearance of the document.

Users can improve the quality of their written product by using the word processor's many features. A full-featured word processor includes ways to check spelling and grammar, look up synonyms, write tables of contents, automatically number pages, and apply citations. The readability of the document can be quickly measured, which allows the user to make edits to improve readability. A full-featured word processor also has methods to easily incorporate graphics and photographs as well as ways to perform basic edits to these elements. This chapter discusses the process of creating a document.

MICROSOFT OFFICE SPECIALIST OBJECTIVES

Word

Create and Manage Documents

1.1 Create a Document
- **1.1.1** Create a blank document
- **1.1.2** Create a blank document using a template
- **1.1.3** Open a PDF in Word for editing
- **1.1.4** Insert text from a file or external source

1.2 Navigate Through a Document
- **1.2.3** Create bookmarks
- **1.2.4** Move to a specific location or object in a document

1.3 Format a Document
- **1.3.1** Modify page setup
- **1.3.2** Apply document themes
- **1.3.3** Apply document style sets
- **1.3.4** Insert headers and footers
- **1.3.6** Format page background elements

Format Text, Paragraphs, and Sections

2.1 Insert Text and Paragraphs
- **2.1.3** Replace text by using AutoCorrect
- **2.1.4** Insert special characters

2.2 Format Text and Paragraphs
- **2.2.1** Apply font formatting
- **2.2.3** Set line and paragraph spacing and indentation
- **2.2.5** Apply a text highlight color to text selections
- **2.2.6** Apply built-in styles to text

2.3 Order and Group Text and Paragraphs
- **2.3.1** Format text in multiple columns
- **2.3.2** Insert page, section, or column breaks
- **2.3.3** Change page setup options for a section

Create Tables and Lists

3.1 Create a Table
- **3.1.1** Convert text to tables
- **3.1.2** Convert tables to text
- **3.1.3** Create a table by specifying rows and columns
- **3.1.4** Apply table styles

3.2 Modify a Table
- **3.2.2** Configure cell margins and spacing
- **3.2.3** Merge and split cells
- **3.2.4** Resize tables, rows, and columns
- **3.2.5** Split tables
- **3.2.6** Configure a repeating row header

Access

Create Forms

4.3 Format a Form
- **4.3.7** Insert headers and footers

Create Reports

5.3 Format a Report
- **5.3.6** Insert header and footer information
- **5.3.8** Apply a theme

Excel

Create and Manage Worksheets and Workbooks

1.5 Configure Worksheets and Workbooks for Distribution
- **1.5.5** Display repeating row and column titles on multipage worksheets

Create Tables

3.1 Create and Manage Tables
- **3.1.3** Add or remove table rows and columns

3.2 Manage Table Styles and Options
- **3.2.1** Apply styles to tables

SECTION 5.1

CREATING A DOCUMENT

Making a document more readable is the goal of using word-processing software. Being able to control exactly how and where the words will appear on the page is beneficial. Choosing where to start a new page and adding a photo or illustration also increases interest in the document.

Word-processing software can be used to create many types of documents. The most common type of document written with word-processing software contains text only, such as a business letter or research report. Both of these documents are discussed in detail later. However, word-processing software can also be used to create documents that incorporate graphics or photographs, such as business cards, newsletters, and advertising flyers.

Goodluz/Shutterstock.com

TERMS

desktop publishing
font
justification
leading
line spacing
margins
master page
orphan
page break

page layout
serif
style sheet
tabs
touch system
typeface
visual design
widow

LEARNING GOALS

After completing this section, you will be able to:
- Explain how to start a document in Microsoft Word.
- Identify elements of a table.
- Discuss the use of templates.
- Describe desktop publishing.

Starting a Document

As discussed in Chapter 2, word-processing software assists the user with composing, editing, designing, printing, and publishing documents. There are many terms associated with word-processing software. Some common terms and their explanations are shown in Figure 5-1.

To create a new document in Microsoft Word 2016, click **New** in the **File** tab. The backstage view displays many templates as well as the choice of starting a blank document. Click the Blank document tile. The default display is the print layout view showing a simulated sheet of paper. The **Home** tab in the ribbon is active by default because it contains the most common tools for creating a document. The groups on the **Home** tab are **Clipboard**, **Font**, **Paragraph**, **Styles**, and **Editing**.

Word

1.1.1, 1.3.4

FYI

When Microsoft Word 2016 is launched, a startup screen is displayed that allows the user to begin a new blank document.

Access

4.3.7, 5.3.6

Alignment	How text or other element is positioned on the page. Horizontally, the element may be flush left, flush right, or centered left-to-right. Vertically, the element may be flush top, flush bottom, or centered top-to-bottom.
AutoCorrect	A feature in the software that automatically replaces certain text with specified text.
Citation	A notation indicating the source of information in a document.
Endnote	A notation placed at the end of the document. May be a citation or other information.
Font	A set of characters of a typeface in one specific style and size.
Footer	Text that appears at the bottom of every page in a document or section of a document.
Footnote	A citation placed at the bottom of the page.
Format	The appearance of text or other element.
Grammar-check	A feature in the software that examines the document for proper use of grammar.
Header	Text that appears at the top of every page in a document or section of a document.
Heading	A word or phrase placed at the beginning of a passage to indicate the topic of the passage.
Indentation	The amount text is moved in from the standard margin.
Margin	The locations where text will begin and end and beyond which there is no printing.
Merge	To combine two elements into one, such as two cells in a table into a single cell.
Orientation	The direction in which the page or element is aligned: portrait or landscape.
Pagination	Adding page numbers to a document or the page numbers themselves.
Paragraph	Part of a document that typically deals with a single idea or thought and begins and ends with a hard return.
Spell-check	A feature in the software that examines the document for properly spelled words.
Thesaurus	A feature in the software that suggests alternate words with similar meanings.
Typeface	The design of characters. May be serif, sans serif, or decorative.

Goodheart-Willcox Publisher

Figure 5-1. Common terms related to word processing and a brief explanation of each.

FYI

PDFs can be opened in Word for editing by clicking **File>Open>Browse**. Navigate to the desired file before clicking **Open**. A second window will then appear notifying the user that Word will convert the file, which is dismissed by selecting **OK**.

Word
1.1.3

Word
2.6.8

FYI

To import text from an existing file, select **Insert>Text>Object>Text from File**.

Word
1.1.4

Entering Text

To be proficient in creating a document, the user must learn to enter text. The most efficient users employ the touch system or method for entering text, numbers, and other data. In the **touch system**, the user does not look at the keyboard when entering information because he or she has memorized the location of keys based on hand position. Using the touch system, a person can very quickly enter information because he or she does not need to look for the characters on the keyboard when thinking or reading what needs to be entered.

Efficient users in the accounting area employ the touch system on the number keypad. Since these users do not have to look at the number keys, they can keep their eyes on the data to be entered. This increases their efficiency while entering numerical data.

Many software programs are available to help in becoming more skillful at entering text. These targeted exercises are designed to improve the speed and accuracy of the user in entering text and data.

A word-processing document is based on paragraphs. In Microsoft Word, a paragraph is defined as any text that is followed by a hard return. Pressing the [Enter] key adds a hard return to start a new paragraph. A paragraph in Microsoft Word may consist of one word, one sentence, or several lines of text.

As text is added to a document, it is part of the paragraph where the insertion point is located. When enough text is added, the line of text will wrap to a new line, but will remain part of the same paragraph. This continues until the [Enter] key is pressed to begin a new paragraph. When enough lines of text or paragraphs have been added to the document, a new page is automatically added to make room for the text.

To move through the document one page at a time, press the [Page Up] key to move to the previous page or the [Page Down] key to move to the following page. When working with long documents, it is helpful to be able to move quickly to the end or the beginning of the document. The [Ctrl][End] shortcut key combination moves the insertion point to the end of the document. The [Ctrl][Home] shortcut key combination moves the insertion point to the beginning of the document. The arrow keys and the mouse wheel can also be used to navigate.

HANDS-ON EXAMPLE 5.1.1

ENTERING TEXT

The purpose of a word processor is to create a document. Therefore, the most basic skill when using a word processor is entering text.

1. Insert your MS-OFFICE flash drive into the computer.
2. Applying what you have learned, create a folder on the flash drive named Chap05.
3. Launch Microsoft Word, and begin a new blank document.

HANDS-ON EXAMPLE 5.1.1 (CONTINUED)

Show/
Hide

4. Click **Home**>**Paragraph**>**Show/Hide** in the ribbon to activate it. A paragraph symbol should appear at the end of the first line in the document.
5. Add your name, and press the [Enter] key to begin a new line.
6. Add your street address, and press the [Enter] key.
7. Add your city, state abbreviation, and ZIP code.
8. Applying what you have learned, save the file as MyLetterhead.docx in the Chap05 folder on your flash drive.

Formatting Text

When people used typewriters, the choice in formatting was limited to selecting uppercase or lowercase characters. In some cases, the user could choose between blue, black, or red ink. If the size, formatting, and color of the text had to be controlled, professional printers and typesetters composed the document. Word-processing software was a revolutionary development. It allowed users to control the size, formatting, and color of text as well as many other aspects of formatting a document.

As discussed in Chapter 4, the **typeface** is the design of characters. The technical definition of a **font** is a set of characters of a typeface in one specific style and size. For example, Garamond may be the typeface, and the font may be bold, 11 point. In common usage, *font* is used to mean *typeface*, but this is not technically correct. In software such as Microsoft Word, when you select the *font*, you are technically selecting the *typeface*. By applying formatting, such as bold or italic, and setting the size of the characters, you are technically selecting the font of the current typeface.

Typefaces are divided into three broad categories: serif, sans serif, and decorative. **Serifs** are small marks that extend from the end strokes of characters, as shown in Figure 5-2. A sans serif typeface does not have serifs. Most text should be set in either a serif or sans serif typeface. Serif typefaces tend to be used for long passages. Sans serif typefaces tend to

| GS5 |
| Key Applications |
| 2.1, 2.3 |

| Word |
| 2.2.1 |

FYI

It is a good practice to limit the number of typefaces in a document to two or three.

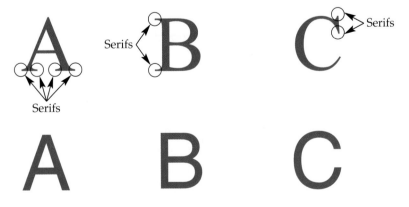

Goodheart-Willcox Publisher

Figure 5-2. A comparison of serif and sans serif typefaces.

be used for short text, such as headings. Decorative typefaces, such as script typefaces, have limited applications and should be used only for artistic presentations.

The height of the characters is called the *text size*. The text size is measured in points. Recall from Chapter 4 that there are 72 points per inch. The main body text in a document is usually between 10 and 12 points, and 11 points is very common. For younger and older readers, the text may need to be a bit larger than 12 points. Headings and titles should be larger than the body text.

Formatting that can be applied to text includes bold, italic, underlined, and color. Bold text, or boldface text, is the typeface with thicker lines. Italic is the typeface with the characters tilted or slanted. Underlined is a horizontal line underneath the characters in the typeface. If the characters are not bold, italic, or underlined, the typeface is said to be roman. Figure 5-3 shows a comparison of roman, bold, italic, and underlined type. These formats can be combined. The characters can also be set in any color. This is a common practice by accountants who use black characters to show positive amounts and red characters to show negative amounts.

To highlight text is to place a colored background behind it. This is similar to taking a highlighter marker to a printed page. Highlighting places much emphasis on the text. It should be used sparingly. Many people apply highlighting only for their own use, such as a reminder of an important sentence or paragraph.

Word
2.2.5

roman   underlined

bold   ***bold, italic***

italic

Goodheart-Willcox Publisher

Figure 5-3. A comparison of several fonts in the Times New Roman typeface. These examples are all 14 point type.

HANDS-ON EXAMPLE 5.1.2

FORMATTING TEXT

There are many times when the formatting of certain text within a document must be changed. This is easy to do using the commands in the ribbon in Microsoft Word.

1. Navigate to the student companion website at www.g-wlearning.com, download the data files for this chapter, and save them in the Chap05 folder on your flash drive.
2. Launch Microsoft Word, and open the Lighting1.docx file from the Chap05 folder on your flash drive.
3. Applying what you have learned, save the document as *LastName*Lighting.docx in the Chap05 folder on your flash drive.
4. Applying what you have learned, select the whole document.
5. Click the **Font** drop-down arrow in the **Font** group on the **Home** tab of the ribbon, and click **Times New Roman** in the drop-down list. The typeface for the entire document is changed.
6. Click the **Font Size** drop-down arrow in the **Font** group on the **Home** tab of the ribbon, and click **11** in the drop-down list. The size of all text is changed to 11 points.

Hands-On Example 5.1.2 (continued)

Bold

7. Select the title Home Lighting, and click **Home>Font>Bold** in the ribbon. The font is made boldface.
8. Applying what you have learned, change the point size for the title to 14.
9. Press the [Enter] key twice to leave a blank space, and add your name.
10. Applying what you have learned, format your name as not bold in 12 points.

Font Color

11. Select your name, and click the drop-down arrow next to **Home>Font>Font Color** in the ribbon. In the color palette that is displayed, click the color swatch for a dark color of your choice. The font color is changed.
12. Applying what you have learned, use the format painter to copy the formatting on the title to these headings: Interior Lighting, Exterior Lighting, Lighting for Energy Efficiency, and Summary.
13. Save the file.

> **FYI**
>
> The background of a page can be modified by selecting a tool from **Design>Page Background**.
>
> **Word**
> **1.3.6**

Page Layout

Page layout refers to how the type is placed on the page. Formatting an entire document includes deciding on page orientation, setting up margins, and adjusting tabs. A tool that is useful when formatting a document is the ruler.

> **GS5**
> Key Applications
> **2.2**
>
> **Word**
> **1.3.1**

Ruler

The ruler displays inch divisions for the page. It shows the user where the text is on the page. It also shows where the margins are located as well as any indents. It also displays if any tabs have been set up, and the types of tabs. To display the ruler, check the **Ruler** check box in the **Show** group on the **View** tab of the ribbon. The horizontal ruler can be displayed in the draft, print layout, and web layout views. The vertical ruler can only be displayed in the print layout view.

> **GS5**
> Key Applications
> **2.5.5**

The horizontal ruler can be used as a shortcut for changing the margins, indents, and tabs. By sliding the triangles that mark the indents and left and right margins, the user can change those values without using the ribbon. The vertical ruler can be used to slide the bottom and top margins up or down. However, it should be noted that these adjustments are style overrides. Style overrides are discussed later in this chapter.

Orientation

The orientation is how the document will be placed on the sheet. This is similar to the page layout for printing discussed in Chapter 4. The orientation can be portrait or landscape. By default, new blank documents in Microsoft Word are set up in portrait orientation on a letter-size sheet

> **GS5**
> Key Applications
> **2.5.6**

of paper. This means the paper is 8.5″ × 11″ with the long edge along the side. In landscape orientation, the long edge is along the top.

To set the orientation, click **Page Layout>Page Setup>Change Page Orientation** in the ribbon. Then, click either **Landscape** or **Portrait** in the drop-down menu. The change in orientation will only be visible in the page layout view.

Page Margins

Each new blank document in Microsoft Word is formatted with preset margins. **Margins** are the points at the top, bottom, left, and right of the page beyond which text is not placed. The default value in Word for all margins is 1″, but the value for each margin can be changed.

The easiest way to change the page margins in Microsoft Word 2016 is to use the ruler. It is a good idea to be at the beginning of the document so the overall effect can be seen.

Click and drag to change the margin

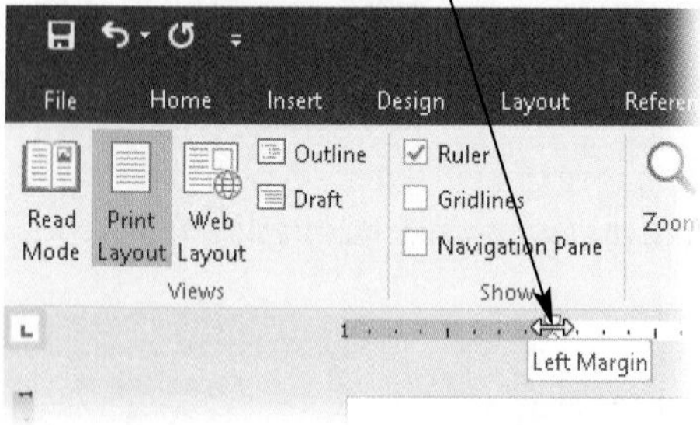

Goodheart-Willcox Publisher

Figure 5-4. Using the ruler to change the left-hand margin.

To change the left-hand margin using the ruler, hover the cursor on the left-hand side of the ruler between the upward- and downward-pointing triangles until the double-arrow cursor appears, as shown in Figure 5-4. The help text will display Left Margin. The downward-pointing triangle controls the first line indent. The upward-pointing triangle controls the hanging indent. If both of these markers are at the same location, as they are by default, it can be difficult to position the cursor for adjusting the left-hand margin.

Once the double-arrow cursor appears and the help text reads Left Margin, click, hold, and drag to adjust the left-hand margin.

The other margins are similarly adjusted. To adjust the right-hand margin, hover the cursor on the right-hand side of the ruler until the double-arrow cursor is displayed and the help text displays Right Margin. To adjust the top margin, hover the cursor on the top end of the ruler until the double-arrow cursor is displayed and the help text displays Top Margin. To adjust the bottom margin, hover the cursor on the bottom end of the ruler until the double-arrow cursor is displayed and the help text displays Bottom Margin. Then, click, hold, and drag to adjust the margin.

The margins can also be adjusted using the **Page Layout** tab. This allows for a precise adjustment of the top and bottom margins, where the ruler allows for only an approximation. Click **Layout>Page Setup>Adjust Margins** to display a drop-down menu. Then, click a new margin arrangement in the drop-down menu or click **Custom Margins...** to display the **Page Setup** dialog box. This dialog box allows the user to set the margins to values not offered in the drop-down menu.

FYI

Adjusting the left- and right-hand page margins should not be confused with adjusting the indentation of a paragraph.

HANDS-ON EXAMPLE 5.1.3

ADJUSTING MARGINS

For some documents, the default margin values are fine. However, for many documents, the margin values need to be changed.

1. Launch Microsoft Word, and open the MyLetterhead.docx file from the Chap05 folder on your flash drive, if it is not already open.
2. Applying what you have learned, display the page layout view, if it is not already displayed.
3. If the rulers are not visible along the top and left sides of the document, check the **Ruler** check box (**View>Show>Ruler**).
4. Scroll to the beginning of the document.
5. Hover the cursor over the top margin indicator in the vertical ruler. The portion of the ruler that is outside the margin is darker than the portion that is inside the margin.
6. When the double-arrow cursor is displayed and the help text displays Top Margin, click, hold, and drag the margin indicator down approximately .5". Notice how the ruler shifts as you drag, so you can only approximate the new margin value.

Adjust Margins

7. Click the ribbon, and click **Custom Margins…** in the drop-down menu.
8. Enter 1.5" in the **Top:** text box of the **Page Setup** dialog box (**Layout>Page Setup**). This precisely adds .5" to the default 1" margin.
9. Click the **OK** button to update the margin setting.

Tabs

Tabs help to organize and space the text, which improves the readability of the document. For example, the beginning of each paragraph in the body of the letter can be indented with a tab. **Tabs** are preset horizontal locations across the page in a document. The term is more accurately *tab stops* because these are the locations where the insertion point will stop when the [Tab] key is pressed. The term originated with typewriters where a metal tab would be pulled out to set the stops.

There are several types of tabs, as shown in Figure 5-5. The most commonly used tab is the left tab, which left-aligns the text to the tab position. Microsoft Word has default left tabs at half-inch intervals. As the [Tab] key is pressed, the insertion point moves across the page one-half inch at a time.

Tabs can be easily added to a document in Microsoft Word. First, select the type of tab to add using the selector at the left-hand end of the ruler. Then, click on the horizontal ruler at the location where the tab should be. A tab indicator is added to the ruler. The default tabs up to that point are removed, but there will be no visible indication of this. Once a tab is added to the ruler, it can be moved left or right to adjust the location.

GS5
Key Applications
2.5.5

FYI

In most cases, the tab stops should be set in the style, not manually added using the ruler.

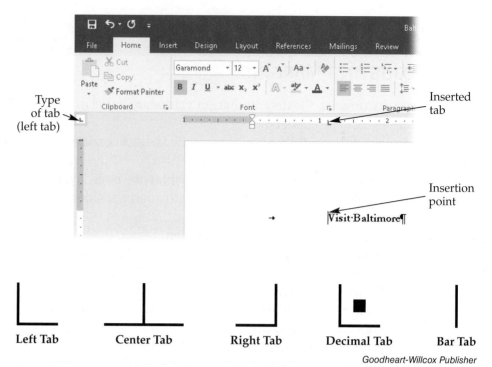

Type of tab (left tab)

Inserted tab

Insertion point

Visit·Baltimore¶

| Left Tab | Center Tab | Right Tab | Decimal Tab | Bar Tab |

Goodheart-Willcox Publisher

Figure 5-5. There are several different types of tabs that can be added.

GS5

Key Applications

2.5.4, 2.5.7

Word

2.2.3

FYI

In most cases, line spacing and alignment should be set in the style, not manually set using the commands in the ribbon.

Modifying Line Spacing and Paragraph Alignment

How much space is present between lines or paragraphs can be changed. **Line spacing** is the amount of space between lines of text. The space between paragraphs is controlled by the *space before* and *space after* settings. **Leading**, pronounced *led-ing*, is the technical term for vertical spacing between lines of text and paragraphs. The term comes from early printing technology when slabs of metal were placed between lines of text. Long passages of text can be made easier to read by adding more spacing between lines. Adding space between paragraphs also makes long passages easier to read and helps define where a paragraph begins and ends.

To change the line spacing for a paragraph, place the insertion point within the paragraph. Then, click **Home>Paragraph>Line Spacing** in the ribbon to display a drop-down menu. The numbered entries in the drop-down list refer to the line spacing, and the current setting is checked. Options include single spaced (**1**), double spaced (**2**), and one-and-a-half spaced (**1.5**), among others. Space before or after the paragraph can be removed or added using this drop-down menu as well.

A paragraph can be aligned to the left margin, to the right margin, centered, or fully justified (aligned left and right). **Justification** is the technical term for paragraph alignment. The easiest way to read text is to have it left-justified. Titles or headings are sometimes centered for emphasis. There are four buttons in the **Paragraph** group on the **Home** tab of the ribbon that control justification: **Align Text Left**, **Center**, **Align Text Right**, and **Justify**. The current setting for the paragraph in which the insertion point is located is indicated by which button is on (depressed).

HANDS-ON EXAMPLE 5.1.4

ADJUSTING LINE SPACING

The default line spacing in Microsoft Word 2016 is 1.08. This is okay for short lines of text, but for multiple lines and paragraphs, the line spacing may need to be increased.

1. Launch Microsoft Word, and open the MyLetterhead.docx file from the Chap05 folder on your flash drive, if it is not already open.
2. Select the three lines of text (name and address).

Line and Paragraph Spacing

3. Click **Home>Paragraph>Line and Paragraph Spacing** in the ribbon, and click **1.5** in the drop-down menu. This sets the line spacing to one-and-a-half times that of single-spaced text.
4. Select the first line of text, click the **Line Spacing** button again, and click **Add Space Before Paragraph** in the drop-down menu. The paragraph shifts down slightly as space is added before it.
5. Save the file.

Paragraph Styles

As discussed in Chapter 4, a *paragraph style* defines the formatting for a paragraph. Paragraph formatting includes indentation, line spacing, text formatting, and tabs, among other things. Using styles saves time. All of the formatting can be applied to text in one step. Using styles also ensures that similar parts of a document will be consistently formatted.

Microsoft Word contains default styles. Many of these are displayed in the style gallery in the **Styles** group on the **Home** tab of the ribbon. To see additional styles, click the **More** button on the gallery. Clicking the dialog box launcher in the **Styles** group displays the **Styles** palette, as shown in Figure 5-6. To apply a style, click it in the gallery or the **Styles** palette.

> Word
> 1.3.3, 2.2.6
>
> **FYI**
>
> A different style set can be selected by clicking it in the gallery in the **Document Formatting** group on the **Design** tab of the ribbon.

TITANS OF TECHNOLOGY

In 1979, Rob Barnaby of MicroPro International created WordStar for a microprocessor platform. It was the first commercially successful word-processing software produced for microcomputers. To users of a current word processor, such as Microsoft Word, WordStar would seem clunky and hard to use. For example, it had no mouse support, no function keys, and could not use arrow keys. Navigation was accomplished by a combination of the [Ctrl] key and letter keys. In addition, there were no font choices or other advanced features that are taken for granted today. However, at the time, WordStar was a significant step forward as it was the first what you see is what you get (WYSIWYG) text editor. Within three years of its release, WordStar was the most popular word-processing software. Other companies began developing word-processing software to compete with WordStar. An early leader was WordPerfect, which is now part of the Corel office suite. Microsoft also developed Word.

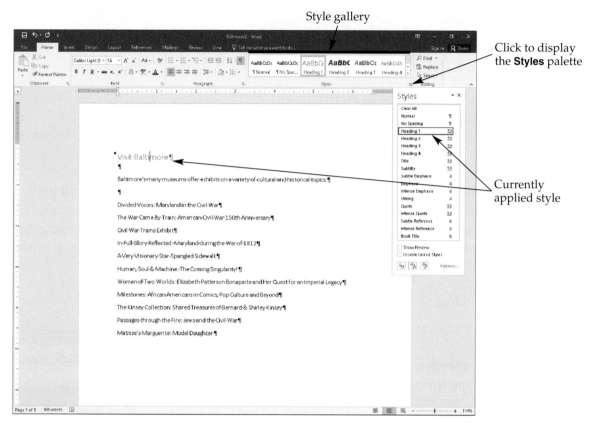

Style gallery

Click to display the **Styles** palette

Currently applied style

Figure 5-6. The **Styles** palette can show all of the styles in the document, but by default will show recommended styles.

FYI

To create a new style, click the **New Style** button in the **Styles** palette or click the **More** button in the styles gallery in the **Styles** group on the **Home** tab of the ribbon and click **Create a Style** in the expanded gallery.

The settings for a default style can be changed or a new style can be created. To modify a style, right-click on it in the gallery (**Home>Styles**) or in the **Styles** palette, and click **Modify…** in the shortcut menu. The **Modify Style** dialog box is displayed, as shown in Figure 5-7. This is the same dialog box used to create a new style, except the name is different. Set the formatting for the style, and click the **OK** button to update (or create) the style. Some formatting can be changed directly in this dialog box. Clicking the **Format** button displays a menu for selecting additional formatting options to change. Each option in this menu opens a new dialog box related to the menu entry.

Applying formatting using the commands in the ribbon is called *style override*. When one of these formatting elements is changed using the commands in the ribbon, the settings of the style are overridden. The best way to make these changes is by modifying the style or by creating a new style to apply to the paragraph.

Goodheart-Willcox Publisher

Figure 5-7. This dialog box is used to modify a style. The same dialog box (with a different name) is used to create a new style.

HANDS-ON EXAMPLE 5.1.5

CREATING A STYLE

Styles are an effective and efficient way to control formatting. Creating a style is easy in Microsoft Word.

1. Launch Microsoft Word, and open the MyLetterhead.docx file from the Chap05 folder on your flash drive, if it is not already open.
2. Place the insertion point at the end of the ZIP code, press the [Enter] key to start a new line, and add the text Introduction.
3. Click the dialog box launcher on the **Styles** group on the **Home** tab of the ribbon to display the **Styles** palette.
4. Click the **New Style** button in the **Styles** palette. The **Create New Style from Formatting** dialog box is displayed. The default name for the style being created is Style*x*, where *x* is a sequential number.

New
Style

HANDS-ON EXAMPLE 5.1.5 (CONTINUED)

5. Click in the **Name:** text box, and enter Introduction, as shown. Each style must have a unique name.

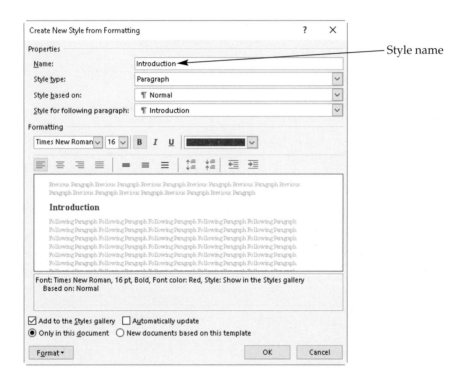

Style name

6. Using the formatting commands in the dialog box, change the typeface to Arial Black and the font size to 20 points. The changes appear in the window.
7. Click the **OK** button. The style is created and applied to the current selection.
8. Save the file.

Word
2.3.2

Adding Breaks

There are several types of breaks that may appear in a document. A break is a location where there is a change, such as when the document changes from one page to the next. A break may also occur where the page layout changes, such as when the text changes from one column to two columns. This is called a section break.

Word
1.2.3

Page Breaks

A **page break** is where the document changes from one page to another. Word processors automatically add page breaks when enough text is added to the document to need an additional page. Microsoft Word and most other word processors also allow the user to set where a page will end and a new page begins. This is called a manual page break and can be added at any place in the document.

To add a manual page break in Microsoft Word, place the insertion point at the location where the break should be. Then, click **Insert**>**Pages**>**Page Break** in the ribbon. Or, click **Layout**>**Page Setup**>**Breaks** in the ribbon and choose the type of page break. The shortcut key for adding a page break is [Ctrl][Enter]. In page layout view, a new simulated page is visible. In draft view, a horizontal line and the text Page Break are added if nonprinting elements are displayed (**Show/Hide** button).

Section Breaks

A section break is a point in the document where page formatting changes. One document can have several different sections. Each section can have its own header and footer, page orientation, margins, page borders, and number of columns. Using section breaks allows much more control of the document and how you want it to look.

To add a section break, place the insertion point at the location where the break should occur. Then, click **Page Layout**>**Page Setup**>**Insert Page and Section Breaks** in the ribbon. The types of section breaks appear on the lower part of the drop-down menu that is displayed. Select the type of section break to add.

GS5
Key Applications
2.5.2

Word
2.3.3

FYI

Some actions, such as changing the number of columns for selected text, automatically add section breaks.

HANDS-ON EXAMPLE 5.1.6

ADDING A PAGE BREAK

In many cases, the content in a document should begin on a new page even if the previous page is not full. For example, an introduction to a technical report may be less than one page, but often this type of introduction appears on a page by itself.

1. Launch Microsoft Word, and open the Library1.docx file from the Chap05 folder on your flash drive.
2. Applying what you have learned, save the file as *LastName*Library in the Chap05 folder on your flash drive.
3. Place the insertion point after the word Sincerely and the following comma.
4. Press the [Enter] key twice to add two blank lines.
5. Add your first and last names followed by a comma, a space, and the word Director.
6. With the insertion point after the word *Director*, press the [Ctrl][Enter] key combination to insert a manual page break.
7. Applying what you have learned, display the draft view.
8. Press the [Page Up] key to display the previous page.
9. Click the **Home**>**Paragraph**>**Show/Hide** in the ribbon so it is on (depressed). Notice code in the document for the page break.
10. Save the file.

Show/Hide

GS5
Key Applications
2.9

Tables

A table in a word-processing document is similar to a spreadsheet. Tables increase readability for complex or mathematical text. Data are organized in columns and rows, and the box where a row and column intersect is called a cell. Being able to view data in columns and rows helps the reader find information. A table can list numerical information or organize the appearance of text on a page.

Creating and working with a table in Microsoft Word is simple. A table is added at the insertion point. When creating a table, you should have an idea of its dimensions. However, adding or deleting extra rows and columns is easy. The column and row widths are easy to manipulate. Colors and shading can be added to rows, columns, and cells.

Word
3.1.1, 3.1.3

Creating a Table

To create a table, click **Insert**>**Tables**>**Add a Table** in the ribbon. A drop-down menu containing a grid is displayed, as shown in Figure 5-8. Move the cursor to highlight the number of columns and rows desired, and click to create the blank table. The table is ready for data to be entered.

Data in the columns can be aligned to the right or centered. Left alignment is the default. To change the width and height of the table or cells within it, move the cursor over a cell margin line. When the cursor changes to a resizing cursor, click and drag to change the size.

To convert text into a table, there should be some type of punctuation to tell the software how to separate the text into columns and rows. Commas or tabs can be used to indicate where columns will be. Hard returns indicate where rows will be. Once this is set up, select the text. Then, click **Insert**>**Tables**>**Add a Table** in the ribbon, and click **Convert Text to Table...** in the drop-down menu. The **Convert Text to Table** dialog box is displayed, as shown in Figure 5-9. At the bottom of the dialog box, choose

FYI

The [Tab] key, [Shift][Tab] key combination, and arrow keys can be used to navigate a table.

Word
3.1.2

FYI

Users can split tables by placing the cursor at the desired splitting point and clicking **Layout**>**Merge**>**Split Table**.

Word
3.2.5

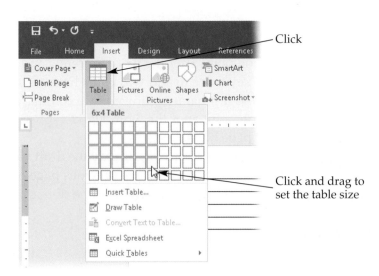

Goodheart-Willcox Publisher

Figure 5-8. Adding a table to a document by specifying the number of columns and rows.

how the text is separated, then click the **OK** button to create the table.

Tables can be converted to text. Select the table, and click **Layout**>**Data**>**Convert to Text** in the ribbon. In the **Convert Table to Text** dialog box that is displayed, choose how the text will be separated, and click the **OK** button.

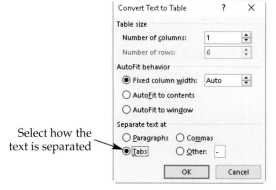

Select how the text is separated

Figure 5-9. Converting text into a table.

HANDS-ON EXAMPLE 5.1.7

Excel Word
3.2.1 3.1.4

CREATING A TABLE

There are many times when a table can improve the presentation of information in a document. For example, a schedule may be better presented as a table than as a bulleted list.

1. Launch Microsoft Word, and open the file FitnessOpportunities.docx from the Chap05 folder on your flash drive.
2. Applying what you have learned, save the file as *LastName*FitnessOpportunities.docx in the Chap05 folder on your flash drive.
3. Place the insertion point at the end of the paragraph that begins with the text *The following*.
4. Press the [Enter] key to add a blank line.

5. Click **Insert**>**Tables**>**Add a Table** in the ribbon to display a drop-down menu, as shown.
6. Move the cursor over the grid in the drop-down menu until two columns and six rows are highlighted. The top of the grid should display **2 × 5 Table**. Then, click to add the blank table.

Add a Table

7. Enter this text into the table:

Volleyball Area	2 hours
Soccer Fields	2 hours
Baseball Diamonds	2 hours
Basketball Courts	1 hour
Tennis Courts	1 hour

8. Select the right-hand column by moving the cursor to the top of the column until it changes to a downward pointing arrow, and then click.

9. Click **Home**>**Paragraph**>**Align Right** in the ribbon. Notice how the table is too wide. With this text alignment, the right-hand text is too far from the left-hand text.
10. Move the cursor over the right-hand border until it changes to a double arrow.

Align Right

11. Click and drag the right-hand border to the left to narrow the column. When the column is about as wide as the longest entry, release the mouse button.
12. Select the entire table by moving the cursor to the top of the left-hand column until it changes to a downward pointing arrow, and then click and drag to the right-hand column.

13. Click the **More** button in the styles gallery in the **Table Styles** group on the **Design** on-demand tab of the ribbon to show the expanded gallery.

More

HANDS-ON EXAMPLE 5.1.7 (CONTINUED)

14. Click **Grid Table 4 – Accent 4** in the expanded gallery. The design is applied, and the table rows are shaded in color.
15. Save the file.

Excel
3.1.3

FYI

A shortcut to adding a row at the end of a table is to place the cursor in the bottom-right cell, and press the [Tab] key.

Word
3.2.3

FYI

If a table spans multiple pages, consider adding a repeating row header. This is accomplished by right-clicking the table and selecting **Table Properties** from the shortcut menu. From there, select the **Row** tab and check the box next to **Repeat as header row at the top of each page** under **Options**.

Excel
1.5.5

Word
3.2.6

Adding Columns and Rows

To add a column or row to a table, click in the table, and then click the **Layout** on-demand tab. The **Rows & Columns** group on this tab contains buttons for adding a row above or below the current cell and adding a column to the right or left. Click the appropriate button.

Another way to add a row or column is to use the shortcut menu. Right-click on the cell to use as the reference point for the insertion. Then, click **Insert** in the shortcut menu to display a cascading menu, and click the appropriate command for adding a row or column.

Splitting and Merging Cells

Occasionally, one cell must be split into two or two cells must be combined into one. To split a cell, click in the cell. Then, click **Layout**>**Merge**>**Split Cells** in the ribbon. In the **Split Cells** dialog box that is displayed, set the number of columns and rows to create, and click the **OK** button.

To merge cells, first select which cells will be combined. Then, click **Layout**>**Merge**>**Merge Cells** in the ribbon. The cells are combined into one cell. If multiple cells contained data, the data from each cell is placed on its own line within the new single cell.

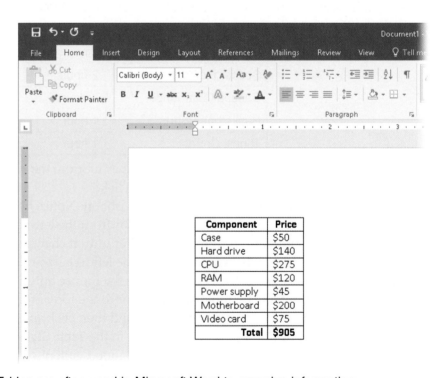

Component	Price
Case	$50
Hard drive	$140
CPU	$275
RAM	$120
Power supply	$45
Motherboard	$200
Video card	$75
Total	**$905**

Tables are often used in Microsoft Word to organize information.

HANDS-ON EXAMPLE 5.1.8

MODIFYING A TABLE

Sometimes you will need to make changes to an existing table. For example, a table may need additional columns, descriptive column headings, and adjustments to the column widths.

1. Launch Microsoft Word, and open the file *LastName*FitnessOpportunities.docx from the Chap05 folder on your flash drive, if it is not already open.
2. Click anywhere within the first row of the table.
3. Click **Layout>Rows & Columns>Insert Rows Above** in the ribbon. A new row appears at the top. Notice that the new first row assumes the dark shading set by the table style.
4. Add the text Fitness Area into the first cell in the first row. Do not press the [Enter] key because that will start a new line in the same cell.
5. Press the [Tab] key to move to the second cell in the first row.
6. Add the text Reservations.
7. With the insertion point in the right-hand cell in the first row, click **Layout>Rows & Columns>Insert Columns to the Left** in the ribbon. A middle column is added to the table.
8. Add the text Description to the middle cell in the first row. Notice that the columns are not equal widths.
9. With the insertion point anywhere within the table, click **Layout>Cell Size>Autofit** in the ribbon, and click **AutoFit Contents** in the drop-down menu. Each column is resized to fit the widest cell content in the column.
10. Save the file.

Insert
Rows
Above

Insert
Columns
to the
Left

Autofit

Resizing a Table

Tables can be resized as needed in a number of ways. To adjust cell margins and spacing, right-click the table and select **Table Properties** from the shortcut menu. In the **Table** tab of the **Table Properties** dialog box, select the **Options** button near the bottom. Once in **Table Options**, check the **Allow spacing between cells** box and enter the desired amount of space. Cell margins can also be adjusted here. Select **OK** to close the dialog box.

To resize rows and columns, rest the cursor on the row or column boundary that needs to be adjusted. The cursor will change to a double-sided arrow. Click and drag the boundary to resize as needed. If a specific height or width is desired, that size can be entered in the **Cell Size** group of the **Layout** tab.

Word
3.2.2, 3.2.4

Templates

As discussed in Chapter 4, a document template is a document preformatted for a specific use and may contain placeholder text or images the user replaces with actual content. They are designed to aid the user in creating professional-looking documents. Templates are available for brochures, flyers, newsletters, reports, invitations, certificates, calendars, and many other types of documents. A template typically contains some basic instructions on how to use it to the best advantage.

GS5
Key Applications
2.10.2
Word
1.1.2

For example, a template can be used to create an academic calendar for next month and add some personal events. The template can be easily updated for any month and year. Depending on the template used, it may include room for notes or display the previous and next months as thumbnails for at-a-glance scheduling.

Another example of using a template is to create a newsletter or flyer. These templates may have placeholders for text, images, and a logo. To replace any placeholder text with your own, click the placeholder and enter text. To replace a photo or logo, typically the procedure is to right-click on the placeholder, and then click **Change Picture** or similar command in the shortcut menu.

HANDS-ON EXAMPLE 5.1.9

GS5
Key Applications
2.10.2

CREATING A DOCUMENT FROM A TEMPLATE

Templates provide a quick way to create a professional-looking document. The user can focus on the content instead of the format.

1. Launch Microsoft Word 2016.
2. On the startup screen, click in the search text box, enter Academic Calendar, and click the **Search** button. Note: the computer must be connected to the Internet.
3. In the list of returned results, click **Academic Calendar (one month, any year, Monday start)** in the list of templates.
4. In the preview that is displayed, click the **Create** button to start a new document based on the template, as shown.

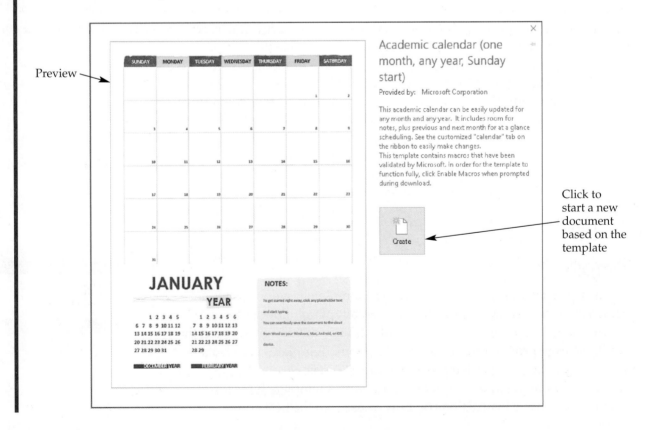

Preview

Click to start a new document based on the template

HANDS-ON EXAMPLE 5.1.9 (CONTINUED)

5. In the **Select Calendar Dates** dialog box that appears, choose next month and the current year in the drop-down lists, and then click the **OK** button. If a message appears, click the **OK** button to dismiss it.

6. Click the **Calendar** tab in the ribbon, if it is not already active.

7. Click the placeholder text in the Notes: area of the template. The placeholder text states Click here to add notes.

8. Add the note Study for Chapter 5 test.

9. Save the file as *LastName*MonthCalendar.docx in the Chap05 folder on your flash drive.

10. Applying what you have learned, begin a new document based on the Event flyer template.

11. Replace the placeholder text in the upper-right box with this text, one line per placeholder:

    Earth Day is an annual event

    Events are held worldwide

    Demonstrate support for environmental protection

    Now observed in 192 countries

    Be a part of a better environment

12. In the lower-left area of the template, add the date as April 22, the event as Earth Day, the paragraph heading as School-Wide Meeting, and the paragraph text as:

    Meet with other environmentally minded students to complete a community replanting and clean-up project. Wear work clothes and bring gloves if you have them. We'll see you at the Student Center at 9:00 a.m.

13. Right-click on the placeholder at the top of the flyer, and click **Change Picture...** in the shortcut menu.

14. In the **Insert Pictures** dialog box that is displayed, click the **Browse** link in the **From a file** area. In the standard open dialog box that is displayed, navigate to the Chap05 folder on your flash drive, select the EarthDayImage.jpg image file, and click the **Insert** button. The placeholder image is replaced with the Earth Day image.

15. Applying what you have learned, replace the placeholder logo image with the EarthDayLogo.jpg image file in the Chap05 folder on your flash drive.

16. Applying what you have learned, replace the placeholder text in the lower-right box on the flyer with your own personal information.

17. Save the document as *LastName*Flyer.docx in the Chap05 folder on your flash drive.

Overview of Desktop Publishing

Most letters, reports, and similar documents are formatted using word-processing software. However, if a document is being created for a formal purpose or large audience, desktop-publishing software should be used. **Desktop publishing** is using software to lay out text and graphics for professional-looking documents, such as newspapers, books, or brochures. Microsoft Publisher and Adobe InDesign are examples of desktop-publishing software.

Desktop-publishing software often includes writing and publishing features. Certain aspects of desktop-publishing software make designing documents fast and easy. Using templates and text controls speed up the

FYI

Themes are predetermined formatting choices that are applied to an entire document. This takes the guesswork out of making decisions regarding layout, font, colors, and other choices. Users can add themes by clicking **Layout>Theme>Themes**.

Word
1.3.2

Access
5.3.8

Word
1.1.2

FYI

Text can be formatted into columns by selecting the text and clicking **Layout>Page Setup>Columns** and choosing the desired number of columns.

Word
2.3.1

process of laying out a document and applying a visual design across several pages. The finished document may be printed or electronically distributed.

When creating a document in desktop-publishing software, the visual design is as important as the content. The **visual design** is the arrangement of the visual and artistic elements used to accomplish a goal or communicate an idea. By applying these design concepts, the message becomes more clear and memorable to the reader:

- Contrast is having two dissimilar elements next to one another.
- Alignment is how items line up with one another, such as on the left side or the right side and horizontally or vertically.
- Repetition creates consistency and pattern.
- Proximity is how near or far two design elements are from each other.

An effective visual design will improve the clarity of the messages and be visually appealing.

Using Templates

When creating documents in desktop-publishing software, it can be a time-consuming challenge to get everything just right. In order to make it easier and faster to lay out documents, templates are used to automate much of the process. The purpose of creating a template is so repeated elements, such as heading styles, page numbers, font choices, and graphical elements, do not have to be created for each new page. It takes time to create a template, but the amount of time saved is generally much greater. The two most useful portions of a desktop-publishing template are the master page and the style sheet.

The **master page** defines the page size, recurring areas for type and graphics, and placement of recurring elements, such as page numbers. Sometimes the master page is simply called the *master*. Depending on the needs of the document, multiple master pages can be created within a single template. For example, one template may have a master for the section opener, a master for the pages of the body, and a master for the works cited and index pages.

A style sheet is a part of a template that deals only with font characteristics. A **style sheet** is a desktop-publishing file that saves the attributes of every font that will be used in a project. The style sheet defines the typography used in the document. Point size, typeface, leading, letter spacing, alignment, color, and other special customizations can be set in a style sheet. A unique name is created for each font in the style sheet. Each individually named font is called a *style*.

Style sheets allow an individual style to be applied to text so you do not have to select the typeface, point size, and other characteristics of the font every time you want to use it. For example, if every heading in a report will be in 14-point Cambria bold, a style can be created with these characteristics. The style is applied with one click rather than the several clicks necessary to select these characteristics for each heading. This is similar to how styles work in Microsoft Word.

Text Controls

After the template is created, document layout can begin. *Layout* is arranging the text and graphics to create an appealing document. Desktop-publishing software typically has several tools that make this process very simple.

A basic text-control feature sets how pages break for increased readability by eliminating widows and orphans. A **widow** is the last line of a paragraph that falls immediately *after* a page break, making it appear as though it is not part of the previous paragraph. The opposite of a widow is an orphan. An **orphan** is the first line of a paragraph that falls immediately *before* a page break, making it appear as though it is not part of the paragraph on the next page. Widows and orphans are always undesirable because they can cause confusion and reduce readability. The widow and orphan control in the desktop-publishing software can be switched on to automatically prevent widows and orphans. Word-processing software usually includes widow and orphan control.

Another tool is automatic text flow. This allows you to place a large amount of text into controlled portions that fit into the layout. For example, you may need to flow text into columns across several pages. Once the column text boxes are created and linked as necessary, the entirety of the text can be placed in the first text box. The software places enough text to fit into one column, and the text automatically flows into the next column, picking up where the previous one left off. Automatic text flow also works for other text boxes.

Career Skills

School Counselor

Educational, guidance, school, and vocational counselors work to improve the lives of their students. They evaluate a student's current needs, publish a written treatment plan, enact the plan, and follow through. Record keeping is constant and electronic records are essential to the effectiveness and support of these human services workers.

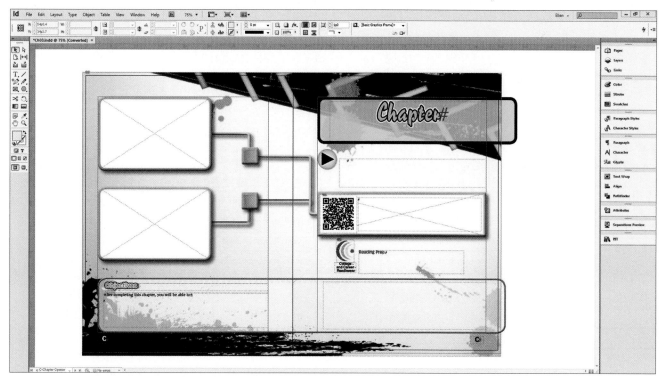

Goodheart-Willcox Publisher

A master page is used in desktop publishing to locate recurring elements in the layout.

Another option for placing text on the page is automatic text wrap. This allows the text to surround the visuals on the page so the text does not have to be broken up. For example, if you need to run text around photographs from a company event, automatic text wrap will allow this.

5.1 | SECTION REVIEW

 ### CHECK YOUR UNDERSTANDING

1. What is the touch system of entering text?
2. What are the two possible orientations for a page?
3. How are data in a table arranged?
4. What is a document template?
5. How is a master page used in desktop publishing?

 ### BUILD YOUR VOCABULARY

As you progress through this course, develop a personal IT glossary. This will help you build your vocabulary and prepare you for a career. Write a definition for each of the following terms and add it to your IT glossary.

desktop publishing
font
justification
leading
line spacing
margins
master page
orphan
page break

page layout
serif
style sheet
tabs
touch system
typeface
visual design
widow

PROOFING TEXT

Goodluz/Shutterstock.com

Proofing is an important part of creating any document. Most word-processing programs provide tools to help in proofing a document, such as finding and correcting spelling and grammar mistakes. Many can correct spelling errors as soon as they are entered. Some users prefer to have the software check for spelling and grammar errors as they enter text. Other users prefer to wait until the end to check spelling and grammar.

Word-processing software uses a dictionary to check for spelling errors. Words can be added to this dictionary. This is helpful when writing a document that contains many words a standard dictionary would not contain, such as technical terms.

TERMS

kerning
proofing
readability
track changes

LEARNING GOALS

After completing this section, you will be able to:
- Identify proofing options that can be set.
- Describe how to track changes in Microsoft Word.
- Perform a spelling and grammar check.
- Explain readability measurements.

Proofing Options

Proofing is the process of checking the document for errors, such as misspellings, grammar mistakes, and formatting problems. There are tools in word processors to help in proofing a document. However, these tools should be considered aids and not replacements for manually reviewing a document for accuracy.

Editing the Final Document

Once the project is complete, whether created in a word processor or desktop-publishing software, review the document for any errors. It is necessary to review both the content and the layout. Read through the final product. Spelling and grammatical errors should be fixed by the proofing tools in the word-processing program. However, do not depend on software to "think" for you. Read for spelling and grammatical errors that the spell-checker may not find.

Review the layout and visual design. When editing a desktop-publishing project, check the following aspects of the design.

- Every item appears as intended.
- Typefaces and font styles are appropriately applied.
- Correct templates are used for each page.
- Graphics are appropriately labeled.
- Headings are accurate.
- There is consistency in typefaces, spacing, and other important elements.

As you become more proficient at document creation and desktop publishing, add additional criteria to this list. This will help to ensure your final projects look as professional as possible.

Setting Proofing Options

GS5
Key Applications
1.4

As introduced in Chapter 4, there are various options that can be set in Microsoft Word. One of the categories in the **Options** dialog box is **Proofing**. This category contains settings related to how Word handles proofing functions.

Throughout the writing of a document, Microsoft Word, by default, attempts to identify errors in spelling and grammar. Words that are not recognized are underlined in red. Phrases identified as possible grammatical errors are underlined in green. Words that might be misused are underlined in blue. Many users find these underlines distracting. These actions can be disabled. In the **Options** dialog box, display the **Proofing** category. Then, locate the **When correcting spelling and grammar in Word** area, as shown in Figure 5-10. To prevent Word from flagging spelling errors while text is being entered, uncheck the **Check spelling as you type** check box. Uncheck the **Mark grammar errors as you type** check box to prevent Word from flagging possible grammatical mistakes. Uncheck the **Frequently confused words** check box to prevent Word from flagging words that may be misused.

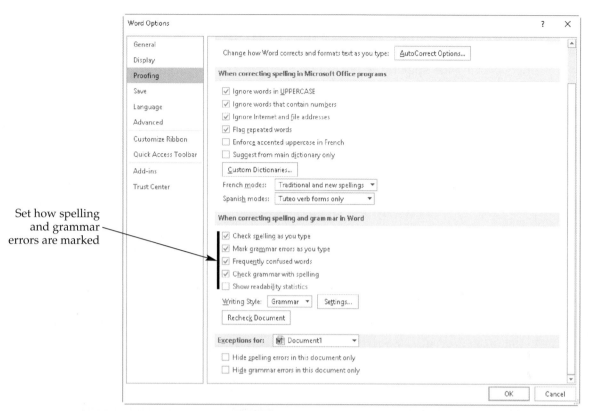

Figure 5-10. The **Proofing** category in the **Options** dialog box contains settings for how spelling and grammar errors are marked.

A powerful proofing feature of Microsoft Word is AutoCorrect. The AutoCorrect feature replaces certain text, usually a common misspelling of a word, with specified text. For example, a common error in entering text is hte for the. One of the default AutoCorrect entries is to replace hte with the as soon as the space bar is pressed after hte is added. Another default AutoCorrect entry is to replace (c) with the copyright symbol ©. Additional AutoCorrect entries can be created by clicking the **AutoCorrect Options...** button in the **Proofing** category in the **Options** dialog box.

Word

2.1.3, 2.1.4

HANDS-ON EXAMPLE 5.2.1

PROOFING SETTINGS

There are several options related to proofing a document that can be set in Microsoft Word. It is important that these options are correctly set before proofing a document.

1. Launch Microsoft Word, and open the file *LastName*Library.docx from the Chap05 folder on your flash drive, if it is not already open.
2. Click **Options** in the **File** tab. The **Word Options** dialog box is displayed.
3. Click the **Proofing** category on the left side of the dialog box.
4. Check these check boxes: **Check spelling as you type**, **Mark grammar errors as you type**, **Frequently confused words**, **Check grammar with spelling**, and **Show readability statistics**.

HANDS-ON EXAMPLE 5.2.1 (CONTINUED)

5. Uncheck the **Hide spelling errors in this document only** check box.
6. Click the **Recheck Document** button. A message appears indicating this action resets the spelling and grammar checker so all words will be examined. Click the **Yes** button.
7. Click the **OK** button.
8. Save the file.

GS5
Key Applications
1.4, 2.8.1, 2.8.2

Tracking Changes

When more than one person is writing or editing a document, it is very useful to keep track of what was original text as well as what has changed. Many other word processors have the ability to record changes to a document. These changes are called markups.

In Microsoft Word, the feature for logging markups is called **track changes**. This feature not only logs markups, it tracks who made the change. Each user is assigned a color, and his or her changes are highlighted in that color, as shown in Figure 5-11.

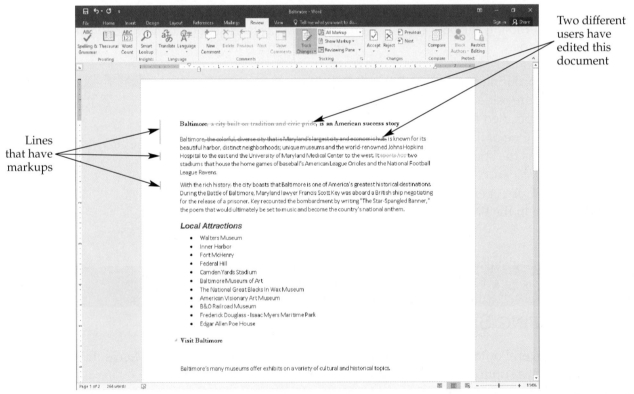

Lines that have markups

Two different users have edited this document

Goodheart-Willcox Publisher

Figure 5-11. The track changes feature of Microsoft Word logs changes that have been made and who made them.

If you prefer to work without the changes showing, click the drop-down arrow in the **Tracking** group on the **Review** tab of the ribbon, and click **No Markup** in the drop-down list. The changes will still be tracked, but only the end result is visible. To display the changes, click **All Markup** or **Simple Markup** in the drop-down list.

To start tracking changes, click **Review>Tracking>Track Changes** in the ribbon. This is a toggle button. To stop tracking changes, click the **Track Changes** button again. When track changes is off, any existing markups are kept. However, any new changes are not tracked as markups. Turning track changes on begins logging markups again. Only markups made with track changes on will be logged.

When the editing is complete, the track changes must be set as final. This is done by accepting or rejecting each change. Move to the beginning of the document. Then, click **Review>Changes>Next Change** in the ribbon. This locates the first markup in the document. If the change is okay, click **Review>Changes>Accept and Move to Next** in the ribbon. If the markup should not be made, click the **Reject and Move to Next** button in the same group. The change is either applied or not applied, and then the next markup is located. Continue doing this until there are no more markups in the document.

Checking Spelling and Grammar

Spelling and grammar mistakes distract readers. More importantly, they show a lack of quality and concern for the work. To help find spelling and grammar errors, use the spell-check feature of the word processor. However, it is important to keep in mind that a spell-check may not find all mistakes. It is a tool to help you, but it should not be a substitute for manually reviewing and proofreading the document.

Many word-processing programs, including Microsoft Word, check spelling and grammar as words are entered by default. When these words are flagged, you can right-click on the word, and alternate spellings or words will be displayed in the shortcut menu. However, a manual spell-check should always be the last thing you do to a document before declaring it completed.

To start a manual spell-check, click **Review>Proofing>Spelling & Grammar** in the ribbon or press the [F7] key. If no errors are found, a message is displayed indicating this. If errors are found, the **Spelling** pane is displayed with the first error display, as shown in Figure 5-12. The error is also selected in the document. Select the correct spelling from the options displayed, and click the **Change** button. If the word is not an error, click the **Ignore** button. If this spelling will appear many times in the document, click the **Ignore All** button so the spell-checker will not stop on all of the instances. After clicking the **Change**, **Ignore**, or **Ignore All** button, Word will locate the next error. Continue making changes as needed until there are no more errors found in the document.

Ethics

Altering Documents

The track changes feature in word-processing software records which user made each change to a document. The user is set in the options for the software. It is unethical to change the user name in the software to make it appear as if a different person has made changes to a document. It is also unethical to accept or reject changes by any user unless you are the one who has the authority to do so.

GS5

Key Applications

1.3

Questioned word   Suggestions

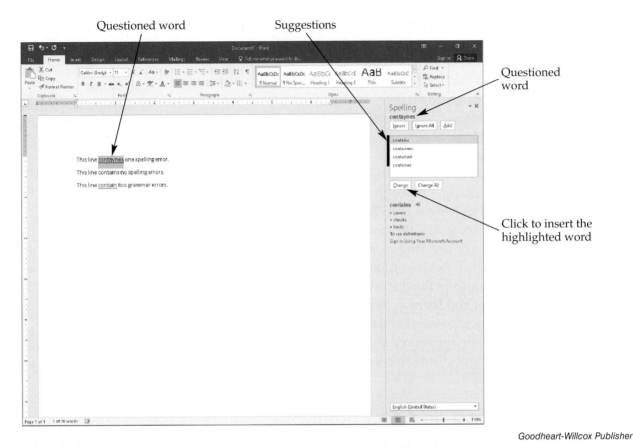

Questioned word

Click to insert the highlighted word

Figure 5-12. The spell-check feature is used to check for misspellings and can be set to check for proper grammar as well.

HANDS-ON EXAMPLE 5.2.2

CHECKING SPELLING AND GRAMMAR

It is important to use proper spelling and grammar in all documents. Misspelled words or improper usage of grammar are signs of lack of quality and professionalism.

1. Launch Microsoft Word 2016, and open the file *LastName*Library.docx from the Chap05 folder on your flash drive, if it is not already open.
2. Place the insertion point at the beginning of the document.

ABC ✓

Spelling & Grammar

3. Click **Review>Proofing>Spelling & Grammar** in the ribbon or press the [F7] key. Because there are spelling errors in this document, the **Spelling** pane is displayed on the right-hand side of the window, and the first questionable word is highlighted in the document. Note: earlier versions of Microsoft Word will display the **Spelling and Grammar** dialog box.
4. In the list of spelling alternatives offered, select the correct spelling, and click the **Change** button. The word is changed, and the next questionable word is highlighted in the document.

HANDS-ON EXAMPLE 5.2.2 (CONTINUED)

5. Continue correcting the document. If the questioned word is correct, click the **Ignore** button. If the correct word does not appear in the list of spelling alternatives, click in the document and manually correct the word. When the last questionable word has been addressed, the **Spelling** pane is closed, and the **Readability Statistics** dialog box is displayed.
6. Make note of the reading level and reading ease scores, and then close the **Readability Statistics** dialog box.
7. Save the file.

Readability

Readability is a measure of how easy it is for the reader to understand and locate information within a document. It includes the visual appearance of text on the page, but also included are the length of words, sentences, and paragraphs. When proofing a document, it is important to remember that somebody will be reading the document. Therefore, readability should always be considered.

Visual Appearance

The arrangement of information in relation to the white space on the page contributes to readability. White space includes margins, space between paragraphs, and any other blank space on the page.

Kerning is the amount of space between two letters. Letters in words that have little space between them create a crowded look. Letters in words with too much space between them can be hard to read.

As discussed earlier in this chapter, leading is the amount of space between lines of text and paragraphs. Similar to kerning, lines of text that have little space between them create a crowded look. Lines with too much space between them also can be difficult to read.

Also discussed earlier in this chapter is paragraph alignment. Alignment can affect readability. The pages may be left aligned, right aligned, or centered. Additionally, text may be *ragged*, meaning there are uneven end points for each line, or fully justified. How these aspects affect readability vary based on other factors, such as the typeface, point size, length of text, and page and text color.

Reading Level and Readability Scores

Readability and reading level scores help authors and educators adjust a document so it fits the needs of the target audience. These scores predict how difficult the material is to read. The two publications

Green Tech

Repurpose Electronics
Most electronics cannot just be thrown away. They have to be recycled due to harmful chemicals. Sometimes they can be repurposed. For example, a wireless router can be reprogrammed and repurposed to act as a signal amplifier or repeater. By repurposing electronics, a company can save hundreds of dollars on the disposal of old products and even more on the purchasing of new ones.

with the largest circulations, *TV Guide* (13 million) and *Reader's Digest* (12 million), are written at the ninth-grade level. This means that anybody with education of at least ninth grade should be able to read the material without difficulty. Some of the most popular novels are written at the seventh-grade level. Two common measures of readability are Flesch Reading Ease and Flesch-Kincaid Grade Level.

The Flesch Reading Ease test produces a rating based on a 100-point scale. The higher the score, the easier it is to understand the document. For most audiences, the target score should be between 60 and 70.

The Flesch-Kincaid Grade Level test produces a rating that corresponds to a school grade level in the United States. For example, a score of 8.0 means the average eighth grader should be able to understand the material. For most audiences, the target grade should be between 7.0 and 8.0.

These tests look at the average number of syllables per word and the number of words per sentence. To improve the readability of a document, edit it to reduce the number of words used in each sentence. Also, try to use words that have no more than two syllables. Words with one or two syllables do not affect the scores.

To set up Microsoft Word to display readability statistics, click **Options** in the **File** tab. In the **Options** dialog box, select **Proofing** on the left-hand side. Under the **When correcting spelling and grammar in Word** heading, check the **Check grammar with spelling** check box. This enables the **Show readability statistics** check box. Check this check box, and then close the **Options** dialog box. The next time a document is spell-checked, the readability statistics dialog box will be displayed after the spell-check is completed, as shown in Figure 5-13.

FYI

Microsoft Outlook can also be set up to display readability statistics for composed e-mails.

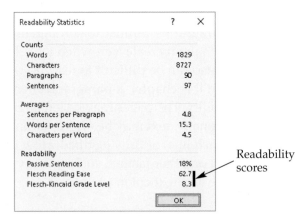

Readability scores

Figure 5-13. Readability statistics can be displayed after a spell-check. In this example, the document has a high reading level.

5.2 | SECTION REVIEW

CHECK YOUR UNDERSTANDING

1. What does proofing a document involve?
2. How is Microsoft Word set to check spelling as text is entered?
3. What are the two things that the track changes feature logs?
4. What are two ways to start a manual spell-check?
5. How can the reading level of a passage be reduced?

BUILD YOUR VOCABULARY

As you progress through this course, develop a personal IT glossary. This will help you build your vocabulary and prepare you for a career. Write a definition for each of the following terms and add it to your IT glossary.

kerning

proofing

readability

track changes

5 REVIEW AND ASSESSMENT

Chapter Summary

Section 5.1
Creating a Document

- Starting with a blank document, text can be entered and formatted. The page layout can be modified, and paragraph styles can be used to control the formatting of the text.
- Tables can be added to a document. A table can be created from existing text, and an existing table can be converted into text.
- A document template is a document preformatted for a specific use. It is intended to be an aid in creating professional-looking documents, such as brochures, flyers, newsletters, reports, invitations, certificates, and calendars.
- Desktop publishing is using software to lay out text and graphics for professional-looking documents, such as newspapers, books, or brochures. As important as the content in a desktop-publishing document is the visual design, which is the arrangement of the visual and artistic elements used to accomplish a goal or communicate an idea.

Section 5.2
Proofing Text

- Proofing is the process of checking the document for errors, such as misspellings, grammar mistakes, and formatting problems. The tools in word processors that help in proofing a document should be considered aids, not replacements for manually reviewing a document for accuracy.

- The track changes feature of word processors is used to log markups made to the document. When finalizing the document, review the markups and either accept or reject each one.
- Spelling and grammar mistakes not only distract readers, they show a lack of quality and concern for the work. A spell-checker can help find spelling and grammar errors along with a manual review of the document.
- Readability is a measure of how easy it is for the reader to understand and locate information within a document. The visual appearance of the document affects readability, and readability scores can be used to assign a score.

Now that you have finished this chapter, see what you know about computer applications by taking the chapter posttest. Access the posttest by visiting www.g-wlearning.com. ↗

Chapter 5 Test

Multiple Choice
Select the best response.

1. Which of the following key combinations moves the insertion point to the end of the document?
   A. [Page Down]
   B. [Ctrl][Page Down]
   C. [End]
   D. [Ctrl][End]

2. Which of the following is not a category of typefaces?
   A. serif
   B. bold
   C. decorative
   D. sans serif

3. Which of the following should be checked when editing a desktop-publishing project?
   A. Typefaces and font styles are appropriately applied.
   B. Graphics are appropriately labeled.
   C. Headings are accurate.
   D. All of the above.

4. Which proofing feature can be used to automatically change a misspelled word to the correct spelling?
   A. spell-check
   B. AutoCorrect
   C. AutoChange
   D. SmartCorrect

5. In order for readability statistics to be displayed, what additional function must be done?
   A. Use the **Readability** command.
   B. Apply correct styles.
   C. Check grammar with spelling.
   D. None of the above.

Completion

Complete the following sentences with the correct word(s).

6. The vertical ruler can only be displayed in the _____ view.

7. A(n) _____ is a desktop-publishing file that saves the attributes of every font that will be used in a project.

8. _____ is examining a document for misspellings and grammatical mistakes.

9. To start a manual spell-check, press the _____ key.

10. In the Flesch Reading Ease measurement, the _____ the score, the easier it is to understand the document.

Matching

Match the correct term with its definition.

A. typeface
B. orientation
C. tabs
D. kerning
E. Flesch-Kincaid Grade Level

11. The amount of space between two letters.

12. How the document will be placed on the sheet.

13. The design of characters.

14. A measure of readability.

15. Preset horizontal locations across the page in a document.

Application and Extension of Knowledge

1. Create a three-column table in a Microsoft Word document that outlines each hour of your day. The cells in the left-hand column should indicate the hour. The middle column should list the name of each activity. The right-hand column should include any notes, such as "study for test tomorrow" or "bring new shoes to practice." Resize each column as needed. For example, the notes column may need to be wider than the other two columns.

2. Begin a new blank document. Create four new styles: *LastName*Heading1, *LastName*Heading2, *LastName*Heading3, and *LastName*Body. Set the formatting of each to your preference. Do not use more than two typefaces. Vary the formatting to make each style look different. Save the file in a location where you will be able to access it in the future.

3. Begin a new blank document. Change the page orientation to landscape. Create a new style named TabStops. Set the line spacing for the style to double. In the style, add a left tab at 1″, a center tab at 4.5″, and a right tab at 8″. Change the typeface and formatting to your preference. Save the file in a location where you will be able to access it in the future.

4. Research three local attractions that your local tourism board may highlight to encourage visitors. Write a report describing what a visitor might find at each of the three sites. Include an introduction and a separate page for each of the three attractions. Use page breaks. Spell-check the document, and display the readability statistics.

5. Research careers that may interest you. Select one career. Write a brief summary of what types of activities are involved in the career. Include a table that outlines the educational requirements, average entry-level salary, number of current jobs in the field, and expected number of jobs in the future. Create styles as needed to format the document. Spell-check the document.

Online Activities

Complete the following activities, which will help you learn, practice, and expand your knowledge and skills.

Vocabulary. Practice vocabulary for this chapter using the e-flash cards, matching activity, and vocabulary game until you are able to recognize their meanings.

Communication Skills

Writing. There will be many instances when you will be required to persuade the reader. Prepare a letter about who should be responsible for paying for collection or pickup and then disposal of electronic waste. Ask for assistance to help you argue your case and show solid reasoning.

Reading. Imagery is descriptive language that indicates how something looks, feels, smells, sounds, or tastes. After you have read this chapter, find an example of how the author used imagery to appeal to the five senses. Describe how it influenced your mood.

Speaking. Word-processing software is used to create written documents. How can a written document help you prepare for an oral presentation? Prepare for and participate in a discussion describing your answer to this question.

Internet Research

Famous Speakers. Research famous speakers and select one that captures your attention. Listen to a speech this individual has given. Using presentation software, summarize this speech and explain why it was effective.

Teamwork

Collaborating with your team, make a list of the various types of reading materials that you regularly use to find specific information. Examples include a bus schedule, on-screen TV guide, blogs, text messages, newspapers, and magazines. For each type of medium, list the information you are reading to find and discuss strategies for finding it quickly.

Activity Files

Visit www.g-wlearning.com/informationtechnology/ to download the activity files for this chapter. These activities will expand your learning of the material presented in this chapter and allow you to practice what you have learned. Follow the instructions provided in each file to complete the activity.

Activity File 5-1 Typefaces

Activity File 5-2 Tab Stops

Activity File 5-3 Advanced Autocorrect Options

Activity File 5-4 Templates

Activity File 5-5 Improving Your Formatting Skills

CAPSTONE PROJECT

The capstone project builds from one chapter to the next. It allows you to apply the skills you have learned to create a complete project in a desired career area. Read the instructions below for the career area you chose to work in for this course. Work in the same career area in each chapter.

Agriculture, Food, and Natural Resources

In this activity, you will create a business letter template, and you will create and implement a company style and logo. These documents will be used to draft a response letter to a local 4H group that has inquired about raising chickens. Access the *Introduction to Microsoft Office 2016* companion website (www.g-wlearning.com/informationtechnology/) to view the instructions for this chapter's Agriculture, Food, and Natural Resources capstone project.

Business, Management, and Administration

In this activity, you will create stationery files that promote and present a professional image for the company. These templates will need to be saved for easy, future access as you progress in your comprehensive capstone project. Access the *Introduction to Microsoft Office 2016* companion website (www.g-wlearning.com/informationtechnology/) to view the instructions for this chapter's Business, Management, and Administration capstone project.

Health Science

In this activity, you will create a business letter template, and you will create and implement a company style and logo. You will then write a professional response to a local physician regarding non-pharmaceutical alternatives to viral illness. Access the *Introduction to Microsoft Office 2016* companion website (www.g-wlearning.com/informationtechnology/) to view the instructions for this chapter's Health Science capstone project.

Science, Technology, Engineering, and Mathematics

In this activity, you will create stationery files that promote and present a professional image for the company. These templates will need to be stored in an easily accessible folder for future access as you progress in your capstone project. Access the *Introduction to Microsoft Office 2016* companion website (www.g-wlearning.com/informationtechnology/) to view the instructions for this chapter's Science, Technology, Engineering, and Mathematics capstone project.

6

FORMAL DOCUMENTS

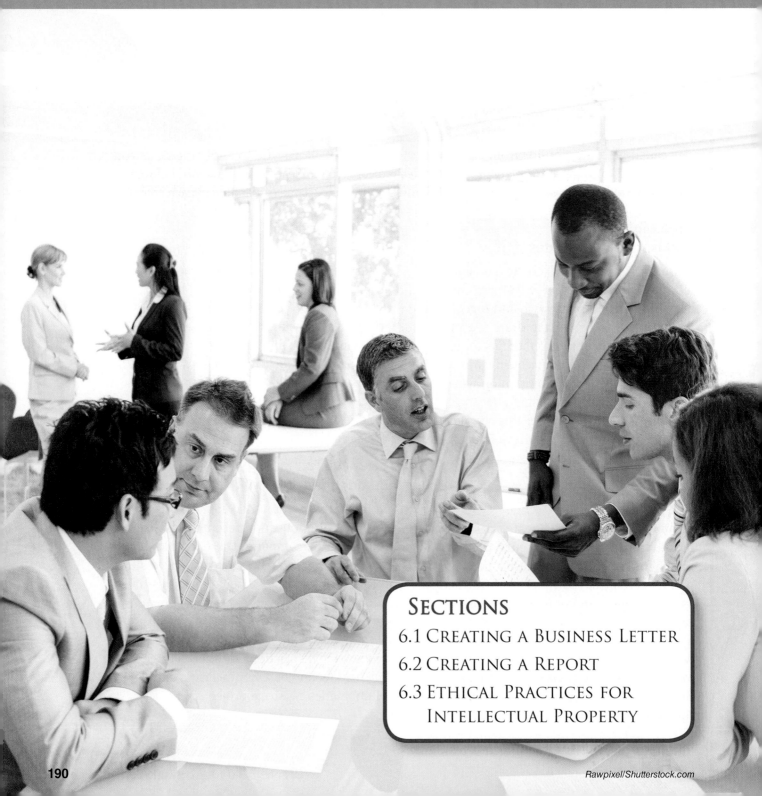

SECTIONS

6.1 CREATING A BUSINESS LETTER

6.2 CREATING A REPORT

6.3 ETHICAL PRACTICES FOR INTELLECTUAL PROPERTY

In the modern world of text messaging and other real-time communication, it is common to see invented spelling and improper grammar. For informal communication between family and friends, these behaviors are accepted. However, formal business communication should reflect a high level of written communication skill. When employers are asked what they are looking for in a new hire, most say they want workers who can show up on time, work a good day, and have excellent oral and written communication skills.

Good communications skills include use of clear, concise sentences with proper sentence structure. Good communicators use proper grammar and spelling. Words are spelled out, not abbreviated. No slang is used. Fortunately, as discussed in the previous chapter, Microsoft Word has built in features to assist with proper written communication. The format of formal communication is commonly used in business. Business letters and interoffice memos use this formal way of communicating. This chapter assists in the development of good written communication for business.

MICROSOFT OFFICE SPECIALIST OBJECTIVES

Word

Create and Manage Documents

1.3 Format a Document
  1.3.5 Insert page numbers

Create and Manage References

4.1 Create and Manage Reference Markers
  4.1.1 Insert footnotes and endnotes
  4.1.2 Modify footnote and endnote properties
  4.1.3 Create bibliography citation sources
  4.1.4 Modify bibliography citation sources
  4.1.5 Insert citations for bibliographies
  4.1.6 Insert figure and table captions
  4.1.7 Modify caption properties

4.2 Create and Manage Simple References
  4.2.1 Insert a standard table of contents
  4.2.2 Update a table of contents
  4.2.3 Insert a cover page

SECTION 6.1

CREATING A BUSINESS LETTER

One of the most common uses for word-processing software in the professional world is to create a letter. Readers expect professional documents to appear a certain way. By using the appropriate format, the reader can immediately tell what type of document is being received. Standard formatting is a generally accepted way to format a document so its appearance follows a convention. Writers use standard formatting so their business documents are consistent in appearance with what the reader expects.

The appearance of a document is the first impression your writing makes on the reader. That first glance at the message should be an open invitation to the receiver. The arrangement of text in relation to the white space on the page determines the visual appeal to the reader. Without properly formatted elements, the reader can easily become lost or distracted.

Rob Marmion/Shutterstock.com

TERMS

block-style letter
body
complimentary close
copy notation
enclosure notation
inside address
letterhead
mixed punctuation

modified-block-style letter
open punctuation
postscript
reference initials
salutation
signature block
subject line

LEARNING GOALS

After completing this section, you will be able to:

- Describe the standard business letter formats.
- Identify standard letter elements.
- Discuss elements beyond standard letter elements.
- Format a business letter.

Standard Business Letter Format

Letters are messages printed on stationery and should conform to workplace standards. Stationery used for business purposes is often letterhead stationery. A **letterhead** includes information about an organization, such as its name, address, contact information, and a logo. Letterhead is preprinted on high-quality paper so organizations do not have to add this information on every correspondence. In the case of a letter concerning personal business, the letterhead is replaced by the return address of the sender.

Businesses generally use one of two standardized letter formats: block or modified block. The **block-style letter** is formatted so all lines are flush with the left-hand page margin, as shown in Figure 6-1. No indentions are used. The **modified-block-style letter** places the date, complimentary close, and signature to the right of the center point of the letter. All other elements of the letter are flush with the left-hand page margin. Figure 6-2 shows a letter formatted in the modified-block style.

Standard Letter Elements

Standardized letter formats contain various elements. Block-style and modified-block-style letters include the same elements:

- date
- inside address
- salutation
- body
- complimentary close
- signature
- notations

If not using a letterhead, a return address should also be included.

TITANS OF TECHNOLOGY

Charles Simonyi and Butler Lampson were early developers of word-processing software. Many people would say that word processing began with the electric typewriter, which allowed, for the first time, someone to edit his or her work and reprint the document. However, others claim the first true word processors were the software programs for the minicomputers and microcomputers that allowed formatting of a document. Simonyi and Lampson were two researchers at Palo Alto Research Center (PARC), the research arm of Xerox Corporation, when they developed Bravo in 1974 for the Alto minicomputer. However, the earliest word processor for home microcomputers was Electric Pencil, which was developed by Michael Shrayer, a computer club enthusiast. Other early word-processing programs included WordStar, Word Perfect, Apple Writer, and Easy Writer. The word-processing programs of today are descendants of these early software applications.

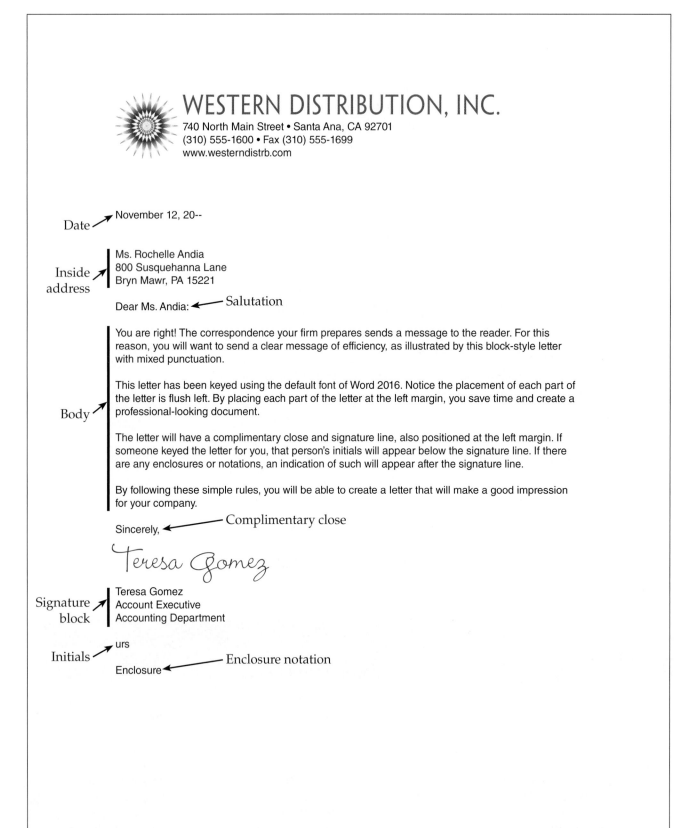

Figure 6-1. This letter is formatted in block style with mixed punctuation.

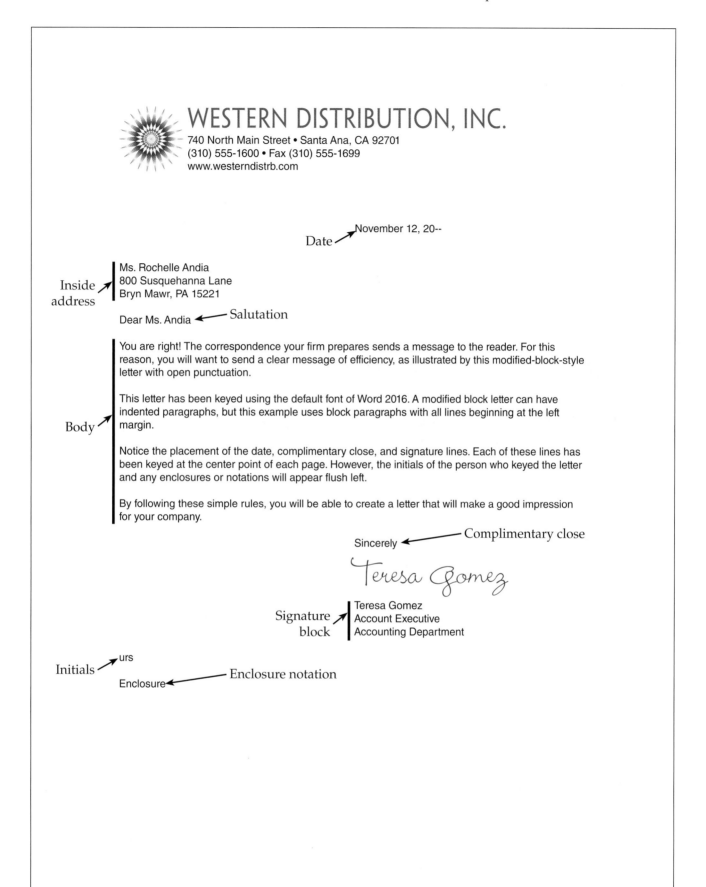

WESTERN DISTRIBUTION, INC.
740 North Main Street • Santa Ana, CA 92701
(310) 555-1600 • Fax (310) 555-1699
www.westerndistrb.com

Date → November 12, 20--

Inside address ↗ Ms. Rochelle Andia
800 Susquehanna Lane
Bryn Mawr, PA 15221

Dear Ms. Andia ← Salutation

Body ↗ You are right! The correspondence your firm prepares sends a message to the reader. For this reason, you will want to send a clear message of efficiency, as illustrated by this modified-block-style letter with open punctuation.

This letter has been keyed using the default font of Word 2016. A modified block letter can have indented paragraphs, but this example uses block paragraphs with all lines beginning at the left margin.

Notice the placement of the date, complimentary close, and signature lines. Each of these lines has been keyed at the center point of each page. However, the initials of the person who keyed the letter and any enclosures or notations will appear flush left.

By following these simple rules, you will be able to create a letter that will make a good impression for your company.

Sincerely ← Complimentary close

Teresa Gomez

Signature ↗ Teresa Gomez
block Account Executive
Accounting Department

Initials ↗ urs

Enclosure ← Enclosure notation

Figure 6-2. This is similar to the letter shown in Figure 6-1, but formatted in modified-block style with open punctuation.

Career Skills

Destination Marketing Manager

A destination marketing manager works for a variety of employers to attract visitors to a particular destination. They coordinate the destination activities of agencies, convention bureaus, or marketing firms who choose their particular destination. Using business communications standards and promotional materials, these marketing managers target travelers within a certain budget range.

Date

The date consists of the month, day, and year. The month is spelled in full. The day is written in figures and followed by a comma. The year is written in full and consists of numbers. For example:

> December 18, 20xx

where xx is the current year. This is the standard for the United States. International uses may require a different format for the date.

Inside Address

The **inside address** is the name, title, and address of the recipient. The two examples that follow show how to format an inside address.

> Mr. Angelo Costanzo, Manager
> Griffin Plumbing Supply Co.
> 1987 Susquehanna Avenue
> Wilkes-Barre, PA 18701

> Ms. Denise Rodriquez
> President & CEO
> Urban Development Council
> 150 Grosvenor Avenue
> Washington, DC 30005

For addresses in the United States, the last line must be the city, state, and ZIP code. Note that the state abbreviation is always two letters and in all capital letters.

Salutation

The **salutation** is the greeting in a letter and always begins with *Dear*. This is followed by the recipient's first name or, according to your relationship, title and last name.

There are two types of punctuation used in letters. **Mixed punctuation** is a style in which a colon is placed after the salutation and a comma after the complimentary close. **Open punctuation** is a style in which there is no punctuation after the salutation or complimentary close.

Always address a letter to a specific person unless it is being intentionally directed to an organization. It may take a phone call or Internet search to get the correct name, but it is worth the effort to personalize business messages. Also, make sure the receiver's name is correctly spelled and the appropriate title used, such as *Dr.*, *Mr.*, or *Ms.* The title *Mrs.* is rarely used in business writing. Spell out and capitalize titles, such as *Professor* and *Reverend*. If you are unsure of a person's gender, use the full name.

If you need to write a letter without the name of a specific person, do not use generic greetings, such as *Dear Sir* or *Gentlemen*. You may use *Ladies and Gentlemen*; however, the best course is to use words that describe the role of the person:

Dear Customer:
Dear Circulation Manager:
Dear Editor:

Body

The **body** of the letter is the message. Format the body according to the block or modified-block style. Most businesses use the block style. Single-spaced letters are standard. However, some businesses prefer the default setting of the word-processing software used. In Microsoft Word 2016, this is 1.08.

Complimentary Close

The **complimentary close** is the sign-off for the letter. Only the first word is capitalized. The style used in the complimentary close—mixed or open punctuation—must match the salutation. The complimentary close follows the body of the letter and is appropriately spaced, as shown in Figure 6-1 and Figure 6-2. The most commonly used closings are as follows.

Mixed Punctuation
Sincerely,
Sincerely yours,
Cordially,
Cordially yours,

Open Punctuation
Sincerely
Sincerely yours
Cordially
Cordially yours

Signature Block

The writer's name and title are called the **signature block** or *signature*. The writer's job title and department appear beneath the name, unless a letterhead is used that contains this information. Begin the signature block below the complimentary close. The blank lines of space are used for the handwritten signature.

Sincerely,

Margaret Shaw
Coordinator
Business Development

When the message is from the company rather than an individual, the company name may appear in all-capital letters below the complimentary close. In this situation, there is no signature.

Sincerely,

JIMENEZ-BRADFORD REALTY

Notations

Letters may include reference initials. **Reference initials** indicate the person who keyed the letter. If the writer keyed the letter, initials are not included. Reference initials are lowercase letters.

Cordially yours,

Margaret Shaw
Senior Vice President

smb

An **enclosure notation** alerts the reader to materials that are included in the mailing along with the letter. Spell out and capitalize the word *Enclosure*. If there is more than one enclosure, indicate the number of items included or list them. The word *Attachment* may be used instead of the word *Enclosure*.

Enclosures
Enclosures: 3
Enclosures: Statement
               Check
               Letter

A **copy notation** is needed when others are being sent a copy of the letter. The notation appears below the signature block, as shown in Figure 6-1 and Figure 6-2. If there are enclosure notations or reference initials, the copy notation appears below these. Use *c* for copy or *cc* for carbon copy or courtesy copy. The copy notation is followed by a colon and a list of the full names of individuals receiving copies.

cc: Tina Ricco
       Gary Kowalski

Additional Letter Elements

The previously described elements are the most common elements of a business letter. However, there are three additional letter elements that are sometimes used in a business letter. These are the attention line, subject line, and postscript.

Attention Line

There is a wealth of resources available to the writer, such as the Internet and company databases, that make it largely unnecessary to address correspondence without an individual's name. However, if this circumstance does occur, substituting a position or department title for a specific name is a good solution. For example, you may know the marketing manager is to receive the letter, but cannot find the name of the person. In this situation, it is appropriate to include an attention line that says *Attention Marketing Manager*. This line is positioned as part of the inside address.

> Attention Marketing Manager
> Urban Development Council
> 150 Grosvenor Avenue
> Washington, DC 30005

Subject Line

A **subject line** in a letter helps the reader know the content of the message before reading. The subject line may be in all caps or initial caps and the word *subject* is optional. The subject line appears after the salutation and before the body of the letter.

> Dear Mr. Ramito:
>
>
> SUBJECT: MINUTES OF SUMMER MEETING
>
>
> Thank you for attending the summer meeting of the Green Entrepreneur that was held last month in Orlando. We appreciate your attendance and your contribution to this meeting…

Postscript

Postscript means *after writing* and is information included after the signature. In business letters, the postscript is no longer used to represent an afterthought. For example, in the past, a writer may have included an omission as a postscript, such as:

> P.S. I forgot to tell you we're moving. After June 1, you can reach us at our new address.

With the advent of word-processing software, the need for postscripts disappeared. If you discover that something important was omitted from the body of a letter, simply edit the letter and include it.

Occasionally, however, a writer uses a postscript to emphasize or personalize a point. Sales letters often use postscripts for special effect.

> P.S. Remember, our sale ends this Thursday. Don't miss the wonderful savings in store for you!

Use postscripts sparingly. Frequent use of postscripts may suggest to the reader that you did not plan your message.

HANDS-ON EXAMPLE 6.1.1

CREATING A PERSONAL BUSINESS LETTER

There will be many times throughout your career when you will need to create a business letter. The ability to create a proper business letter is an important skill to develop.

1. Launch Microsoft Word, and begin a new blank document.
2. Save the file as *LastName*BusinessLetter.docx in the Chap06 folder on your flash drive.
3. Add the text University of New Hampshire, and press the [Enter] key.
4. Add a one-line street address, and press the [Enter] key.
5. Add a city, a state abbreviation, and a ZIP code, and press the [Enter] key.
6. Enter today's date. Notice that when Word recognizes you are entering a month, it suggests the current month. Accept this by pressing the [Enter] key. Then, once you press the space bar, Word suggests today's date. Accept this by pressing the [Enter] key.
7. Enter the following text on separate lines. The body should be two paragraphs.

> Dr. Kathleen Augustino
> University of Baltimore
> 1420 North Charles St.
> Baltimore, MD 21201
>
> Dear Dr. Augustino,
>
> Please let me know who on your faculty is in charge of coordinating student internships for international studies for the spring and summer semesters. We have several very good candidates who are bilingual.
>
> Our candidates are fluent in French, Spanish, German, and Arabic. They are all US citizens. Several have grown up in bilingual households. Others have spent time learning the languages through total immersion. You can reach me through e-mail at languages@arc.xyz or 999-555-1234. Thank you.
>
> Sincerely,

8. Enter your name. The letter is now composed, but it needs to be properly formatted. This will be done in the next exercise.
9. Save the document.

GS5
Key Applications
2.1

Formatting a Business Letter

There is an accepted standard format for business letters. It is important to follow the accepted standard. Using nonstandard formatting makes the letter appear unprofessional. As a result, the reader may not take the letter seriously or the message of the letter may not be effectively communicated.

If you will be creating letters on a regular basis, the best approach is to create paragraph styles for each element of the letter. Also set up the page margins. Then, save the document as a template. Whenever a letter needs to be created, begin a new blank document based on this letter template. All of the paragraph styles and page formatting will be set up automatically.

Then, simply write the letter and apply the proper paragraph styles to each element. However, if you do not frequently write letters, you may choose to manually format the page and paragraphs each time.

Common Formatting

The left- and right-hand page margins should be 1″. The bottom page margin should also be 1″. The top page margin should be 2″. However, if the letterhead extends more than 2″ from the top edge of the page, the date line should be placed two lines below the bottom of the letterhead. If the letter is longer than one page, the top margin on the second and remaining pages should be 1″.

The typeface used in a letter is largely a personal preference, but many people use the default typeface in the word processor. The typeface may be a serif typeface or a sans serif typeface, as discussed in Chapter 5. A common serif typeface is Times New Roman. A common sans serif typeface is Arial. Do not use decorative typefaces, such as Flemish Script, Monotype Corsiva (a calligraphy-style typeface), or Comic Sans. These typefaces are not appropriate for a business letter and their use decreases the readability of text.

Business letters should have single line spacing. However, some word-processing software has a default setting that is not single spaced. For example, the default line spacing in Microsoft Word 2016 is 1.08, as shown in Figure 6-3. Many companies use the default setting for line spacing, but single line spacing is the traditional standard. To use single line spacing, either modify the paragraph setting or style or use the [Shift] [Enter] key combination to add a soft return.

If writing a personal business letter with a return address, leave two blank lines between the return address and the date. Otherwise, the date should begin at the top margin. There should be two blank lines between the date and the inside address. After the inside address, there should be one blank line before the salutation. Leave one blank line after the salutation and begin the body. If the body is longer than one paragraph, leave one blank line between each paragraph. After the body, leave one blank line and then add the complimentary close. Between the complimentary close and the signature block, there should be two blank lines. This is the space where the writer will sign the letter. For additional elements, such as reference initials or an enclosure notation, leave one blank line between each element.

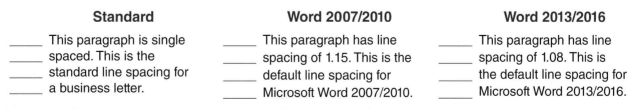

Standard	Word 2007/2010	Word 2013/2016
_____ This paragraph is single _____ spaced. This is the _____ standard line spacing for _____ a business letter.	_____ This paragraph has line _____ spacing of 1.15. This is the _____ default line spacing for _____ Microsoft Word 2007/2010.	_____ This paragraph has line _____ spacing of 1.08. This is _____ the default line spacing for _____ Microsoft Word 2013/2016.

Goodheart-Willcox Publisher

Figure 6-3. The standard line spacing for business letters is single spaced, but some companies allow the Microsoft Word default setting to be used.

Block Style versus Modified-Block Style

In a block-style letter, all elements are flush to the left-hand page margin. There should be no indentation on any line. This can be set up in the paragraph styles. If manually formatting the letter, it is easiest to remove the indentation before writing the letter so each new line will not be automatically indented.

In a modified-block-style letter, the date, complimentary close, and signature are flush left with the center point of the page. The horizontal center of the page for a standard letter-size sheet is 4.25", which becomes 3.25" on the ruler when the 1" page margin is subtracted. This point can be set in the paragraph style or the left indentation can be manually shifted over by 3.25". All other elements are flush to the left-hand page margin. The first line of body paragraphs may be indented or not. If indentation is used, the indent should be .5". This can be set up in the paragraph styles or, if manually formatting the letter, a tab stop can be manually added at this location.

HANDS-ON EXAMPLE 6.1.2

FORMATTING A BUSINESS LETTER

Composing the message in a letter is only an initial step. The letter must be properly formatted following accepted guidelines to be final.

1. Launch Microsoft Word, and open the *LastName*BusinessLetter.docx file in the Chap06 folder on your flash drive, if it is not already open.

Adjust Margins

2. Click **Layout>Page Setup>Adjust Margins** in the ribbon, and click **Custom Margins** in the drop-down menu. The **Page Setup** dialog box is displayed with the **Margins** tab selected, as shown.

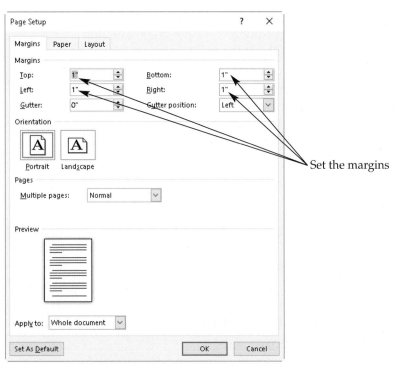

Set the margins

HANDS-ON EXAMPLE 6.1.2 (CONTINUED)

3. Click in the **Top:** text box, and enter 2. This sets the top page margin to 2″.
4. Enter 1 in the **Bottom:**, **Left:**, and **Right:** text boxes to set the corresponding page margins to 1″.
5. Click the **OK** button to close the dialog box and set the margins. The first line should shift down slightly to match the new top margin.
6. Click at the end of the first line in the return address, press the [Shift][Enter] key combination, and press the [Delete] key. This adds a soft return and makes the first and second lines of the return address in the same paragraph. Essentially, this two-line paragraph becomes single spaced.
7. Applying what you have learned, make the third line in the return address part of the same paragraph as the first two lines.
8. Click after the ZIP code in the return address, and press the [Enter] key twice. This manually adds two blank lines between the return address and the date.
9. Click after the date, and press the [Enter] key twice to manually add two blank lines between the date and the inside address.
10. Applying what you have learned, add soft returns to single space the inside address.
11. Click after the ZIP code in the inside address, and press the [Enter] key once. This manually adds one blank line between the inside address and the salutation.
12. Click after the salutation, and press the [Enter] key once to manually add one blank line between the salutation and the body.
13. Click at the end of the first paragraph of the body, and press the [Enter] key once to manually add one blank line between the paragraphs in the body.
14. Applying what you have learned, select all of the text in the document, including blank lines.
15. Click the dialog box launcher in the **Paragraph** group on the **Home** tab of the ribbon. The **Paragraph** dialog box is displayed with the **Indents and Spacing** tab selected, as shown.

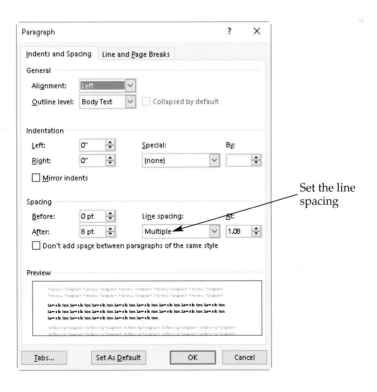

Set the line spacing

HANDS-ON EXAMPLE 6.1.2 (CONTINUED)

16. Click the **Line spacing:** drop-down arrow, and click **Single** in the drop-down list. This manually sets the line spacing for the selected text, which is the entire document, to single spaced.
17. Enter 0 in the **Before:** and **After:** text boxes. This sets the amount of space (in points) that appears before and after each paragraph.
18. Click the **OK** button to update the line spacing.
19. Click at the end of the last line in the body, and press the [Enter] key to manually add one blank line between the body and the complimentary close.
20. Click at the end of the complimentary close, and press the [Enter] key twice to add two blank lines between the complimentary close and your name. The letter is now properly formatted in block style.

6.1 | SECTION REVIEW

CHECK YOUR UNDERSTANDING

1. What are the two standardized letter formats used by businesses?
2. Which standard letter element contains the address of the person for whom the letter is intended?
3. What is the purpose of the subject line on a letter?
4. If you will be creating letters on a regular basis, what is the best approach to formatting the text of the letters?
5. What is the traditional line spacing used in a business letter?

BUILD YOUR VOCABULARY

As you progress through this course, develop a personal IT glossary. This will help you build your vocabulary and prepare you for a career. Write a definition for each of the following terms and add it to your IT glossary.

block-style letter
body
complimentary close
copy notation
enclosure notation
inside address
letterhead
mixed punctuation

modified-block-style letter
open punctuation
postscript
reference initials
salutation
signature block
subject line

CREATING A REPORT

Air Images/Shutterstock.com

Reports provide facts and information from which conclusions are drawn. They also discuss problems and recommend solutions. In the workplace, reports are often used to convey information that is used as the basis for making business decisions. In school, students are often required to write reports to provide information on specific topics related to coursework.

Reports may be developed for use inside an organization. They may also be sent to people outside of the organization, such as governmental agencies, stockholders, members, investors, clients, customers, and to the media. No matter who the audience is for a report, the manner in which the report is presented represents the writer. A properly formatted report will communicate professionalism. It may also set the stage for how the reader will view the validity of the information presented in the report.

LEARNING GOALS

After completing this section, you will be able to:
- Describe the process of creating a report.
- Format a report.

TERMS

analytical report	introduction
citation	primary research
conclusion	proposal
data	qualitative data
endnote	quantitative data
folio	recommendation
footnote	secondary research
heading	table of contents
informational report	

Creating a Report

Reports are documents used to present information in a structured format to a specific audience for a defined purpose. There are three common types of reports:

- informational reports
- analytical reports
- proposals

Informational reports contain facts, data, or other types of information. They do not attempt to analyze the data or persuade the reader. **Analytical reports** contain both information and analysis of the data. They often provide conclusions or recommendations drawn from the analysis. **Proposals** typically contain a specific idea and attempt to persuade the reader to take a certain course of action. Extensive research and analysis often go into a proposal.

A choice must be made when planning the document in order to achieve the desired outcome. The direct or indirect approach can be applied to the content of a report. When using the direct approach, start with a general statement of purpose. Follow this with supporting details. The direct approach is desirable when the reader is expecting a straightforward message. When using the indirect approach, discuss supporting details upfront to prepare the reader for your general statement of purpose or conclusions.

FYI

The outline view in Microsoft Word can be useful in organizing the content of a report.

Planning a Report

Planning is the most important stage of preparing a report. It involves focusing on the subject and outlining the content. Writing a report should always follow the steps of the writing process, shown in Figure 6-4. Begin planning by completing the first step in the writing process, which is prewriting. Prewriting helps you identify the purpose and audience of the report. In prewriting, answer the questions of who, what, when, where, why, and how.

- Who is the audience?
- What do you want to communicate?

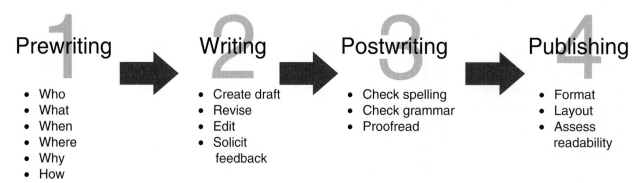

1 Prewriting
- Who
- What
- When
- Where
- Why
- How

2 Writing
- Create draft
- Revise
- Edit
- Solicit feedback

3 Postwriting
- Check spelling
- Check grammar
- Proofread

4 Publishing
- Format
- Layout
- Assess readability

Goodheart-Willcox Publisher

Figure 6-4. There are four stages in the writing process.

- When must the report be complete?
- Where is the information?
- Why are you writing?
- How should the information be organized?

The questions can be answered in any order. After you have completed the prewriting steps, you will be able to begin the research.

Researching a Report

Collecting data is an important step in preparing to write a report. **Data** are the pieces of information gathered through research. Research techniques include studying written information on the topic and conducting surveys, focus groups, or interviews. Research might include consulting experts or convening a taskforce or committee to work on different aspects of the report.

Whatever the length or purpose of a formal report, the goal is to prepare a valid, useful, and informative document. Consider the type of information needed to make the report credible. Information usually falls into one of two categories: qualitative or quantitative data. **Qualitative data** are the information that provides insight into how people think about a particular topic. An example of qualitative data is a customer's feelings after speaking with a customer service agent. **Quantitative data** are the facts and figures from which conclusions can be drawn. An example of quantitative data is the number of customers who requested to speak with a customer service agent after using a certain product.

Primary research is first-hand research conducted by the writer in preparation for writing a report. The most common methods of primary research for a business report are interviews, surveys, and experiments.

Secondary research is data and information already assembled and recorded by someone else. This might include published materials or resources available to you on the job. In many cases, you will conduct secondary research first to find credible information to support your ideas. You will conduct primary research only when key data are not found.

Writers can reference material from other authors provided proper credit is given. This is done by summarizing the work in your own words, which is called *paraphrasing*, or by directly quoting a small part of the work. It is necessary to credit, or cite, sources when referencing or paraphrasing someone else's work. In general, the following information is needed to create citations.

- author's name
- publication title
- name and location of the publisher
- publication year
- website name, URL, and date of retrieval

Citations are discussed later in this section. Ethical use of information is discussed later in this chapter.

FYI

The root of the word *qualitative* is *quality*. The root of the word *quantitative* is *quantity*.

Writing a Report

Once the research is completed and the sources are organized, you are ready to continue the writing process and compose the report. Complete a first draft and revise the document as many times as necessary to create the final product.

Title Page

Word
4.2.3

All formal reports should have a title page designed for readability and visual appeal. These elements belong on the title page:

- name of the report
- name of the person or group for whom the report was written
- name of the author of the report
- date the report is distributed

Sometimes other information, such as the location of the company, organization, or school, may also be needed. A sample title page is shown in Figure 6-5.

Table of Contents

The **table of contents**, or TOC, lists the major sections and subsections within the report with page numbers, as shown in Figure 6-6. A table of contents is necessary so the reader knows what is included in the report. This page may be referred to as *table of contents* or *contents*.

Introduction

Capture the reader's attention by giving an overview of the report's contents. A formal report usually contains an introduction. The **introduction** discusses the purpose of the report and the benefits of the ideas or recommendations you are presenting. The introduction of the report often covers the following information, but what is included in the introduction varies based on the needs of the report.

- History or background that led to the preparation of the report.
- Scope of the report, including what is covered and, if necessary, what is not covered.
- Purpose for which the report was written, including the need or justification for the report.
- Method of gathering information, facts, and figures for the report.
- Definitions of terms that may present problems for certain readers.

Refer to Figure 6-7 for an example of an introduction. Note that the order of information in an introduction may differ based on the requirements for the report you are writing.

Green Tech

Unplug Electronics
Electronics that are plugged into an outlet use standby power, which is the minimum power usage when the item is plugged in. That means that even if it is turned off, an electronic device is still drawing power and costing money to run. To make sure that electronics will not waste power, unplug them entirely.

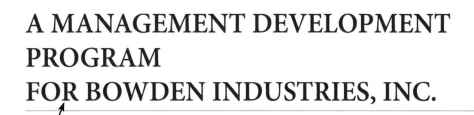

Name of
the report

A Report to the
President's Advisory Committee

Who the
report is for

Author of
the report

Prepared by

Susan Chen

Director, Development & Training
Bowden Industries, Inc.

June 17, 20--

Date the report
was published

Figure 6-5. This is an example of a title page.

Begin introduction on page 1 and use roman numerals for preceding pages

CONTENTS

Executive Summary iii
  Introduction 1
Job Requirements 5
  Senior Executives 5
  Vice Presidents 6
  Managers 6
  Supervisors 7
  Employees 8
On-the-Job Training 8
  Establishing Objectives 10
  Organization Planning 12
  Delegation of Authority 12
  Job Counseling 13
Company Training Programs 14
Company Structure and Objectives 14
  Basic Management Techniques 15
  Professional Development Courses 15
  Job-Specific Training 16
  Job Rotation 17
Career Paths 18
  Career Ladders at Bowden 22
  Studies on Promotion and Retention 24
  Succession Planning 25
Recommendations 27
Conclusion 29
Works Cited 30
Appendix 31

ii

Goodheart-Willcox Publisher

Figure 6-6. This is an example of a table of contents (TOC).

INTRODUCTION

Bowden Industries, Inc., is often referred to as "a family that keeps outgrowing its home." This implies little planning, innovation, and management leadership in the company's 12 years of existence, which is simply not true. Product diversification, innovative marketing and manufacturing, and sound financial management all attest to the effective leadership with which the company has been blessed.

At the May 9 meeting of the President's Advisory Committee, the question was asked, "Where will the managerial expertise needed for future growth and expansion come from?" The purpose of this report is to provide possible answers to that vital question.

History

In the past, Bowden has depended largely on universities and executive placement agencies for sources of managerial talent—and, of course, on its own promotion-from-within policy. By and large, these have been good sources of talent and, no doubt, will continue to be used. However, training and developing those new management hires has been through hit-or-miss, largely unstructured, on-the-job supervision. The results are mixed. Some people were well trained and quickly moved up when positions became available. Others languished and, seeing no opportunity for growth, left the company.

Scope

The term "management" in this report refers to all positions from first-line supervisors (classified as Levels 13 and 14 by the Human Resources Department) right on up to the top executive positions. No attention has been given to lower-level jobs in this report, although this is obviously a subject that deserves full exploration later.

Statement of Problem

During the past year, 44 vacancies occurred in management positions. Of that number, 22 were the result of retirement because of age or health, 13 resigned to accept positions in other companies, and the remaining nine were the result of newly created positions within the company.

It is interesting to find that 27 of the 44 openings had to be filled from the outside. In other words, only 17 employees were considered ready to accept the greater responsibilities of management. Actually, few of the people recruited from the outside were actually ready either (the unknown often looks better than the known); many required a long break-in period. Besides having a negative effect on employees who were denied promotion, outside recruiting and on-the-job adjustment are very expensive.

Goodheart-Willcox Publisher

Figure 6-7. An introduction states the purpose of the report. A page number does not appear on the first page of the introduction.

Body

The body of the report contains all of the information, data, and statistics you assemble. Organize ideas in a logical manner. Provide supporting facts and figures from reliable sources for all information. Do not report your position based solely on opinion. In many formal reports, a conclusion must be drawn, but it should be based on facts presented in the report.

If the topic you are writing about is very high level, such as a detailed proposal that will cost a great deal of money, a conversational tone could take away from the objectivity that the audience might expect. You want to convince the reader you have thoroughly studied the matter and that your facts and figures are highly trustworthy. A more formal tone is more likely to achieve this goal.

If, on the other hand, you are writing a report on activities that boost morale and create a sense of team, a conversational tone would be appropriate. This tone is friendlier and will help set the stage for the theme of the report.

A report addressed to the company president is likely to be formal in tone. If you have a friendly relationship with your supervisor or instructor, a report you write for her or him may be more conversational.

Conclusion

The closing should summarize the key points. In some cases, the report will close with conclusions and recommendations based on your study or analysis. **Conclusions** are the writer's summary of what the audience should take away from the report. **Recommendations** are actions the writer believes the reader should take, as shown in Figure 6-8. Both of these should follow logically from the information presented in the body of the report. If you make a leap in logic, you risk losing credibility with the audience.

RECOMMENDATIONS

On the basis of this study, there would appear to be a definite need for a well-rounded education program at Bowden Industries, Inc. There are numerous possible methods of operating and conducting it. The following recommendations are offered.

1. Appoint a Director of Management Development, preferably a person with sound academic credentials (possibly a Ph.D.), teaching experience in management at the undergraduate and graduate levels, and broad business experience in supervision and management. The appointed person would report directly to the Executive Vice President or to the President.

2. Appoint a Management Education Committee, consisting of the top executive of each of the six divisions in the company and the Executive Vice President (ex officio). This committee would advise the Director of Management Development in planning and operating the program, using as many of the sources described in this report as feasible.

Goodheart-Willcox Publisher

Figure 6-8. Recommendations provide the writer's suggestions for a course of action.

Formatting a Report

The appearance of the document is important. Many organizations have formatting guidelines for reports, while other organizations use templates provided in Microsoft Word or other word processing software. When the topic covers more than one key point or important issue, headings should be used as a design element.

Headings

Headings are words and phrases that introduce sections of text. Headings are tiered, beginning with the section opener title and continuing with the main heading and subheadings. They organize blocks of information in a document and serve as guideposts to alert the reader to what is coming.

Most narrative text can be divided into main topics and subtopics usually with no more than three levels of headings. Figure 6-9 shows examples of different head levels in a document. If a given heading has subheads, it should have at least two subheads. Never have only one subhead below any heading.

Headings are formatted so the main heads have a greater visual impact than the subheads. The lowest level of subhead should have the least visual impact. For example, Heading 1 is in a much larger point size than Heading 3.

The report title is usually set in the default Title style of the word processor. The default settings for this style in Microsoft Word 2016 are 28 points, Calibri Light, and font color Automatic (black).

The first level of head, usually called a *level 1 head* or a *side head*, should begin at the left-hand page margin. Capitalization should follow *title case* in which the first word and all main words in the head are

GS5
Key Applications
2.1

FYI

If planning to use Microsoft Word's automated table of contents feature, it is very important to use the built-in heading styles.

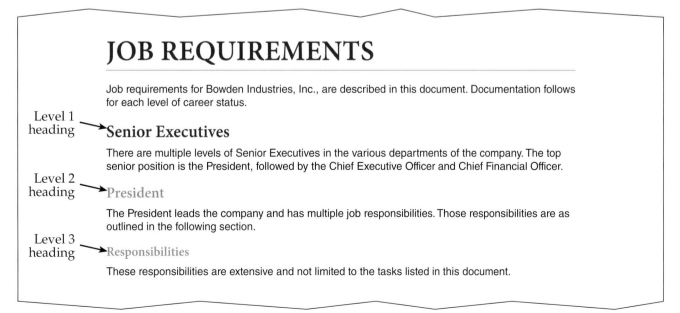

JOB REQUIREMENTS

Job requirements for Bowden Industries, Inc., are described in this document. Documentation follows for each level of career status.

Level 1 heading → **Senior Executives**

There are multiple levels of Senior Executives in the various departments of the company. The top senior position is the President, followed by the Chief Executive Officer and Chief Financial Officer.

Level 2 heading → President

The President leads the company and has multiple job responsibilities. Those responsibilities are as outlined in the following section.

Level 3 heading → Responsibilities

These responsibilities are extensive and not limited to the tasks listed in this document.

Goodheart-Willcox Publisher

Figure 6-9. Levels of headings within the body of a document help to organize information and guide the reader.

capitalized. The default Heading 1 style of the word processor can be used. In Microsoft Word 2016, the default settings are 16 point, Calibri Light, and font color Blue Accent 1 Darker 25%.

The second level of head, usually called a *level 2 head*, should begin at the left-hand page margin. Capitalization should follow title case. The default Heading 2 style of the word processor can be used. In Microsoft Word 2016, the default settings are 13 point, Calibri Light, and font color Blue Accent 1 Darker 25%.

The third level of head, usually called a *level 3 head*, should begin at the left-hand page margin. Capitalization may follow title case or sentence case. In *sentence case*, only the first letter on the line is capitalized. The default Heading 3 style of the word processor can be used. In Microsoft Word 2016, the default settings are 12 point, Calibri Light, and font color Blue Accent 1 Darker 50%.

In most cases, a report should not contain more than three levels of headings. However, if a level 4 head, or paragraph head, is needed, a run-in style should be used. A run-in head is the first sentence in a paragraph. The line should begin at the left-hand page margin. The typeface should be the same as the body text and in the same point size, but should be bolded and is often italicized as well. The font color is usually black, but may be a color if the formatting guidelines allow it. The first word of the run-in head is capitalized, as are any proper nouns. The run-in head should end with a period even though it is not a complete sentence.

Spacing

The left- and right-hand page margins of a report should be 1″ each. The bottom page margin should not be less than 1″. A bottom page margin greater than 1″ is acceptable for pages on which it would be impossible to have the margin be exactly 1″. For example, a heading should not be at the bottom of the page and the first line of body copy underneath it starting at the top of the next page. In this case, add a manual page break before the heading to run the page short and keep the heading with the first line of text beneath it. The top page margin on the first page should be 2″. On all other pages of the report, the top page margin should be 1″.

The report should be single spaced, but the default setting for line spacing of the word processor can be used. In Microsoft Word 2016, the default line spacing is 1.08. Leave a blank line between paragraphs in the report. This can be easily achieved with a paragraph style.

FYI

If the report is to be placed in a binder, the left-hand page margin should be increased to allow for the binding.

HANDS-ON EXAMPLE 6.2.1 ➲

FORMATTING A REPORT

The formatting of a report sets the stage for how the reader will view the information. A properly formatted report communicates professionalism to the reader.

1. Navigate to the student companion website at www.g-wlearning.com, download the data files for this chapter, and save them in the Chap06 folder on your flash drive.
2. Launch Microsoft Word, and open the LandscapeOptions.docx file from the Chap06 folder on your flash drive.
3. Place the insertion point in the first line of the document.
4. Click the Title style in the gallery in the **Styles** group on the **Home** tab of the ribbon. The style is applied to the paragraph.
5. Place the insertion point in the first heading, Landscaping as a Weather Barrier.
6. Click the dialog box launcher in the **Styles** group on the **Home** tab of the ribbon. The **Styles** pane is displayed, as shown.

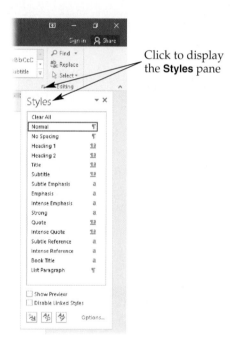

Click to display the **Styles** pane

7. Click the Heading 1 style in the **Styles** pane to apply that style.
8. Applying what you have learned, assign the style Heading 1 to the remaining two headings, Landscaping that Attracts Butterflies and Landscaping to Minimize Water Use.
9. Applying what you have learned, add a blank line between paragraphs in the report. You should add a total of four blank lines.
10. Save the file as *LastName*LandscapeOptions.docx in the Chap06 folder on your flash drive.

GS5
Key Applications
2.5.1

Word
1.3.5

FYI

Page numbers are automatically updated if edits cause pages to change.

Page Numbering

The **folio**, or page number, is placed outside of the body copy. The *header* is at the top of the page, and the *footer* is at the bottom of the page. When content is placed in these areas, it appears on every page. The page number can be placed in the header or footer area, but the standard location is in the header on the second and subsequent pages. The page number should be flush right to the right-hand page margin. A page number is not usually included on the first page of the report. If one is required, it should be placed in the footer and center-aligned.

In addition to the page number, a user may choose to add the document name or a copyright date to the header or footer. For example, a book often displays the chapter number or title in the header along with the page number.

HANDS-ON EXAMPLE 6.2.2

ADDING PAGE NUMBERS

When creating a document for schoolwork, it may be a good idea to include your name in the header or footer. In this way, should the pages of the printout become mixed with those of other students, it will be easy to locate your work.

1. Launch Microsoft Word, and open the *LastName*LandscapeOptions.docx file from the Chap06 folder on your flash drive, if it is not already open.

Add a
Header

2. Click **Insert>Header & Footer>Add a Header** in the ribbon. A drop-down menu is displayed.
3. Click the Blank style in the drop-down menu. The header and footer areas are activated, as shown.

Header area is activated

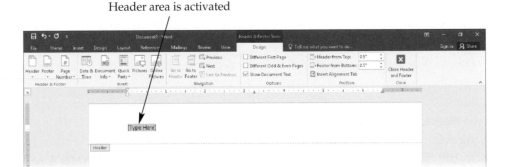

4. Applying what you have learned, replace the placeholder text with your last name, a comma, and a space.
5. Click **Home>Paragraph>Align Right** in the ribbon. The header is aligned to the right-hand margin.

Align
Right

HANDS-ON EXAMPLE 6.2.2 (CONTINUED)

Add Page Numbers

6. With the insertion point at the end of the header, click **Design>Header & Footer>Add Page Numbers** in the ribbon. A drop-down menu is displayed.

7. Click **Current Position>Plain Number** in the drop-down menu that is displayed. A page number is added after your last name.

Close Header and Footer

8. Click **Design>Close>Close Header and Footer** in the ribbon. The header and footer areas are deactivated, and the page layout view of the document is displayed.

9. Scroll through the document, and verify that your name and the page number appear on every page.

10. Save the file.

Title Page

The title of the report should be the first item on the title page. It should begin 2" from the top page margin and be aligned to the left-hand page margin. The font should be 14 points and bold. The text should be set in all uppercase.

Below the title, place the target audience. This is the group or organization for whom the report was written. The text should be center-aligned, and the font should be 11 points.

Below the target audience, place the author's name. The name should begin 5" from the top page margin and be center-aligned. The font should be 11 points, and the text should be set in title case. Using the same formatting, leave a blank line after the author's name, and place the name of the organization to which the author belongs. Below that, using the same formatting, place the date of the report. The date should begin 9" from the top page margin.

Table of Contents

The table of contents (TOC) usually lists the level 1 and level 2 heads in the document. It is not common to list level 3 heads, but if needed these can be included as well. The page number on which the head appears is placed to the right of the head listing in the table of contents. A dotted line, called a leader, is placed between the head listing and its page number. The table of contents usually begins on a new page and ends with a page break so the report content begins on the following page.

Enter the text Table of Contents 2" below the top page margin. Leave two blank lines, and then enter the first level 1 head of the document. Enter a tab and the page number for the heading. On the next line, enter the next head. If a level 2 head, indent the line .5". Level 3 heads should be indented an additional .5".

Many word processors have a feature that automates the creating of a table of contents. The automatic table of contents feature of Microsoft Word is based on the use of predefined styles. Many organizations

> ## FYI
>
> The leader style is set with the tab formatting.
>
>
> **Word**
> 4.2.1

allow the default settings to be used, but the styles can be modified to match accepted standards. When Word generates a table of contents, it will include any text that has been assigned the Heading 1, Heading 2, or Heading 3 style. The page numbers are automatically included.

HANDS-ON EXAMPLE 6.2.3

Word
4.2.2

CREATING A TABLE OF CONTENTS

The table of contents is an important element for long reports. It allows the reader to quickly locate information within the report.

Table of Contents

1. Launch Microsoft Word, and open the *LastName*LandscapeOptions.docx file from the Chap06 folder on your flash drive, if it is not already open.
2. Place the insertion point at the beginning of the document. The table of contents will be added at the insertion point. Note: when the title page is added later, it should come before the table of contents.
3. Click **References>Table of Contents>Table of Contents** in the ribbon. A drop-down menu is displayed.
4. Click **Automatic Table 2** in the drop-down menu. The table of contents is automatically generated. Note what is included. Also make note of the page numbers listed.
5. Applying what you have learned, add a manual page break after the table of contents and before the title text.
6. Scroll to the table of contents, and click anywhere in it. The table of contents changes into a table format, which is used to update the TOC.
7. Click the **Update Table...** button above the TOC. The **Update Table** dialog box is displayed.
8. Click the **Update entire table** radio button, and click the **OK** button. The page numbers in the TOC are updated to reflect the addition of the page break.
9. Click anywhere outside of the table of contents to deselect it.
10. Save the file.

Word
4.1

Citations

When writing a research paper, many ideas and factual information come from other publications. The author must tell the reader exactly where the information originated. This is done through citations. **Citations** generally include the author, publication date, source document, URL, and other relevant information for material that is referenced or paraphrased within the document. It is necessary to provide citations for both print and electronic sources.

Citations usually appear as footnotes or endnotes. **Footnotes** are numbered annotations that appear once at the bottom of a page, as shown in Figure 6-10. **Endnotes** perform the same job, but appear at the end of the document, and contain the same information as a bibliography. Many word processors, including Microsoft Word, have a function to automatically create a bibliography of the sources used to write a report.

WORKS CITED

Arbor, Jonathan Cole, "Training That Works." *Train the Trainer* (March 20--) pp. 23–25.

Coletta, Nicole, *The Essentials of Performance Management*. New York: Future Publishing, 2010.

Newberg, Alexis, "Formal Training Programs at Bowden Industries," Report Submitted to the Executive Board, Bowden Training Department, 2009.

Goodheart-Willcox Publisher

Figure 6-10. Always cite works that are referenced in the document.

There are many ways to format citations. In general, it is best to follow the formatting specified by a style guide. Style guides are specifications for formatting, word usage, and other aspects of creating a document. Common style guides include APA, MLA, Chicago, and AP. Microsoft Word allows the user to select among many common style guides to control how automatically generated bibliographies appear.

APA Style

The *Publication Manual of the American Psychological Association*, which is usually simply called the APA style guide, is popular in many fields, including the sciences. The writing style dictated by this guide is also known as the Harvard Style of writing.

The APA style guide calls for reports to be double-spaced on 8 1/2 × 11 inch paper set in Times New Roman typeface in 10 or 12 points. Note that this differs from the specifications outlined in this chapter. The paper should have a title page, an abstract, a main body, and references. The report title and the folio should appear in the header right-aligned.

A citation is listed in a bibliography at the end of the document. Where the citation is referenced in the body of the document, the notation is placed within the sentence so it is clear what information is being quoted or paraphrased and whose information is being cited. Many other specifications appear in the guide.

MLA Style

The *MLA Style Manual and Guide to Scholarly Publishing* is popular for English classes, graduate classes, and general papers. It is published by the Modern Language Association of America.

The MLA style calls for no title page or abstract section. The author's name, the instructor's name, the course, and the date are placed in the upper left-hand corner of the first page. The author's last name followed by a space and page number is placed in the header and right-aligned. This is similar to the header created earlier. The bibliography is called Works Cited and appears at the end of the document. Many other specifications appear in the guide.

FYI

Footnote and endnote properties can be modified by selecting a footnote or endnote style by selecting the **Manage Styles** button from the Styles pane. Select a footnote or endnote style from the list in the **Manage Styles** menu, then select **Modify**.

Word
4.1.2

HANDS-ON EXAMPLE 6.2.4

ADDING CITATIONS

When other information is paraphrased in a report, the source of the information must be cited. This provides validity to the information and acknowledges the owner of the material.

1. Launch Microsoft Word, and open the *LastName*LandscapeOptions.docx file from the Chap06 folder on your flash drive, if it is not already open.
2. Click **References>Citations & Bibliography>Bibliography Style:** in the ribbon, and click **MLA** in the drop-down list. This sets the style guide to use.
3. In the numbered list in the document, place the insertion point after the final *d* in the line *Willow hybrid*.

Insert Citation

4. Click **References>Citations & Bibliography>Insert Citation** in the ribbon, and click **Add New Source...** in the drop-down menu. The **Create Source** dialog box is displayed, as shown.

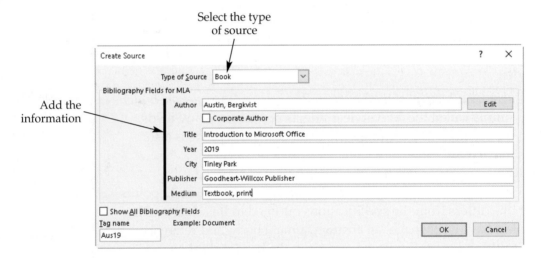

Select the type of source

Add the information

5. Click the **Type of Source** drop-down list at the top of the dialog box, and click **Book** in the list.
6. Fill in the fields in the dialog box using information for this textbook. Notice that information appears at the bottom of the dialog box related to which text box is active. Use this to help fill in the proper information.
7. Click the **OK** button to add the citation. The author's name appears in parentheses where the insertion point was.
8. Applying what you have learned, add a new page to the end of the document.

Bibliography

9. Click **References>Citations & Bibliography>Bibliography** in the ribbon, and click **Works Cited** in the drop-down menu. The bibliography is automatically created and follows the MLA style for citations.
10. Save the file.

Captions

Users can create captions for figures and tables directly in Microsoft Word without having to insert a text box. This is especially helpful in describing visual aids that accompany reports and other formal documents. To insert a caption, click **References**>**Captions**>**Insert Caption**. In the drop-down list next to the **Label** field, select the desired caption type. Enter the caption in the **Caption** field and select **OK**. Once a caption has been added, a new style will appear in the style gallery called Caption. To modify the properties of this style, right-click the style and select **Modify** in the shortcut menu. From here, the user can adjust the font, size, color, and type, as well as other properties.

> **Word**
>
> 4.1.6, 4.1.7

6.2 | SECTION REVIEW

 ### CHECK YOUR UNDERSTANDING

1. What are the three common types of reports?
2. What is the first step in the writing process, and what is its purpose?
3. What is the folio?
4. How many levels of headings are usually listed in the table of contents?
5. When is a citation needed?

BUILD YOUR VOCABULARY

As you progress through this course, develop a personal IT glossary. This will help you build your vocabulary and prepare you for a career. Write a definition for each of the following terms and add it to your IT glossary.

analytical report	introduction
citation	primary research
conclusion	proposal
data	qualitative data
endnote	quantitative data
folio	recommendation
footnote	secondary research
heading	table of contents
informational report	

SECTION 6.3

ETHICAL PRACTICES FOR INTELLECTUAL PROPERTY

With so much information available on the Internet, it is possible to read about almost any topic. At one time, this information was only found in encyclopedias or reference volumes in libraries. The ease of access to information as well as the ability to copy material reinforces the importance of properly using the information. Just because information can be quickly located and accessed from home does not mean the information is free to use. Laws are in place to protect information. Improper use of information is not only unethical; in most cases, it is illegal.

Ethical use of computers and information is an important part of society. Ethics are common standards of moral behavior. Computer ethics defines how people use computers in morally acceptable ways. What users do with information, how they acknowledge its source, and to whom they give it all have ethical implications.

Dragon Images/Shutterstock.com

TERMS

antipiracy technology

common knowledge

copyright

Creative Commons (CC) license

Electronic User's Bill of Rights

fair use doctrine

intellectual property

licensing agreement

open source

paraphrasing

patent

piracy

plagiarism

public domain

quotation

service mark

trademark

LEARNING GOALS

After completing this section, you will be able to:
- Explain intellectual property.
- Identify software piracy.
- Properly use information.
- Discuss the Electronic User's Bill of Rights.

222

Copyright Goodheart-Willcox Co., Inc.

Intellectual Property

The Internet provides countless sources for obtaining text, images, video, audio, and software. Even though this material is readily available, this does not make it free to use however you choose. The creators or owners of this material have certain legal rights. **Intellectual property** is something that comes from a person's mind, such as an idea, invention, or process. Intellectual property laws protect a person's or a company's inventions, artistic works, and other intellectual property. These laws apply not only to material on the Internet, but to printed materials, broadcast media, and materials in any form.

Copyright

A **copyright** acknowledges ownership of a work and specifies that only the owner has the right to sell the work, use it, or give permission for someone else to sell or use it. Any use of copyrighted material without permission is called *infringement*. Copyright laws cover all original work, whether it is in print, on the Internet, or in any other form.

Most information on the Internet is copyrighted, whether it is text, graphics, illustrations, or digital media. This means you cannot reuse it without first obtaining permission from the owner. Sometimes, the owner of the material has placed the material on the Internet for others to reuse. However, if this is not explicitly stated, assume the material is copyrighted and cannot be freely used.

Copyrighted material is indicated by the © symbol or the statement "copyright by." However, lack of the symbol or statement does not mean the material is not copyrighted. All original material is automatically copyrighted as soon as it is in tangible form. An idea cannot be copyrighted. It is the expression of an idea that is copyrighted. A copyright can be registered with the US Copyright Office, which is part of the Library of Congress. However, original material is still legally protected whether or not the copyright is registered or the symbol or statement is included.

Fair use doctrine allows individuals to use copyrighted works without permission in limited situations under very strict guidelines. Fair use doctrine allows copyrighted material to be used for the purpose of describing or reviewing the work. For example, a student writing about the material in an original report falls under fair use doctrine. Another is a product-review website providing editorial comment. Fair use doctrine does not change the copyright or ownership of the material used under the doctrine.

In some cases, individuals or organizations may wish to allow others to use their intellectual property without needing permission. Sometimes, this type of use assignment is called copyleft, which is a play on the word copyright. One popular method of allowing use of intellectual property is a Creative Commons license. A **Creative Commons (CC) license** is a specialized copyright license that allows free distribution of copyrighted work. If the creator of the work wants to give the public the ability to use, share, or advance his or her original work, a Creative Commons license provides that flexibility. The creator maintains the copyright and can specify how the copyrighted work can be used. For example, one type of Creative Commons license prohibits commercial use.

Public domain refers to material that is not owned by anybody and can be used without permission. Material can enter the public domain when a copyright expires and is not renewed. Additionally, the owner of material may choose to give up ownership and place the material in the public domain. Much of the material created by federal, state, or local governments is often in the public domain. This is because taxpayer money was used to create it. However, in some cases, material from governmental sources may be copyrighted, so be sure to verify the status before using the material.

Patent

A **patent** gives a person or company the right to be the sole producer of a product for a defined period of time. Patents protect an invention that is functional or mechanical. The invention must be considered useful and nonobvious, and it must be operational. This means that an idea may not be patented. A process can be patented under certain conditions. The process must be related to a particular machine or transform a substance or item into a different state or thing.

Trademark

A **trademark** protects taglines, slogans, names, symbols, or any unique method to identify a product or company. A **service mark** is similar to a trademark, but it identifies a service rather than a product. Trademarks and service marks do not protect a work or product, they only protect the way in which the product is described. The term "trademark" is often used to refer to both trademarks and service marks. Trademarks never expire.

The symbols used to indicate a trademark or service mark are called graphic marks. Some graphic marks can be used without being formally registered, as shown in Figure 6-11.

Correct Usage of Graphic Marks	
TM	Trademark, not registered
SM	Service mark, not registered
®	Registered trademark

Goodheart-Willcox Publisher

Figure 6-11. Graphic marks are symbols that indicate legal protection of intellectual property.

Software Piracy

Piracy is the unethical and illegal copying or downloading of software, files, or other protected material. Examples of protected material include images, movies, and music. It is illegal to copy protected material or download it from the Internet if the owner has not given permission to do so. Software installed at your school or office is licensed to that entity. It is piracy to take that software and install it at home. Piracy is a form of stealing and carries a heavy penalty, including fines and incarceration.

A software or video game developer will work for months, investing time and money, to make a program or a game. The developer not only owns the software, but also wants to earn a return on the investment of time and money. Piracy hurts the developer because it is the theft of the developer's product. To counter piracy, **antipiracy technology** has been developed that makes it very difficult for someone to use pirated software. Common antipiracy technology for software includes the activation key and the device ID. An activation key is a code the user must enter during the installation process. A device ID is a unique identifier based on the machine on which the software is installed, and the software will function only on that machine.

An organization called the BSA/The Software Alliance is an advocate for the software industry. Among its many efforts, it tracks pirated software. In its most recent report, dated 2016, it concluded that 39% of all software used in the world is pirated. It estimates 90% of the computers in one country use pirated software. Conversely, in the United States, an estimated 17% of the computers use pirated software. Even though this figure is lower, it still represents that nearly one-fifth of all software in the United States is being used illegally. The commercial value of software used illegally worldwide is estimated to be nearly $63 billion, which is money lost to the software industry.

There is legislation in place in most countries to prevent software piracy. However, the laws have to be strongly enforced by the local government. The use of pirated software is most prevalent in developing countries.

Licensing Agreement

A **licensing agreement** is a contract that gives one party permission to market, produce, or use the product or service owned by another party. The agreement grants a license in return for a fee or royalty payment. When buying software, the purchaser is agreeing to follow the terms of a license, which is the legal permission to use a software program. All software has terms of use that explain how and when the software may be used. Figure 6-12 explains the characteristics of different software licensing.

Characteristics of Software Types			
Characteristics	**Software Type**		
	For-Purchase	**Freeware**	**Shareware**
Cost	• Must be purchased to use • Demo may be available	• Never have to pay for it	• Free to try • Pay to upgrade to full functionality
Features	• Full functionality	• Full functionality	• Limited functionality without upgrade

Goodheart-Willcox Publisher

Figure 6-12. Each type of software has specific licensing permissions.

Alternative-usage rights for software programs are typically covered by the GNU General Public License (GNU GPL). The GNU GPL guarantees all users the freedom to use, study, share, and modify the software. The term **open source** applies to software that has had its source code made available to the public at no charge and with no restrictions on use or modification. Open-source software can be downloaded and used for free and can also be modified and distributed by anyone. However, part or all of the code of open-source software may be owned by an individual or organization.

Ethics

Terms of Use

All software has a terms of use agreement. Social media sites also have terms of use agreements. Most websites that you have to "join" have terms of use agreements. It is unethical, and in many cases illegal, to violate the terms of use.

Terms of Use

Many websites list rules called the *terms of use* that must be followed for downloaded files or for participating in the online community. The agreement may come up automatically, for example, if you are downloading a file or software application. If you want to use an image or text from a website, look for the terms of use. Unless the terms of use specifically states that you are free to copy and use the material, assume the material cannot be reused without permission.

Proper Usage of Information

Scanning or photocopying a document does not make the content yours. Similarly, copying someone's published work is unethical and illegal. It is very easy to copy and paste text from electronic resources. Therefore, it is important for users to know what constitutes proper usage of information.

GS5
Living Online
1.1.8

Plagiarism

Plagiarism is claiming another person's material as your own, which is both unethical and illegal. If you must refer to someone else's work, follow intellectual property laws to ethically acquire the information. Use standard methods of citing sources, as discussed earlier in this chapter. However, if you *copy* the work of others without permission, even if you credit the source, you are committing plagiarism.

Computer technology has also made it fairly easy to detect plagiarism. There are services that scan for plagiarism. Educators can use these services to check the originality of a student's paper. Businesses can use the services to check the originality of submitted material. Programs such as Turnitin, Grammarly, Dustball, Dupli Checker, and Viper can check documents. There are student versions of this type of software that can be used so a student can determine if an assignment contains all required citations. Some are free. However, they must be downloaded on a personal system.

Another way of using the Internet to find the original source of published text is to enter that text directly into a search engine. Depending on the search engine's capabilities, it may locate a source for the text.

HANDS-ON EXAMPLE 6.3.1

LOCATING INFORMATION'S SOURCE

The Internet is a great resource for locating information. It can be used to find material to support your original work or to locate the source of information.

1. Launch a web browser, and navigate to a search engine.
2. Enter the following quotation into the search box *exactly* as shown, including punctuation. Be careful not to mistype or misspell anything.

> But where do we stand today? The government's official measure of poverty shows that poverty has actually increased slightly since the Johnson administration, rising from 14.2 percent in 1967 to 15 percent in 2012.

3. Count the number of websites that contain these exact words.
4. Identify the publication in which the original work appeared.
5. Identify the authors of the original work.

Common Knowledge

Common knowledge consists of notions and factual information that can be found in a variety of places. Nobody can claim ownership of common knowledge and, therefore, it can be used by anybody. When using ideas that are common knowledge, the author does not need to let the reader know the source. A citation is not required for common knowledge.

An example of common knowledge is that a water molecule is composed of hydrogen and oxygen. Another example is Jupiter is the largest planet that revolves around the Sun. These are both examples of factual information.

Paraphrasing

Paraphrasing means expressing an idea using different words. It is summarizing the work in your own words. When using someone else's material as the basis for your own work, such as a report, do not copy the material. Instead, paraphrase portions of the work and use that to support your own original material. Note, however, that extensive paraphrasing is generally considered to be the same as copying the original material. In other words, use limited paraphrasing to *support* your original work, but do not use paraphrasing as a *replacement* for your original work.

When something has been paraphrased, the thought or research is not original. Therefore, a citation is required. This properly credits the original source of the material.

Quotation

In some cases, the best way to present another's words is exactly as they were originally written. A **quotation** is an exact repeat of a passage of another author's work. A quotation should generally be short, such as a single sentence or a brief paragraph. While there is no set rule as to the acceptable length of a quote, presenting a quote longer than this is generally considered to be a *copy* of the original material, not a quotation of it. It is important that the quotation not be used out of context or in a manner that changes its meaning or implies an intention not present in the original work. As with paraphrasing, a quotation should support your original work, not be a substitute for your original work.

The quotation must be placed within opening and closing quotation marks ("…"). Often, quotations are indented from the body text on both the left- and right-hand sides. Quotations must be properly cited to credit the original source.

Electronic User's Bill of Rights

The **Electronic User's Bill of Rights** details the rights and responsibilities of both individuals and institutions regarding the treatment of digital information. It was originally proposed in 1993 by Frank W. Connolly of American University. It is modeled after the original United States Bill of Rights, although it contains only four articles. The articles are not legally binding, but contain guidelines for appropriate use of digital information. The articles in the Electronic User's Bill of Rights are:

- Article I: Individual Rights
- Article II: Individual Responsibilities
- Article III: Rights of Educational Institutions
- Article IV: Institutional Responsibilities

Article I focuses on the rights and freedoms of the users of computers and the Internet. It states "citizens of the electronic community of learners" have the right to access computers and informational resources. They should be informed when their personal information is being collected. They have the right to review and correct the information that has been collected. Users should have freedom of speech and have rights of ownership for their intellectual property.

Article II focuses on the responsibilities that come with those rights outlined in Article I. A citizen of the electronic community is responsible for seeking information and using it effectively. It is also the individual's responsibility to honor the intellectual property of others. This includes verifying the accuracy of information obtained electronically. It also includes respecting the privacy of others, and using electronic resources wisely.

Article III states the right of educational institutions to access computers and informational resources. Like individuals, an educational institution retains ownership of its intellectual property. Each institution has the right to use its resources as it sees fit.

Article IV focuses on the responsibilities that come with the rights granted in Article III. Educational institutions are held accountable for the information they use and provide. Institutions are responsible for creating and maintaining "an environment wherein trust and intellectual freedom are the foundation for individual and institutional growth and success."

6.3 SECTION REVIEW

CHECK YOUR UNDERSTANDING

1. What acknowledges ownership of a work and specifies that only the owner has the right to sell the work, use it, or give permission for someone else to sell or use it?
2. How does the fair use doctrine allow the use of protected material?
3. What illegal act is a person committing who creates an unauthorized copy of software?
4. If you submit somebody else's term paper as your own, what have you committed?
5. What does the Electronic User's Bill of Rights describe?

BUILD YOUR VOCABULARY

As you progress through this course, develop a personal IT glossary. This will help you build your vocabulary and prepare you for a career. Write a definition for each of the following terms and add it to your IT glossary.

antipiracy technology
common knowledge
copyright
Creative Commons (CC) license
Electronic User's Bill of Rights
fair use doctrine
intellectual property
licensing agreement

open source
paraphrasing
patent
piracy
plagiarism
public domain
quotation
service mark
trademark

6 REVIEW AND ASSESSMENT

Chapter Summary

Section 6.1
Creating a Business Letter

- Letters are messages printed on stationery, often letterhead, and should conform to workplace standards. The two standard formats for a business letter are block style and modified-block style.

- Standardized letter formats contain various elements. Block-style and modified-block-style letters include: date, inside address, salutation, body, complimentary close, signature, and notations.

- Beyond the standard elements, a business letter may contain other elements. The attention line, subject line, and postscript may or may not be included.

- It is important to follow the accepted standard format for business letters. Using nonstandard formatting makes the letter appear unprofessional, and the message of the letter may not be effectively communicated.

Section 6.2
Creating a Report

- The three common types of reports are informational reports, analytical reports, and proposals. Informational reports contain facts, data, or other types of information; analytical reports contain both information and analysis of the data; and proposals typically contain a specific idea and attempt to persuade the reader.

- Many organizations have formatting guidelines for reports or a template can be used. When the topic covers more than one key point or important issue, headings should be used as a design element.

Section 6.3
Ethical Practices for Intellectual Property

- Intellectual property is something that comes from a person's mind, such as an idea, invention, or process. Intellectual property laws apply not only to material on the Internet, but to printed materials, broadcast media, and materials in any form.

- Piracy is the unethical and illegal copying or downloading of software, files, or other protected material. To counter piracy, antipiracy technology has been developed that makes it very difficult for someone to use pirated software.

- Plagiarism is claiming another person's material as your own, which is both unethical and illegal. The work can be paraphrased to support your own work, but it must be properly cited.

- The Electronic User's Bill of Rights details the rights and responsibilities of both individuals and institutions regarding the treatment of digital information. Its articles are Article I: Individual Rights, Article II: Individual Responsibilities, Article III: Rights of Educational Institutions, and Article IV: Institutional Responsibilities.

Now that you have finished this chapter, see what you know about computer applications by taking the chapter posttest. Access the posttest by visiting www.g-wlearning.com. ⤤

Chapter 6 Test

Multiple Choice

Select the best response.

1. Which of the following is not included in a letterhead?
   A. Company name
   B. Date
   C. Address
   D. Logo

2. What always begins a salutation?
   A. Hello
   B. Dear
   C. Hi
   D. There is no beginning to a salutation.

3. Which of the following is primary research?
   A. Reading a newspaper article.
   B. Locating an analytical report on the Internet.
   C. Interviewing several people who witnessed an event.
   D. Watching a documentary on an event.

4. Which of the following styles will be automatically included in the table of contents in a Microsoft Word document?
   A. Normal
   B. Title
   C. Footnote
   D. Heading 1

5. What is the term describing something that comes from a person's mind, such as an idea, invention, or process?
   A. Intellectual property
   B. Copyright
   C. Plagiarism
   D. Common knowledge

Completion

Complete the following sentences with the correct word(s).

6. In a(n) _____-style letter, all elements are to be flush to the left-hand page margin.

7. _____ are words and phrases that introduce sections of text in a document.

8. APA, MLA, Chicago, and AP are examples of _____, which contain specifications for formatting, word usage, and other aspects of creating a document.

9. _____ is copying information and claiming it as your own.

10. The act of copying video games without permission of the author is considered _____.

Matching

Match the correct term with its definition.

A. endnotes
B. table of contents
C. fair use doctrine
D. complimentary close
E. MLA

11. Sign-off for a letter.

12. Lists the major sections and subsections within the report with page numbers.

13. Numbered annotations that appear at the end of document.

14. A style guide for formatting, word usage, and other aspects of creating documents.

15. Allows individuals to use copyrighted works without permission in limited situations under very strict guidelines.

Application and Extension of Knowledge

1. Start a new document, and create paragraph styles for the parts of a business letter. Define each style according to the formatting described in this chapter. Write a two-paragraph letter to your instructor explaining how useful word processing is in your schoolwork.

2. Use the help feature in Microsoft Word to find out how to print an envelope for the letter you created in #1. Using what you learned, print the envelope, enclose the letter, and give it to your instructor.

3. Conduct research comparing and contrasting desktop-publishing software and word-processing software. Prepare a presentation illustrating the similarities and differences.

4. Identify a well-known business of your choosing. Investigate the company to see if it has any trademarks and patents. Based on your findings, prepare for a class discussion to describe how this company protects its intellectual property.

5. Use the help feature in Microsoft Word to find out how to add a table of contents to a document. List the steps for creating a TOC. Include an explanation of how to update the TOC after changes have been made to the document.

Online Activities

Complete the following activities, which will help you learn, practice, and expand your knowledge and skills.

Vocabulary. Practice vocabulary for this chapter using the e-flash cards, matching activity, and vocabulary game until you are able to recognize their meanings.

Communication Skills

Writing. Writing style is the way in which a writer uses language to convey an idea. Select a page or pages of notes you have taken during a class. Evaluate your writing style and the relevance, quality, and depth of the information. Once you have done so, write a one-page paper that synthesizes your notes into complete sentences and thoughts.

Reading. After you have read this chapter, determine the central ideas and review the conclusions made by the author. Demonstrate your understanding of the information by retelling or summarizing what you read.

Speaking. To become career ready, it is necessary to utilize critical-thinking skills in order to solve problems. Give an example of a problem that you needed to solve that was important to your success at work or school. Explain your solution to the class.

Internet Research

Skills Search. Self-assessment tools can help you decide which career opportunities might be a good fit for you. Visit the O*NET Resource Center online and select one of their assessments called Career Exploration Tools. Create a chart listing skills you possess, careers that match those skills, and skills you will need to develop for those careers. Share your findings with the class.

Teamwork

Meet with a group of your classmates and take turns describing IT skills that you have acquired in school or elsewhere, such as volunteer or after-school work, or in your free time. Using word-processing software, list one or two skills for each team member. Working together, write a description of each skill.

Activity Files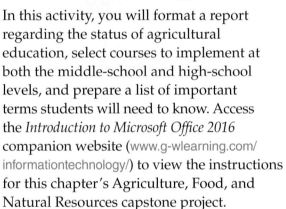

Visit www.g-wlearning.com/informationtechnology/ to download the activity files for this chapter. These activities will expand your learning of the material presented in this chapter and allow you to practice what you have learned. Follow the instructions provided in each file to complete the activity.

Activity File 6-1 Downloading and Using Templates

Activity File 6-2 Modifying Templates

Activity File 6-3 Drafting Business Letters

Activity File 6-4 Software Piracy

CAPSTONE PROJECT

The capstone project builds from one chapter to the next. It allows you to apply the skills you have learned to create a complete project in a desired career area. Read the instructions below for the career area you chose to work in for this course. Work in the same career area in each chapter.

Agriculture, Food, and Natural Resources

In this activity, you will format a report regarding the status of agricultural education, select courses to implement at both the middle-school and high-school levels, and prepare a list of important terms students will need to know. Access the *Introduction to Microsoft Office 2016* companion website (www.g-wlearning.com/informationtechnology/) to view the instructions for this chapter's Agriculture, Food, and Natural Resources capstone project.

Business, Management, and Administration

In this activity, you will assume the role of an administrator in a small, growing, widget-manufacturing business. You will create letters and reports for the company and use these to communicate the reorganization process planned for the company. Access the *Introduction to Microsoft Office 2016* companion website (www.g-wlearning.com/informationtechnology/) to view the instructions for this chapter's Business, Management, and Administration capstone project.

Health Science

In this activity, you will format a report of medical testing results, draft business letters to patients outlining test results and definitions, conduct research of advanced courses you can take, and learn how to cite other health science professionals. Access the *Introduction to Microsoft Office 2016* companion website (www.g-wlearning.com/informationtechnology/) to view the instructions for this chapter's Health Science capstone project.

Science, Technology, Engineering, and Mathematics

In this activity, you will assume the role of a NASA communications team member for the Near-Earth Object Project. You will create letters and reports for the communications department that will be used to communicate internally and to the public. Access the *Introduction to Microsoft Office 2016* companion website (www.g-wlearning.com/informationtechnology/) to view the instructions for this chapter's Science, Technology, Engineering, and Mathematics capstone project.

7

PRESENTATION SOFTWARE

SECTIONS

7.1 CREATING A PROFESSIONAL PRESENTATION

7.2 ADDING TRANSITIONS AND ANIMATIONS

7.3 CHARTS, TABLES, AND HANDOUTS

CHECK YOUR IT IQ

Before you begin this chapter, see what you already know about computer applications by taking the chapter pretest. Access the pretest by visiting www.g-wlearning.com. ↗

Presentation software is used to present information in a visual medium. When given to an audience, the presentation is usually projected on a large screen or screens for the audience to see. A presentation can also be distributed for individual viewing. A presentation is commonly posted on a website so the audience can access it later or for those who could not attend. This is also a way to distribute the presentation instead of delivering it in front of an audience in a room.

Presentation software provides the ability to create, edit, and display the slides. The three major functions of the software are: a text editor, allowing words to be inserted and formatted; a technique for adding and manipulating graphic images; and a slide-show system to display the contents. Graphic and textual elements can be animated with smooth transitions between slides. Handouts can be created from a presentation to provide the audience with a copy of the presentation to take with them.

MICROSOFT OFFICE SPECIALIST OBJECTIVES

PowerPoint

Create and Manage Presentations

1.1 Create a Presentation
- **1.1.1** Create a new presentation
- **1.1.2** Create a presentation based on a template
- **1.1.3** Import Word document outlines

1.2 Insert and Format Slides
- **1.2.1** Insert specific slide layouts
- **1.2.2** Duplicate existing slides
- **1.2.3** Hide and unhide slides
- **1.2.4** Delete slides
- **1.2.5** Apply a different slide layout
- **1.2.6** Modify individual slide backgrounds
- **1.2.7** Insert slide headers, footers, and page numbers

1.3 Modify Slides, Handouts, and Notes
- **1.3.1** Change the slide master theme or background
- **1.3.2** Modify slide master content
- **1.3.3** Create a slide layout
- **1.3.4** Modify a slide layout
- **1.3.5** Modify the handout master
- **1.3.6** Modify the notes master

1.4 Order and Group Slides
- **1.4.1** Create sections
- **1.4.2** Modify slide order
- **1.4.3** Rename sections

1.5 Change Presentation Options and Views
- **1.5.1** Change slide size

1.6 Configure a Presentation for Print
- **1.6.1** Print all or part of a presentation
- **1.6.2** Print notes pages
- **1.6.3** Print handouts
- **1.6.4** Print in color, grayscale, or black and white

1.7 Configure and Present a Slide Show
- **1.7.1** Create custom slide shows
- **1.7.2** Configure slide show options
- **1.7.3** Rehearse slide show timing
- **1.7.4** Present a slide show by using Presenter view

Insert and Format Text, Shapes, and Images

2.1 Insert and Format Text
- **2.1.1** Insert text on a slide
- **2.1.4** Format text in multiple columns
- **2.1.6** Insert hyperlinks

2.2 Insert and Format Shapes and Text Boxes
- **2.2.1** Insert or replace shapes
- **2.2.5** Apply styles to shapes and text boxes

2.3 Insert and Format Images
- **2.3.1** Insert images
- **2.3.2** Resize and crop images

Insert Tables, Charts, SmartArt, and Media

3.1 Insert and Format Tables
- **3.1.1** Create a table
- **3.1.2** Insert and delete table rows and columns
- **3.1.3** Apply table styles
- **3.1.4** Import a table

3.2 Insert and Format Charts
- **3.2.1** Create a chart
- **3.2.2** Import a chart
- **3.2.3** Change the Chart Type
- **3.2.4** Add a legend to a chart
- **3.2.5** Change the chart style of a chart

3.4 Insert and Manage Media
- **3.4.1** Insert audio and video clips
- **3.4.2** Configure media playback options
- **3.4.3** Adjust media window size
- **3.4.4** Set the video start and stop time
- **3.4.5** Set media timing options

Apply Transitions and Animations

4.1 Apply Slide Transitions
- **4.1.1** Insert slide transitions
- **4.1.2** Set transition effect options

4.2 Animate Slide Content
- **4.2.1** Apply animations to objects
- **4.2.2** Apply animations to text
- **4.2.3** Set animation effect options
- **4.2.4** Set animation paths

4.3 Set Timing for Transitions and Animations
- **4.3.1** Set transition effect duration
- **4.3.2** Configure transition start and finish options
- **4.3.3** Reorder animations on a slide

Manage Multiple Presentations

5.1 Merge Content from Multiple Presentations
- **5.1.1** Insert slides from another presentation
- **5.1.2** Compare two presentations

5.2 Finalize Presentations
- **5.2.3** Proof a presentation
- **5.2.5** Export presentations to other formats

Excel

Create Tables

3.2 Manage Table Styles and Options
- **3.2.1** Apply styles to tables

Word

Create and Manage Documents

1.2 Navigate Through a Document
- **1.2.2** Insert hyperlinks

Access

Build Tables

2.1 Create Tables
- **2.1.4** Import tables from other databases

CREATING A PROFESSIONAL PRESENTATION

Presentation software is used to create presentations in a slide-show format. The Microsoft Office software used to create presentations is Microsoft PowerPoint. This software contains features to present information in colorful, interesting formats. Text and graphics can be added to slides to enhance the information. Graphics can also be used to improve the visual interest and provide a mood for the presentation.

Creating a professional presentation begins with defining the purpose and planning the presentation. Everything added to the presentation should support the purpose. It is easy to add graphics, animations, and transitions, but this does not mean that the presentation should be filled with these elements. This section discusses how to create a professional presentation by modifying an existing presentation.

VGstockstudio/Shutterstock.com

LEARNING GOALS

After completing this section, you will be able to:
- Plan a formal presentation.
- Discuss how to navigate through a presentation.
- Explain how to rearrange, delete, and copy slides.

TERMS

attention grabber
clincher
external audience
graphic
internal audience
presentation
scope
slide master
theme

Purpose and Planning

A **presentation** is a speech, address, or demonstration given to a group. This type of presentation is sometimes called *public speaking.* Presentation software is used to create a slide show to accompany a presentation. The goal of creating a slide show, or visual presentation, is to educate or entertain an audience. To accomplish this requires engaging both visual and auditory learning mechanisms of the audience. A visual presentation is an excellent teaching tool because it can be used to simplify complex material. Presentation software can help create a strong impression through use of color, and it can help a speaker make efficient use of the time during a presentation. There are many terms associated with presentation software, as shown in Figure 7-1.

When designing a presentation, it is important to consider who the intended audience is and where the presentation will be viewed. A large audience in an auditorium will see and hear things differently than a small group in a classroom. The speaker can maximize readability by formatting the presentation so it can be easily viewed by everyone, regardless of the size of the room.

Planning a Formal Presentation

Formal presentations vary greatly in length, topic, and level of formality. Sometimes one speaker does all of the talking. In other presentations, two or more people share the responsibility, as in a panel discussion. Often the presentation includes a question-and-answer

Green Tech

Green Presentations
Many companies find that being good stewards of the environment can help increase sales and profits. This is because consumers often hold companies in higher regard when they have environmentally friendly policies. Green presenters post presentations to a website. Interested audience members can review information about the presentation online. This saves a number of resources.

Alignment	How text or another element is positioned on the slide. Horizontally, the element may be flush left, flush right, or centered left-to-right. Vertically, the element may be flush top, flush bottom, or centered top-to-bottom.
Bulleted list	Separate lines of text with a small graphic, such as a dot, in front of the line. Also called an unordered list.
Citation	A notation indicating the source of information in a document.
Font	A set of characters of a typeface in one specific style and size.
Footer	Text that appears at the bottom of every slide in a presentation.
Format	The appearance of text or other elements.
Heading	A word or phrase placed at the beginning of the slide to indicate the topic of the slide; also called a title.
Indentation	The amount text is moved in or out from the standard margin.
Margin	The points at the top, bottom, left, and right of the slide beyond which text is not placed.
Numbered list	Consists of separate lines of text with numbers in sequential order in front of the text. Also called an ordered list.
Orientation	How the slide will be placed on the sheet when printed and on screen.
Typeface	The design of characters. May be serif, sans serif, or decorative.

Goodheart-Willcox Publisher

Figure 7-1. Common terms related to presentations and a brief explanation of each.

session, allowing the audience to participate. The audience may be coworkers or customers. It may be professionals from other companies or some other group with a shared interest in the topic.

Why Are You Presenting?

When writing a formal presentation, first determine the purpose. Speeches are generally made for the purpose of informing or persuading the listener. Speaking to inform usually includes sharing descriptions or definitions about a topic. The content is structured and may sound like the speaker is telling a story. Speaking to persuade involves convincing a person to take the course of action you propose. A persuasive speech requires that the presenter be clear about what is needed from the audience. It has the goal of trying to convince the listeners to agree with the information that is being shared.

Who Is the Audience?

It is important to identify who will be attending your presentation. First, note whether the individuals are internal or external to the organization. An **internal audience** has a specific background and experience. It can be assumed the listeners have a basis for and can relate to at least some of the information that is being conveyed. An **external audience** will probably need more background information about your topic. Analyze the audience to evaluate interest in what you have to say. You can then determine the best way to gain their attention.

What Is the Topic?

Before writing a presentation, the subject must be selected. The subject is a broad idea of what the presentation will be about. Many times, the subject will be assigned to you. There may be other times when it is necessary for you to select the subject. After the subject is selected, narrow the larger idea to a specific topic.

Next, consider the scope of the content for the presentation. The **scope** of the presentation is the guideline of how much information will be included. It will be necessary to narrow the topic so that the content is manageable as well as meaningful. Will the information be detailed or general? Scope defines what should be included and what should be left out of the presentation.

Where Is the Information?

Once the topic of the presentation is set, research will be necessary to support the points made in the presentation. Researching for a presentation is similar to researching for a written report. Chapter 6 explains the research process. The same steps are applied to gathering information for a presentation.

You may need to conduct primary research, secondary research, or both. Remember the importance of crediting secondary sources. Mention

Career Skills

Management Analyst
Management analysts work with managers to improve an establishment's efficiency. They identify ways to cut costs and raise revenues. The analysis process is supported by use of all productivity tools, especially spreadsheets and databases. Analysts often communicate with managers through presentation software and documents created with word-processing software.

the source during the presentation when you discuss your research findings. Source citations add to speaker credibility and the overall believability or acceptance of the presentation. Formally cite the sources in any handouts or printed reports accompanying the presentation.

When Is the Presentation?

Most often, formal presentations must be given on a certain date, at a certain place, and for a specific occasion. Time is an important element when preparing for a presentation. When you begin prewriting, identify the date of the presentation. If you are not given a date to have the presentation finished, select a date of your own.

Writing a presentation takes time, so do not underestimate the effort that will be required. Schedule your writing or preparation time just as you would schedule appointments or activities. Allow appropriate time to research, write, and practice the presentation. Rushing through the writing process could result in a presentation that appears unprofessional.

How Should the Presentation Be Organized?

As you prepare to write the presentation, select an approach that supports the message you want to convey. The approach of the document is how the information is presented. The direct approach works well when delivering an informative speech. The topic is introduced first and then followed by descriptive details. The indirect approach works well for persuasive messages. Details are given first and are then followed by the main idea. Begin with information that prepares the reader to respond in the manner you want him or her to respond.

Next, prepare an outline. The outline will serve as a guideline to identify the information to be presented and its proper sequence. One way to create an outline is to make a numbered list of the key points. These should be the main ideas about the topic. If using the direct approach, start with the main ideas followed by the details, as shown in Figure 7-2. If using the indirect approach, do the reverse. These will be considered as the headings in the outline. Start recording the main ideas in the order in which you think of them. Then, reorder the points until they reflect the order in which the information will be presented.

As you compose the outline, keep in mind how much time has been allotted for the presentation. The amount of detail in certain parts of the presentation may need to be adjusted so the presentation will fit into the available time. Facts and figures might need to be provided to the audience as handouts instead of being explained during the presentation.

Presentation Outline

I.   First main point
   a. Subpoint
   b. Subpoint
II. Second main point
   a. Subpoint
   b. Subpoint
III. Third main point
   a. Subpoint
   b. Subpoint

Goodheart-Willcox Publisher

Figure 7-2. Developing an outline helps organize a presentation.

Preparing Content for a Presentation

When the outline is completed, it is time to begin the writing stage for the presentation. To begin drafting the presentation, follow the outline. Write sentences, words, or phrases next to each topic on the outline to act as cues for what you want to say. If you are a beginning speaker or if the topic is complex, you might opt to draft your presentation word for word. As you write, think about how spoken language differs from written language. Aim for a less formal, more conversational delivery. Be sure to identify any words that might be unfamiliar to the audience and plan to explain them.

Introduction

The introduction of the presentation serves several purposes. It should introduce the topic of the presentation and preview the main points. In other words, "tell them what you are going to tell them."

The introduction should also draw the listener into the presentation. This important function is often overlooked. Include something to arouse the interest of the audience. This is often called an **attention grabber**. Common attention grabbers include asking a question, citing a surprising statistic, reciting a relevant quote, and telling a story. If you are giving a presentation to coworkers about team-building methods, the attention grabber might be to ask, "What do you think you know about teamwork?"

Body

The body of the presentation is where the main points are made and supported. These points should be presented using the direct or indirect approach. Having too many main points can lead to a long, drawn-out presentation. This usually loses the attention of the audience. Be concise. Keep the number of main points manageable. Following each main point, briefly summarize it.

Two techniques that can enhance a presentation are the use of facts and humor. Using reliable, informative facts is an important part of any good presentation. Humor can also be a way to win over an audience, provided you use it correctly.

Conclusion

The conclusion summarizes the entire presentation. In other words, "tell them what you said." Conclude the presentation by restating the main points. Relate each point back to the purpose of the presentation. This will help the audience more easily retain the information.

The conclusion is often where the presenter will answer audience questions. Having time for questions helps engage the audience with the presentation. It also allows the audience to get clarification on any points that were not understood.

After you have adequately concluded the speech and answered any audience questions, close with a clincher. A **clincher** is a statement to finish the presentation that will make an impact on the audience. It is similar to the attention grabber in the introduction. This is the chance to leave a lasting, positive impression on the audience.

Tips

Use a simple typeface, as shown in Figure 7-3. A sans serif typeface is commonly used in presentations because these are generally easy to read. Do not use decorative typefaces, such as Comic Sans. Make sure the point size of the text is large enough to allow all of the audience, even those at the back of a large room, to read the slides.

Use the 7 × 7 rule for textual elements. This rule limits you to no more than seven items on a slide or seven words per item. That means if the slide has a title, there should not be more than six bullets below it. Split the information over two or more slides with the same title if needed. Also, do not have more than seven words in a bullet. Often articles—*the*, *a*, and *an*—are omitted from presentations. This helps reduce the number of words on the screen.

When adding text, highlight the important points. The speaker is the one with the message. If there is a large amount of text on a slide, the audience will tend to read instead of listen.

Create focus on slides with large images. This can draw attention to the presentation. The images should help the audience relate to the topic.

Just because images can be easily added using the software, this is not a reason to do so. Unnecessary graphics may distract from the

Some experts recommend the 4 × 5 rule over the 7 × 7 rule: no more than four lines and no more than five words per line.

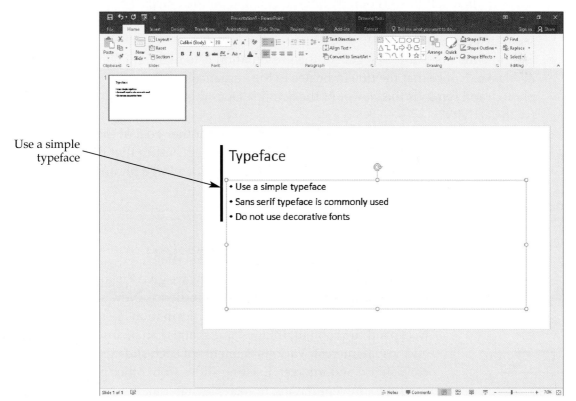

Figure 7-3. A simple, sans serif typeface is easy to quickly read, so often the choice for a presentation.

FYI

Slide size can be changed by selecting **Design**>**Customize**> **Slide Size**. Users can select either **Standard (4:3)** or **Widescreen (16:9)** as the slide size.

PowerPoint
1.5.1

message. Only include graphics that add to or support the message. Do not clutter the slides.

Elements in a presentation can be animated. However, too much animation or too many different types of animation may distract from the message. Use animation to add interest to the presentation, but use it sparingly.

Consider the makeup of the audience when designing the presentation. A business presentation or academic presentation should be polished and professional. Do not overuse cartoons or silly photographs in these types of presentations.

HANDS-ON EXAMPLE 7.1.1 ☞

PowerPoint
5.1.2

COMPARING SLIDE COMPOSITION

The design of a presentation can have an impact on how the audience receives the message. One of the best ways to develop a sense for the impact a design can have is by comparing two presentations.

1. Insert your MS-OFFICE flash drive into the computer.
2. Applying what you have learned, create a folder on the flash drive named Chap07.
3. Navigate to the student companion website at www.g-wlearning.com, download the data files for this chapter, and save them in the Chap07 folder on your flash drive.
4. Launch Microsoft PowerPoint by double-clicking on the Comparison.pptx file in the Chap07 folder on your flash drive. Each slide in this presentation represents the title slide of a separate presentation.
5. Examine the first slide. The goal of the presentation is to highlight features of a bicycle tour in Alaska. Notice that the title indicates to the audience the slide topic with text details. The photograph reminds the viewer of the activity. Does this image make the viewer want to try the activity?
6. Press the [Page Down] key to view the second slide. Another goal of the presentation is to make the participants want to go to Alaska for bicycling. Notice that the text is minimal. Instead, the message of the experience is conveyed with a large photograph. What details can be learned by viewing this slide?

Working with a Presentation

The features of presentation software give the author enormous possibilities to create interest for an audience. New slides can be added to the presentation to include more information. Text can be easily added to expand the content. Images and shapes can be inserted onto slides to add visual interest. Various elements of each slide can be formatted for consistency and interest. Existing slides from other presentations can be reused to prevent having to recreate material.

Navigating a Presentation File

A presentation will usually contain many slides. To navigate through the presentation file, use the scroll bar along the side of the application window. The up and down arrow keys on the keyboard can also be used to navigate through the file. Pressing the key will display either the next or previous slide in the file. The [Ctrl][Home] key combination displays the first slide in the file. The [Ctrl][End] key combination displays the last slide in the file.

In the default view of Microsoft PowerPoint, the current slide is displayed on the right-hand side of the application window. The slide takes up most of the space in the window. As the user navigates through the file, the current slide is always displayed on the right-hand side of the window. A highlight surrounds the thumbnail on the left for the current slide.

Most presentation software has a slide-sorter feature. In Microsoft PowerPoint, the slide sorter is displayed as a separate view, but it also includes thumbnails along the left-hand side of the application window, which serves as a slide sorter. The slide sorter can be used to navigate through the presentation file. To display a slide, click its thumbnail.

Adding New Slides and Text

When adding a new slide in most presentation software, there are several styles or templates to choose for the new slide. These styles or templates are usually called slide masters. A **slide master** is a predefined slide on which the position and formatting of text boxes and graphics is specified. Whatever appears on the slide master will appear on each slide in the presentation based on that master.

For example, Microsoft PowerPoint 2016 offers nine slide masters when inserting a new slide, as shown in Figure 7-4. Two of these are most commonly used. The Title Slide slide master is used for a title and subtitle for the presentation. Whenever a new blank presentation is started, the default slide in the presentation is based on the Title Slide slide master. The Title and Contents slide master is set up to allow the user to enter a title for the slide and associated bullet points. This is the slide master most people use to add content to the presentation.

Slides can be added in any location in the presentation file. In Microsoft PowerPoint, an inserted slide will be placed after the current slide. So, navigate to the slide after which the slide should be inserted, and then insert the new slide. Slides can be rearranged. If a slide is inserted in the wrong location, it is easy to move it to the correct location.

Text is added to a slide in Microsoft PowerPoint through the use of text boxes. The default slide masters all contain text boxes, with the exception of the Blank slide master. The placeholder text in a text box will be Click to add. To add text, click in the text box. The text box is activated, the placeholder text disappears, and the insertion point within the text box indicates where text will be added.

Despite text appearing in text boxes, it can still be formatted into columns, like in Microsoft Word. To list text in columnar format, right-click on the placeholder and select **Format Shape** from the shortcut menu.

FYI

Slide masters and slide layouts can be created or modified by selecting **View>Master Views>Slide Master**. Once in Slide Master view, the user can modify existing layouts or create new ones. The **Insert Placeholder** button allows the user to place and size text boxes.

PowerPoint
1.3.2, 1.3.3, 1.3.4, 1.3.5

GS5
Key Applications
5.5.1, 5.6.1, 5.7.2

PowerPoint
1.2.1, 1.2.5, 2.1.1

FYI

In Microsoft PowerPoint, the [Ctrl][M] key combination can be used to insert a new slide based on the same slide master as the last inserted slide.

PowerPoint
2.1.4, 1.1.3

Styles can be applied to shapes and text boxes by selecting **Format>Shape Styles>More**.

PowerPoint
2.2.5

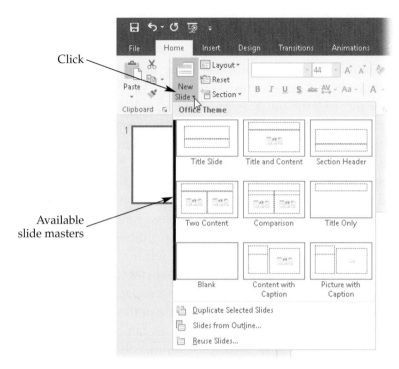

Goodheart-Willcox Publisher

Figure 7-4. When inserting a new slide, you can select a slide master on which to base the new side.

On the right side of the resulting window, select **Text Options**, then **Text Box**. Click on the **Columns** box and enter the number of columns as well as the space of each column in the designated fields. Then select **OK**.

PowerPoint
1.1.3

Instead of manually adding and creating new slides, the user can import an outline created in Microsoft Word that will retain the specific heading levels in PowerPoint. To import an outline, select **Home>Slides>New Slide>Slides from Outline**. Navigate to and select the desired Word document and click **Insert**. If the Word document does not contain any text tagged with the Heading 1 or Heading 2 styles, PowerPoint will automatically generate one slide for each paragraph of content.

HANDS-ON EXAMPLE 7.1.2

ADDING SLIDES AND TEXT

One of the most basic skills for creating a presentation is the ability to add slides and content. Slides and content are added when creating a presentation from a blank starting point and when modifying an existing presentation.

1. Launch Microsoft PowerPoint, and open the Presentation1.pptx file in the Chap07 folder on your flash drive.
2. Save the file as *LastName*Presentation.pptx in the Chap07 folder on your flash drive.
3. Use the arrow keys, scroll bar, or [Page Up] and [Page Down] keys to navigate through the slides in the file. Notice that the first slide has a different format from the rest. The Title Slide slide master was used for this slide. The Title and Content slide master was used for the remaining slides. Each slide contains text boxes in which text is placed.

HANDS-ON EXAMPLE 7.1.2 (CONTINUED)

4. Navigate to the first slide.

5. Click after the *t* in the word PowerPoint to place the insertion point there. The text box is activated, and its extents are indicated by the dashed rectangle.

6. Press the [Enter] key, and add your name to the text box.

7. Press the [Enter] key, and add today's date.

8. Navigate to the last slide, which is slide 4.

New Slide

9. Click **Home**>**Slides**>**New Slide** in the ribbon. Do not click the drop-down arrow next to the button. A new slide is added after slide 4. Notice that the same slide master as slide 4, which is Title and Content, is used for the new slide.

10. Click the placeholder text in the title text box, and add the text What Are the Features? to the text box.

11. Click the placeholder text in the content text box, and add the following text on separate lines. The content will be automatically formatted as a bulleted list.

> Presents information in colorful, interesting format
> Creates handouts for distribution to audience
> Can be set to run continuously
> Does not require PowerPoint be installed

12. Applying what you have learned, add a new slide to the end of the presentation, enter the title How Do I Write a Presentation?, and add the following text on separate lines.

> Identify the purpose
> Identify the audience
> Determine what the audience needs to know
> Know where presentation will be given

13. Save the file.

Adding Graphics

Graphics are illustrations, photographs, and drawing shapes, as shown in Figure 7-5. Graphics add interest and provide a realistic view of the information being presented. An audience should be able to interpret the graphics and understand what is conveyed. Some viewers will look at the graphics first, so each image should be clear and well-designed. Consider the audience and the purpose of the information when choosing graphics. Select the most appropriate visual for the content being presented.

While visuals can add interest and emphasis, care must be taken to avoid overuse. Too many visuals in a presentation will become distracting, and the information will lose its effectiveness. If a presentation is cluttered, the message can be lost.

Illustrations are also called line art. Line art is an image created by drawing lines of various widths and colors. Often, colors fill in the space between the lines.

Photographs are still images created by capturing a real-life scene. Photographs are usually created with a digital camera, either a dedicated

| GS5 |
| Key Applications |
| 5.5.2 |
| PowerPoint |
| 2.3.1, 2.3.2 |

FYI

Graphics can be downloaded from various online sources and inserted into a presentation. Properly credit the source.

device or a device that is part of a mobile device, such as a smartphone. However, continuous tone photographs (printed) may be scanned and used in digital form.

PowerPoint
2.2.1

Drawing shapes are basic forms created in the software, such as rectangles and circles. Shapes are a basic type of line art created directly within the software application, not imported or inserted from another source.

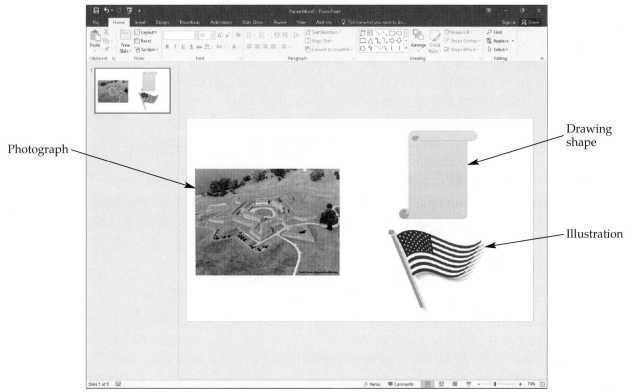

Photograph

Drawing shape

Illustration

Figure 7-5. Illustrations, photographs, and drawing shapes are called graphics, which can add interest to a presentation.

HANDS-ON EXAMPLE 7.1.3

ADDING GRAPHICS

When properly used, graphics can enhance the message of a presentation. Be sure not to overuse graphics to avoid cluttering the presentation.

1. Launch Microsoft PowerPoint, and open the *LastName*Presentation.pptx file in the Chap07 folder on your flash drive, if it is not already open.
2. Navigate to the What Is Presentation Software? slide, which is slide 3.

HANDS-ON EXAMPLE 7.1.3 (CONTINUED)

Shapes

3. Click **Insert>Illustrations>Shapes** in the ribbon. A drop-down menu is displayed containing the various drawing shapes that can be inserted, as shown.

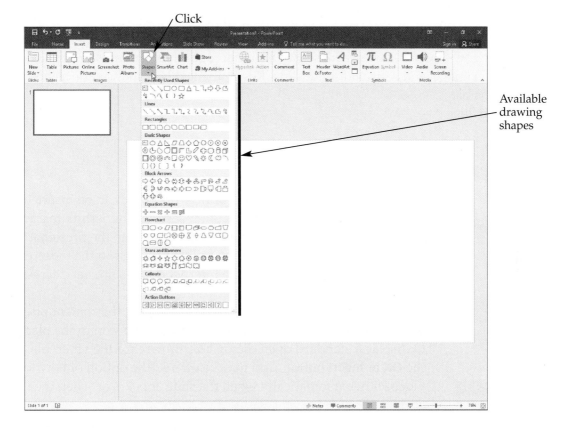

4. Click the **Right Arrow** shape in the **Block Arrows** area of the drop-down menu. The cursor changes to indicate a shape can be drawn.
5. Click to the left of the third bullet, drag to the left, and release. An arrow drawing shape is added to the slide.
6. Navigate to the What Are the Features? slide, which is slide 5.

Online
Pictures

7. Click **Insert>Pictures>Online Pictures** in the ribbon. The **Insert Pictures** dialog box is displayed, which contains a search box.
8. Click in the search box, enter printers, and click the **Search** button (magnifying glass).
9. Scroll through the list of results to find a photograph of a printer producing handouts, click the image, and then click the **Insert** button. The photograph is placed on the slide. It is automatically selected with resizing handles displayed.
10. Click and drag one of the corner handles on the image to resize it. The corner handles maintain the height-to-width ratio, and the image is proportionally resized. Resize the image so it is about one-half of the height of the slide.
11. Click and hold on the image and drag it to the right of the bulleted list. The image will likely overlap the text.
12. Click anywhere in the bulleted list in the text box. Handles appear on the text box.

HANDS-ON EXAMPLE 7.1.3 (CONTINUED)

13. Drag the right-center handle to the left to resize the text box. When the right-hand edge of the text box clears the image, release the mouse button. The lines of text will wrap as the text box is resized.
14. Navigate to the last slide. Notice that the word audience is used twice on this slide. This would be a good topic of a graphic to place on this slide.
15. Applying what you have learned, search for a photograph of students in a classroom, insert the image, and resize it for the slide. Resize the text box on the slide as needed so all text is visible.
16. Save the file.

GS5
Key Applications
5.5.2

PowerPoint
3.4

PowerPoint
3.4.2

GS5
Key Applications
5.6.1, 5.7.5

PowerPoint
1.3.1

Adding Video

Video files saved on a local or network drive can be inserted into presentations. This is different from inserting a hyperlink to a video stored online. The video itself can be inserted into the presentation. Anyone opening the presentation will have access to the video even if the computer is not connected to the Internet or does not have access to the original video file.

The easiest way to insert a video is by using the content placeholder on a Title and Content slide. Click the **Insert Video** icon in the placeholder to display a standard open dialog box. Browse for the video file, and click the **OK** or **Insert** button. You may be offered the option of how to play the video, either automatically when the slide appears or when the video is clicked.

Once a video has been inserted, it can be configured to the needs of the presentation. For example, if the user needs the video's window size to be made larger or smaller, the window size can be adjusted by clicking and dragging the resizing handles. Additional customization can be accomplished by selecting **Video Tools>Playback**. From this area, the user can configure playback options, including controlling whether the video plays on a loop or rewinds at the conclusion. The user can also set the start and stop times by selecting **Trim Video**.

Formatting a Presentation Using a Theme

A presentation can be enhanced by the use of themes. A **theme** is a set of specified colors, fonts, and effects, as shown in Figure 7-6. Themes are used to standardize these items across all slides in a presentation. By having consistency throughout the presentation, the message of the presentation can be reinforced. Inconsistency leads to distraction, and the audience may not fully receive the message of the presentation. Themes add professionalism to the final product.

Themes can be added before creating the presentation or at any other time. Microsoft PowerPoint is supplied with many default themes. Additional themes can be downloaded from the Internet. Additionally, the user can create and save themes. The default themes in Microsoft

Available
themes

Variations for
current theme

Figure 7-6. A theme can be applied to standardize colors, fonts, and effects. There may be variations available for the current theme.

PowerPoint also have variants. Variants are based on the main theme, but have some of the elements changed. For example, the background may be lighter or darker than the main theme. They offer the same design with different color schemes.

A dark blue background with light-colored lettering is the easiest on the eyes of the audience. Red should be used sparingly and only for emphasis. The eye tires from seeing too much red.

HANDS-ON EXAMPLE 7.1.4

APPLYING A THEME

The use of a theme is an easy way to maintain consistency in a presentation. It is very easy to apply a theme to a presentation at any point.

1. Launch Microsoft PowerPoint, and open the *LastName*Presentation.pptx file in the Chap07 folder on your flash drive, if it is not already open.
2. Navigate to the first slide of the presentation.
3. Click the **More** button in the gallery in the **Themes** group on the **Design** tab of the ribbon. Several themes are displayed in the expanded gallery. The name of each theme is displayed as help text when the cursor is hovered over the preview.
4. Scroll through the expanded gallery, and click the Damask theme. If this theme is not available, choose a different theme. The theme is applied to all slides in the presentation.
5. In the gallery in the **Variants** group on the **Design** tab of the ribbon, click the preview for the variation you prefer. The slides are updated.
6. Navigate through the presentation to see how the titles and text are formatted on the slides. Text should always begin in the same location from slide to slide. Otherwise, the text will appear to jump or bounce during the presentation.
7. Move text boxes on each slide as needed so the text begins in the same location. To move a text box, click in it to display the handles and border, then click and drag the border.
8. Navigate to the How Do I Write a Presentation? slide, which is slide 6.
9. Click the photograph to select it.
10. Click **Simple Frame, White** in the gallery in the **Picture Styles** group on the **Format** tab of the ribbon. A white frame is added around the photograph to emphasize the image.
11. Save the file.

More

GS5
Key Applications
5.5.1

PowerPoint
1.2.2, 5.1.1

Reusing Slides

Information in a presentation may need to be repeated in a different presentation. Slides in existing presentations can be reused in a new presentation. This saves the time needed to recreate what already has been created. The content can be copied and pasted. However, in Microsoft PowerPoint, there is a function that allows inserting slides from an existing presentation. The reused slides automatically take on the formatting of the new presentation.

HANDS-ON EXAMPLE 7.1.5

REUSING SLIDES

If needed information already exists on slides in another presentation, it is more efficient to reuse those slides than to recreate them. It is easy to reuse slides in Microsoft PowerPoint.

1. Launch Microsoft PowerPoint 2016, and open the *LastName*Presentation.pptx file in the Chap07 folder on your flash drive, if it is not already open.
2. Navigate to the last slide.
3. Click the drop-down arrow next to the **New Slide** button on the **Home** tab of the ribbon, and click **Reuse Slides…** in the drop-down menu. Note: do not press the **New Slide** button. The **Reuse Slides** pane is displayed on the right-hand side of the application window, as shown.

New Slide

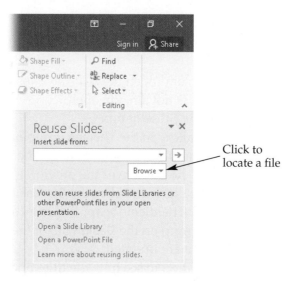

4. Click the **Browse** button on the **Reuse Slides** pane, and then **Browse File…** in the drop-down menu that is displayed. In the standard open dialog box that is displayed, navigate the Chap07 folder on your flash drive, select the InsertPresentation.pptx file, and open it. The slides in the file are displayed in the **Reuse Slides** pane.
5. Click each preview in the **Reuse Slides** pane one at a time. Each slide is added to the presentation after the current slide. There should be a total of 11 slides after inserting the reused slides.

HANDS-ON EXAMPLE 7.1.5 (CONTINUED)

6. Close the **Reuse Slides** pane.
7. Applying what you have learned, review the inserted slides for formatting and adjust text boxes and images as needed.
8. Save the file.

Proofing and Displaying a Presentation

Before displaying the presentation, review it for any errors. It is necessary to review both the content and the layout. Review the layout and visual design to:

- ensure every item appears as intended;
- check that typefaces and font styles are appropriately applied;
- examine consistency in typefaces, spacing, and other important elements; and
- look for correct slide masters used for all slides.

Read through the final product. Run the spell-check function to locate spelling errors, but do not depend on software to "think" for you. Read for spelling and grammatical errors that the spell-checker may not find.

To run the spell-checker in Microsoft PowerPoint, click **Review>Proofing>Spelling** in the ribbon. If any spelling errors are identified, they are displayed one by one in the **Spelling** pane. The function of the spell-checker is similar to the same function in Microsoft Word, as discussed in Chapter 5. Note, however, grammar-checking is not part of the function.

When ready to display the presentation, Microsoft PowerPoint gives you the option to view the entire presentation from the beginning or only the portion of the presentation from the current slide forward. The option to view the presentation from the current slide is useful for testing only a portion of the presentation. For example, to test only the current slide, use this option and then press the [Esc] key after viewing the current slide. The [Esc] key always exits the playback.

To view the entire presentation, click **Slide Show>Start Slide Show>Start From Beginning** in the ribbon. The presentation is displayed in full-screen mode starting with the first slide, as shown in Figure 7-7. To view the presentation starting with the current slide, click **Slide Show>Start Slide Show>Start From This Slide** in the ribbon. During presentation playback, left-click, press the space bar, or press the down arrow or [Page Down] key to advance to the next slide. In some cases, depending on how the slides have been set up, the slides may automatically advance. If there is a need to return to the previous slide, press the up arrow or [Page Up] key.

Viewing the presentation provides the opportunity to get an idea as to what will be needed for showing the final presentation. For example, if a presentation is being given in a room that allows for the use of external monitors and speakers, the speaker will need to know and connect the presentation device to these components. This can be accomplished

PowerPoint
5.2.3

FYI

The [F7] key is a shortcut for launching the spell-checker in most Microsoft Office applications.

FYI

To present a slide show by using Presenter View, select **Slide Show** at the bottom of the PowerPoint slide window, click the ellipsis icon (...) at the bottom-left corner of the control bar, and select **Show Presenter View**.

PowerPoint
1.7.4

PowerPoint
1.7.2

GS5
Key Applications
5.2.1, 5.2.2

by inserting cables into the proper audio and video ports. Audio ports connect headphones, microphones, and speakers. Some devices, such as certain speakers, may be connected using Bluetooth or infrared technologies. The computer must be equipped with Bluetooth or infrared cards in order to use these technologies. Video ports traditionally include video graphics array (VGA), which is used by older LCD monitors; digital video interface (DVI), which is used by new-model monitors as well as televisions, DVD players, and projectors; and high-definition multimedia interface (HDMI), which carries high-definition video and uncompressed digital audio in one cable. Once the speaker understands what additional components, if any, are needed, the slide show can be configured in a way that seamlessly integrates the additional technology. To configure slide show options, select **Slide Show>Set Up>Set Up Slide Show**.

Users can compare two different presentations by selecting **Review> Compare>Compare**. In the **Choose File to Merge with Current Presentation** dialog box, navigate to and select the desired presentation, then select **Merge**. The second presentation will appear in the Revisions pane.

PowerPoint
5.1.2

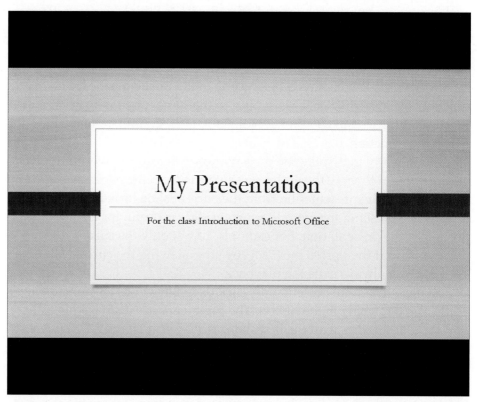

Goodheart-Willcox Publisher

Figure 7-7. When the slide show is played, the presentation is displayed in full-screen mode.

HANDS-ON EXAMPLE 7.1.6

DISPLAYING A PRESENTATION

The end result of creating a presentation is to display the presentation. Before displaying the presentation, be sure to proof it for errors.

1. Launch Microsoft PowerPoint 2016, and open the *LastName*Presentation.pptx file in the Chap07 folder on your flash drive, if it is not already open.

Spelling

2. Click **Review**>**Proofing**>**Spelling** in the ribbon. Because there are spelling errors in this document, the **Spelling** pane is displayed on the right-hand side of the window, and the first questionable word is highlighted in the document. Note: earlier versions of PowerPoint will display the **Spelling and Grammar** dialog box.

3. In the list of spelling alternatives offered, select the correct spelling, and click the **Change** button. The word is changed, and the next questionable word is highlighted in the document.

4. Continue correcting the document. If the questioned word is correct, click the **Ignore** button. If the correct word does not appear in the list of spelling alternatives, click in the document and manually correct the word. When the last questionable word has been addressed, the **Spelling** pane is closed.

5. Navigate to the third slide in the presentation.

6. Click **Slide Show**>**Start Slide Show**>**From Beginning** in the ribbon or press the [F5] key. Playback of the presentation begins with the first slide.

7. Left-click, press the space bar, or press the down arrow or [Page Down] key to advance slides. Notice that some of the slides include animations. You will learn how to do this later in this chapter.

8. Press the [Esc] key to exit playback. Notice that the current slide in PowerPoint was the last slide displayed during playback.

9. Save the file.

Sharing a Presentation

After a presentation is completed, it can be saved in a PDF format for sharing with others who do not have the presentation software. A PDF can be viewed on any computer or can be used to prepare the file for commercial printing. This format does not permit the presentation to be edited. Other ways to share a presentation include saving it as a show, which can be viewed without PowerPoint, or as image files. A presentation can also be shared through e-mail, posted to the web, or saved in the cloud and shared.

The presentation can be saved to a CD using a special function in PowerPoint. This is an important option to allow viewing of the presentation, slide by slide, on most any other computer. Instead of saving the file, the presentation is exported using the **Package Presentation for CD** option. During the process, instructions are added to the file to tell other computers how to run the presentation. Exporting a presentation can also be used to create a video of the file if narration needs to be added.

GS5
Key Applications
5.1.1, 5.1.2, 5.7.1

PowerPoint
5.2.5

GS5
Key Applications
5.3

FYI

Double-clicking a slide thumbnail in the Slide Sorter view will display the Normal view with that slide current.

Managing the Presentation

Microsoft PowerPoint offers several ways in which to view a presentation during development. The Normal view is the default view. This view displays the current slide in a large size as well as thumbnails of the other slides in the presentation. The Outline view also displays the current slide in a large size, but in place of the thumbnails the text content of all slides is displayed on the left. The Slide Sorter view displays only thumbnails of all slides, as shown in Figure 7-8. This view is very helpful when looking at the presentation as a whole. Most often, the Normal view along with the Slide Sorter view are used to manage the presentation, which includes inserting, rearranging, deleting, and copying slides. Inserting slides is discussed earlier in this chapter.

To change views in Microsoft PowerPoint, click the **View** tab in the ribbon. The buttons for changing views are located in the **Presentation Views** group on this tab. Buttons for displaying the Normal and Slide Sorter views are also located in the lower-right corner of the application window. These buttons are always visible no matter which tab is active in the ribbon, which makes it easy to restore one of these views at any time.

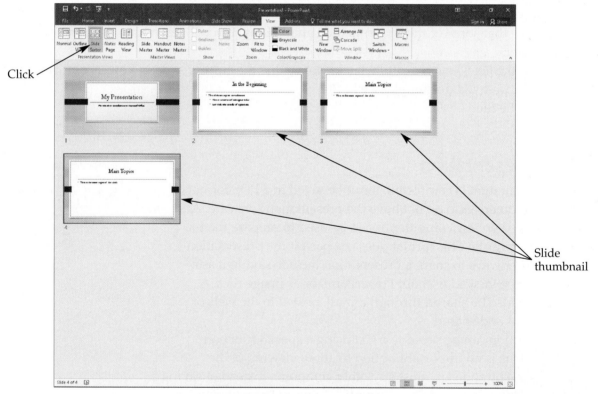

Goodheart-Willcox Publisher

Figure 7-8. The Slide Sorter view displays all of the slides in the presentation and can be used to rearrange slides.

TITANS OF TECHNOLOGY

John W. Thompson's education is in business management, but he has always worked with, and ultimately led, some of the most productive technology companies in the world. In 2014, Thompson was named Chairman of the Board of Microsoft Corporation, replacing Bill Gates in that position. Concurrently, since 2012 he has been the CEO of Virtual Instruments. His career has also included tenures at IBM, serving as Vice President and General Manager of IBM Americas, and Symantec, where he was President and CEO leading the cloud security giant. Thompson began his career working in sales at IBM and would spend the next 28 years in various positions at the company before leaving for the CEO position at Symantec.

After leaving Symantec in 2009, Thompson joined Virtual Instruments. He was named CEO in 2010. Virtual Instruments was a startup company in 2009, having been founded one year earlier. Virtual Instruments is an information technology company that helps other companies migrate to cloud computing.

Rearranging Slides

As a presentation is developed, slides often need to be rearranged in a different order. Sometimes this is because a slide is accidentally inserted in the wrong order. However, frequently the writer will decide the overall order of content needs to be changed. In Microsoft PowerPoint, slides can be rearranged in the Normal or Slide Sorter view. To move a slide to a different order, click and hold the thumbnail for the slide to move, drag it to the new location, and drop to reorder the slides.

Deleting Slides

There are times when all of the content on a slide is no longer needed. The easiest way to remove this content from the presentation is to delete the slide. Slides can be deleted in the Normal, Slide Show, or Outline view in Microsoft PowerPoint. In the Normal and Slide Show views, click the thumbnail for the slide to delete. In the Outline view, click the square next to the slide number in the outline. When a slide is selected, the thumbnail or the square will be outlined. With the correct slide selected, press the [Delete] key to remove the slide.

Copying Slides

Slides can be copied. This is useful if the slide contains a significant amount of information, but the user wants to make subtle changes to it to enhance the visual flow. Slides can be copied in the Normal, Slide Show,

GS5
Key Applications
5.7.4

PowerPoint
1.4.2

FYI

Slides can be rearranged in the Outline view in Microsoft PowerPoint by dragging the square in front of the content.

GS5
Key Applications
5.7.3

PowerPoint
1.2.4

FYI

Slides can be hidden from a presentation by right-clicking the desired slide and choosing **Hide Slide** from the shortcut menu. This same action will reveal hidden slides.

PowerPoint
1.2.3

or Outline view in Microsoft PowerPoint. First, select the slide to copy. Then, click **Home**>**Clipboard**>**Copy** in the ribbon or press the [Ctrl][C] key combination. Next, select the slide *after* which the copy should be placed. Finally, click **Home**>**Clipboard**>**Paste** in the ribbon or press the [Ctrl][V] key combination.

In Microsoft PowerPoint, there is also a duplicate function. This function is used to create a copy of a slide and automatically paste it after the current slide in one step. First, select the slide to copy. Then, click the drop-down arrow next to **Home**>**Clipboard**>**Copy** in the ribbon, and click **Duplicate** in the drop-down menu. The slide is automatically copied and pasted after the current slide.

HANDS-ON EXAMPLE 7.1.7

MANAGING A PRESENTATION

Managing a presentation involves many tasks, including inserting, rearranging, deleting, and copying slides. These are common tasks throughout development of a presentation.

Slide Sorter View

1. Launch Microsoft PowerPoint 2016, and open the *LastName*Presentation.pptx file in the Chap07 folder on your flash drive, if it is not already open.
2. Click **View**>**Presentation Styles**>**Slide Sorter View** in the ribbon. The Slide Sorter view is displayed in which all slides are displayed as thumbnails.
3. Select the last slide in the presentation by clicking on it. The thumbnail will be outlined to indicate the slide is selected.
4. Press the [Delete] key to remove the selected slide.
5. Applying what you have learned, select the To Create an Effective Presentation slide (slide 8).
6. Click and hold on slide 8, drag to the end of the presentation, and drop the slide. The slides are automatically rearranged with the To Create an Effective Presentation slide at the end.
7. Applying what you have learned, view the slide show.
8. Click **View**>**Presentation Styles**>**Normal View** in the ribbon.
9. Save the file.

Normal View

7.1 | SECTION REVIEW

 ### CHECK YOUR UNDERSTANDING

1. What are the six questions that should be asked when planning a formal presentation?
2. What is the 7 × 7 rule?
3. If an object appears on a slide master, where else will it appear?
4. What happens if too many graphics are used in a presentation?
5. How are slides rearranged in a presentation?

 ### BUILD YOUR VOCABULARY

As you progress through this course, develop a personal IT glossary. This will help you build your vocabulary and prepare you for a career. Write a definition for each of the following terms and add it to your IT glossary.

attention grabber

clincher

external audience

graphic

internal audience

presentation

scope

slide master

theme

SECTION 7.2

ADDING TRANSITIONS AND ANIMATIONS

Presentation software is not only used to create a presentation that communicates information, it is used to make the information more educational or entertaining for the audience. A presentation that is only text on the screen is not very engaging for the audience. The message of the presentation is likely to be lost. There are many ways to improve the visual aspect of the presentation.

There are also ways to provide information that is not part of or that supports the main focus. As with most types of documents, there are header and footer areas in a presentation that can be used to provide supplemental information, such as the name of the speaker. This section covers designing a presentation from scratch and including advanced features to improve a presentation.

Stephen Coburn/Shutterstock.com

LEARNING GOALS

After completing this section, you will be able to:
• Create a new presentation.
• Discuss advanced features of presentation software.

TERMS

animating
background image
hyperlink
transition

Creating a New Presentation

PowerPoint
1.1.1, 1.1.2, 1.7.1

Creating a presentation from scratch first requires writing. Before writing the text, create an outline of the important points. As discussed earlier, answer these questions:

- Why are you presenting?
- Who is the audience?
- What is the topic?
- Where is the information?
- When is the presentation?
- How should the presentation be organized?

From the answers, formulate the introduction, body, and conclusion.

In Microsoft PowerPoint 2010 and earlier, a blank presentation is automatically started whenever the software is launched. To create a new presentation in Microsoft PowerPoint 2016, launch the software. The startup screen is displayed. A template can be selected in the startup screen if appropriate. To begin a blank presentation, click Blank Presentation on the right-hand side of the startup screen, as shown in Figure 7-9. A new blank presentation is started and displayed in the Normal view. To create a presentation from a template, select **File>New**. Under **New Presentation**, select the desired template from the **Templates** drop-down menu.

By default, a blank presentation in PowerPoint includes a slide based on the Title Slide slide master, as shown in Figure 7-10. If a title slide is not required, a different slide master can be applied to the default slide or the slide can be deleted. Add slides and content as needed to develop the presentation.

FYI

A theme can be applied to a blank presentation at any point to add color and visual interest.

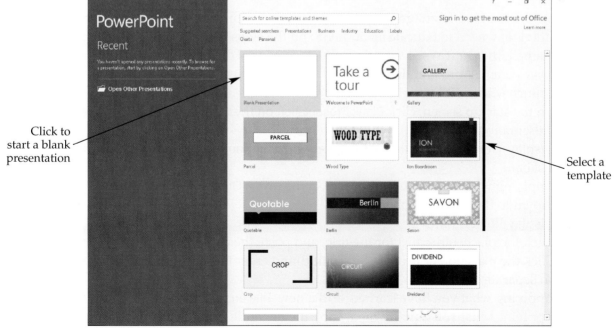

Click to start a blank presentation

Select a template

Goodheart-Willcox Publisher

Figure 7-9. Starting a new, blank presentation in Microsoft PowerPoint 2016.

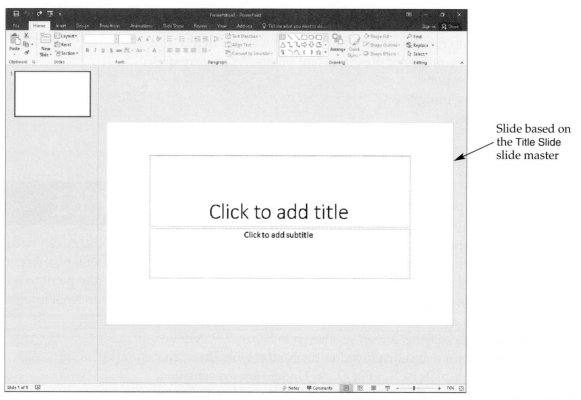

Figure 7-10. A slide based on the Title Slide master slide is automatically included in a new, blank presentation.

HANDS-ON EXAMPLE 7.2.1

CREATING A NEW PRESENTATION

There are many different goals for which a presentation may be created. For example, a presentation may need to educate an audience on the steps to take in preparing a presentation.

1. Launch Microsoft Word, and open the Seminar.docx file in the Chap07 folder on your flash drive. Leave Word and this file open.
2. Launch Microsoft PowerPoint 2016.
3. On the startup screen, click Blank Presentation on the right-hand side to begin a new presentation.
4. Display Word by using the [Alt][Tab] key combination or by clicking the button on the taskbar.
5. Applying what you have learned, select the text A Guide to Winning Business Seminar, and copy it to the system clipboard.
6. Display PowerPoint.
7. Click the placeholder text for the title, and paste the copied text.
8. Click the placeholder text for the subtitle, and enter Presented by *your name* and today's date on separate lines.
9. Applying what you have learned, add a new Title and Content slide.
10. Applying what you have learned, copy the next title from Word, and paste it into PowerPoint.

HANDS-ON EXAMPLE 7.2.1 (CONTINUED)

11. Copy the bulleted text from Word, and paste it into PowerPoint as the content.
12. Applying what you have learned, add a new Title and Content slide.
13. Applying what you have learned, copy the next title and content from Word, and paste it into PowerPoint.
14. Applying what you have learned, add a new Title and Content slide.
15. Applying what you have learned, copy the final title and content from Word, and paste it into PowerPoint.
16. Navigate to slide 2.
17. Click **Insert**>**Images**>**Pictures** in the ribbon. A standard open dialog box is displayed.
18. Navigate to the Chap07 folder on your flash drive, and open the Seminar.jpg image file.

Pictures

19. Move and resize the image as needed.
20. Applying what you have learned, insert the Idea.jpg image file on slide 3.
21. Applying what you have learned, insert the Leader.jpg image file on slide 4.
22. Applying what you have learned, apply the Wisp theme and the blue variant. If this theme is not available, select one of your own choice.
23. Click **File**>**Save** in the ribbon, and save the file as *LastName*Seminar.pptx in the Chap07 folder on your flash drive. Since this is the first time the file has been saved, the **Save As** option is automatically used.

Advanced Features

Most presentation software contains many techniques to add sophisticated features. In Microsoft PowerPoint, these techniques include adding effects that appear when moving from slide to slide, including hyperlinks, and inserting a background image. Other presentation software will typically include these or similar features.

Adding Transitions

Transitions are the methods of shifting from one slide to the next. Rather than abruptly showing the next slide, the software can make the slides gradually move from one to the next, as shown in Figure 7-11. There are many types of transitions that can be applied. Slides can dramatically split, come in from the top or bottom, fly in from the left or right, or one of many other entrances.

Transitions can add visual interest to a presentation. However, do not overuse transitions. Also, limit the types of transitions used in a presentation. Generally, one or two types of transitions are fine for most applications. Some transitions may be harsh. Harsh transitions are dramatic, but they tend to focus the audience's attention away from the message. Simple transitions are best in most cases.

GS5
Key Applications
5.4

PowerPoint
4.1.1

FYI

The **Effect Options** button in the **Transition** tab on the ribbon allows the user to set transition options, including duration of transition, sound effects, and whether it should occur automatically or on a mouse click.

PowerPoint
4.1.2, 4.2.3

Slide appears from the center outward

Goodheart-Willcox Publisher

Figure 7-11. Transitions can be used to gradually shift from one slide to another.

HANDS-ON EXAMPLE 7.2.2

PowerPoint
4.3.1, 4.3.2

ADDING SLIDE TRANSITIONS

While transitions can add visual interest, they should not be overused. A subtle animation from one slide to the next is interesting, but not distracting.

1. Launch Microsoft PowerPoint, and open the *LastName*Seminar.pptx file in the Chap07 folder on your flash drive, if it is not already open.
2. Applying what you have learned, display the Slide Sorter view.
3. Select slide 1.
4. Click **Transitions>Transitions to This Slide>Split** in the ribbon. The transition is previewed and applied. If desired, though not necessary for this activity, the duration of the transition can be established by selecting **Transitions>Timing>Duration**. Clicking **Apply to All** will set the transition duration for all slides. The **Transitions** tab is also where users can configure start and finish options.
5. Applying what you have learned, apply a split transition to slide 2.
6. Applying what you have learned, apply a glitter transition to slide 3. You will need to expand the gallery to locate this transition. Glitter is a harsher transition compared to split.
7. Save the file.

PoiwerPoint
4.2.1, 4.2.2,
4.2.4

Animating Objects

Text and graphics can be made to move on the screen. **Animating** is the process of adding motion to an object. An animation is the resulting scene.

A common animation used in presentations is each bullet point entering the slide one at a time. This is a good way to focus the audience on the new topic. Shapes can be animated to provide a simple demonstration. This may more effectively communicate the action than describing it with text. Combining the use of slide transitions with animated objects can add drama to the flow of the presentation.

The number of animations should be kept to a minimum. Overuse of moving objects tends to distract the audience. Also, motion should be used for a purpose, such as emphasizing a bullet point. Just because an object *can* be animated does not mean it *should* be animated. Motion without a purpose is likely to be distracting to the audience.

Animation paths can be established to objects to enhance the presentation. For example, if a user needs to animate objects moving from one side of the slide to the other, an animation path can do this more efficiently than an animation. To set these paths, click **Animations>Add Animation** from the ribbon. In the drop-down menu, scroll down to **Motion Paths** and select the desired path. Selecting **Custom Path** will allow the user to draw an original path. Additional options can be found by selecting **More Motion Paths** at the bottom of the gallery. After making a selection, click **OK**.

FYI

Be sure not to overpower the purpose of the presentation with unneeded graphics, transitions, and animations.

HANDS-ON EXAMPLE 7.2.3

PowerPoint
4.3.3

ADDING ANIMATIONS

An effective use of motion in a presentation is to animate bullet points to appear one at a time. Combining a slide transition with this animation can make the presentation more dramatic.

1. Launch Microsoft PowerPoint, and open the *LastName*Seminar.pptx file in the Chap07 folder on your flash drive, if it is not already open.
2. Applying what you have learned, navigate to slide 4, and display the Normal view.
3. Click at the beginning of the first bullet, press the [Shift] key, and click at the end of the last bullet. This selects the bulleted list.
4. Click **Animations>Animation>Appear** in the ribbon. The animation is previewed and applied. Notice the number 1 appears next to each bullet. This indicates the order in which animations will be applied. In this case, all bullets are animated together, which is why they all have the number 1 next to them.
5. Click **Animations>Timing>Start** in the ribbon, and select **On Click** in the drop-down list. Now the bullets are numbered 1 through 6, as shown. This indicates the animation will be applied individually. In this case, one bullet will appear each time the mouse is clicked. If animations need to be reordered, simply drag and drop the desired animation to the new location in the list. A red line will appear in the new location.

Animation order

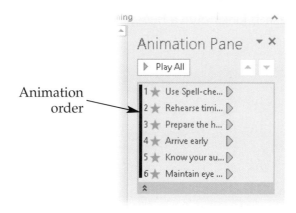

HANDS-ON EXAMPLE 7.2.3 (CONTINUED)

6. Applying what you have learned, view the presentation from the beginning. Verify that the bullets on slide 4 appear one at a time as the mouse is clicked.
7. Navigate to slide 3. This slide currently has a glitter transition applied, which is a harsh transition.
8. Applying what you have learned, apply the Origami transition to slide 3.
9. Applying what you have learned, view the presentation from this slide forward.
10. Save the file.

PowerPoint
2.1.6

Word
1.2.2

Ethics

Ethical Messages

Sometimes it is necessary to write a sales message or other type of document for your company. Embellishing a message about a product or service or intentionally misrepresenting a product or service is unethical and possibly illegal. There are truth-in-advertising laws that must be followed. Focus on the truths of the message to generate interest.

Creating a Hyperlink

Another tool for an effective presentation is the ability to add a link to additional information. A **hyperlink** is an electronic link between a marked place in a document to another place in the document or to another document, file, or web page.

For example, it may be appropriate to show the audience an informative video on the topic being discussed. Instead of embedding the video in the presentation, a hyperlink can be placed in the presentation. That link is clicked to access the video on the Internet or as a file saved on the hard drive. In another example, you may wish to show the audience how to locate information on a website. By including a hyperlink to the site, you can quickly access the site. A hyperlink can also be used to navigate to a different slide in the presentation, such as a slide containing glossary definitions.

A hyperlink is attached to a word or object in the presentation. For the presentation to be able to find the linked information, it must know the path. The path is found in the hyperlink. When the object containing the hyperlink is clicked during the slide show, the target is opened. The target may be an Internet address, a file on the local drive or a network drive, or another location in the current presentation or a different presentation.

An object that acts as the trigger must be set up and placed on a slide. In most presentation software, the procedure is to select the object, initiate the command for attaching a hyperlink, and enter the path to the target. In Microsoft PowerPoint, the command is initiated by clicking **Insert>Links>Add a Hyperlink** or by pressing the [Ctrl][K] key combination.

HANDS-ON EXAMPLE 7.2.4

ADDING A HYPERLINK

Many times it is important to show more information than is appropriate to include in the presentation itself. While showing a video may enhance the presentation, embedding it in the file will increase the file size.

1. Launch Microsoft PowerPoint, and open the *LastName*Seminar.pptx file in the Chap07 folder on your flash drive, if it is not already open.
2. Applying what you have learned, add a new Title and Content slide at the end of the presentation, and display the Normal view.
3. Applying what you have learned, insert an online picture of a microphone. Place the image in the center of the slide.
4. Launch a web browser, navigate to www.YouTube.com, and locate the video entitled "4 Steps to Improve Your Public Speaking" by Conor Neill. If you cannot locate this video, search for another professional video that discusses public speaking.
5. Watch the video to see that it is suitable. Click the **Share** link below the video player. The URL of the video appears in a text box.
6. Select the URL, and copy it to the system clipboard.
7. Close the web browser, and return to PowerPoint.

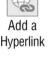

Add a
Hyperlink

8. Select the microphone image, and click **Insert>Links>Add a Hyperlink** in the ribbon. The **Insert Hyperlink** dialog box is displayed, as shown.

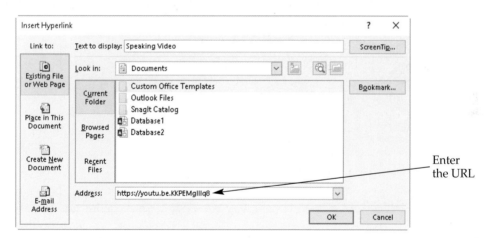

9. Click in the **Address:** text box, and paste the URL copied from the web browser. Click the **OK** button to attach the hyperlink to the image.
10. Applying what you have learned, view the presentation from the current slide.
11. Hover the cursor over the microphone image. The URL is displayed as help text.
12. Click the image to activate the hyperlink. The default web browser is launched, the YouTube page is displayed, and the video is played.
13. Close the web browser, and end the PowerPoint presentation.
14. Save the file.

PowerPoint

1.2.6

Inserting a Background Image

A **background image** is an overall image that appears behind all other elements on the slide. It is usually included as a way to make the presentation attractive. A background image can enhance the feeling of a presentation. It can draw increased attention to the presentation or it can be soothing to the audience.

A background image usually should not be the main focus of the slide. It should be visible, but it should not compete with the content on the slide for the audience's attention, as shown in Figure 7-12. If a photograph is used as a background image, a level of transparency is usually assigned to it. This allows the image to recede into the background yet be visible to the audience.

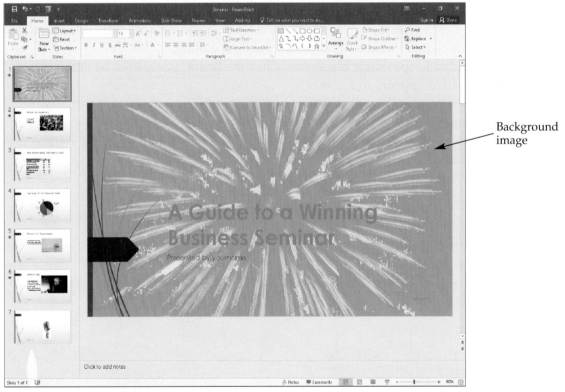

Background image

Goodheart-Willcox Publisher

Figure 7-12. A background image can be used to enhance a presentation, but it should not be the main focus.

HANDS-ON EXAMPLE 7.2.5

INSERTING A BACKGROUND IMAGE

A background image on the title slide can set the mood for a presentation. For example, a background image of fireworks will communicate excitement.

1. Launch Microsoft PowerPoint 2016, and open the *LastName*Seminar.pptx file in the Chap07 folder on your flash drive, if it is not already open.
2. Navigate to the title slide (slide 1).

HANDS-ON EXAMPLE 7.2.5 (CONTINUED)

3. Right-click on the slide or its thumbnail image, and click **Format Background** in the shortcut menu. The **Format Background** pane is displayed on the right-hand side of the application window, as shown. Note: in Microsoft PowerPoint 2010 and earlier, the **Format Background** dialog box is displayed.

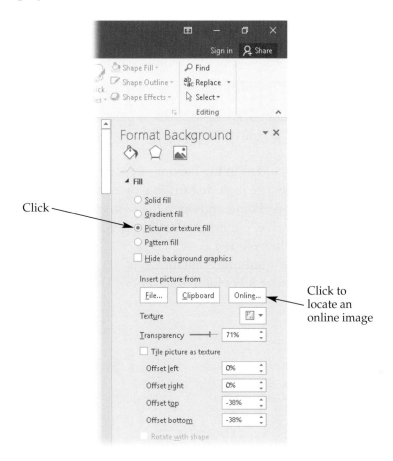

4. Click the **Picture or texture fill** radio button in the **Format Background** pane. The options in the pane change to reflect the selection.
5. Click the **Online...** button in the pane. The **Insert Pictures** dialog box is displayed.
6. Applying what you have learned, locate an image of holiday celebration fireworks and insert it. The image is added to the slide behind all other elements. Notice how the image is fully visible and the slide text is hard to read.
7. Click the **Transparency** slider, and drag to the right until the text on the slide is readable. The value in the **Transparency** text box increases as you drag, and the effect is previewed on the slide.
8. Close the **Format Background** pane.
9. Save the file.

PowerPoint
1.2.7

FYI

Headers and footers are commonly omitted from presentations.

Adding Headers and Footers

The *header* is at the top of the slide, and the *footer* is at the bottom of the slide. Each is outside of the area where the main content is placed. When content is placed in the header or footer, it appears on every slide. The header and footer can be used to include slide numbers, a date, or information about the presentation file. This information may be useful if the presentation is to be distributed for individual viewing instead of displayed to an audience.

HANDS-ON EXAMPLE 7.2.6

ADDING A HEADER AND FOOTER

Sometimes information is included in the header or footer as a courtesy to those viewing the presentation. Information may also be included to state ownership of the material.

1. Launch Microsoft PowerPoint, and open the *LastName*Seminar.pptx file in the Chap07 folder on your flash drive, if it is not already open.
2. Navigate to the title slide (slide 1).
3. Delete the date from the subtitle content.

Header & Footer

4. Click **Insert>Text>Header & Footer** in the ribbon. The **Header and Footer** dialog box is displayed, as shown.

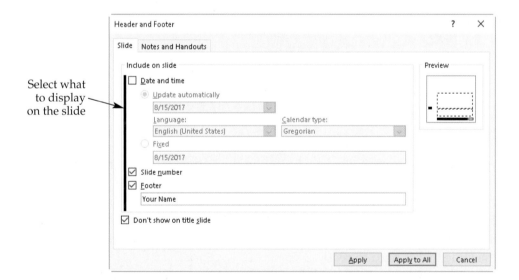

Select what to display on the slide

5. Check the **Slide number**, **Footer**, and **Don't show on title slide** check boxes. This specifies the footer and slide number will be placed on all the slides except the title slide.
6. Click in the **Footer** text box, and enter your name.
7. Click the **Apply to All** button.
8. Applying what you have learned, view the presentation from the beginning. Notice the slide number appears in the upper-left corner of the slide, and your name appears in the lower-left corner.
9. End the playback, and navigate to the title slide.
10. Applying what you have learned, open the **Header and Footer** dialog box.

HANDS-ON EXAMPLE 7.2.6 (CONTINUED)

11. Check the **Date and time** check box.
12. Click the **Update automatically** radio button.
13. Click the **Update automatically** drop-down arrow, and select the month, day, year format in the drop-down list.
14. Uncheck the **Don't show on title** slide check box.
15. Click the **Apply** button, *not* the **Apply to All** button. The **Apply** button applies the settings to only the current slide.
16. Applying what you have learned, view the presentation from the beginning. Notice on the title slide that there is no slide number and the date is in the footer instead of your name.
17. Save the file.

Creating Sections

PowerPoint
1.4.1, 1.4.3

When necessary, sections can be added to a PowerPoint presentation. Sections can help keep slides organized by content. To add a section to a presentation, right-click between the two slides where the section will begin and select **Add Section** from the shortcut menu. Alternatively, the user can use the keyboard shortcut [Ctrl][<]. Established sections can be renamed by selecting **Rename Section** from the shortcut menu.

7.2 | SECTION REVIEW

↪ CHECK YOUR UNDERSTANDING

1. What slide is included by default in a blank Microsoft PowerPoint file?
2. What is the difference between a transition and an animation?
3. What can a hyperlink be attached to in a Microsoft PowerPoint presentation?
4. Where does a background image appear on a slide?
5. Where are the header and footer located on a slide?

↪ BUILD YOUR VOCABULARY

As you progress through this course, develop a personal IT glossary. This will help you build your vocabulary and prepare you for a career. Write a definition for each of the following terms and add it to your IT glossary.

animating
background image
hyperlink
transition

CHARTS, TABLES, AND HANDOUTS

Properly used, assembled, and presented, statistics and other types of numerical data can be powerful devices in a presentation. A great number of data can be illustrated so that many individual items can be dealt with as one thought. Lists of numbers are not visually appealing or easy to understand in a presentation. However, presentation software makes it possible to visualize summary statistics.

Many people in the audience will want to take notes during a presentation. If the audience is provided with a hard copy of the presentation, that can be used for notes. Most presentation software is capable of printing the presentation with several slides per page to use as a handout for the audience. This section covers creating tables, charts, speaker notes, and handouts.

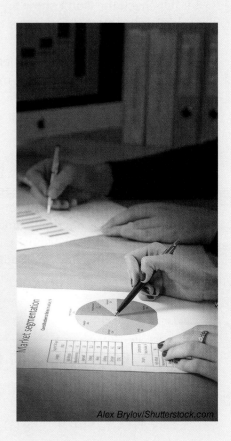

Alex Brylov/Shutterstock.com

LEARNING GOALS

After completing this section, you will be able to:
- Describe how to create a table.
- Explain the purpose of charts in a presentation.
- Discuss when to use speaker notes.
- Create handouts for a presentation audience.

TERMS

chart
handout
presentation notes

Creating Tables

Tables are often used to present data, such as numerical figures or statistics. The table format makes it easy for the audience to view this type of information. A table, which looks similar to a spreadsheet, consists of columns, rows, and cells.

Tables are easy to add to a presentation. A table in a presentation is similar to a table in a word-processing document, as discussed in Chapter 5. The standard format for a table sets the first row as a header row, as shown in Figure 7-13. A header row is used to indicate what the data in each cell mean. The spacing, font, and column and row sizing for a table can all be customized.

There are a couple of ways to add a table to a presentation in Microsoft PowerPoint. The commands on the **Insert** tab of the ribbon can be used. Click **Insert>Tables>Table** in the ribbon. The drop-down menu that is displayed contains a grid representing rows and columns. Highlight the number of rows and columns for the table using this grid. The table is previewed on the slide as the grid is highlighted. When the correct number of rows and columns are highlighted in the grid, click to insert the table.

Another way to add a table is by clicking **Insert Table...** in the drop-down menu. This displays the **Insert Table** dialog box. Enter the number of rows and columns for the table, and click the **OK** button to insert the table.

Also, any of the content text boxes on the default slide masters contain embedded helper icons, as shown in Figure 7-14. One of these is the **Insert Table** icon, which looks like a small table. This is a shortcut for inserting a table into the text box. Clicking the icon displays the **Insert Table** dialog box. If this icon is present, using it is the most efficient way to access the command.

PowerPoint

3.1.1, 3.1.2

FYI

Navigating the table is done with the arrow keys, the mouse, or the [Tab] and [Shift][Tab] key combinations.

FYI

The number of rows and columns in a table can be adjusted after the table is inserted.

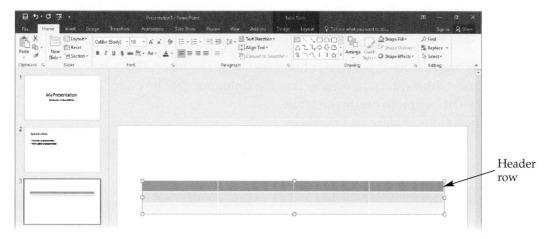

Header row

Goodheart-Willcox Publisher

Figure 7-13. A header row is the first row in a table, which indicates what the data in each column mean.

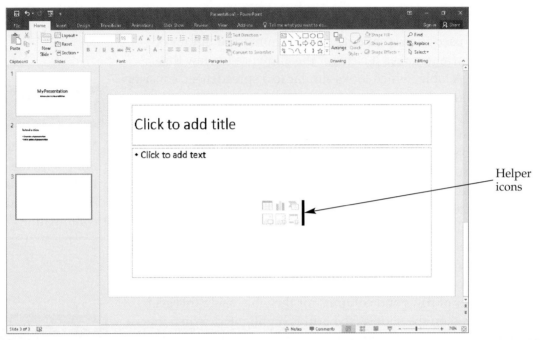

Figure 7-14. Content text boxes contain helper icons, which are shortcuts to adding content.

HANDS-ON EXAMPLE 7.3.1

Excel	PowerPoint
3.2.1	3.1.3

ADDING A TABLE

Tables can be used in a presentation to present numerical data. However, a table can also be used to organize textual information as well.

1. Launch Microsoft PowerPoint, and open the *LastName*Seminar.pptx file in the Chap07 folder on your flash drive, if it is not already open.
2. Applying what you have learned, add a new Title and Content slide after slide 2.
3. Enter How Presentation Software Is Used as the title content.
4. Click the **Insert Table** icon in the content text box. The **Insert Table** dialog box is displayed.
5. In the **Insert Table** dialog box, enter 3 in the **Columns:** text box and 9 in the **Rows:** text box. Click the **OK** button to create the table.
6. Enter the following data into the table.

	Employees	Students
Education and teaching	72	97
Talks and meetings	70	32
Private ceremonies	32	40
Company presentations	43	11
Conferences and trade fairs	39	7
Product presentations	30	8
Entertainment	8	10
Other	1	1

HANDS-ON EXAMPLE 7.3.1 (CONTINUED)

7. Select all text in the table by clicking in the upper-left cell and dragging to the bottom-right cell.

8. Click **Home>Font>Font Size** in the ribbon, and click **16** in the drop-down list to change the size of the text.

9. Applying what you have learned, select the numerical data in the table.

Align Right

10. Click **Home>Font>Align Right** in the ribbon.

11. Move the cursor to the top of the right-hand column until it changes to a downward arrow, and click to select the column.

12. Click **Layout>Cell Size>Width:** in the ribbon, and enter 1.2".

13. Applying what you have learned, reduce the width of the middle column to 1.4".

14. Applying what you have learned, select the entire table.

15. Choose **Design>Table Styles>Light Style 2 – Accent 3** in the ribbon. The table is complete, as shown.

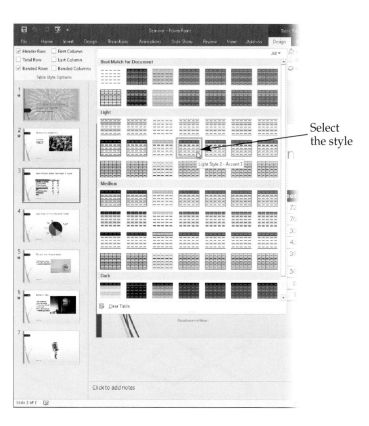

Select the style

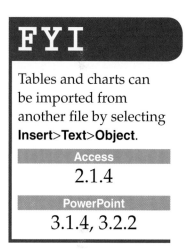

FYI

Tables and charts can be imported from another file by selecting **Insert>Text>Object**.

Access
2.1.4

PowerPoint
3.1.4, 3.2.2

Creating Charts

PowerPoint
3.2.1

Charts are another way to present data. A **chart**, or *graph*, illustrates data in a picture-like format. Many times it is easier to understand the data if they are shown in graphical form instead of in numerical form in a table. The meaning of the data can be absorbed in one glance without

FYI

Legends can be added to charts from the drop-down menu in the **Chart Elements** button.

PowerPoint
3.2.4

PowerPoint
3.2.3, 3.2.5

reading each number. For example, a line chart can be used to show the trend of financial markets over time. Common charts include bar, line, and pie, as shown in Figure 7-15.

Most presentation software has commands to create various charts. In Microsoft PowerPoint, either click the **Insert Chart** icon in a content text box or click **Insert>Illustrations>Insert Chart** in the ribbon. The **Insert Chart** dialog box is displayed, which is used to select the type of chart to create. Once the type of chart is selected, a placeholder chart is added to the slide, and a spreadsheet is displayed for entering data, as shown in Figure 7-16. As data are entered in the spreadsheet, the placeholder chart is updated to reflect the data. When all data have been entered, close the spreadsheet.

Once a chart is created, it can be formatted. In Microsoft PowerPoint, there are various options on the **Design** and **Format** on-demand tabs for changing the appearance of the chart. The basic formatting style of the chart can be changed. The colors used in the chart can be changed. Even the type of chart can be changed. The same data will be represented in the new type selected.

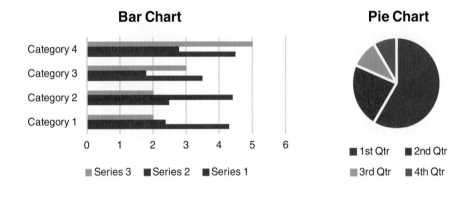

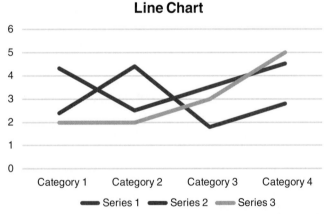

Goodheart-Willcox Publisher

Figure 7-15. The most common types of charts are bar, line, and pie.

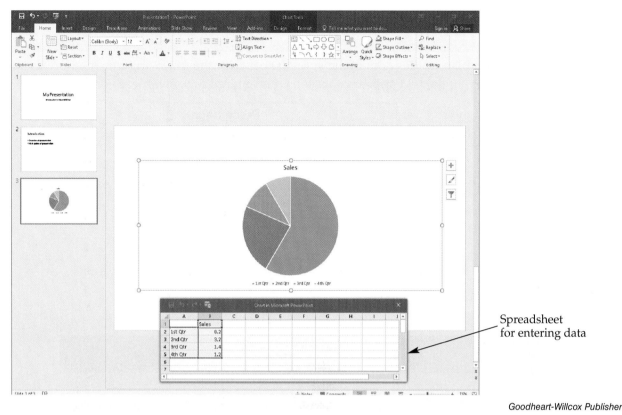

Goodheart-Willcox Publisher

Figure 7-16. When inserting a chart, an embedded spreadsheet is used to enter the data.

HANDS-ON EXAMPLE 7.3.2

ADDING A CHART

Charts can provide a way for the audience to quickly understand the meaning of data. For example, a pie chart can be used to quickly show the occurrence of various phobias among the general population.

1. Launch Microsoft PowerPoint, and open the *LastName*Seminar.pptx file in the Chap07 folder on your flash drive, if it is not already open.
2. Applying what you have learned, add a new Title and Content slide after slide 3.
3. Enter Top Fears of the General Public as the title content.
4. Click the **Insert Chart** icon in the content text box, which appears as a small bar chart, to display the **Insert Chart** dialog box.
5. Click **Pie** in the **Insert Chart** dialog box to specify the type of chart to create.
6. Click the **OK** button. A placeholder pie chart is added to the slide, and a spreadsheet containing placeholder data is displayed below the chart.

HANDS-ON EXAMPLE 7.3.2 (CONTINUED)

7. Replace the placeholder data in the spreadsheet with the following information, as shown. Do not worry if the text appears cut off as it is entered, it will appear correctly in the chart.

	Percentage
Public speaking	71
Heights	32
Insects	24
Finances	23
Deep water	22
Sickness	20
Death	19
Flying	18

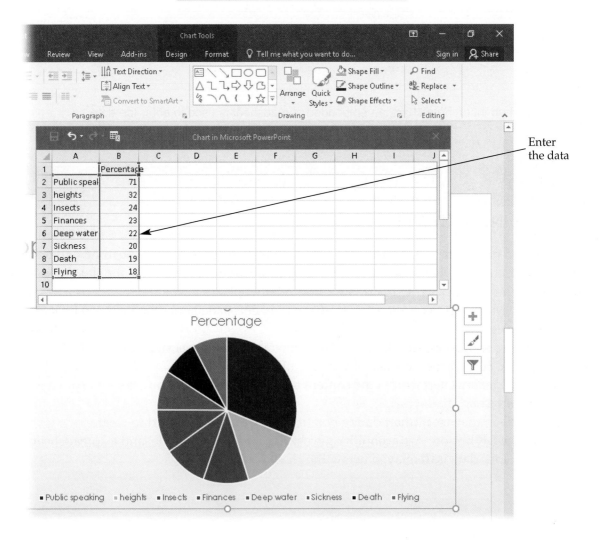

Enter the data

HANDS-ON EXAMPLE 7.3.2 (CONTINUED)

8. Close the spreadsheet by clicking the close button (X) for the spreadsheet. The spreadsheet is automatically saved when the presentation is saved.
9. With the chart selected, three buttons appear on the right-hand side of the chart. Click the **Chart Elements** button, which looks like a plus sign (+). The **Chart Elements** pane appears on the left-hand side of the chart.
10. In the **Chart Elements** pane, uncheck the **Chart Title** check box. The title Percentages is no longer displayed on the chart.
11. Click the **Chart Styles** button on the right-hand side of the chart, which looks like a paintbrush. The **Style/Color** pane is displayed on the left-hand side of the chart.
12. Click **Style 9** in the list of styles in the **Style/Color** pane. To see the name of a style, hover the cursor over the preview to display the name as help text. This style places the names of the different fears next to the corresponding slices in the pie chart.
13. Save the file.

Creating Speaker Notes

Most speakers do not memorize their speeches. Instead, they rely on notes. **Presentation notes,** or speaker notes, are notes used to keep the speaker on topic. They are used during the presentation to help you keep your place and to remind yourself of points should you forget anything.

Most presentation software offers a feature to help the speaker create presentation notes. In Microsoft PowerPoint, this feature is called speaker notes. These notes will not be visible during the presentation, but they can be printed beforehand for the speaker to use. They can also be used as notes to yourself during the development process, such as "add a photograph to this slide."

In Microsoft PowerPoint, notes can be entered below each slide. Notes can be entered for all slides or just the ones that require further explanation. The text in a presentation note should be kept to a minimum. The purpose of a note is to be a reminder, not full sentences to read to the audience.

To create a speaker note in Microsoft PowerPoint, click in the **Notes** area at the bottom of the PowerPoint window, as shown in Figure 7-17. If this area is not displayed, click the **Notes** button in the bar at the bottom of the PowerPoint window. With the insertion point in the **Notes** area, enter the text for the note. Limited formatting is available for note text. The text can be made bold, italic, underlined, or any combination of these. However, the size cannot be changed, nor can the color of the text.

FYI

Having the printed presentation with speaker notes available during the presentation can help make for a professional delivery.

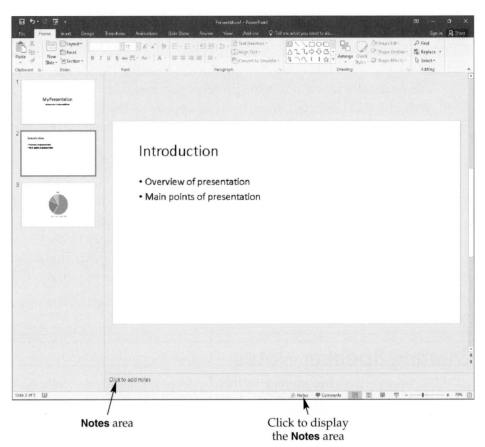

Notes area   Click to display
                    the Notes area

Goodheart-Willcox Publisher

Figure 7-17. The **Notes** area is displayed below the slide at the bottom of the window.

HANDS-ON EXAMPLE 7.3.3

PowerPoint
1.6.1, 1.6.2

ADDING SPEAKER NOTES

Speaker notes can be used as reminders of important points to make during a presentation. Speaker notes will not be visible during a presentation, but they can be printed beforehand.

1. Launch Microsoft PowerPoint, and open the *LastName*Seminar.pptx file in the Chap07 folder on your flash drive, if it is not already open.
2. Navigate to slide 4, and display the Normal view, if it is not already displayed. Speaker notes must be added in the Normal view.
3. If the notes area is not displayed at the bottom of the window, click the **Notes** button.

Notes

4. Click in the notes area. The placeholder text Click to Add Notes is replaced by the insertion point.
5. Enter this text:
   The word for speech anxiety, glossophobia, comes from the Greek glossa, meaning tongue, and phobos, meaning fear or dread.
6. Click **File>Print** in the ribbon.
7. Under **Settings**, click the first drop-down arrow, and click **Print Current Slide** in the drop-down list.

HANDS-ON EXAMPLE 7.3.3 (CONTINUED)

8. Click the second drop-down arrow, and click **Notes Pages** in the drop-down menu. Notice the print preview shows slide 4 (the current slide) and the speaker notes added below the slide.
9. Click the **Print** button.
10. Save the file.

Creating Handouts

Handouts, also called *leave-behinds,* are printed materials that are distributed to the audience. Generally, handouts are used to help the listener understand the information in the presentation, provide additional information about the topic, or both. They are useful for providing an outline of key points or supplemental information that is not covered in the presentation. Figure 7-18 provides some guidelines for using handouts.

Handouts can be valuable to the audience. They serve as a review of the speaker's key points. They give the audience something to take away from the presentation. They are an important way for participants to be reminded of the key messages. Handouts are especially useful if the presentation is highly technical or complex.

However, do not overload people with a large amount of reading material. The audience should be paying attention to the key points of the presenter, not trying to read material. If listeners need the information during the presentation, distribute the materials before you begin. Place handouts on a table at the front or hand them out as people enter. If you intend to distribute the handout during the presentation, inform the listeners at the beginning of the presentation. Then they will know that they do not need to take notes. This makes it possible for them to focus their attention completely on the speaker. For distribution after the presentation, pass them out while people are still seated.

GS5
Key Applications
5.1.1

FYI

Speaker notes can be used as handouts to provide additional information.

Using Handouts

- Do not assume audience members will read your handouts.
- Keep handouts as short as possible; be concise.
- Use a format that presents the information in a way that is visually appealing and professional.
- Include your contact information and the date of the presentation.
- If the handout or presentation is available on a website, include the appropriate URL.
- Before the presentation, plan when and how you will use handouts.
- Have a plan for quickly distributing materials without distraction.
- Before referring to a handout during your presentation, be sure each person has a copy.

Goodheart-Willcox Publisher

Figure 7-18. Follow these tips when using handouts with a presentation.

FYI

Clicking **View>Master Views>Handout Master** allows a user to change the layout, orientation, headers and footers, and background of presentation handouts.

PowerPoint
1.3.5

FYI

Users can rehearse the pace and timings of presentations by selecting **Slide Show>Set Up>Rehearse Timings**.

PowerPoint
1.7.3

Most presentation software has a function to create handouts from the slides in the presentation. This can be done to provide the audience with a copy of the presentation on which to make notes or to help those who may be in the back of the room follow the presentation. In Microsoft PowerPoint, creating handouts is part of the printing function. When selecting to print handouts, the number of slides that will appear on each printed page must be selected, from one to nine slides per page. The option for three slides per page also includes lines the audience can use to take notes. This is a good option for handouts distributed at the beginning of a presentation. The printout can be generated in color, grayscale, or pure black and white, as shown in Figure 7-19.

Option	Explanation
Color	Choose this option to output in color on a color printer. If this option is used to print on a black-and-white printer, the printout will be grayscale, but of a lower quality than when printing in grayscale.
Grayscale	Choose this option to print all objects on the page in shades of gray. This option should be used with a black-and-white printer, but it can also be used with a color printer if the output does not need to be in color.
Pure Black and White	This option prints slides in black and white. There are no shades of gray. As a result, some objects in the design theme of the slide, such as embossing and drop shadows, will not print. Text will print as black even if the text is in color.

Goodheart-Willcox Publisher

Figure 7-19. When creating a handout, decide how the color will be printed.

HANDS-ON EXAMPLE 7.3.4

PowerPoint
1.6.3, 1.6.4

PRINTING HANDOUTS

Handouts can be valuable for the audience. The handout function in Microsoft PowerPoint can be used to generate a copy of the presentation for the audience.

1. Launch Microsoft PowerPoint, and open the *LastName*Seminar.pptx file in the Chap07 folder on your flash drive, if it is not already open.
2. Click **File>Print** in the ribbon.
3. Under **Settings**, click the first drop-down arrow, and click **Print All Slides** in the drop-down list.
4. Click the second drop-down arrow, and click **3 Slides** in the drop-down menu. Notice the print preview shows the first three slides in the presentation as well as lines next to each slide. The audience can use these lines to write notes.
5. Click the bottom drop-down arrow, and click **Grayscale** in the drop-down list. All colors in the presentation will be output as shades of gray.
6. Click the **Print** button.
7. Save the file.

7.3 | SECTION REVIEW

 CHECK YOUR UNDERSTANDING

1. What type of information is presented in a table?
2. How does a chart present data?
3. When creating a chart in Microsoft PowerPoint, how is a spreadsheet used?
4. How are speaker notes used?
5. In general, what is the purpose of a handout?

 BUILD YOUR VOCABULARY

As you progress through this course, develop a personal IT glossary. This will help you build your vocabulary and prepare you for a career. Write a definition for each of the following terms and add it to your IT glossary.

chart
handout
presentation notes

7 REVIEW AND ASSESSMENT

Chapter Summary

Section 7.1
Creating a Professional Presentation

- A presentation is a speech, address, or demonstration given to a group. Begin by planning the presentation, and then create the content for the presentation.

- Knowing how to navigate a presentation is important when creating and presenting. You must also be able to add slides, text, and graphics as well as be able to format the presentation.

- Managing the presentation involves rearranging, deleting, and copying slides. There are many tools available to help in managing the presentation.

Section 7.2
Adding Transitions and Animations

- A new presentation can be started from scratch or a template can be used. The new presentation will contain several slide masters that can be applied to slides in the presentation.

- Transitions are the methods of shifting from one slide to the next, while animations are objects with motion added to them. Hyperlinks can be assigned to elements in a presentation, and a background image can be added behind all other elements on a slide.

Section 7.3
Charts, Tables, and Handouts

- Tables are often used to present data, such as numerical figures or statistics. A table is similar to a spreadsheet, consisting of columns, rows, and cells.

- A chart, or graph, illustrates data in a picture-like format. This allows the meaning of data to be absorbed in one glance without reading individual numbers.

- Presentation notes help to keep the speaker on topic. They are used during the presentation to help you keep your place and to remind yourself of points should you forget anything.

- Handouts, also called leave-behinds, are printed materials that are distributed to the audience. They are useful for providing an outline of key points or supplemental information that is not covered in the presentation.

Now that you have finished this chapter, see what you know about computer applications by taking the chapter posttest. Access the posttest by visiting www.g-wlearning.com.

Chapter 7 Test

Multiple Choice

Select the best response.

1. When identifying who will attend a presentation, what are the two types of audiences?
   A. Students and professionals.
   B. Internal and external.
   C. Experienced and novice.
   D. Top-down and bottom-up.

2. Which of the following is the key combination to navigate to the beginning of a presentation in Microsoft PowerPoint?
   A. [Ctrl][Page Up]
   B. [Home]
   C. [Ctrl][Home]
   D. [Shift][Home]

3. Overuse of moving objects tends to do what?
   A. Distract the audience.
   B. Emphasize a point.
   C. Add interest to the presentation.
   D. Create visual appeal.

4. What happens when the item containing a hyperlink is clicked during the slide show?
   A. The hyperlink is inactive during the slide show.
   B. The target defined in the hyperlink is opened.
   C. A new presentation window is opened.
   D. The presentation is closed and the target is opened.

5. Where are speaker notes entered in Microsoft PowerPoint?
   A. As a comment on the slide.
   B. In the **Notes** dialog box.
   C. Below the slide.
   D. In the Notes view.

Completion

Complete the following sentences with the correct word(s).

6. The introduction should also draw the listener into the presentation with a(n) _____.

7. _____ are used to standardize colors, fonts, and effects across all slides in a presentation.

8. Rather than abruptly showing the next slide, a(n) _____ can make the slides gradually move from one to the next.

9. A table is similar to a(n) _____, consisting of columns, rows, and cells.

10. Speaker notes are intended to be used by the _____.

Matching

Match the correct term with its definition.

A. presentation
B. theme
C. transition
D. hyperlink
E. chart

11. Technique for showing data in a picture-like format.

12. Set of specified colors, fonts, and effects.

13. Method of moving from one slide to the next.

14. Electronic link between a marked place in a document to another place in the document or to another document, file, or web page.

15. Speech, address, or demonstration given to a group.

Application and Extension of Knowledge

1. Go to the Bureau of Labor Statistics website (www.bls.gov), and investigate four careers of interest to you. Create a presentation that describes these careers. Include a title slide, a slide for each career describing the skills needed, and a summary slide that compares the median salaries of the four careers. Apply the principles outlined in this chapter, including the 7×7 rule.

2. Visit a software store, either online or a physical store, and look for presentations software. Make a list of the available software. Compare the price and available features for the software you found. Choose which software you would use and prepare for a class discussion explaining your choice.

3. Select a topic of interest to you, such as a hobby or activity. Outline the three parts of a presentation explaining the topic: introduction, body, and conclusion. Make note of what you will use as an attention grabber and a clincher. Then, create the presentation applying the principles outlined in this chapter.

4. Think of a short scene that can be animated, such as a dog chasing a ball. Create a presentation, and insert images, clipart, and drawing shapes to create the scene. Then, animate the objects as needed. Use the help function as needed to investigate animation features and functions. Think of ways to use transitions between slides to help with animating the scene. When completed, prepare to present the slide show to the class and explain how you animated the scene.

5. Select one of the presentations you created. Generate handouts to distribute when you give the presentation. Determine when you will distribute the handouts and how, and follow through with this when you give your presentation.

Online Activities

Complete the following activities, which will help you learn, practice, and expand your knowledge and skills.

Vocabulary. Practice vocabulary for this chapter using the e-flash cards, matching activity, and vocabulary game until you are able to recognize their meanings.

Communication Skills

Reading. Using technology in the workplace can help employees be more productive. In other instances, technology can be a distraction. Read about types of technology and how people can use each to be more productive in the workplace. What did you learn?

Listening. Practice active-listening skills while listening to your teacher present this chapter. Focus on the message and monitor it for understanding. Were there any barriers to effective listening? Share your ideas in the group discussion.

Speaking. What role do you think ethics and integrity have in deciding which graphics to use in a presentation? What process did you use to make the decision? Make an informal presentation to your class to share your thoughts.

Internet Research

Netiquette. Research the term *netiquette* using various Internet resources. Write several paragraphs to describe what the term means, where it came from, and how it has evolved this century.

Teamwork

With your team, conduct research on the phrase *Silicon Valley*. Create a presentation that explains what Silicon Valley is, how it got its name, and the significance of it to information technology.

Activity Files

Visit www.g-wlearning.com/informationtechnology/ to download the activity files for this chapter. These activities will expand your learning of the material presented in this chapter and allow you to practice what you have learned. Follow the instructions provided in each file to complete the activity.

Activity File 7-1 Modifying Premade Themes

Activity File 7-2 Applying Transitions

Activity File 7-3 Adding Animations

Activity File 7-4 Inserting Hyperlinks

Activity File 7-5 Analyzing Handouts

CAPSTONE PROJECT

The capstone project builds from one chapter to the next. It allows you to apply the skills you have learned to create a complete project in a desired career area. Read the instructions below for the career area you chose to work in for this course. Work in the same career area in each chapter.

Agriculture, Food, and Natural Resources

In this activity, you will assume the role of a farm owner and create presentations discussing the topics of public speaking and raising poultry. Then, you will modify and customize these presentations for specific needs. Access the *Introduction to Microsoft Office 2016* companion website (www.g-wlearning.com/informationtechnology/) to view the instructions for this chapter's Agriculture, Food, and Natural Resources capstone project.

Business, Management, and Administration

In this activity, you will assume the role of an administrator in a small, growing, widget-manufacturing business. You will create a presentation for the company and communicate the new reorganization to the company at large. Access the *Introduction to Microsoft Office 2016* companion website (www.g-wlearning.com/informationtechnology/) to view the instructions for this chapter's Business, Management, and Administration capstone project.

Health Science

In this activity, you will assume the role of a patient educator to create presentations discussing the topics of public speaking and recovery from a heart attack. Then, you will modify and customize these presentations for specific needs. Access the *Introduction to Microsoft Office 2016* companion website (www.g-wlearning.com/informationtechnology/) to view the instructions for this chapter's Health Science capstone project.

Science, Technology, Engineering, and Mathematics

In this activity, you will continue your role of a NASA communications team member for the Near-Earth Object Project. You will create a presentation for the communications department that communicates and explains the status of near-earth objects. Access the *Introduction to Microsoft Office 2016* companion website (www.g-wlearning. com/informationtechnology/) to view the instructions for this chapter's Science, Technology, Engineering, and Mathematics capstone project.

8

SPREADSHEET SOFTWARE

SECTIONS

8.1 INTRODUCTION TO SPREADSHEETS

8.2 MANAGING DATA IN SPREADSHEETS

CHECK YOUR IT IQ

Before you begin this chapter, see what you already know about computer applications by taking the chapter pretest. Access the pretest by visiting www.g-wlearning.com. ↗

Microsoft Excel is the most popular software for creating computerized spreadsheets, but spreadsheets have a long history, originating hundreds of years before computers. Spreadsheets are used to organize, calculate, and communicate information. An individual cell in a computerized spreadsheet where a row and a column intersect can contain a variety of data, including text, numbers, or formulas to perform calculations. After data are entered, it is easy to update or edit the spreadsheet.

The data in a computerized spreadsheet can be formatted in many ways. The color of cells and the text and numbers they contain can be changed. Numbers can be formatted as percentages, currency, and many other formats. The size of individual cells can be changed, and cells can be merged. The size of rows and columns can be changed, and rows and columns can be inserted or deleted. Data in a computerized spreadsheet can be sorted and filtered as needed to display only needed information.

MICROSOFT OFFICE SPECIALIST OBJECTIVES

Excel

Create and Manage Worksheets and Workbooks

1.1 Create Worksheets and Workbooks
- **1.1.1** Create a workbook
- **1.1.2** Import data from a delimited text file
- **1.1.3** Add a worksheet to an existing workbook
- **1.1.4** Copy and move a worksheet

1.2 Navigate in Worksheets and Workbooks
- **1.2.1** Search for data within a workbook
- **1.2.2** Navigate to a named cell, range, or workbook element
- **1.2.3** Insert and remove hyperlinks

1.3 Format Worksheets and Workbooks
- **1.3.1** Change worksheet tab color
- **1.3.2** Rename a worksheet
- **1.3.3** Change worksheet order
- **1.3.4** Modify page setup
- **1.3.5** Insert and delete columns and rows
- **1.3.6** Change workbook themes
- **1.3.7** Adjust row height and column width
- **1.3.8** Insert headers and footers

1.4 Customize Options and Views for Worksheets and Workbooks
- **1.4.1** Hide or unhide worksheets
- **1.4.2** Hide or unhide columns and rows
- **1.4.4** Change workbook views
- **1.4.5** Change window views
- **1.4.6** Modify document properties
- **1.4.8** Display formulas

1.5 Configure Worksheets and Workbooks for Distribution
- **1.5.1** Set a print area
- **1.5.2** Save workbooks in alternative file formats
- **1.5.3** Print all or part of a workbook
- **1.5.4** Set print scaling

Manage Data Cells and Ranges

2.1 Insert Data in Cells and Ranges
- **2.1.1** Replace data
- **2.1.2** Cut, copy, or paste data
- **2.1.4** Fill cells by using Auto Fill
- **2.1.5** Insert and delete cells

2.2 Format Cells and Ranges
- **2.2.1** Merge cells
- **2.2.2** Modify cell alignment and indentation
- **2.2.4** Wrap text within cells
- **2.2.5** Apply number formats
- **2.2.6** Apply cell formats
- **2.2.7** Apply cell styles

2.3 Summarize and Organize Data
- **2.3.2** Outline data
- **2.3.3** Insert subtotals

Create Tables

3.3 Filter and Sort a Table
- **3.3.1** Filter records
- **3.3.2** Sort data by multiple columns
- **3.3.3** Change sort order

Perform Operations with Formulas and Functions

4.1 Summarize Data by using Functions
- **4.1.1** Insert references

INTRODUCTION TO SPREADSHEETS

Spreadsheets have long been used to record financial data. They display data in columns and rows for easy viewing and analysis. Computerized spreadsheets are basically the same as manual spreadsheets, with data arranged in rows and columns. However, computerized spreadsheets offer significant advantages.

Data can be quickly added to a computerized spreadsheet, and the spreadsheet can be easily navigated using the keyboard or mouse. One of the greatest advantages of a computerized spreadsheet is the ability to include formulas that automatically perform calculations. Another great advantage lies in the ease of editing data, either correcting errors or updating figures.

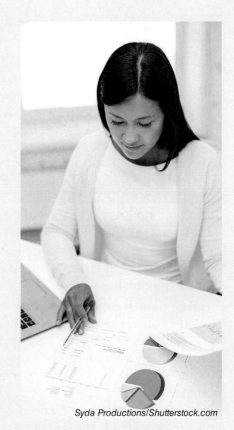

Syda Productions/Shutterstock.com

LEARNING GOALS

After completing this section, you will be able to:
- Discuss the origin of spreadsheets.
- Describe a spreadsheet.
- Enter data into a spreadsheet.
- Explain how to create a formula in a spreadsheet.
- Edit data to correct errors and update information.

TERMS

active cell	row
cell	spreadsheet
column	text
formula	what-if analysis
killer app	
numbers	workbook
range	worksheet

Origin of Spreadsheets

A **spreadsheet** is a collection of data arranged in rows and columns. Spreadsheets originated with bookkeepers, who recorded financial data in a ledger in rows and columns that spanned two facing pages or a single oversized page. Data were manually entered, with columns representing categories of expenditures, rows representing invoices, and cells containing the money amount; worksheets are added to a workbook by selecting the **New Sheet** button. If any changes needed to be made or mistakes corrected, bookkeepers had to erase several entries and rerecord data.

Manual spreadsheets continued to be used after the advent of computerized spreadsheet software in the 1960s. Early spreadsheet software was for large mainframe computers, not personal computers. In 1978, Dan Bricklin was watching his professor at Harvard Business School solve a complex math problem on a blackboard. When the professor found an error or wanted to change a value, he had to erase several numbers and recalculate the result. Bricklin realized he could make a computer do that for him.

Bricklin and Bob Frankston invented spreadsheet software named VisiCalc for the Apple II personal computer in just two months. It became the first killer app. A **killer app** is a software application so compelling that people buy a computer just to be able to use it. VisiCalc helped change the Apple II computer from a hobbyist's device to a useful business tool. It also helped launch the widespread transition from manual spreadsheets to computerized spreadsheets.

Using Spreadsheets

A spreadsheet is very helpful whenever a job requires a great deal of calculation, a graph or chart to visually display relationships, or numerical data that change from time to time. Businesses collect lots of data. Some numerical data that has to be totaled, multiplied, or otherwise analyzed include amounts of money, quantities of inventory, and numbers of hours. Spreadsheet software contains the features which make this possible. The most valuable advantage is its ability to automatically recalculate formulas and reprocess data.

Spreadsheet Overview

A sample computerized spreadsheet containing data and a chart is shown in Figure 8-1. The arrangement of the spreadsheet is similar to a manual spreadsheet based on a bookkeeper's ledger. The grid is the arrangement of vertical and horizontal lines. This is where the work is done. In Microsoft Excel, this grid, which is the spreadsheet, is called a **worksheet**. A **workbook**, which is the Excel file, may contain one or several worksheets.

Columns are the spaces between the vertical grid lines. In Microsoft Excel, these are named alphabetically from left to right. **Rows** are the spaces between the horizontal grid lines. In Microsoft Excel, these are sequentially numbered from top to bottom. Where a column and row

Excel

1.1.3

FYI

The word *spreadsheet* comes from the publishing term *spread*, which means two facing pages of a publication, such as a book, magazine, or newspaper.

GS5

Key Applications

3.13

GS5

Key Applications

3.1.1, 3.1.2, 3.1.3, 3.1.5, 3.1.6

Funds Tracking

Name	January	February	March	Total	Percentage
Jimmy	$ 25.50	$ 36.25	$ 18.75	$ 80.50	37%
Carlos	$ 15.50	$ 22.00	$ 36.75	$ 74.25	34%
Stevie	$ 20.75	$ 12.75	$ 28.50	$ 62.00	29%
Monthly Total	$ 61.75	$ 71.00	$ 84.00	$ 216.75	

Goodheart-Willcox Publisher

Figure 8-1. A spreadsheet consists of columns and rows, and where they intersect is a cell.

intersect is a **cell**. Each cell has an address named for the column and row. For example, cell B2 is located in the second row (row 2) of the second column (column B), as shown in Figure 8-2. The **active cell** is the currently selected cell, which is indicated by an outline around the cell.

Navigating a Spreadsheet

A spreadsheet may be very small, consisting of just a few columns and rows, or very large, consisting of thousands of columns and rows. When a blank spreadsheet is started, only the upper-left corner of it can be seen. A few rows and columns are visible, but many more are available for use.

The mouse can be used to navigate a spreadsheet. To select a different cell, click the cell. Double-click the cell to activate its contents for editing.

GS5

Key Applications

1.6, 3.1.7

Excel

1.2.2

FYI

Microsoft Excel 2010 and later versions are able to accommodate 16,384 columns and over one million rows of data.

FYI

Users can switch workbook views by clicking **View>Workbook Views** in the ribbon and choosing the desired view.

Excel

1.4.5

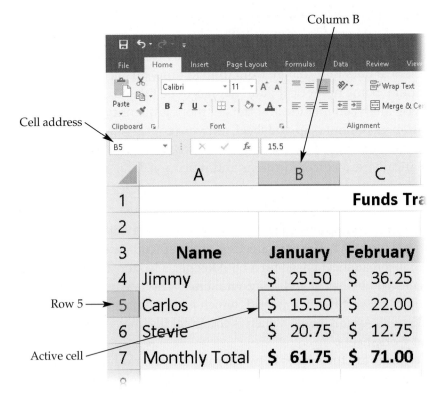

Goodheart-Willcox Publisher

Figure 8-2. A cell's address is based on the column and row where it is located.

To see rows or columns not visible in the current view, use the scroll bars to pan the view. The mouse wheel can also be used to scroll downward. If at any time a different view is needed, the user can select the desired view by clicking **View**>**Workbook View**.

However, the most efficient users primarily navigate a spreadsheet with the keyboard. Figure 8-3 shows ways in which to use a keyboard to navigate a spreadsheet.

Saving a Spreadsheet

A spreadsheet is saved in Microsoft Excel in the same manner as a document in any Microsoft Office application. Click **File**>**Save** in the ribbon, and then click **Computer** followed by the **Browse** button in the backstage view. If the file has not yet been saved, the save as function is started. Navigate to the folder where you wish to save the spreadsheet, enter a file name, and save the file. Microsoft Excel automatically adds the .xlsx extension. If the file has previously been saved, clicking **Save** will automatically save the file under the same name. To save the file under a different name, click **File**>**Save As** in the ribbon.

Entering Data

There are several common data types used in computer programming:
- Integers are the positive and negative counting numbers and zero.
- Floating point numbers are decimal numbers.
- Boolean types only hold values for true or false.
- Characters are single letters, digits, or other symbols.
- Strings hold alphabetic and numeric text, along with special symbols.
- Date types hold time and date information.

Data types are also important in a computerized spreadsheet. The data type, or *format*, for a cell determines what the data entered in the cell mean. Microsoft Excel sets the default data type for the cell by the characters entered in the cell.

In general, data entered into a spreadsheet are either text, numbers, or formulas. **Text** is a string data type. It may consist of any letters, digits, or other keyboard characters. Text is used for titles, labels, and

Excel
1.4.4

FYI

Spreadsheets usually represent many hours of work, so save your work often!

Excel
2.1.4

GS5
Key Applications
3.6

Excel
1.1.1, 2.1.1

FYI

It is possible to format numbers and formulas as text, so if a formula is not working, be sure this is not the case.

[Enter]	Move down one row
[Tab]	Move one column to the right
[Shift][Tab]	Move one column to the left
Arrow keys	Move one cell in the direction of the arrow
[Ctrl][Home]	Move to cell A1
[Ctrl][End]	Move to the last cell that contains data (highest row number and highest column letter)
[F2] (PC), [Ctrl][U] (Mac)	Activate the current cell's content for editing

Goodheart-Willcox Publisher

Figure 8-3. The most efficient way to navigate a spreadsheet is using the keyboard.

FYI

Rather than entering information manually, data can be imported from a delimited text file by running the Import Text Wizard. This resource can be found by clicking **Data**>**Get External Data**>**From Text**. After the desired file has been selected, select the **Delimited** radio button and follow the steps in the Import Text Wizard.

Excel
1.1.2

Excel
2.1.2, 2.1.4

Excel
1.4.8

GS5
Key Applications
3.5.1, 3.5.2, 3.5.3

explanations. **Numbers** are a floating point number data type. Numbers can be used as data in calculations. **Formulas** are equations. The formula defines the calculation, and the result of the calculation is displayed as the value for the cell.

To enter data, first select the cell where the data are to be added. Next, use the keyboard to enter the data. Once another cell is selected, the content is set. In Microsoft Excel, data for the cell can also be entered in the formula bar, as shown in Figure 8-4, or by double-clicking to activate the cell for editing.

When text is entered, it is automatically left justified in the cell. When a number is entered, it is automatically right justified in the cell. When entering data, it may appear to extend beyond the edge of the cell. The data are contained within the cell, it just *appears* as if the data extend beyond the cell. The width of columns and height of rows can be adjusted and cells can be set to wrap text, which are discussed later in this chapter.

Auto Fill is a function of Microsoft Excel that automatically generates information for a given cell range. To use Auto Fill, select and hold the small block at the bottom-right corner of a cell or range. This block is called the *fill handle*. Drag the fill handle to the desired cell and release the mouse button. All cells between the source and destination cells will be automatically filled with pertinent information.

To display formulas within their respective cells, press the tilde key [~] while simultaneously pressing the [Ctrl] key. This key combination will toggle formulas on and off.

Using Formulas

Formulas often look like the expressions seen in math class. When a formula is entered into a cell, the software automatically executes the calculation and displays the result as the cell value. The formula can be viewed in the formula bar by selecting the cell. Double-clicking the cell to activate it for editing displays the formula in the cell.

The most basic formulas are for simple algebra: addition, subtraction, multiplication, and division. Addition is represented in a formula with the plus sign (+). Subtraction is represented with the dash or minus sign (–). Multiplication is represented with the asterisk (*). Division is represented with the forward slash (/). These characters can be entered using the standard keyboard keys or the number pad keys. All formulas in Microsoft Excel begin with an equals sign (=).

For example, assume cell A1 contains the number 5 and cell A2 contains the number 4. To create a formula that finds the sum of cells A1 and A2, select a different cell in which to add the formula, such as cell A3. Next, use the keyboard to enter this formula:

=A1+A2

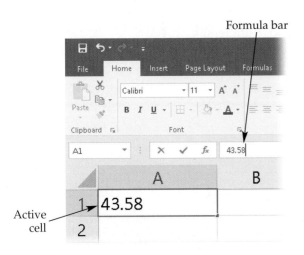

Goodheart-Willcox Publisher

Figure 8-4. The formula bar can be used to enter or edit data or a formula. When done, press the [Enter] key or click the check mark button.

As soon as the [Enter] key is pressed, the calculation is performed, and the answer displayed as the value of cell A3, as shown in Figure 8-5. Also, cell B3 is made the current cell. A different navigation key, such as an arrow key or the [Tab] key, could be used instead of the [Enter] key to set the formula and initiate the calculation.

When the data entered represent dollar amounts, do not include the dollar sign ($). The dollar sign means something special in an Excel spreadsheet. Also, for decimal numbers that end in zero, such as 34.900, the trailing zeros to the right of the decimal point are not displayed unless the cell is formatted to display them. Formatting cells is discussed later in this chapter.

FYI

Although all numbers in a spreadsheet are floating point, they can be formatted to look like integers.

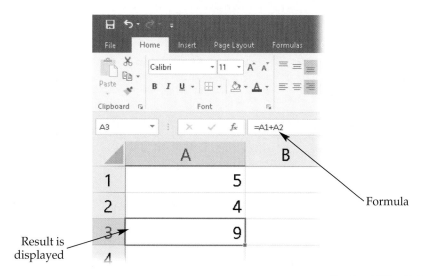

Goodheart-Willcox Publisher

Figure 8-5. When a formula is entered into a cell, the cell displays the result of evaluating the formula.

HANDS-ON EXAMPLE 8.1.1

Excel
1.1.2

CREATING A SPREADSHEET

Microsoft Excel can be used to calculate many things. For example, a student with a part-time job can keep track of how much money has been made.

1. Insert your MS-OFFICE flash drive into the computer.
2. Applying what you have learned, create a folder on the flash drive named Chap08.
3. Launch Microsoft Excel, and click Blank Spreadsheet on the startup screen. Note: Excel 2010 and earlier versions automatically open a blank spreadsheet when launched.
4. Click **File>Save** in the ribbon, and click **Computer** and then the **Browse** button in the backstage view. The **Save As** dialog box is displayed.
5. Save the file as Earnings.xlsx in the Chap08 folder on your flash drive.
6. Cell A1 should be automatically selected, as indicated by the outline surrounding the cell. Cell A1 is located where column A and row 1 intersect, which is the upper-left cell in the spreadsheet. If cell A1 is not the current cell, click it to select it.
7. Add the text Earnings History using the keyboard, and press the [Enter] key.
8. Applying what you have learned, add the text Week to cell A3 and the text Amount of Take-Home Pay to cell B3.

HANDS-ON EXAMPLE 8.1.1 (CONTINUED)

9. In cells A4 through A8, add the text First, Second, Third, Fourth, and Total Earnings.
10. In cells B4 through B7, add the numbers 52.83, 34.90, 23.89, and 44.32.
11. In cell B8, enter this formula: =B4+B5+B6+B7. The weekly earnings are in cells B4 through B7, so this formula finds the sum of all earnings. As soon as the [Enter] key is pressed to set the formula, the cell will display the total of 155.94.
12. Select cell B8. The cell displays the result of the calculation, but the formula is displayed in the formula bar, as shown.

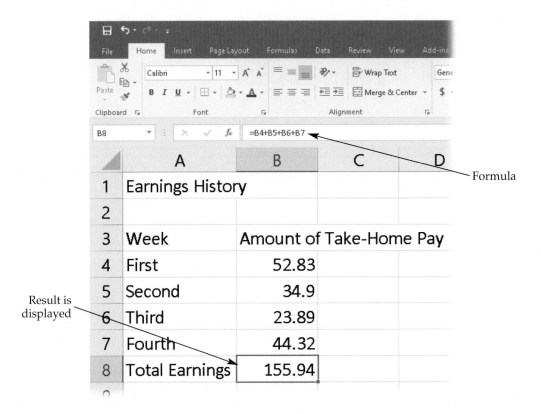

Formula

Result is displayed

13. Save the file.

GS5

Key Applications

3.6

Editing Data

One of the biggest advantages of a computerized spreadsheet is the ability to correct errors quickly when creating the spreadsheet. However, creating the spreadsheet is usually only the first step. The real power of a computerized spreadsheet lies in the ability to change repeatedly or update data.

Correcting Errors

It is not uncommon to make an error when entering data into a spreadsheet. Fortunately, correcting errors is easy. First, locate the cell with the error and make it the active cell. Next, press the [F2] key or double-click to activate the cell for editing. Use the arrow keys or click with the mouse to position the insertion point where the edit is to be made. Then, use the [Delete] or [Backspace] key to remove the unwanted data. Finally, enter the correct data. To set the change, press the [Enter] key.

The formula bar can also be used to edit the content of a cell, as shown in Figure 8-6. First, select the cell to edit. Then, click in the formula bar and edit the data. Press the [Enter] key or click the **Enter** button (check mark) to the left of the formula bar.

The content in a cell can be erased with one keystroke. Select the cell, and press the [Delete] key. Similarly, the content in several cells can be deleted. Select the cells by clicking and dragging. To select cells that are not next to each other, click the first cell, hold down the [Ctrl] key, and click the other cells. When more than one cell is selected, the selection is called a **range** of cells. Finally, press the [Delete] key to erase the content in all selected cells. You can also right-click on the selected cells, and then click **Clear Contents** in the shortcut menu.

FYI

To cancel editing a cell, press the [Esc] key or click the **Cancel** button (X) in the formula bar.

GS5
Key Applications
3.1.4

Green Tech

Carbon Footprints

A *carbon footprint* is a measurement of how much the everyday behaviors of an individual, company, or community impact the environment. This includes the amount of carbon dioxide put into the air from the consumption of energy and fuel used in homes, for travel, and for business.

Updating Data

One of the best features of a computerized spreadsheet is the automatic update that occurs when changing one of the values. This allows a what-if analysis. A **what-if analysis** is changing a parameter in a data model to see how the outcome will be altered. When data are changed in a Microsoft Excel spreadsheet, Excel not only recalculates all formulas that reference those data, but also redraws any charts using those data.

Using a what-if analysis is a very valuable tool for predicting costs and other monetary scenarios. For example, if a homebuilder wants to keep track of the cost of materials to construct a particular house, each item would be listed in the spreadsheet, how many of each item is needed, and how much each item costs. A formula would be entered into

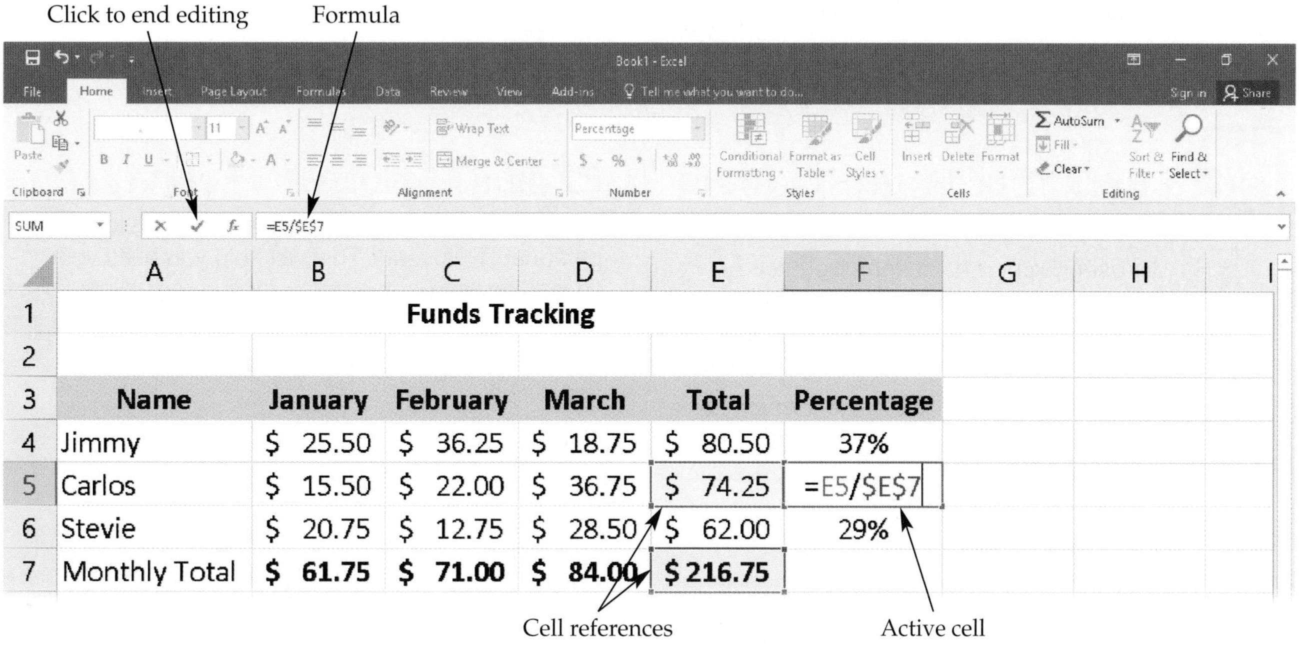

Goodheart-Willcox Publisher

Figure 8-6. Editing a formula using the formula bar. Notice the color-coding used to indicate the cells referenced in the formula.

the spreadsheet to multiply the quantity of each item by the cost of each item. Another formula would be entered to add the cost of all materials to yield the total cost of the house. If the price of a sheet of plywood increases, for example, the cell containing the per-item cost of that item can be quickly updated. With only this one change, the entire cost of the house would be instantly and accurately updated.

HANDS-ON EXAMPLE 8.1.2

EDITING DATA

Correcting errors is easy in Microsoft Excel. It is also easy to change or update data to create a what-if analysis.

1. Launch Microsoft Excel, and open the Earnings.xlsx file in the Chap08 folder on your flash drive, if it is not already open.
2. Select cell B3, and press the [F2] key to activate the cell for editing.
3. Press the left arrow key until the insertion point is to the left of the T in the word *Take*. You can also click at that point with the mouse.
4. Press the [Backspace] key to erase the text *Amount of* from the cell.
5. Press the [Enter] key to set the change.
6. Click cell B6 to select it.
7. Enter 32.58 to change the data in the cell. Notice how the total earnings value in cell B8 automatically changes as soon as the [Enter] key is pressed.
8. Save the file.

8.1 SECTION REVIEW

 ### CHECK YOUR UNDERSTANDING

1. Which software is considered the first killer app?
2. In Microsoft Excel, what is the difference between a worksheet and a workbook?
3. Which data type can be used in calculations in a spreadsheet?
4. In Microsoft Excel, how would the formula be written to subtract the value of cell D3 from the value of cell A5?
5. How do you select cells that are not next to each other?

 ### BUILD YOUR VOCABULARY

As you progress through this course, develop a personal IT glossary. This will help you build your vocabulary and prepare you for a career. Write a definition for each of the following terms and add it to your IT glossary.

active cell	row
cell	spreadsheet
column	text
formula	what-if analysis
killer app	workbook
numbers	worksheet
range	

MANAGING DATA IN SPREADSHEETS

wavebreakmedia/Shutterstock.com

The data in a spreadsheet can be formatted in many ways. Microsoft Excel is part of the Microsoft Office suite of tools, so it supports many of the same formatting options found in other applications in the suite. The color of text and numbers can be changed, as can the color of cells. Numbers can be formatted as numbers, dates, percentages, and other formats. The size of rows and columns can be changed. Cells can be merged, copied, and moved. Rows and columns can be inserted and deleted.

A computerized spreadsheet can be a powerful analysis tool. It is easy to find data in the spreadsheet. Additionally, data can be sorted and filtered to focus on the needed information. A spreadsheet can be printed when a hardcopy is needed.

TERMS

absolute cell address
ascending order
descending order
filtering
fraction
merge
percentage
relative cell address
sorting
wrap text

LEARNING GOALS

After completing this section, you will be able to:
- Discuss ways to customize the appearance of a spreadsheet.
- Change data locations by copying and moving cells.
- Explain how to rearrange data.
- Describe ways to locate and organize data.
- Identify options for printing a spreadsheet.

GS5
Key Applications
3.10.1

Excel
1.4.6, 2.2.6

Excel
1.3.6, 2.2.4, 2.2.7

FYI

Many of the formatting choices are available in the mini toolbar displayed for a selection, which may be more efficient than using the ribbon.

Customizing the Appearance

Once data have been entered into the spreadsheet, in most cases, it will be necessary to format the spreadsheet to make the data understandable. This may be as simple as adjusting the column and row sizes to ensure all data are visible. However, column and row headings can be emphasized by changing styles, size, or color. Cells can be formatted to clarify the meaning of the data they contain. Additionally, rows and columns can be added to the spreadsheet to promote readability.

Formatting Text

It is not necessary to use the default text formatting. The alignment, orientation, wrapping, and background color can be changed. The color, style, and size of the typeface can be changed as can the typeface itself. To format text, first select the cell or cells to which the formatting will be applied.

In Microsoft Excel, to change the typeface or the color, background color, size, style, or alignment of the text or the typeface, use the commands in the **Font** and **Alignment** groups on the **Home** tab of the ribbon, as shown in Figure 8-7. These commands function the same way as in Microsoft Word or Microsoft PowerPoint. Applying a theme will unify the look of the spreadsheet as a whole. To select a theme, click **Page Layout>Themes**. Additionally, users can apply cell styles, which function similarly to paragraph and character styles in Word, by right-clicking a cell and selecting **Format Cells** from the shortcut menu.

One way to correct text that extends beyond the edges of a cell is to wrap it. When a cell is set to **wrap text**, a new line within the cell will be automatically started when the length of the text exceeds the width of the cell. To turn on text wrapping for the selected cell, click **Home>Alignment> Wrap Text** in the ribbon.

By default, text is automatically left-aligned and numbers are automatically right-aligned. Additionally, all cells are by default bottom-aligned, which means the data will be placed at the bottom of the cell. To change the horizontal alignment of the selected cell, click **Home>Alignment>Align Text Left**, **Center**, or **Align Text Right** in the ribbon. Despite the names of these commands, they work for any cell content. To change the vertical alignment of the selected cell, click **Home>Alignment>**

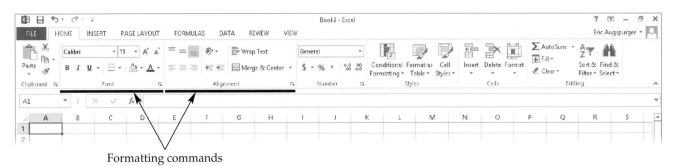

Formatting commands

Goodheart-Willcox Publisher

Figure 8-7. There are many options for formatting text in a spreadsheet.

Top Align, Middle Align, or Bottom Align in the ribbon. If needed, users can link files or websites directly to the spreadsheet. Hyperlinks can be added by right-clicking the cell in which the link will be placed and selecting **Hyperlink** from the shortcut menu. To remove an existing link, simply right-click the hyperlink and select **Remove Hyperlink** from the shortcut menu.

Excel
1.2.3, 2.2.7

Word
1.2.2

HANDS-ON EXAMPLE 8.2.1

FORMATTING TEXT

In some cases, the default text formatting is sufficient for a spreadsheet. However, in most cases, some or all of the default formatting needs to be changed to improve the appearance of the spreadsheet.

1. Launch Microsoft Excel, and open the Earnings.xlsx file in the Chap08 folder on your flash drive, if it is not already open.
2. Right-click on cell A1. In the mini toolbar, click the **Font** drop-down list, and click **Arial Black** in the list. The typeface of the text in the cell is changed.
3. Click the **Font Size** drop-down list, and click **14** in the list. The size of the text in the cell is changed.
4. Click cell A3, hold, and drag to cell B3. This selects the range A3:B3 (A3 to B3).
5. Applying what you have learned, change the font to 12 point italic.
6. Applying what you have learned, select the range A4:A8, and change the font to 12 point.
7. With range A4:A8 selected, click **Home>Font>Fill Color** in the ribbon, and click a light-orange color tile in the palette that appears. The spreadsheet is now formatted for better readability, as shown. Expand column A to see all of the text in cell A8.

Fill
Color

Fill
applied →

	A	B	C
1	**Earnings History**		
2			
3	*Week*	*Take-Home Pay*	
4	First	52.83	
5	Second	34.9	
6	Third	32.58	
7	Fourth	44.32	
8	Total Earnings	164.63	

8. Save the file.

Formatting Numbers

When entering numerical data, there are many choices for formatting them. Common formatting for numbers includes currency, dates, percentages, and fractions. Other formatting is also often available, depending on the spreadsheet software. Options for formatting are depicted in Figure 8-8.

Number	12.576
Currency	$12.58
Accounting	$ 12.58
Date	6/6/1934
Time	01:49:26 PM
Percentage	1257.60%
Fraction	12 4/7
Scientific	1.26E+1

Goodheart-Willcox Publisher

Figure 8-8. There are several options for formatting a number. Here, the number 12.576 is entered in each cell, and the formatting indicated has been applied.

FYI

The dollar sign signifies a special meaning in certain situations, so the currency symbol should be added through formatting.

In Microsoft Excel, the commands for applying numerical formatting to a cell are located in the **Number** group on the **Home** tab of the ribbon. The full range of cell formatting is available in the **Format Cells** dialog box, which is displayed by clicking the dialog box launcher in the **Number** group or by right-clicking on a cell and then clicking **Format Cells...** in the shortcut menu.

If the numerical data represent currency, the displayed value can be made to look as such by adding a currency symbol. In Microsoft Excel, if the currency symbol is directly entered with the data, the cell will be formatted as currency with the symbol. The symbol is automatically removed from the entered data, but the displayed value will contain the symbol. It may be easier, however, to format the cell to automatically add the currency symbol before entering the data.

Currency is most often expressed with either two decimal places or no decimal places. Choices for formatting values allow decimal places to be added or removed. In Microsoft Excel, numbers, including currency, can be formatted to contain up to 30 decimal places. To increase the number of decimal places shown in a cell, click **Home>Number>Increase Decimal** in the ribbon. To decrease the number of decimal places, click **Home>Number>Decrease Decimal** in the ribbon.

Numbers over 1,000 are usually rendered with commas separating each thousands place. Separating large numbers in this manner makes them more readable. In Microsoft Excel, if the commas are directly entered with the data, the cell will be formatted as a number with commas. The comma is automatically removed from the entered data, but the displayed value will contain the comma. It may be easier, however, to format the cell to automatically add the commas before entering the data.

The most common way to enter a date into a spreadsheet is as numbers separated by hyphens (dashes) or forward slashes. However, there are many ways in which the displayed value can be formatted, as shown in Figure 8-9. In Microsoft Excel, if a date is entered as mm/dd/yy, mm/dd/yyyy, mm-dd-yy, or mm-dd-yyyy, where *mm* is the numerical month, *dd* is the numerical day, and *yy* or *yyyy* is the numerical year, the cell will be automatically formatted as a date with forward slashes separating the month, day, and year with the year in a four-digit format. A cell can be formatted before or after entering the date so the displayed value will be in a different format.

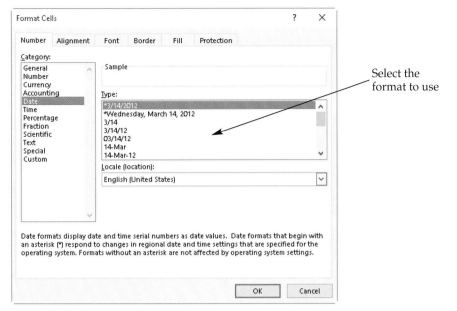

Select the format to use

Goodheart-Willcox Publisher

Figure 8-9. When formatting a cell as a date, there are many different formats from which to choose.

A **fraction** is the number of parts of a whole. For example, the fraction 3/4 represents three parts of the whole number four. The number on the top is the numerator, or number of parts. The number on the bottom is the denominator, or the whole. In Microsoft Excel, the fraction formatting must be applied to the cell. Usually, the formatting is applied before entering data. In this way, a fraction, such as 3/4, will be accepted as a fraction, not the date March 4 of the current year.

A **percentage** is a fraction of 100. For example, 20 percent is the same as 20/100. This may also be written as .2, which is the decimal fractional equivalent. In Microsoft Excel, if the percentage is entered with the symbol, such as 20%, the cell will be automatically formatted for a percentage. The symbol is retained as part of the data. If percentage formatting is applied after the data are entered, the symbol is automatically added to the data. A data entry of .1, for example, will be converted to 10%, *not* 0.1%.

Ethics

Integrity

Integrity is defined as the honesty of a person's actions. Integrity and ethics go hand-in-hand in both personal and professional lives. Employees and employers both help establish the reputation of a business in the community. Company employees who display integrity help create a positive culture for the business, customers, and community.

FYI

A decimal fraction is the result of dividing the numerator by the denominator, such as .75 for the fraction 3/4.

HANDS-ON EXAMPLE 8.2.2

FORMATTING NUMBERS

Numbers can represent many different things. Proper cell formatting can help give meaning to the numerical data displayed in a cell.

1. Launch Microsoft Excel, and open the Earnings.xlsx file in the Chap08 folder on your flash drive, if it is not already open.
2. Applying what you have learned, select the range B4:B8.
3. Right-click on the selection, and click **Format Cells...** in the shortcut menu. The **Format Cells** dialog box is displayed.

HANDS-ON EXAMPLE 8.2.2 (CONTINUED)

4. On the **Number** tab of the dialog box, click **Currency** in the **Category:** list, as shown. This specifies the number formatting for the selected cells.

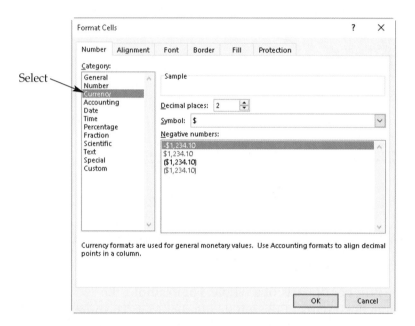

Select

5. Click the **Symbol:** drop-down arrow, and click **$** in the drop-down list. This specifies the currency symbol to be used.
6. Click in the **Decimal places:** text box, and enter 2. Dollar values are usually represented with two decimal places.
7. Click the **OK** button to apply the formatting. Dollar signs appear in front of the value displayed in each cell. Also notice that the displayed value in cell B5 includes the trailing zero where before this was hidden.
8. Save the file.

GS5

Key Applications

3.3

Excel

1.3.7, 2.2.2

In Microsoft Excel, double-clicking between rows or columns in the header area will automatically reduce the size of the row or column to the minimum size.

Formatting Cell Size

If part of the cell content is cut off on the right-hand side of the cell or if several pound signs (#######) appear in the cell, the cell is not wide enough. The cell width is controlled by the column width. The column must be wide enough to allow all of the characters to be visible. If part of the cell content is cut off on the bottom, the cell is not tall enough. The cell height is controlled by the row height. In Microsoft Excel, column width and row height are similarly adjusted in one of three ways.

The first method involves dragging the row or column to resize it. Move the cursor to the header area of the column or row and place it on the edge to move, as shown in Figure 8-10. When the double-arrow resizing cursor appears, click, hold, and drag to resize the column or row.

The second method allows for more precise adjustment of column width or row height. Right-click on the column or row in the header area. This selects the column or row and displays a shortcut menu. Click **Column Width...** or **Row Height...** in the shortcut menu. In the **Column**

Width or **Row Height** dialog box that is displayed, enter the numerical value for the height or width, and click the **OK** button.

The column width and row height can also be changed using commands in the ribbon. Click **Home>Cells>Format** in the ribbon. Then, click either **Row height...** or **Column width...** in the drop-down menu. Finally, enter the new height or width in the dialog box that appears.

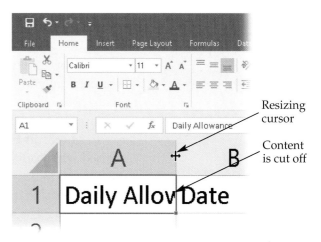

Goodheart-Willcox Publisher

Figure 8-10. A row or column can be dragged to manually resize it.

HANDS-ON EXAMPLE 8.2.3

ADJUSTING COLUMN WIDTH

Adjusting the column width or row height is often needed to improve the readability of the spreadsheet. In some cases, this is done to display hidden content, while in other cases doing so helps the reader locate data.

1. Launch Microsoft Excel, and open the Earnings.xlsx file in the Chap08 folder on your flash drive, if it is not already open.
2. Move the cursor to the line between columns A and B in the header row. The double-arrow cursor is displayed.
3. Click and drag the edge of column A to the right until all of the text in cell A8 is visible. Release the mouse button to set the new width of the column.
4. Save the file.

Adding Columns and Rows

After the spreadsheet is initially created, rows or columns may need to be added to allow for more data or to improve readability of the spreadsheet. To add a column in Microsoft Excel, select the column to the right of where the new column should be added. Then, click **Home>Cells> Insert Cells** in the ribbon, and click **Insert Sheet Columns** in the drop-down menu. The new column is added to the *left* of the selected column.

To add a row in Microsoft Excel, select the row below where the new row should be added. Then, click **Home>Cells>Insert Cells** in the ribbon, and click **Insert Sheet Rows** in the drop-down menu. The new row is added above the selected row.

Another way to insert a column or row in Microsoft Excel is to right-click on the column or row in the header area. Then, click **Insert** in the shortcut menu. If right-clicking on a cell, select **Insert...** in the shortcut menu to display the **Insert** dialog box. Then, in the dialog box, choose to insert an entire row or column.

GS5
Key Applications
3.2

Excel
1.3.5, 2.1.5

FYI

Clicking the **Insert Cells** button instead of the drop-down arrow automatically inserts a column or row, depending on which is selected.

GS5
Key Applications
3.9.1

Excel
2.2.1

Merging Cells

To **merge** cells is to combine them into a single cell. Cells can be merged horizontally, vertically, or both, as shown in Figure 8-11. Merging cells is usually done to improve the readability of the spreadsheet or to group columns or rows under a title. For example, the title Income may be placed across three rows that represent sources of income.

In Microsoft Excel, the content is automatically horizontally center-aligned when cells are merged. If more than one cell contains data, only the content in the upper-left selected cell is retained. If only one cell contains data, that content is retained regardless of the cell's position in the selection. The **Merge & Center** command is located in the **Alignment** group on the **Home** tab of the ribbon.

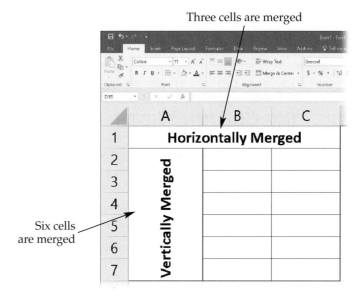

Goodheart-Willcox Publisher

Figure 8-11. Cells can be merged to improve the readability of the spreadsheet.

HANDS-ON EXAMPLE 8.2.4

ADDING COLUMNS

Frequently, a column or row must be added between existing columns or rows in a spreadsheet. Also, it is common to merge cells to improve readability of the spreadsheet.

1. Launch Microsoft Excel, and open the Earnings.xlsx file in the Chap08 folder on your flash drive, if it is not already open.
2. Click the column B header to select the column.
3. Click **Home>Cells>Insert Cells** in the ribbon. A column is added to the left of the selected column. Notice that the new column is column B. All columns are automatically renamed. Also notice the formatting of column A, which was the column to the left, is automatically applied to the new column.
4. Right-click the row 3 header to select the row and display the shortcut menu.
5. Click **Insert** in the shortcut menu. A new row is added above the selected row. Notice the new row is row 3 and the formatting of row 2 is automatically applied.

Insert
Cells

HANDS-ON EXAMPLE 8.2.4 (CONTINUED)

6. Applying what you have learned, add the text April to cell A2.
7. Applying what you have learned, add a new row at the top of the spreadsheet.
8. Applying what you have learned, add the text Budget to the first empty cell (A1).
9. Select the range A1:D1.

Merge & Center

10. Click **Home**>**Alignment**>**Merge & Center** in the ribbon. The cells are merged, and the content is centered.
11. Save the file.

Modifying Worksheets

In addition to modifying the appearance of cells, worksheet tab names and colors can be customized. To rename or recolor worksheet tabs, right-click the desired tab and select either **Rename** or **Tab Color**. It is also possible to hide and reveal worksheet tabs. To hide a worksheet, select the desired tab to activate it, and click **Home**>**Cells**>**Format** in the ribbon. Under Visibility, select **Hide & Unhide**, then **Hide Sheet**. To reveal a hidden worksheet, select **Unhide Sheet** in the Visibility section.

> Excel
> 1.3.1, 1.3.2, 1.4.1

Deleting Columns and Rows

Just as there are times a column or row must be added to a spreadsheet, there are times when one must be deleted. Deleting a column or row also deletes all data within the cells. In Microsoft Excel, columns and rows are deleted in a similar manner. Right-click on the header for the column or row to delete, and click **Delete** in the shortcut menu. A selected column or row can also be deleted by clicking **Home**>**Cells**>**Delete Cells** in the ribbon.

Alternatively, instead of deleting a column or row, the user can simply hide it by right-clicking the desired column or row and selecting **Hide** from the shortcut menu. If the column or row needs to be made visible again, the user can do so by selecting and right-clicking the columns or rows on each side of the hidden cells and choosing **Unhide** from the shortcut menu.

> Excel
> 1.4.2

> **FYI**
>
> Pressing the [Delete] key when a column or row is selected will clear the contents, but will not remove the column or row.

Changing Data Locations

Data that are already present in the spreadsheet can be copied. This is often more efficient, especially for complex data, than reentering the data. Data can also be moved from one location to a different location. Any cell content can be copied or moved. The new data will look exactly the same as the original. When moving content, any formulas that reference the content are automatically updated to the new content location.

> GS5
> Key Applications
> 3.9.2

> Excel
> 2.1.2

Copying Cells

When a cell is copied, a duplicate appears in the new location. However, the original cell is unaffected, and there is no reference between the original and copied data. Any formula referencing the original cell will continue to reference the original cell.

To copy a cell in Microsoft Excel, select the source cell. Next, press the [Ctrl][C] key combination, click **Home**>**Clipboard**>**Copy** in the ribbon, or right-click on the cell and click **Copy** in the shortcut menu. A marquee appears around the original cell to indicate this is what will be pasted, as shown in Figure 8-12. Next, select the destination cell. Finally, press the [Ctrl][V] key combination, click **Home**>**Clipboard**>**Paste** in the ribbon, or right-click on the destination cell and click **Paste** in the shortcut menu. As long as the marquee appears on the source cell, the contents can be pasted into several locations. To end the operation, press the [Esc] key.

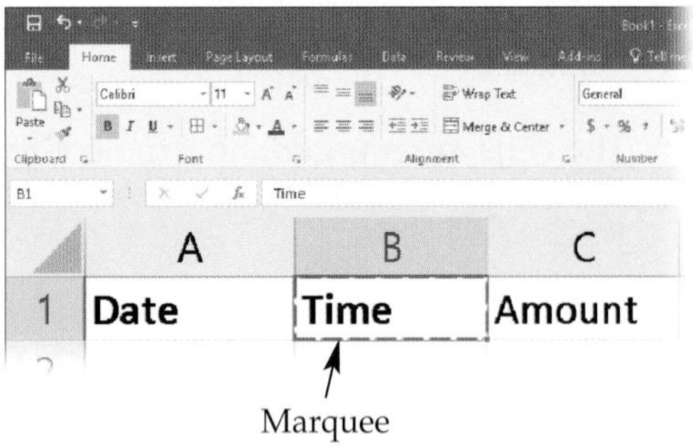

When copying a formula in Excel, any cell references in the formula will be altered based on the new location. For example, if the formula in cell A3 is =A1+A2 and is copied to cell B3, the new formula will be =B1+B2. This is because the destination cell is one column to the right of the source (from column A to column B). If the formula is copied to cell B2, a reference error will be displayed. Because the destination cell is one column to the right (from column A to B) and one row above (from row 3 to 2) the source, the formula would in essence become =B0+B1. There is no cell B0, so Excel displays the reference error. This is an important concept to remember in Excel.

Marquee

Goodheart-Willcox Publisher

Figure 8-12. The marquee indicates the cell has been copied and is ready to be pasted.

Moving Cells

When a cell is moved, a duplicate appears in the new location and content in the original cell is erased. Any formula referencing the original cell will be automatically updated to reference the cell in the new location. However, unlike when a cell is copied, if the moved cell contains a formula, cell references within the formula are *not* altered based on the new location.

To move a cell in Microsoft Excel, the cut function is used. First, select the source cell. Next, press the [Ctrl][X] key combination, click **Home**>**Clipboard**>**Cut** in the ribbon, or right-click on the cell and click **Cut** in the shortcut menu. A flashing marquee appears around the cut cell. Next, select the destination cell. Finally, press the [Ctrl][V] key combination, click **Home**>**Clipboard**>**Paste** in the ribbon, or right-click on the destination cell and click **Paste** in the shortcut menu. The operation is immediately ended. A cut cell cannot be repeatedly pasted in multiple locations.

FYI

A cell can be moved in Microsoft Excel by selecting it, clicking and dragging the outline around the cell, and dropping it in the new location.

Excel
1.1.4, 1.3.3

Copying and Moving Worksheets

It is possible to copy and move entire worksheets instead of individual cells. To copy a worksheet, select **Home**>**Format**>**Move or Copy**. Alternatively, the user can right-click a selected sheet tab and select **Move or Copy** from the shortcut menu. In the **Move or Copy** dialog box, select the sheet that should come immediately after the affected sheet. If copying the sheet, select the Create a copy checkbox; otherwise, select **OK**. The result will be a reordered set of worksheet tabs. Another option of moving worksheets is to drag-and-drop a worksheet tab to the desired location.

HANDS-ON EXAMPLE 8.2.5

COPYING CELLS

Cells are often copied once a section of a spreadsheet is complete. For example, the income for one month is set up in rows and columns; these cells can be quickly copied as a starting point for the next month.

1. Launch Microsoft Excel, and open the Earnings.xlsx file in the Chap08 folder on your flash drive, if it is not already open.
2. Add the text May to cell A13.
3. Applying what you have learned, remove the background color from cell A13.
4. Select the range A4:A10.
5. Press the [Ctrl][C] key combination. A marquee appears around the range to indicate the selection is copied.
6. Select cell A14.
7. Press the [Ctrl][V] key combination. The selected range is pasted with cell A14 as the upper-left corner of the range. In this case, there is only one column in the range, so A14 is the upper cell in the pasted range.
8. Press the [Esc] key to end the operation.
9. Save the file.

Rearranging Data

On occasion, it is advantageous to copy a particular formula from one place to another in a spreadsheet. For example, when keeping a running tab of checkbook activity, each row is similar. The pattern is to add a credit or subtract a debit from the checkbook total.

What if a cell reference is used in the formula? As discussed earlier, the software will automatically update the cell reference, but what if the reference should *not* be updated? In this case, it is necessary to tell the software not to change the cell reference. In Microsoft Excel, the dollar sign ($) is used in a formula to tell Excel which references can be updated and which ones must not be changed. This character does not change the calculation, but instead acts like glue to keep the formula stuck to the original reference. The two types of cell references are relative cell addresses and absolute cell addresses.

Relative Cell Addresses

A **relative cell address** is specified as the number of rows and columns that the second cell is from the first cell. For example, if the formula stored in cell B1 is =D5–F8, D5 refers to the content of cell D5. Cell D5 is located two columns to the right and four rows below cell B1. Another way to state this is cell D5 is plus two columns and plus four rows *relative* to cell B1. Refer to Figure 8-13A.

Excel

4.1.1

Career Skills

Purchasing Manager
Purchasing managers, purchasing agents, and buyers acquire materials for agencies to use. They assess suppliers, evaluate product quality, and negotiate product acquisition contracts. They use technology to manage budgets, search for products, track purchases, and maintain supplier relationships. Often the program of choice is spreadsheet software because of its ability to rapidly update totals and keep track of spending.

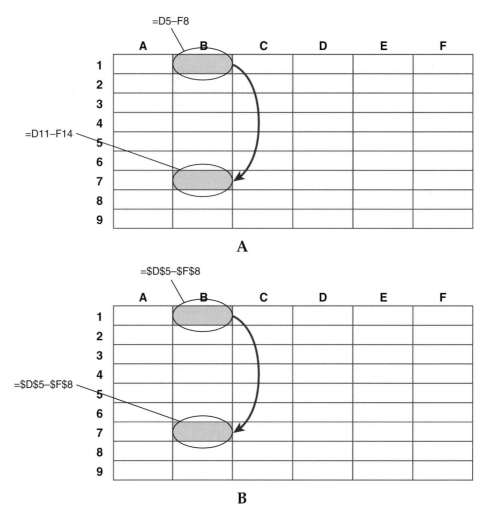

Goodheart-Willcox Publisher

Figure 8-13. A—If relative cell addresses are used, the references are automatically updated if the formula is copied. B—If absolute cell addresses are used, the references are not changed if the formula is copied.

If the formula in cell B1 is copied to cell B7, the cell references in the formula will maintain this relative addressing. Therefore, the formula references cells D11 and F14. Cell D11 is two columns to the right of and four rows below cell B7. Cell F14 is four columns to the right of and seven rows below cell B7, which is the same relative address used in the original formula.

Absolute Cell Addresses

If a formula must always use the content of a specific cell, an absolute cell address must be entered. An **absolute cell address** indicates the formula will refer to the specified cell no matter where the formula is moved or copied. In Microsoft Excel, the dollar sign ($) specifies an absolute cell address. Enter dollar signs before the column letter and row number, as shown in Figure 8-13B.

For example, if the formula in cell B1 is =$D$5–$F$8, $D$5 refers to the content of the cell located in column D and row 5. If the formula in cell B1 is copied to cell B7, the cell references in the formula remain cells D5 and F8. The dollar signs tell Excel not to update the cell addresses.

A formula in a cell may contain a combination of relative and absolute cell addressing, such as =MAX(A2:A12)/$B$1. This formula tells Excel to locate the largest value of the cells in the range A2:A12 and that value is divided by the content in cell B1. If this formula is moved from cell D4 to cell D5, the formula is updated to =MAX(A3:A13)/$B$1. Notice that the relative cell address of the range is updated, but the absolute cell address of cell B1 is not updated.

HANDS-ON EXAMPLE 8.2.6

RELATIVE AND ABSOLUTE CELL ADDRESSES

Copying existing formulas is an efficient way to develop a spreadsheet. When doing so, it is important to understand how relative and absolute cell addresses are used by the software.

1. Launch Microsoft Excel, and begin a new blank spreadsheet.
2. Save the spreadsheet as Fundraising.xlsx in the Chap08 folder on your flash drive.
3. Add the text Funds Tracking to cell A1.
4. Add the text Name to cell A3.
5. Add the text January, February, and March to cells B3 through D3.
6. Add the text Total to cell E3.
7. Add your first name and the first names of two classmates to cells A4 through A6.
8. Add the text Monthly Total to cell A7.
9. Applying what you have learned, adjust the columns as needed to be as wide as the widest text entry.
10. Add dollar amounts of your own choosing to the cells in the range B4:D6. Format the cells as appropriate.
11. Enter the formula =B4+C4+D4 in cell E4. This formula totals the three values.
12. Applying what you have learned, copy cell E4 and paste it into cells E5 and E6.
13. Activate cell E6 for editing. Notice the relative cell addresses in the formula were automatically updated, as shown.

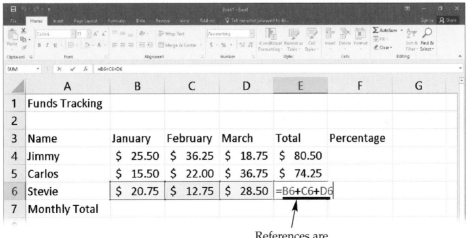

References are automatically updated

HANDS-ON EXAMPLE 8.2.6 (CONTINUED)

14. Applying what you have learned, add formulas to cells B7 through E7 to total each month and calculate the grand total. Use copy and paste as appropriate to improve your efficiency.
15. Add the text Percentage to cell F3. This column will be used to calculate what part of the total each student submitted.
16. Applying what you have learned, format the range F4:F6 for percentages.
17. Enter the formula =E4/E7 to cell F4. This formula calculates percentage of the whole by dividing the individual's total by the grand total.
18. Copy the formula in cell F4 to cells F5 and F6. Cells F5 and F6 will display a divide by zero error of #DIV/0!.
19. Select cell F5, and examine the formula in the formula bar. When the formula was copied from cell F4, both cell references were updated; however, the cell containing the grand total has not moved and remains cell E7. The solution is to use an absolute cell address in the formula for cell E7.
20. Applying what you have learned, edit the formula in cell F4 so there is a $ before the column and row reference to cell E7: =E4/$E$7.
21. Copy the updated formula in cell F4 to cells F5 and F6. Notice calculated values are now displayed instead of the error message.
22. Select cell F6, and examine the formula in the formula bar. Notice the relative cell address is updated to cell E6, which is the student's total, but the absolute cell address is not updated and remains cell E7, which is the grand total.
23. Save the file.

<table>
<tr><td>GS5
Key Applications
3.4</td></tr>
</table>

Locating and Organizing Data

A large spreadsheet may contain hundreds or thousands of data. In order to use the spreadsheet, the data must be located. Instead of scrolling through the spreadsheet, the search or find function of the software can be used to locate data.

Often data are entered into a spreadsheet in the order received. This may not be the best order for evaluating the data. For example, if compiling an inventory, each item is entered when it is tallied. However, after all of the items are entered, it may make sense to view the data with similar items grouped together.

In some cases, only part of the data needs to be viewed. By excluding, or filtering, those data that do not need to be seen, the spreadsheet can be more manageable.

<table>
<tr><td>Excel
1.2.1</td></tr>
</table>

Finding Data

Most software that deals with text and numbers has some sort of search or find function. Spreadsheet software is no different. The basic process for locating data in a spreadsheet is the same as locating a word in a word-processing document. For example, to find all rows that include a particular name, the search or find function can be used with the name as the search phrase to locate the rows containing the name.

To find data in Microsoft Excel, click **Home>Editing>Find & Select** in the ribbon, and click **Find...** in the shortcut menu. The **Find and Replace** dialog box is displayed, as shown in Figure 8-14. Click in the **Find what:** text box, and enter the data to locate. Finally, click the **Find Next** button to locate the next instance of the data from the current cell forward in the spreadsheet.

Sorting Data

Sorting is arranging data in a spreadsheet by criteria. For example, suppose the spreadsheet contains a list of movies, the date each was released, and the starring actors for each. These data can be sorted to place the list in alphabetic order by title.

To use the sort feature in Microsoft Excel, click **Home>Editing>Sort & Filter** in the ribbon to display a drop-down menu, as shown in Figure 8-15. Select the appropriate command in the drop-down menu. The **Sort Smallest to Largest** command arranges the data in **ascending order**, such as A to Z or 1 to 10. The **Sort Largest to Smallest** command arranges the data in **descending order**, such as Z to A or 10 to 1. The **Custom Sort** command provides options for sorting multiple columns and rows rather than columns.

Excel

3.3.2, 3.3.3

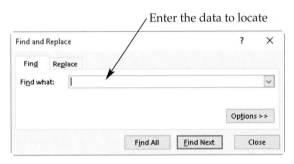

Goodheart-Willcox Publisher

Figure 8-14. The find function can be used to locate specific data.

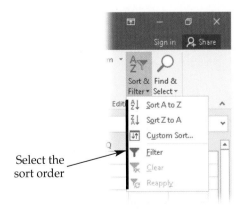

Goodheart-Willcox Publisher

Figure 8-15. Data can be sorted in ascending or descending order.

Excel

3.3.1

FYI

In Microsoft Excel,
a sort can also be
performed using the
filter drop-down menu.

Filtering Data

In many cases, not all of the data need to be viewed at the same time. **Filtering** allows some data to be hidden from view. To use the filter feature in Microsoft Excel, first select a single cell within a range of data. Then, click **Home>Editing>Sort & Filter** in the ribbon, and click **Filter** in the drop-down menu. Excel displays drop-down arrows in the cells it believes to be headings, as shown in Figure 8-16. To filter the data, click the drop-down arrow to display a drop-down menu, and uncheck the items to hide.

Drop-down arrows

Click to display a
drop-down menu

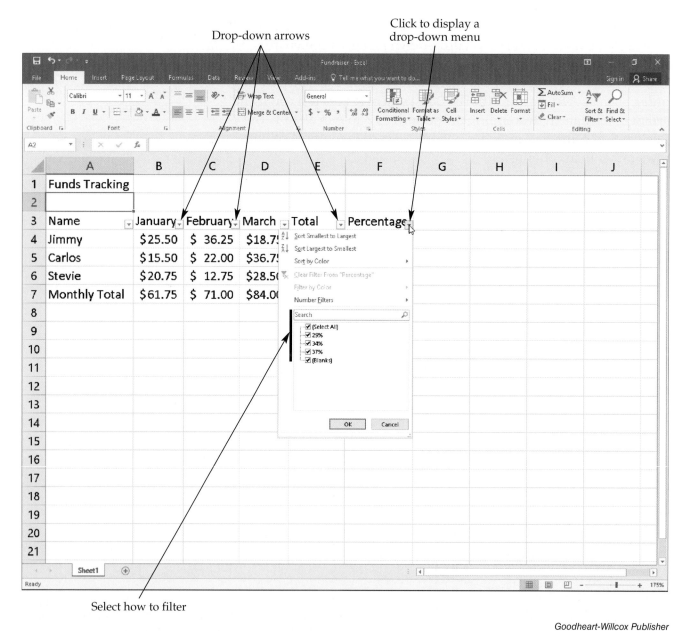

Select how to filter

Figure 8-16. To filter data, click the drop-down arrow, and then select how to filter in the drop-down menu.

HANDS-ON EXAMPLE 8.2.7

GS5
Key Applications
3.12

SORTING DATA

One of the benefits of a computerized spreadsheet is the ability to sort data. For example, in a sales report spreadsheet, it is possible to organize data by products and isolate a certain product from all others.

1. Launch Microsoft Excel 2016.
2. On the startup screen, click in the search text box, enter sales report, and click the **Search** button (magnifying glass).
3. In the list of returned results, locate the Sales report template, and click it. Click the **Create** button in the preview that is displayed to start a new spreadsheet based on this template.
4. Examine the spreadsheet. The first row contains headings for the product, customer, and four fiscal quarters. It is currently sorted on the Product column.
5. Select any cell in the Customer column.

Sort & Filter

6. Click **Home>Editing>Sort & Filter** in the ribbon, and click **Sort A to Z** in the drop-down menu. Notice how the rows of data are rearranged in alphabetical order based on the customer name, as shown.

Sorted by name

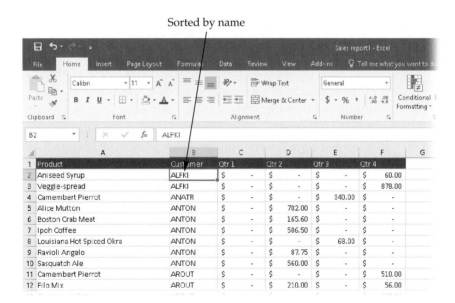

7. Applying what you have learned, sort the Qtr 1 column from largest to smallest.
8. Click **Home>Editing>Sort & Filter** in the ribbon, and click **Custom Sort...** in the drop-down menu.
9. In the **Sort** dialog box that is displayed, click the **Sort by** drop-down arrow, and click **Customer** in the drop-down list.
10. Click the **Order** drop-down arrow, and click **A to Z** in the drop-down list.
11. Click the **Add Level** button to add a second sort criterion.
12. Applying what you have learned, set the second criterion to sort by product in ascending order.
13. Click the **OK** button to apply the custom sort. Notice how the data are arranged first alphabetically by customer and then alphabetically by product name for each customer.

Find & Select

14. Click **Home>Editing>Find & Select** in the ribbon, and click **Find...** in the drop-down menu. The **Find and Replace** dialog box is displayed.

HANDS-ON EXAMPLE 8.2.7 (CONTINUED)

15. Click in the **Find what:** text box, and enter quick.
16. Click the **Find All** button. The locations of all instances of the text *quick* are displayed at the bottom of the **Find and Replace** dialog box.
17. Close the **Find and Replace** dialog box.
18. Select cell A1, which is the Product column heading.

Sort & Filter

19. Click **Home>Editing>Sort & Filter** in the ribbon, and click **Filter** in the drop-down menu. A drop-down arrow appears in all of the heading cells in the first row.
20. Click the drop-down arrow in cell A1, and uncheck the **(Select All)** check box in the list in the drop-down menu.
21. Check the Boston Crab Meat check box in the list in the drop-down menu, and then click the **OK** button. Only the rows containing the product Boston Crab Meat are displayed in the spreadsheet. Two visual hints that the data have been filtered are the row numbers are not consecutive and a filter icon appears in the drop-down arrow at the top of the Product column.
22. Click the drop-down arrow at the top of the Product column, and click **Clear Filter From "Product"** in the drop-down menu. The data are no longer filtered.
23. Close the file without saving it.

Excel
2.3.2, 2.3.3

Group Data

Lists of data can get long in a spreadsheet. There may be times when it is necessary to group selected data to save space in the sheet and time while reading for information. Grouping data in an outline is an efficient way to accomplish this. Similar to an outline in Microsoft Word, the grouped data will be hidden from view until expanded by the user, but is sorted into an outline format with up to eight levels. To group data, select the range of cells that are to be outlined and choose **Data>Outline>Group**.

Another way to group data is to use the **SUBTOTAL** function. The **SUBTOTAL** function returns the subtotal of numbers in a column or row. The type of subtotal created is dictated by the method chosen by the user. The method can be a value ranging from 1–11 or 101–111. The first set of methods includes hidden values in the calculation while the second set ignores them. To perform this function, highlight the cells that will be included in the subtotal, and select **Data>Outline>Subtotal** in the ribbon. In the **At each change in** field, enter the cells to be subtotaled. In the **Use function** field, select the function that should be used to make the calculation. Then, select **OK**. Excel will group the column by adding subtotals for each row and for the column as a whole.

Excel
1.5.3

Printing a Spreadsheet

Often, a spreadsheet is used only in electronic form. However, there may be times when a hard copy of the spreadsheet is needed. To improve the readability of the printed spreadsheet, cells can be outlined or the grid set to print. Without this, there will be no visible definition of the cells on the printout other than the cell content. Additionally, before printing a spreadsheet, it should be previewed.

The steps to print in Microsoft Excel are similar to those used to print in Microsoft Word. Click **File**>**Print** in the ribbon. In the backstage view, set the printing options such as which pages to print, which printer to use, and the paper orientation. A preview of the printed spreadsheet also appears in the backstage view.

Outlining Cells

A border can be drawn around cells. This can be done for emphasis or to improve readability, either on-screen or when the spreadsheet is printed. See Figure 8-17.

To add a border to cells in Microsoft Excel, first select the cell or range to which the border will be applied. Next, click **Home**>**Font**>**Bottom Border** in the ribbon. Note: the name of this button will change based on the last selection made in the drop-down menu. In the drop-down menu, click the type of border to apply. There are many choices for borders.

If a range of cells is selected, it is considered as one cell for applying a border. For example, if three cells are selected and the **Outside Borders** option is selected, a border is placed around the group, not each individual cell.

Printing the Grid

By default, the grid is displayed in Microsoft Excel, but will not be printed. However, the grid can be set to print. This can be an alternative to applying borders to cells.

To set the grid to print, click **Page Layout**>**Sheet Options**>**Gridlines**>**Print** in the ribbon. When this is checked, the grid will be printed in an area from the first upper-left cell containing data to the last lower-right cell containing data, as shown in Figure 8-18.

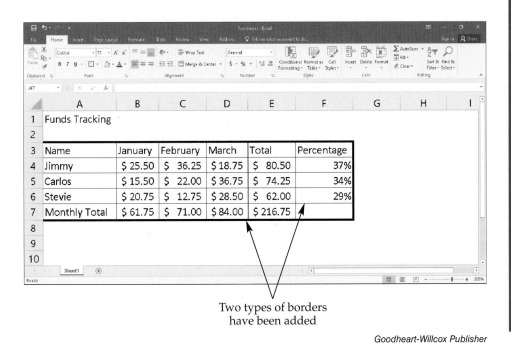

Two types of borders have been added

Goodheart-Willcox Publisher

Figure 8-17. Borders can be used to emphasize parts of the spreadsheet or make it easier to read.

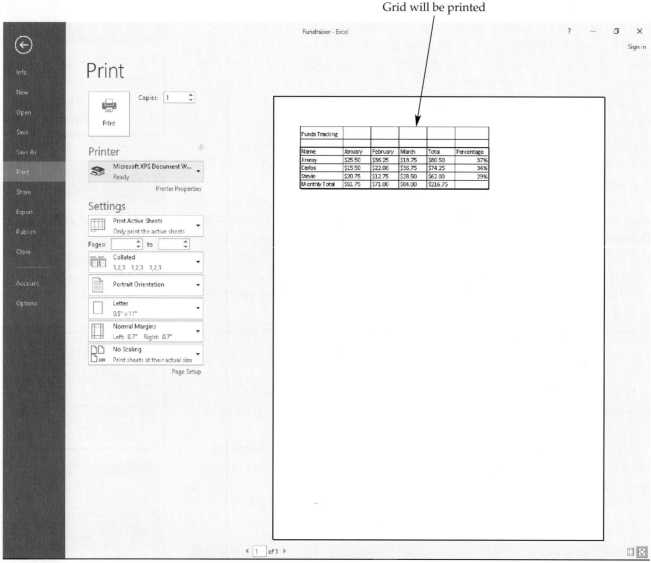

Goodheart-Willcox Publisher

Figure 8-18. The grid can be set to print. This is done in the **Page Layout** tab of the ribbon.

TITANS OF TECHNOLOGY

Edward Rolf Tufte (pronounced *TOUGH-tee*) is an American statistician, political scientist, and professor. He earned his bachelor and master degrees in statistics from Stanford University and his doctorate in political science from Yale. While teaching political economy and data analysis at Princeton University in the 1970s, Tufte was asked to teach a statistics course to a group of journalists who needed to learn economics. He developed lectures on statistical graphics, which became his first book on information design, *The Visual Display of Quantitative Information*. The book quickly became a success, and he became known as an information expert as well as a political scientist. Tufte coined the term *chatjunk*, which refers to elements in graphs and charts that are useless, do not inform, or confuse the data. In 2010, President Obama appointed Tufte to the American Recovery and Reinvestment Act Independent Advisory Panel "to provide transparency in the use" of the funds.

Header and Footer

A header or footer can be added to the printed spreadsheet. Just as with a word-processing document, the header and footer appear on every page. The header and footer can be used to provide information about the spreadsheet, such as the author, the date the spreadsheet was printed, or the file name of the spreadsheet file.

To add a header or footer to a spreadsheet in Microsoft Excel, click **Insert>Text>Header & Footer** in the ribbon. Note: depending on your screen configuration, this group may be collapsed to a single button. The print layout view is displayed, and the center header text box is active. Enter text in this text box or click in the left- or right-hand header text box and enter text. To add text to the footer, click **Design>Navigation>Go to Footer** in the ribbon. The footer similarly has left-hand, center, and right-hand text boxes.

To insert a page number in any of the header or footer text boxes, click **Design>Header & Footer Elements>Page Number** in the ribbon. Other options located in the same group include **Number of Pages**, **Current Date**, **Current Time**, **File Path**, **File Name**, and **Sheet Name**.

8.2 SECTION REVIEW

 ### CHECK YOUR UNDERSTANDING

1. What three properties of a typeface can be changed to format the text?
2. Which key combinations are used to move the content of a cell?
3. Which type of cell address allows a formula to be automatically updated if the formula is moved?
4. What is the difference between sorting and filtering?
5. What is the purpose of adding a border around cells?

 ### BUILD YOUR VOCABULARY

As you progress through this course, develop a personal IT glossary. This will help you build your vocabulary and prepare you for a career. Write a definition for each of the following terms and add it to your IT glossary.

absolute cell address	percentage
ascending order	relative cell address
descending order	sorting
filtering	wrap text
fraction	
merge	

8 REVIEW AND ASSESSMENT

Chapter Summary

Section 8.1
Introduction to Spreadsheets

- A spreadsheet is a collection of data arranged in rows and columns. Manual spreadsheets continued to be used after the advent of computerized spreadsheet software until VisiCalc was created for the Apple II personal computer in the late 1970s.
- Columns are the spaces between the vertical grid lines, rows are the spaces between the horizontal grid lines, and a cell is where a column and row intersect. The mouse can be used to navigate a spreadsheet, but most efficient users primarily navigate with the keyboard.
- The data type for a cell determines what the data entered in the cell mean. There are several common data types used in computer programming.
- The most basic formulas in a spreadsheet are simple algebra. When a formula is entered into a cell, the software automatically executes the calculation and displays the result as the cell value.
- A powerful feature of a computerized spreadsheet is the ease of correcting errors. However, the real power lies in the ability to change or update data repeatedly, which allows a what-if analysis.

Section 8.2
Managing Data in Spreadsheets

- Formatting the spreadsheet may be necessary to make the data understandable. This may involve changing the column and row sizes or changing the styles, size, or color of the values displayed in cells.

- Data can be copied or moved to change their location in a spreadsheet. Any formulas that reference the content are automatically updated to the new content location.
- Data can be rearranged without cell references being automatically updated. An absolute cell address indicates the formula will refer to the specified cell no matter where the formula is moved or copied.
- There are several tools to help in locating data. The search or find function can locate specific data, the sort function displays data in ascending or descending order, and the filter function displays only data that meet certain criteria.
- In many cases, a spreadsheet is only used in electronic form, but a spreadsheet can be printed. Cells can be outlined before printing to improve readability, and headers and footers can be included on the page.

Now that you have finished this chapter, see what you know about computer applications by taking the chapter posttest. Access the posttest by visiting www.g-wlearning.com.

Chapter 8 Test

Multiple Choice
Select the best response.

1. What is used to name each cell?
   A. worksheet name and row
   B. column and row
   C. numbers
   D. letters

2. What determines the meaning of data entered in a cell?
   A. value
   B. format
   C. filter
   D. data type

3. Which of the following is not a common formatting for numbers in a spreadsheet?
   A. currency
   B. dates
   C. absolute
   D. fractions

4. Which of the following is the proper way to write a relative cell address?
   A. C4
   B. $C4
   C. C$4
   D. $C$4

5. What is a way in which to limit the data displayed?
   A. Filtering
   B. Searching
   C. Finding
   D. Sorting

Completion

Complete the following sentences with the correct word(s).

6. _____ is the cocreator of the first computerized spreadsheet software for personal computers.

7. By default, numbers in a cell are aligned to the _____.

8. When more than one cell is selected, the selection is called a(n) _____ of cells.

9. If _____ appear(s) in a cell, the value is wider than the cell.

10. The _____ function is used to locate specific data in a spreadsheet.

Matching

Match the correct term with its definition.

A. active cell
B. what-if scenario
C. wrap text
D. absolute cell address
E. descending order

11. Used to lock the cell reference in a formula.

12. A new line within the cell will be automatically started when the length of the text exceeds the width of the cell.

13. Arranging data from largest to smallest.

14. Currently selected cell.

15. Used to see what happens if cell data are changed.

Application and Extension of Knowledge

1. Create a spreadsheet to keep a running balance of a debit card. Enter the data shown below. Format the cells under the Credit, Debit, and Balance headings as the accounting number format. In the Balance column, enter a formula in each cell that adds the previous balance to any credit in the row or subtracts any debit in the row. What is the formula entered in cell E4? How much money is in the account on April 10?

Item	Date	Credit	Debit	Balance
Beginning balance	April 5	$ 42.56		
Paycheck	April 6	$ 345.10		
Groceries	April 10		$ 68.97	

2. The value of cell A1 is 32, B1 is 42, and C1 is 2. Using a spreadsheet, find the value of each of the following formulas if entered in cell D1.
   A. =(A1+B1)*C1
   B. =A1+B1*C1
   C. =(B1–A1)/C1
   D. =B1–A1/C1

3. Create a spreadsheet to track the amount of time you spent doing certain activities or tasks throughout the day yesterday. Record the time as the number of minutes, such as 5, 30, or 75. Create a formula to calculate the average amount of time spent on each activity.

4. Locate an example of a blank checkbook register. Then, set up a spreadsheet to perform this function. Create formulas as needed to automate your electronic spreadsheet register.

5. The formula for calculating simple interest on a loan is A = P(1+rt), where P is the amount borrowed, r is the annual interest rate as a decimal fraction (such as .05 for 5 percent), and t is the term (time) of the loan. Use a spreadsheet to create a what-if scenario for a simple interest on the loan. See how changing the amount borrowed, interest rate, and length of the loan affect the total amount of money you have to pay the bank.

Online Activities

Complete the following activities, which will help you learn, practice, and expand your knowledge and skills.

Vocabulary. Practice vocabulary for this chapter using the e-flash cards, matching activity, and vocabulary game until you are able to recognize their meanings.

Communication Skills

Reading. Read the Ethics features throughout this text. What role do you think ethics and integrity have in the field of information technology? Think about a time when you used your ideals and principles to make a decision related to information technology, such as software use or a digital download. What process did you use to make the decision?

Writing. Generate ideas for writing a paper that describes the concept of information technology as you understand it. Gather information to support your thoughts and ideas. Create the notes that you could use to write a paper.

Speaking. Create an outline that includes information about using a spreadsheet to track customer data. Consider who will be your audience as you prepare the information. Using the outline, make a presentation to your class.

Internet Research

History of the Internet. Research the history of the Internet using various resources. Write several paragraphs describing what you learned. Use correct punctuation as you write and edit your document.

Teamwork

Working with your team, make a list of the CTSOs that are available at your school. Do any of them relate specifically to information technology? How can your school CTSO help you prepare for life after graduation? Share your findings with the class.

Activity Files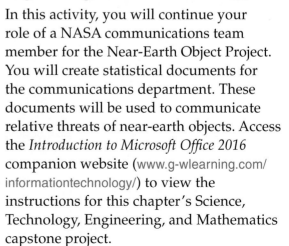

Visit www.g-wlearning.com/informationtechnology/ to download the activity files for this chapter. These activities will expand your learning of the material presented in this chapter and allow you to practice what you have learned. Follow the instructions provided in each file to complete the activity.

Activity File 8-1 Understanding Formulas

Activity File 8-2 Differentiating Cell References

Activity File 8-3 Creating a Budget

Activity File 8-4 Tracking Spending

Activity File 8-5 Assessing a Budget

CAPSTONE PROJECT

The capstone project builds from one chapter to the next. It allows you to apply the skills you have learned to create a complete project in a desired career area. Read the instructions below for the career area you chose to work in for this course. Work in the same career area in each chapter.

Agriculture, Food, and Natural Resources

In this activity, you will assume the role of a chief financial officer of a large agribusiness. You will use Excel to analyze business costs, calculate net worth and owners' equity, and calculate change in medical benefit coverage. Access the *Introduction to Microsoft Office 2016* companion website (www.g-wlearning.com/informationtechnology/) to view the instructions for this chapter's Agriculture, Food, and Natural Resources capstone project.

Business, Management, and Administration

In this activity, you will continue assuming the role of a business administrator. You will create financial documents for your company using Microsoft Office programs. These documents will be used as you communicate with the owner of the company. Access the *Introduction to Microsoft Office 2016* companion website (www.g-wlearning.com/informationtechnology/) to view the instructions for this chapter's Business, Management, and Administration capstone project.

Health Science

In this activity, you will assume the role of the chief financial officer of a large medical-device manufacturer. You will use Excel to create a graph about disease risk, calculate net worth and owners' equity, and calculate change in medical benefit coverage. Access the *Introduction to Microsoft Office 2016* companion website (www.g-wlearning.com/informationtechnology/) to view the instructions for this chapter's Health Science capstone project.

Science, Technology, Engineering, and Mathematics

In this activity, you will continue your role of a NASA communications team member for the Near-Earth Object Project. You will create statistical documents for the communications department. These documents will be used to communicate relative threats of near-earth objects. Access the *Introduction to Microsoft Office 2016* companion website (www.g-wlearning.com/informationtechnology/) to view the instructions for this chapter's Science, Technology, Engineering, and Mathematics capstone project.

9

ADVANCED SPREADSHEET USES

Spreadsheet software makes it possible to complete projects that require repetitive calculations, such as budgeting, processing a payroll, maintaining a grade book, balancing a checkbook, or calculating loan payments. When financial decisions need to be made, spreadsheet software can be used to calculate how much must be paid in taxes or how much a monthly payment would be for a car loan. A what-if analysis can be devised to compare which arrangements are more advantageous before making a monetary commitment.

Spreadsheet software can also create colorful charts. Long columns of numbers can be hard to analyze. The meaning of the data may not be apparent. By displaying the data in a chart, it may be easier to decipher what the data mean. Charts created in spreadsheet software can also be used in word-processing documents. This allows data in a spreadsheet to be represented in graphic form in a report.

MICROSOFT OFFICE SPECIALIST OBJECTIVES

Excel

Manage Data Cells and Ranges

2.3 Summarize and Organize Data
    2.3.1 Insert sparklines
    2.3.4 Apply conditional formatting

Create Tables

3.1 Create and Manage Tables
    3.1.1 Create an Excel table from a cell range
3.2 Manage Table Styles and Options
    3.2.3 Insert total rows
3.3 Filter and Sort a Table
    3.3.4 Remove duplicate records

Perform Operations with Formulas and Functions

4.1 Summarize Data by Using Functions
    4.1.2 Perform calculations by using the SUM function
    4.1.3 Perform calculations by using the MIN and MAX functions
    4.1.4 Perform calculations by using the COUNT function
    4.1.5 Perform calculations by using the AVERAGE function
4.2 Perform Conditional Operations by using Functions
    4.2.1 Perform logical operations by using the IF function
    4.2.2 Perform logical operations by using the SUMIF function
    4.2.3 Perform logical operations by using the AVERAGEIF function
    4.2.4 Perform statistical operations by using the COUNTIF function
4.3 Format and Modify Text by using Functions
    4.3.1 Format text by using RIGHT, LEFT, and MID functions
    4.3.2 Format text by using UPPER, LOWER, and PROPER functions
    4.3.3 Format text by using the CONCATENATE function

Create Charts and Objects

5.1 Create Charts
    5.1.1 Create a new chart
    5.1.2 Add additional data series
    5.1.3 Switch between rows and columns in source data
    5.1.4 Analyze data by using Quick Analysis
5.2 Format Charts
    5.2.1 Resize charts
    5.2.2 Add and modify chart elements
    5.2.3 Apply chart layouts and styles
    5.2.4 Move charts to a chart sheet

CALCULATING WITH FUNCTIONS

One method of adding the values in a column or row of numbers is to write a formula that specifies the individual cell addresses, such as =A3+A4+A5+A6. What if the sum of the content of 100 cells is needed? The address of each of the 100 cells would be in this formula. That would make for a very long formula. To enter this long formula requires some time, and the process would be tedious. The opportunities for errors in writing the formula are great.

Functions, or calculation shortcuts, built into the spreadsheet software simplify the work of creating complex formulas. These shortcuts range from commonly used formulas to complex mathematical and financial calculations. Whenever possible, functions should be used to improve efficiency and accuracy in creating formulas in a spreadsheet.

wavebreakmedia/Shutterstock.com

LEARNING GOALS

After completing this section, you will be able to:
- Describe the use of functions in a spreadsheet.
- Discuss creating complex financial formulas in a spreadsheet.
- Use logical functions in spreadsheet formulas.

TERMS

argument
function
logical function
principal
term

Using Functions

Most spreadsheet software contains many formulas that have already been programmed. A preprogrammed formula in spreadsheet software is called a **function**. Functions are usually divided into categories, including financial, statistical, mathematical, date and time, and logical. All of these are available through the function library.

To see a list of all available functions, click **Formulas>Function Library>Insert Function** in the ribbon. The **Insert Function** dialog box appears, as shown in Figure 9-1. Click the drop-down arrow in the dialog box, and click **All** in the drop-down list. All available functions are listed in the dialog box.

Functions in Microsoft Excel are written in a specific pattern. They begin with an equals sign, just like all formulas, followed by the function name. Next are the parameters or **arguments**, which are values the function needs for the calculation, enclosed in parentheses. Sometimes the arguments can be a range of cells or a cell address that contains critical values. If multiple cell addresses are used as the arguments, they must be separated by commas.

Common Functions

Commonly used functions include **SUM**, **AVERAGE**, **TODAY**, **MIN**, **MAX**, and **IF**. These functions cover calculations for which spreadsheets are often used.

The **SUM** function finds the sum of a list of numbers or the content of a range of cells. For example, to find the sum of the content in cells C4 to C10, or the range C4:C10, the function is written as = SUM(C4:C10).

The **AVERAGE** function finds the average value of the arguments. For example, to find the average of the content in cells B12 to B25, the function is written as =AVERAGE(B12:B25).

The **TODAY** function returns the current date. This function does not require an argument, but it must still have open and closed parentheses. This function is written as =TODAY().

FYI

A shortcut to the **SUM** function in Excel is to click **Home>Editing>AutoSum** in the ribbon.

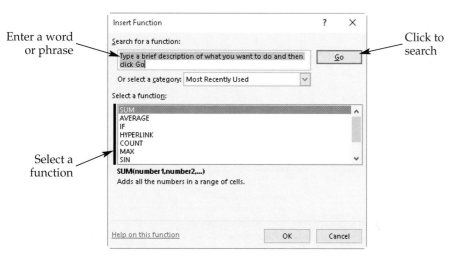

Enter a word or phrase

Click to search

Select a function

Goodheart-Willcox Publisher

Figure 9-1. The **Insert Function** dialog box can be used to help locate and insert functions.

Excel

4.1.3

The **MIN** function returns the lowest value of the range specified in the argument. For example, to find the lowest value in the range A1:D5, the function is written as =MIN(A1:D5). **MIN** is short for *minimum*.

The **MAX** function returns the highest value of the range specified in the argument. For example, to find the highest value in the range C10:G25, the function is written as =MAX(C10:G25). **MAX** is short for *maximum*.

The **IF** function is a logical function, which is used to make a decision. Logical functions are discussed later in this section.

GS5
Key Applications
3.5.3

Entering Functions

To add a function to the spreadsheet in Microsoft Excel, select the cell to which the formula will be added. Then, enter the function. If you know the correct syntax of the function and arguments, the function can be directly entered using the keyboard. For example, the correct syntax to find the minimum value is =MIN(*arguments*), not =MINIMUM(*arguments*).

If you are unsure of the syntax or do not know the name of the function, use the **Insert Function** dialog box. To display this dialog box, click **Formulas>Function Library>Insert Function** in the ribbon.

The drop-down list in the middle of the dialog box can be used to filter the list at the bottom of the dialog box. Click the drop-down arrow, and select the category of functions to show.

If the name of the function is not known, click in the **Search for function:** text box at the top of the box, and enter keywords for what you want to do. Then, click the **Go** button. Excel will display the functions it believes are related to the action you entered in the list at the bottom of the dialog box.

For example, if you want to find the number of cells in a range that are blank, enter blank cells in the **Search for function:** text box, and click the **Go** button. In the list at the bottom of the dialog box, select a function. The function is displayed below the list along with a description of what it does, as shown in Figure 9-2.

To insert a function, select it in the list at the bottom of the dialog box. Then, click the **OK** button. Based on the function, an additional dialog box appears for entering the arguments needed for the function.

> **FYI**
>
> Double-clicking the name of a function in the list in the **Insert Function** dialog box inserts the function.

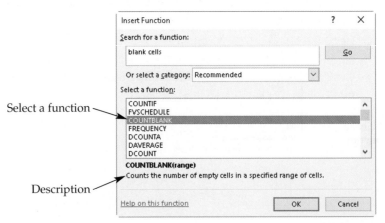

Goodheart-Willcox Publisher

Figure 9-2. A description of the selected function appears at the bottom of the dialog box.

HANDS-ON EXAMPLE 9.1.1

GS5
Key Applications
3.5.3

INSERTING FUNCTIONS

Two commonly used functions are the **SUM** and **AVERAGE** functions. For example, these functions can be used to create a spreadsheet that tracks expenses and displays the total and average expense.

1. Insert your MS-OFFICE flash drive into the computer.
2. Applying what you have learned, create a folder on the flash drive named Chap09.
3. Launch Microsoft Excel, and begin a new blank spreadsheet.
4. Save the file as Expenses.xlsx in the Chap09 folder on your flash drive.
5. Applying what you have learned, format cells B3 through B8 as currency.
6. Add the following content.

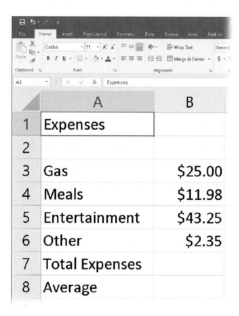

7. Select cell B7. A function will be added to this cell that totals the expenses.
8. Enter the function =SUM(B3:B6) using the keyboard. As soon as the [Enter] key is pressed, the function calculates the total of the range, and the value is displayed in the cell.
9. Select cell B8, and click **Formulas>Function Library>Insert Function** in the ribbon. The **Insert Function** dialog box is displayed.

Insert Function

10. Click in the **Search for a function:** text box, enter average, and click the **Go** button.
11. In the list of results, click the **AVERAGE** entry. Read the description at the bottom of the dialog box to be sure the function is appropriate. In this case, the function should return the average of the arguments supplied to the function, which the **AVERAGE** function does.

HANDS-ON EXAMPLE 9.1.1 (CONTINUED)

12. Double-click the **AVERAGE** entry in the list. The **Function Arguments** dialog box is displayed, as shown.

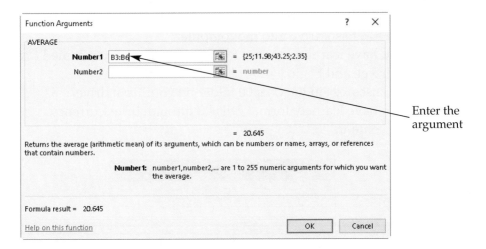

Enter the argument

13. Click in the **Number1** text box, and enter the range B3:B6. Be sure the range ends with cell B6, not cell B7. The range B3:B6 is the argument for the function.
14. Click the **OK** button to finish inserting the function. The value displayed in cell B8 is the average expense. Notice how the function appears in the formula bar: =AVERAGE(B3:B6). This could have been manually entered into the cell like the **SUM** function above to achieve the same result.
15. Save the file.

FYI

When data are entered in a date format, such as 03-14-17, Microsoft Excel will automatically format the cell as a date.

Date and Time

It is possible to insert current, past, and future dates into a spreadsheet through the use of functions. Because the computer has an internal clock, the system always knows the date and time. The computer keeps track of dates by the number of days since January 1, 1900. Time is tracked as a fraction of a day. When a date is entered into a spreadsheet, the software automatically converts it to the number of days since January 1, 1900. When the cell is formatted as a date, this number is displayed as a date. To see the number of days since January 1, 1900, format the cell as a number, as shown in Figure 9-3.

Because dates are stored as numbers, they can be easily used in calculations, such as addition and subtraction. For example, a formula can be created to calculate an age from a person's birthday by subtracting the number for the birthday from the number for today.

In Microsoft Excel, there are several functions related to date and time. These can be accessed through the **Insert Function** dialog box, but there are shortcuts in the ribbon. Click **Formulas>Function Library>Date & Time** in the ribbon, as shown in Figure 9-4. Then, select the function to use in the drop-down menu that is displayed. The function is inserted into the current cell, and the **Function Arguments** dialog box is displayed for entering the arguments.

Formatted
as a date

Formatted
as a number

Goodheart-Willcox Publisher

Figure 9-3. To see the number of days since
January 1, 1900, enter the date and then format the
cell as a number.

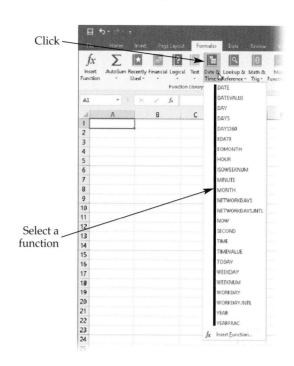

Goodheart-Willcox Publisher

Figure 9-4. The ribbon contains shortcuts for
entering date-related functions.

HANDS-ON EXAMPLE 9.1.2

USING DATE-RELATED FUNCTIONS

There are many functions in Microsoft Excel related to date and time, and these can be used in many different ways. For example, using a function it is easy to see the number of days it has been since January 1, 1900 or to calculate your age in years.

1. Launch Microsoft Excel, and begin a new blank spreadsheet.
2. Save the file as Dates.xlsx in the Chap09 folder on your flash drive.
3. Add the text Date: to cell A1.
4. Enter the function =TODAY() in cell B1. Today's date is displayed in the cell. Every time this spreadsheet is opened, Excel will check for the current date and display it here.
5. Applying what you have learned, format cell B1 as a number. The value displayed in the cell is the number of days since January 1, 1900.
6. Applying what you have learned, format cell B1 as mm/dd/yyyy. The value displayed in the cell is today's date.
7. Enter the function =TODAY() in cell D1.
8. Enter your birthday in cell D2 in the format mm/dd/yy.
9. Enter the formula =D1–D2 in cell D3. This will calculate the number of days between today's date and your birthday. This is how many days you have been alive.

HANDS-ON EXAMPLE 9.1.1 (CONTINUED)

10. Applying what you have learned, edit the formula in D3 to be =(D1–D2)/365, as shown. Be sure the parentheses are correctly placed so the subtraction is carried out before the division. Since ages are not usually expressed in days, dividing by 365 will approximate the number of years you have been alive, including a decimal fraction.

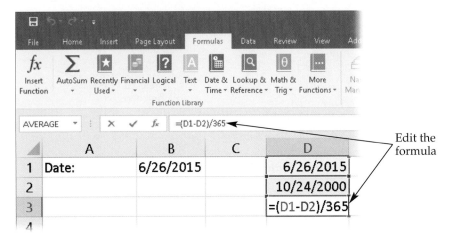

Edit the formula

11. Applying what you have learned, select cell D4, and open the **Insert Function** dialog.
12. Applying what you have learned, search for the phrase round off. In the list of results, select the **INT** function, and read the description. This function converts a decimal to an integer by dropping the decimal places.
13. Double-click the **INT** function and, in the **Function Arguments** dialog box, enter D3 as the argument and click the **OK** button to complete the function. The value displayed in cell D4 is your age as whole number of years.
14. Save the file.

Excel
4.3

Text Functions

Some functions are used not to perform mathematical calculations, but rather to format text or generate information quickly. Formatting functions include **UPPER**, **LOWER**, and **PROPER**. When used properly, these functions take the text of a given cell, for example A15, and change the capitalization of that text to whatever function is being used, as shown in Figure 9-5.

Other text-based functions include **RIGHT**, **LEFT**, **MID**, and **CONCATENATE**. These functions generate a given set of characters based on the information and cell reference in the formula. The **RIGHT** function counts characters from the right side of the text string; the **LEFT** function counts characters from the left side of the text string; and the **MID** function counts characters in the middle of the text string. The formulas for the **RIGHT** and **LEFT** functions include a cell reference and the number of characters needed from the respective end of the text string (as well as the number of characters *into* the text string for the **MID** function). The **CONCATENATE** function joins two or more text strings and merges them into one with the option of inserting new text in the middle. This formula consists of cell references and any text to include in the final output. Examples of how these functions operate are illustrated in Figure 9-5.

Cell Reference	Text	Formula	Result
A15	Excel is an example of spreadsheet software.	=UPPER(A15)	EXCEL IS AN EXAMPLE OF SPREADSHEET SOFTWARE.
A15	Excel is an example of spreadsheet software.	=LOWER(A15)	excel is an example of spreadsheet software.
A15	Excel is an example of spreadsheet software.	=PROPER(A15)	Excel Is An Example Of Spreadsheet Software.
B10	Sat. Jun 8 2019	=RIGHT(B10,4)	2019
B10	Sat. Jun 8 2019	=LEFT(B10,4)	Sat.
B10	Sat. Jun 8 2019	=MID(B10,6,3)	Jun
A6	Interstate 80	=CONCATENATE(A6," by way of ",B12)	Interstate 80 by way of US Route 220
B12	US Route 220		

Figure 9-5. Formatting functions alter or generate text based on the parameters of the formula.

Complex Financial Formulas

One of the benefits of using a computerized spreadsheet is the ability to change the data in cells to create a what-if scenario. It is possible to modify the arguments for a formula to see what the effect will be. This feature of spreadsheets provides the opportunity to analyze a variety of possibilities. It is often helpful to create a what-if scenario when making financial decisions.

An important financial decision is to purchase a car. Cars are very expensive, so many people borrow part of the money to purchase the car. Banks and other organizations that lend money make a profit by charging interest on the money borrowed. For simple interest, they calculate how much interest is owed by multiplying the loan amount by the monthly interest rate and the number of months for the loan. That amount is then added to the loan amount and divided by the number of months for the loan. However, in most cases, interest on a loan is actually calculated on a daily or continual basis, which makes the calculation complex.

Most spreadsheet software contains many preprogrammed functions that can be used to calculate payments. These functions provide an opportunity to look at scenarios to help make a decision. To have the spreadsheet do the math, three values need to be known:

- amount of the loan, also called the **principal**
- interest rate per period
- how many periods it will take to repay the loan, also called the **term**

Interest rates are generally expressed as annual rates. If the spreadsheet function requires the monthly rate, divide the annual rate by 12. The term of a loan is generally stated in years. If the spreadsheet function requires the term to be in months, multiply the number of years by 12 to find the total number of periods.

A function in Microsoft Excel that can be used to calculate payments is **PMT**. The syntax of this function is =PMT(*monthly rate, number of months, principal*). The order of the arguments is very important. Also, notice that

Green Tech

Automatic Lighting
Every building must be well-lighted in order for employees and customers to work and visit safely. Simple changes can make an impact in the cost of lighting. Motion sensors can be a simple solution. If the sensor detects low activity over a period of time, the lights will automatically turn off, saving money and energy.

FYI

Term is also abbreviated as *nper*, for number of periods, in the function list in Microsoft Excel.

the rate and term reference months, not years. Be sure to convert annual rates and terms to monthly rates. Otherwise, the function will return results that are not correct.

HANDS-ON EXAMPLE 9.1.3

CALCULATING A PAYMENT

A what-if scenario can be created to help make decisions when buying a car. You can see what effect changing the principal, interest rate, or term has on the payment.

1. Launch Microsoft Excel, and begin a new blank spreadsheet.
2. Save the file as Payment.xlsx in the Chap09 folder on your flash drive.
3. Enter the following content.

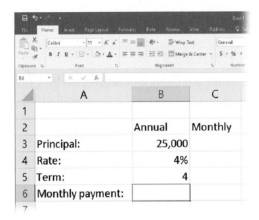

4. Enter the formula =B4/12 in cell C4. This calculates the monthly rate. The result is a decimal fraction.
5. Enter the formula =B5*12 in cell C5. This calculates the number of months for the term.
6. Select cell C6.
7. Applying what you have learned, use the **Insert Function** dialog box to enter the **PMT** function. The arguments are, in order, C4, C5, and B3. After the function is inserted, the correct value that should be displayed in cell C6 is –564.48. The value may be enclosed in parentheses without the minus sign, as (564.48), to indicate a negative value.
8. Applying what you have learned, edit the formula to include a minus sign before the function name: =PMT(C4,C5,B3). This reverses the sign of the result, so the displayed value appears as a positive number instead of a negative number.
9. To perform a what-if scenario, change the loan, rate, and term one at a time. See how each change affects the monthly payment.
10. Save the file.

Logical Functions

In addition to mathematical calculations, a spreadsheet can also determine if certain statements are true or false. Functions that test for true or false are **logical functions**. These functions can be used to add an element of decision making to the spreadsheet.

IF Logical Function

Excel

4.2.1

A commonly used logical function is the **IF** function. In Microsoft Excel, this function has three arguments separated by commas. The first argument is the condition to test. The second argument is the action to perform if the condition is true. The final argument is the action to perform if the condition is false. Any valid logical expression may be used in the first argument of the **IF** statement, as shown in Figure 9-6.

For example, consider the condition where a monthly payment is above or below a certain number. If the payment is less than $325 per month, then the payment is affordable. If the payment is greater than this amount, it is not affordable. The statement is:

Operator	Meaning
=	Equal to
>	Greater than
<	Less than
< >	Not equal to
>=	Greater than or equal to
<=	Less than or equal to

Goodheart-Willcox Publisher

IF p<$325, then it is **TRUE** the payment is affordable, or else it is **FALSE** the payment is affordable.

Figure 9-6. Various operators can be used in a logical expression.

where p represents the payment.

Suppose the monthly payment is in cell C6. In Microsoft Excel, the function for the above statement would be written =IF(C6 <325,"Yes","No"). If the value in cell C6 is less than $325, then the cell containing the function will display the text Yes. If the value is $325 or higher, the cell will display No.

Other Logical Functions

There are several additional logical functions in Microsoft Excel. The **AND** function tests the value of two expressions. If both are true, the function returns the value **TRUE**. If both are false, the function returns the value **FALSE**. The **OR** function also tests the value of two expressions. However, if either expression is true, the function returns the value **TRUE**. If both expressions are false, the function returns the value **FALSE**.

The **NOT** function reverses the value of an expression. If the expression evaluates to **TRUE**, the **NOT** function reverses the value to **FALSE**. If the expression evaluates to **FALSE**, the **NOT** function reverses the value to **TRUE**.

The **IFERROR** function returns a specified value if the expression evaluates to an error. For example, if the expression returns a divide by zero error (#DIV/0), the text Enter a nonzero number could be displayed as the value. If the expression does not return an error, the value of the expression is displayed. In this example, the function could be written as =IFERROR(A1/A2,"Enter a nonzero number"). Notice that the string is contained in quotation marks. If the value of cell A2 is 0, then the text is displayed. If the value of cell A2 is a nonzero number, such as 5, the result of the division is displayed.

The **TRUE** function returns the value **TRUE**. The **FALSE** function returns the value **FALSE**. These functions are provided in Microsoft Excel for compatibility with spreadsheets created in other software. Additional logical functions are outlined in Figure 9-7.

FYI

In computer programming, true-false, yes-no, and on-off all represent the same conditions.

Excel

4.1.4, 4.2.2,
4.2.3, 4.2.4

Function	Purpose	Syntax
COUNT	Counts the number of cells that contain numbers	=COUNT(value1, [value2])
SUMIF	Adds the values in a given range that meet specified criteria	=SUMIF(range, criteria)
AVERAGEIF	Calculates the average of all cells in a given range that meet specified criteria	=AVERAGEIF(range, criteria)
COUNTIF	Counts the number of cells that meet given criteria	=COUNTIF(range, criteria)

Goodheart-Willcox Publisher

Figure 9-7. Logical functions determine if formulas are true or false and generate new expressions based on those results.

HANDS-ON EXAMPLE 9.1.4

USING A LOGICAL FUNCTION

A logical function can be used to determine if a monthly payment is within your budget. Based on the payment, the **IF** function can be used to display either Yes or No in a cell.

1. Launch Microsoft Excel, and open the Payment.xlsx file in the Chap09 folder on your flash drive, if it is not already open.
2. Add the text Affordable? to cell B7.
3. Enter the function =IF(C6<325,"Yes","No") in cell C8. Be sure to include the text in quotation marks. The value displayed in cell C8 should be either Yes or No, depending on whether or not the payment is less than $325.
4. Perform a what-if scenario by changing the principal, rate, and term amounts. Try to find a combination that results in an affordable payment.
5. Save the file.

9.1 | SECTION REVIEW

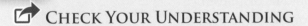

CHECK YOUR UNDERSTANDING

1. What does each function in Microsoft Excel begin with?
2. Which dialog box is used to add a function to a spreadsheet in Microsoft Excel?
3. What three values are needed to calculate loan payments using the **PMT** function in Excel?
4. What does a logical function test for?
5. Which logical function is used to test the values of two expressions?

BUILD YOUR VOCABULARY

As you progress through this course, develop a personal IT glossary. This will help you build your vocabulary and prepare you for a career. Write a definition for each of the following terms and add it to your IT glossary.

argument   principal
function   term
logical function

VISUAL ENHANCEMENTS OF DATA

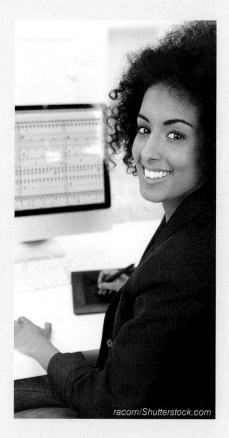

racorn/Shutterstock.com

Most people are visual creatures. Highlighting certain data makes results more visible. It is easy to manually change the color of displayed values or the background color of cells in a spreadsheet. However, some spreadsheet software has the ability to automatically format cells. In Microsoft Excel, this is done through conditional formatting.

Charts graphically represent data. When the data in a spreadsheet are updated, the associated charts are automatically updated. There are several types of charts available in Microsoft Excel, such as column, line, pie, and bar. Each type has a variety of options to make it easy to create and update. The type of chart selected should be appropriate for the data that were entered into the spreadsheet. Excel helps to determine the proper type of chart by displaying tool tips for each type.

TERMS

bar chart
chart
comma-separated values (CSV) file
conditional formatting
embedding
line chart
linking
pie chart

LEARNING GOALS

After completing this section, you will be able to:
- Apply conditional formatting to cells in a spreadsheet.
- Describe how to create a chart from spreadsheet data.
- Explain how to insert a spreadsheet chart into a text document.
- Describe how to create a basic table in a spreadsheet.
- Discuss the use of comma-separated values files.

Excel

2.3.4

Conditional Formatting

Conditional formatting changes the appearance of a cell's value based on parameters set by the user. Conditional formatting allows the user to set up a formula that changes the color of a cell based on the value displayed in the cell. It is often used with the result of the **IF** logical function or another logical function. The result of the logical function is calculated by the software, and the color of the cell's background and content are based on that result, as shown in Figure 9-8.

For example, when looking at a list of names and numbers, conditional formatting makes it possible to have the important cells instantly highlighted. A teacher could create a spreadsheet listing student grades and instantly see who needs extra help. Or, an inventory specialist could create a spreadsheet to track the quantities of products the company has on hand and observe which inventories are low. Conditional formatting makes this possible.

In Microsoft Excel, there are several types of conditional formatting that can be applied. To apply conditional formatting to a cell, select the cell, and click the **Conditional Formatting** button in the **Styles** group on the **Home** tab of the ribbon, as shown in Figure 9-9. Select the type of conditional formatting to apply, and then select the specific formatting in the cascading menu.

Conditional formatting can also be applied using the **New Formatting Rule** dialog box. To display this dialog box, click **New Rule...** in the drop-down menu displayed by clicking the **Conditional Formatting** button in the **Styles** group on the **Home** tab of the ribbon. To create a rule from scratch, click **Use a formula to determine cells to format** in the dialog box. Then, define the formula. For example, the formula =A1<5 tests to see if the value in cell A1 is less than 5. Finally, click the **Format...** button and define the formatting to apply if the condition is true.

An additional benefit of conditional formatting is the ability to remove duplicate records without having to search for them manually. To locate duplicate records, select the range to be searched and select **Home>Conditional Formatting>Highlight Cells Rules>Duplicate Values** from the ribbon. Select the desired formatting in the ensuing dialog box and click **OK**. The selected formatting will then be applied to all duplicate values. With the same set of cells still selected, click **Data>Remove**

FYI

Many experienced users prefer to create conditional formatting from scratch using the **New Formatting Rule** dialog box because doing so offers more control.

Excel

3.3.4

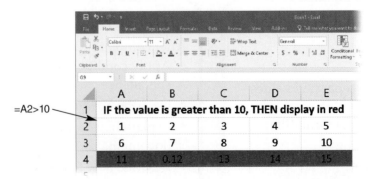

Goodheart-Willcox Publisher

Figure 9-8. Conditional formatting can be used to change the color of a cell's background if a certain condition is met.

Duplicates. In the **Remove Duplicates** dialog box, select the columns from which duplicate values should be removed and click **OK**.

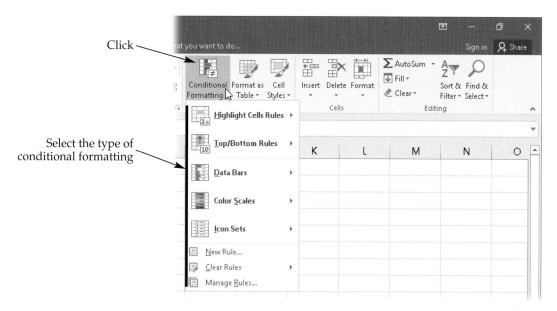

Figure 9-9. There are several ways in which conditional formatting can be applied and used.

HANDS-ON EXAMPLE 9.2.1

APPLYING CONDITIONAL FORMATTING

Conditional formatting can be used to highlight values automatically if they are below a certain point. For example, grades tracked in a spreadsheet can be set up so any grade below 70% will be shown in red.

1. Launch Microsoft Excel, and begin a new blank spreadsheet.
2. Save the file as Formatting.xlsx in the Chap09 folder on your flash drive.
3. Enter the following data.

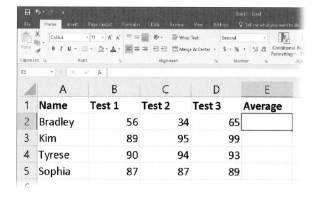

4. Applying what you have learned, insert a function in cell E2 to find the average of the range B2:D2. Use the **Insert Function** dialog box to locate an appropriate function.
5. Applying what you have learned, format cell E2 as a number and decrease the decimal places until only a whole number is displayed.

HANDS-ON EXAMPLE 9.2.1 (CONTINUED)

6. Applying what you have learned, copy the function in cell E2 to cells E3, E4, and E5.

7. Select the range E2:E5, and applying what you have learned, format it as percentages.

Conditional Formatting

8. Click **Home>Styles>Conditional Formatting** in the ribbon. In the drop-down menu that is displayed, click **Highlight Cell Rules** followed by **Less Than...** in the cascading menu. The **Less Than** dialog box is displayed, as shown.

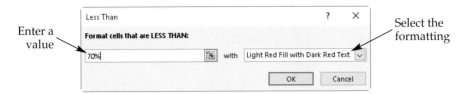

Enter a value

Select the formatting

9. Click in the **Format cells that are less than:** text box, and enter 70%.

10. Click the **with** drop-down arrow, and click **Light Red Fill with Dark Red Text** in the drop-down list.

11. Click the **OK** button to apply the conditional formatting. Any value in the Average column that is less than 70 is highlighted. All other values remain in the default formatting. In this example, only one student is below 70.

12. Change the value in cell C2 to **90**. This student's average is now 70. Notice how the formatting in the Average column changed.

13. Change the value in cell D5 to **34**. This student's average is now below 70. Notice how the formatting in the Average column changed.

14. Change the value in cell D5 to **50**. This student's average is now above 70. Notice how the formatting in the Average column has returned to the default formatting.

15. Save the file.

| GS5 |
| Key Applications |
| 3.7.1, 3.7.2, 3.7.3 |

| Excel |
| 5.1.1 |

FYI

When creating a chart, it is very important to make sure the correct range of cells is selected; otherwise, the software may attempt to include unwanted data.

Charts

Charts are pictures that display numerical data in a graphical format. A chart shows relationships between lists of numbers that may not be easy to see in a table format. The best charts give the viewer the quickest grasp of ideas in the shortest time. They can communicate complex ideas with clarity, precision, and efficiency. For example, financial workers often use charts of the data rather than reading columns and rows of numbers. Charts can enhance information, add visual appeal, and make it easy to analyze data. Creating a chart in spreadsheet software is straightforward:

1. Identify the purpose of the chart.

2. Select the range of cells to chart.

3. Insert the chart on the spreadsheet.

4. Select the chart type.

5. Choose chart elements to clarify data.

6. Change the chart location and size.

Most spreadsheet software can draw many types of charts. The most common types are bar, line, and pie charts, as shown in Figure 9-10. It is important to choose the type of chart that will best represent the selected data and communicate your message.

Bar charts are the best chart type for comparing individual values across categories. The bars can be arranged vertically or horizontally. A bar chart can be used, for example, to show a comparison of total sales of five companies over one year. In Microsoft Excel, a bar chart with vertical bars is called a *column chart*.

Pie charts display the relative size of each fractional part of a whole. Use a pie chart when values represent the division of a category into its parts, such as market share. A pie chart is also useful when displaying only one data series of positive values.

Line charts are used to display trends over time. For example, a line chart can be used to show the annual profit of a company over ten years. Line charts are also used to represent continuous processes rather than individual values. Data points are connected by line segments to show continuous change.

A sparkline is a small graphic that provides an easily read representation of statistical information. Recent versions of Excel offer the opportunity to add sparklines to graphs and charts. To do so, select the empty cell or range in which to insert a sparkline. Next, select the desired type of sparkline (**Line**, **Column**, or **Win/Loss**) from the **Sparklines** group in the **Insert** tab on the ribbon. When prompted, enter the range of cells that house the data the sparkline represents into the **Data** box.

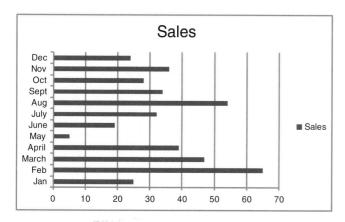

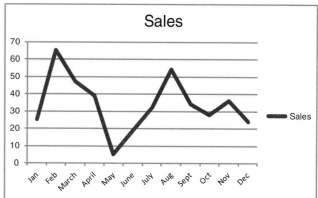

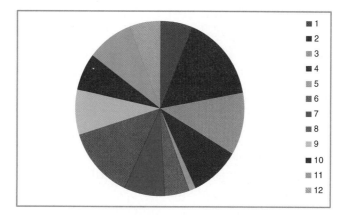

Figure 9-10. The three most common types of chart are, from top to bottom, bar, line, and pie.

HANDS-ON EXAMPLE 9.2.2 📌

Excel
5.1.3, 5.2.1, 5.2.2, 5.2.3

CREATING CHARTS

The Dizzy World Park wants to track the relative popularity of its theme parks among visitors from three regions of the United States and to compare total attendance between parks. A vertical bar chart will be used to track popularity by region, while a pie chart will compare total attendance.

1. Navigate to the student companion website at www.g-wlearning.com, download the data files for this chapter, and save them in the Chap09 folder on your flash drive.
2. Launch Microsoft Excel, and open the ThemePark.xlsx file in the Chap09 folder on your flash drive.
3. Select the range A3:E6. This range includes the attendance at the theme parks as well as the headings. Take care not to select the Total row or Total column.

Insert Column Chart

4. Click **Insert>Charts>Insert Column Chart** in the ribbon, and then click **Clustered Column** in the **2D Column** area of the drop-down menu. This creates a vertical bar chart with the bars grouped in a cluster, as shown. Notice how Excel has selected three ranges within the original selection. Note: though it is not needed in this activity, there may be a situation in which the rows and columns should be switched. To do this, select **Chart Tools>Design>Data>Switch Row/Column** from the ribbon.

> **FYI**
>
> An additional data series can be added to an existing chart by right-clicking the chart and choosing **Select Data** from the shortcut menu to open the **Select Data Source** dialog box.
>
> Excel
> 5.1.2

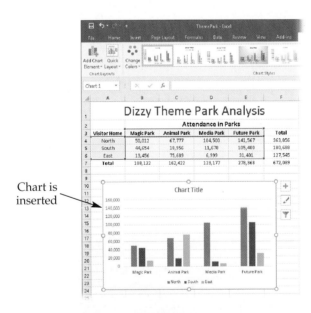

Chart is inserted

5. Double-click the default chart title to activate it for editing, and change the title to Dizzy Theme Park Attendance Analysis.
6. Move the cursor to a corner of the chart until it changes to a resizing cursor, and drag the corner to make the chart smaller.
7. Click and hold on the outside bounding box of the chart, and drag the chart to a position below the data.

HANDS-ON EXAMPLE 9.2.2 (CONTINUED)

8. Click anywhere outside of the chart to deselect the chart.

9. Select the cells containing the headings (B3 through E3) and the totals (B7 through E7). Hold down the [Ctrl] key to select only these cells. These cells will provide headings and data for a pie chart that displays the attendance in percentages of each theme park compared to the whole.

10. Click **Insert>Charts>Insert Pie or Doughnut Chart** in the ribbon, and click **Pie** in the **2D Pie** area of the drop-down menu.

Insert Pie or Doughnut Chart

11. Applying what you have learned, change the default chart title to Attendance by Park.

12. Applying what you have learned, resize the chart to be the same size as the bar chart and move the pie chart below the bar chart.

13. Click the pie in the pie chart. Handles are displayed on all slices of the pie.

14. Click the slice representing Animal Park. Handles are displayed only on that slice.

15. Click and hold on the Animal Park slice, and drag the slice outside of the pie. This is called exploding the chart, and it emphasizes the Animal Park slice.

16. Deselect the chart, and then click the pie to select that element.

17. Click **Design>Chart Layouts>Add Chart Element** in the ribbon, and click **Data Labels** followed by **More Data Label Options...** in the drop-down menu. The **Format Data Labels** pane is displayed on the right-hand side of the Excel window.

Add Chart Element

18. Uncheck the **Value** check box in the **Format Data Labels** pane. The total values are removed from the chart.

19. Check the **Percentage** check box in the **Format Data Labels** pane. Each slice displays a percentage of the whole.

20. To make the chart appear more uniform to a document, layouts and styles can be applied. Select the **Design>Chart Layouts>Quick Layout** from the ribbon.

21. Save the file.

Spreadsheet Charts in Text Documents

The data in a spreadsheet are often used to support a report. The data may support conclusions presented in the report, or the report may explain the data. Spreadsheet software is not suited to create written reports. Therefore, other software must be used to create the report and the data from the spreadsheet must be inserted into the report.

The various applications within an office suite can communicate with each other. This makes it possible to insert objects from one application into documents created by another application. For example, a chart created in Microsoft Excel can be inserted into a Microsoft Word document. There are two ways to achieve this: embedding and linking.

Embedding is a form of copying and pasting. The source object, such as a chart, is copied to the destination document. Once the object is embedded, there is no connection between it and the original from which it was created. If the original is changed, the embedded object will not reflect the changes.

Linking is similar to embedding, but a connection is maintained between the copy and the original source, as shown in Figure 9-11. If

Ethical Communication
Distorting information for a company's gain is an unethical practice. Honesty, accuracy, and truthfulness should guide all communications. Ethically, communication must be presented in an unbiased manner. Facts should be given without distortion. If the information is an opinion, it should be labeled as such.

the original is changed, the linked copy is updated. For example, if the data in Microsoft Excel are updated, a chart based on those data will be updated in Excel, and a linked copy of this chart in a Microsoft Word document will also be updated. Linking is a good option to keep data synchronized. However, if either of the two files is moved or the source file is renamed, the link is broken, so good file management is necessary.

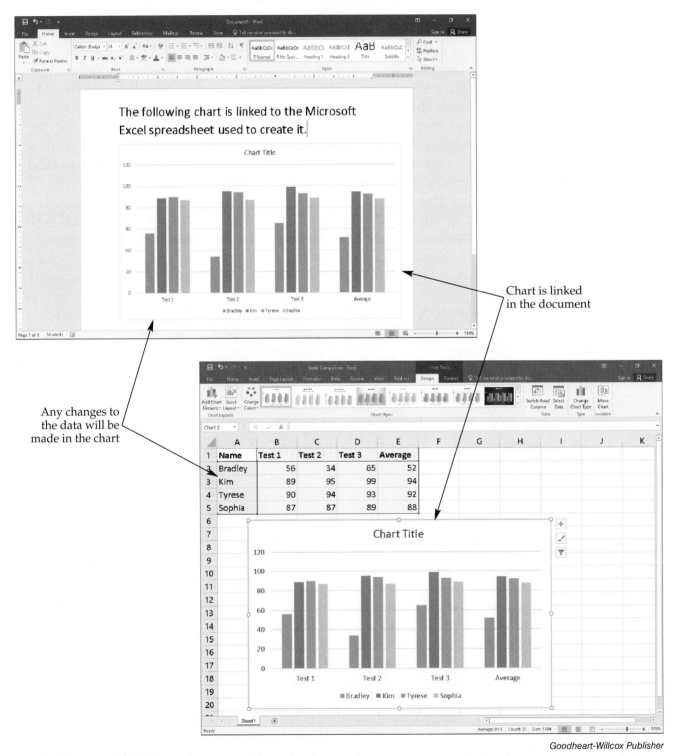

Goodheart-Willcox Publisher

Figure 9-11. A linked object, such as a chart, maintains a connection to the original source. Any changes to the source will be reflected in the linked object.

HANDS-ON EXAMPLE 9.2.3

USING A CHART IN A DOCUMENT

Charts created in a spreadsheet can be inserted into a text document. The chart may be embedded or linked.

1. Launch Microsoft Word, and open the ParkReview.docx file from the Chap09 folder on your flash drive. A pie chart created in Microsoft Excel will be displayed below the text.
2. Launch Microsoft Excel, and open the ThemePark.xlsx file in the Chap09 folder on your flash drive.
3. Click the pie chart to select it.
4. Applying what you have learned, copy the chart to the system clipboard.
5. Return to Microsoft Word.
6. Place the insertion point at the end of the paragraph, and press the [Enter] key to start a new paragraph.
7. Click **Home**>**Clipboard**>**Paste** in the ribbon to display a drop-down menu, as shown.

Paste

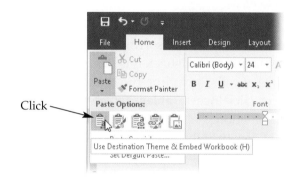

8. Click the **Use Destination Theme & Embed Workbook** button in the drop-down menu. The pie chart is inserted into the document. It is embedded, so there is no connection between it and the original pie chart.
9. Start a new paragraph below the pie chart.
10. Return to Microsoft Excel.
11. Applying what you have learned, copy the bar chart to the system clipboard.
12. Return to Microsoft Word.
13. Click **Home**>**Clipboard**>**Paste** in the ribbon, and click the **Use Destination theme & Link Data** button. The bar chart is inserted into the document. It is linked, so it remains connected to the original bar chart.
14. Return to Microsoft Excel.
15. Change the data in cell B4 to 450,000.
16. Return to Microsoft Word. Notice that the pie chart has not changed, but the bar chart has been updated to reflect the change made in the spreadsheet.
17. Save both files.

TITANS OF TECHNOLOGY

Mitch Kapor launched Lotus 1-2-3 spreadsheet software in early 1983. It was similar in functionality to VisiCalc, but added the capability to generate charts. This software is considered the first killer app for the PC. People were buying PCs only to run Lotus 1-2-3. It soon became clear that PCs were the next big market and Microsoft took notice. Douglas Klunder headed the small team that developed Excel for Microsoft Corporation to take advantage of the PC spreadsheet market. Excel was released in late 1985. The most important elements of a good spreadsheet for advanced developers are speed of recalculations and the availability of many features. Klunder designed a recalculation algorithm that did not recalculate every cell, but only those cells affected by the changes made. This greatly increased the speed of recalculations. When it comes to spreadsheet software, Mitch Kapor and Douglas Klunder are titans of technology.

GS5
Key Applications
3.8.1, 3.8.2, 3.8.3

Excel
3.1.1

Career Skills

Budget Analyst
Budget analysts help private and public institutions manage their finances. Their jobs are both reactive and proactive by studying past spending and making budget projections for management. They use spreadsheets and databases to prepare budget reports and oversee organizational spending. Often their background is a bachelor's degree in accounting and finance.

Tables

A table allows a group of related data to be analyzed. Tables have built-in filtering and sorting functions as well as row shading. To create a table in a spreadsheet, it is easiest to enter the data first. Then, select the range of cells, including the header row, to be in the table. In Microsoft Excel, click **Insert>Tables>Table** in the ribbon or use the [Ctrl][T] key combination.

Once the table is created, row shading can be applied. This can be done manually by setting the fill color for each row, but styles can also be used to control the coloring. There are various other settings that can be changed to alter the appearance of the table. In Microsoft Excel, these are found on the **Design** on-demand tab in the ribbon. The basic style colors are located in the gallery in the **Table Styles** group.

In Microsoft Excel, each cell in the header row of a table contains a drop-down arrow. Clicking the arrow displays a menu that allows the data in the table to be sorted based on the value in the column. Excel recognizes that the cells in each row must remain together. Rows can also be hidden or displayed using this menu.

The **Quick Analysis** feature in Microsoft Excel offers a way to quickly apply conditional formatting to the table. First, select the table to display the **Quick Analysis** button next to the table. Then, click the button and select the type of conditional formatting to apply to the table.

Comma-Separated Values Files

A **comma-separated values (CSV) file** contains data with commas to denote the beginning and end of each datum in a row. Each row is a paragraph in the CSV. A CSV file is used to share data from one application with other software. This type of file is also known as a *comma delimited file*. Other characters may be used instead of a comma, such as tabs or spaces. Figure 9-12 shows how spreadsheet data can be saved to a CSV file.

In addition, a CSV file is used to share spreadsheet data with other software that cannot read the native file format of the spreadsheet software. For example, you may have a word processor that cannot read Microsoft Excel files (XLSx). However, you may need to include the spreadsheet data in a table in the text document. By saving the data from the spreadsheet as a CSV file, the word processor can import the data and create a table.

To create a CSV file in most spreadsheet software, use either the save as or export function. A CSV file has a .csv file name extension. Select the CSV file type, navigate to the folder where the file should be saved, and name the file. In Microsoft Excel, a warning will be displayed indicating that some features of Excel will be lost. Since the CSV file type contains only data, formatting, data types, formulas, and other features are stripped out before the file is saved.

Quarter 1	$ 250
Quarter 2	$ 325
Quarter 3	$ 275
Quarter 4	$ 300

Quarter 1, $250
Quarter 2, $325
Quarter 3, $275
Quarter 4, $300

Datum separator

Goodheart-Willcox Publisher

Figure 9-12. A comma-separated values file contains only the data from a spreadsheet. Commas separate cells in a row, and each row is a separate paragraph.

FYI

Totals can be added to a table by selecting **Design>Table Style Options>Total Row**.

Excel
3.2.3

9.2 | SECTION REVIEW

CHECK YOUR UNDERSTANDING

1. What is used to change the appearance of a cell's value based on parameters set by the user?
2. Name the three most common types of charts.
3. Which type of chart would be best to show trends over time?
4. What is the difference between embedding and linking a chart in a text document?
5. How is each datum in a spreadsheet row separated in a CSV file?

BUILD YOUR VOCABULARY

As you progress through this course, develop a personal IT glossary. This will help you build your vocabulary and prepare you for a career. Write a definition for each of the following terms and add it to your IT glossary.

bar chart
chart
comma-separated
  values (CSV) file
conditional formatting

embedding
line chart
linking
pie chart

9 REVIEW AND ASSESSMENT

Chapter Summary

Section 9.1
Calculating with Functions

- A function is a preprogrammed formula in spreadsheet software. Arguments are values the function needs for the calculation.
- Most spreadsheet software contains many preprogrammed functions that can be used to calculate payments. It is possible to modify the arguments for the formula to create a what-if scenario to see what the effect will be on payments.
- Logical functions test for true or false. These functions can be used to add an element of decision making to the spreadsheet.

Section 9.2
Visual Enhancements of Data

- Conditional formatting changes the appearance of a cell's value based on parameters set by the user. A formula can be created to change the color of a cell based on the value displayed in the cell.
- A chart shows relationships between lists of numbers that may not be easy to see in a table format. The best charts give the viewer the quickest grasp of ideas in the shortest time.
- A chart can be created in spreadsheet software and used in other software. The chart can be embedded, which is a copy, or linked, which maintains a connection to the original chart.

- A table can be inserted into a spreadsheet based on a range of cells. Once inserted, the table can be stylized, including adding shading to rows. Conditional formatting can also be applied to the table.
- A comma-separated values file contains only the data from a spreadsheet. This file type is used to share data with other software that cannot read the spreadsheet software file format.

Now that you have finished this chapter, see what you know about computer applications by taking the chapter posttest. Access the posttest by visiting www.g-wlearning.com.

Chapter 9 Test

Multiple Choice
Select the best response.

1. What are the values the function needs for the calculation called?
   A. pieces
   B. arguments
   C. addresses
   D. logicals

2. Which of the following is *not* a logical function?
   A. **NOT**
   B. **IF**
   C. **MIN**
   D. **AND**

3. How is the **Insert Function** dialog box displayed?
   A. **Formulas>Function Library>Insert Function**
   B. **Insert>Formulas>Functions**
   C. **Formulas>Functions>Insert**
   D. **Insert>Functions**

4. Which type of chart shows the relative size of each fractional part of a whole?
   A. graph
   B. line
   C. bar
   D. pie

5. What is the purpose of a CSV file?
   A. To share data with other software.
   B. To retain formatting and formulas.
   C. To improve readability.
   D. To use logical functions.

Completion

Complete the following sentences with the correct word(s).

6. A(n) _____ is a preprogrammed formula in spreadsheet software.

7. The _____ function returns the lowest value of the arguments.

8. The _____ logical function tests if the value of either of two expressions is true.

9. To create a conditional formatting from scratch, use the _____ dialog box.

10. A _____ is a picture that displays numerical data in a graphical format.

Matching

Match the correct term with its definition.

A. function
B. **MAX** function
C. logical function
D. bar chart
E. linking

11. Tests for true or false.

12. A preprogrammed formula.

13. Best for comparing individual values across categories.

14. Returns the highest value of the arguments.

15. A connection is maintained between the copy and the original source.

Application and Extension of Knowledge

1. Monitor the outside temperature for your area for one 24-hour period. Create a spreadsheet, and enter the data for each hour. Create a line chart in the spreadsheet to illustrate the changes in temperature for the day.

2. Modify the spreadsheet created in #1. Add functions to display the highest and lowest temperatures for the day. Save the spreadsheet under a new file name.

3. Modify the spreadsheet created in #2. Apply conditional formatting to the cells containing the hourly information. Change the background color of

the cells so all data during the day has a light-yellow background and all data during the night has a dark-blue background. Save the spreadsheet under a new file name.

4. Create a spreadsheet to track the amount of time you spend doing certain activities or tasks throughout one week. Be sure to account for all of your time. There are 168 hours in a week. Record the time as the number of hours, such as .25, .5, or 1.25. Use these data to create a pie chart.

5. Open the file created in #4. Create CSV file from the spreadsheet. Open the CSV file in Notepad or other text editor. Write a one-paragraph paper describing what happens to the data in the spreadsheet when the CSV file was created.

Online Activities

Complete the following activities, which will help you learn, practice, and expand your knowledge and skills.

Vocabulary. Practice vocabulary for this chapter using the e-flash cards, matching activity, and vocabulary game until you are able to recognize their meanings.

Communication Skills

Speaking. Participate actively and effectively in a one-on-one oral communication with a classmate about the importance of the technology use for a business. Prepare for the conversation by creating notes that outline your opinions.

Writing. Create a Venn diagram to show the relationships between mobile and desktop computer technology.

Reading. Make a list of the terms and the words that are italicized in this chapter. Use reference guides to confirm the meanings of new words or concepts.

Internet Research

Entering Data into a Spreadsheet. Navigate to Google Trends by keying www.google.com/trends into your web browser. Conduct a search for the term information technology. The numbers along the time line demonstrate the interest in the searched term relative to the highest point on the chart. Build a spreadsheet consisting of the month and search interest indicator for the last 12 months. Then, turn your data into a line graph.

Teamwork

Working with your team, use spreadsheet software to create a list of rules that should be followed when giving criticism to a peer. Next, create a list of rules that should be followed when receiving criticism. Share your findings with the class.

Activity Files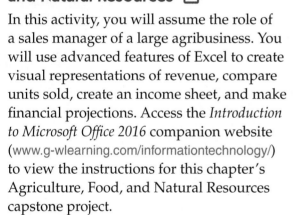

Visit www.g-wlearning.com/informationtechnology/ to download the activity files for this chapter. These activities will expand your learning of the material presented in this chapter and allow you to practice what you have learned. Follow the instructions provided in each file to complete the activity.

Activity File 9-1 Converting Tables

Activity File 9-2 Calculating Payments

Activity File 9-3 Using Functions to Make Decisions

Activity File 9-4 Look-Up Table

Activity File 9-5 Exporting Data

CAPSTONE PROJECT

The capstone project builds from one chapter to the next. It allows you to apply the skills you have learned to create a complete project in a desired career area. Read the instructions below for the career area you chose to work in for this course. Work in the same career area in each chapter.

Agriculture, Food, and Natural Resources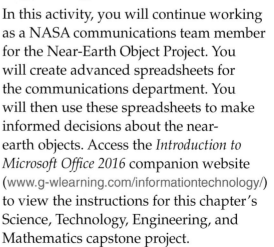

In this activity, you will assume the role of a sales manager of a large agribusiness. You will use advanced features of Excel to create visual representations of revenue, compare units sold, create an income sheet, and make financial projections. Access the *Introduction to Microsoft Office 2016* companion website (www.g-wlearning.com/informationtechnology/) to view the instructions for this chapter's Agriculture, Food, and Natural Resources capstone project.

Business, Management, and Administration

In this activity, you will continue working as a business administrator for a small widget-manufacturing company and create advanced spreadsheets for the company. These advanced spreadsheets will then be used to make informed decisions about the company. Access the *Introduction to Microsoft Office 2016* companion website (www.g-wlearning.com/informationtechnology/) to view the instructions for this chapter's Business, Management, and Administration capstone project.

Health Science

In this activity, you will assume the role of a researcher assessing the stability of pharmaceutical companies. You will use advanced features of Excel to create visual representations of revenue, create filters to compare totals, calculate growth, and make financial projections. Access the *Introduction to Microsoft Office 2016* companion website (www.g-wlearning.com/informationtechnology/) to view the instructions for this chapter's Health Science capstone project.

Science, Technology, Engineering, and Mathematics

In this activity, you will continue working as a NASA communications team member for the Near-Earth Object Project. You will create advanced spreadsheets for the communications department. You will then use these spreadsheets to make informed decisions about the near-earth objects. Access the *Introduction to Microsoft Office 2016* companion website (www.g-wlearning.com/informationtechnology/) to view the instructions for this chapter's Science, Technology, Engineering, and Mathematics capstone project.

10

DATABASE SOFTWARE

SECTIONS

Imagine trying to operate a school without knowing who the students are, who the faculty is, what courses are offered, when the students attended class, or what grades the students earned. All schools have to keep track of this type of data and much more. Schools must have these data available for parents and state officials when they ask for it. Business people also need to keep track of who their customers are, what products they sell, who their employees are, and who owes them money.

Information drives many aspects of society, which is one of the reasons this time in history is called the Information Age. Information systems help schools, businesses, and other organizations arrange information. The data are stored in a database. While similar to a spreadsheet, a database offers many advantages over a spreadsheet. A database allows information to be organized and rapidly retrieved when needed.

MICROSOFT OFFICE SPECIALIST OBJECTIVES

INTRODUCTION TO DATABASES

Databases have many uses, from simple to complex. A simple database may contain information related to recipes and ingredients. A complex database may contain information about the various configurations of a particular model of car and the tens of thousands of parts needed to manufacture each.

A database organizes data in one or more tables. Each table consists of rows and columns, like a spreadsheet. However, database software offers more powerful tools for working with the data than the tools offered by spreadsheet software. The process of creating a database is not difficult, but it may be time-consuming if the database is large.

Ammentorp Photography/Shutterstock.com

LEARNING GOALS

After completing this section, you will be able to:

- Describe the structure of a database.
- Explain how to add, edit, and delete records in a database.
- Create a database structure.

TERMS

database

database management system (DBMS)

design view

field

primary key

record

table

Overview of Databases

A **database** is a structured collection of related information organized for easily locating and retrieving the data. A database can be very large. For example, a database may contain information of sports card collections as well as all details of the related major league sports teams. Before computers became widely used, most organizations kept data on paper. Schools and businesses had to find many places to store the paper. It was also difficult to find specific pieces of information.

An electronic or computerized database is a big improvement over paper-based databases. It not only organizes the data, but offers tools to search and output the data. When people search the computerized card catalog at the library, they are using an electronic database to show, or output, the results. The World Wide Web uses databases to look up website locations. When someone places a food order by phone, a database may be used to check the customer's name, address, and ordering history.

There are many advantages to using an electronic system over a paper system. An electronic database offers faster input with fewer errors. The data are easier to maintain. All calculations are done correctly by the computer, eliminating errors that may occur with manual calculations. When a company's data are kept in an electronic form, the data can be protected by backups. Passwords can be required to provide security for the data. Electronic databases make it easy to search, find specific answers, and create reports.

The software that manipulates the data is called a database management system. A **database management system (DBMS)** handles the collection, storage, sorting, reporting, and organization of data. In a society of "knowledge workers," an understanding of databases and database management systems is critical. This chapter introduces the basic concepts of database management. Some common terms associated with a DBMS and their explanations are shown in Figure 10-1.

Customer relationship management (CRM) software is a type of database designed to manage and analyze customer data and interactions with customers. CRM programs can improve business relationships by compiling information on customers across different points of contact. These points of contact may include the company's website, telephone,

GS5
Key Applications
4.3.3

FYI

To set the desired startup form, select **File>Options**. Navigate to **Current Database**, and in the **Display Form** list, select the desired form and click **OK**.

Access
1.3.3

Field	Contains information about specific characteristics of the entry described in a record.
Form	Database object used to collect or display data one record at a time.
Query	Contains information from one or more tables that meets certain criteria or conditions.
Record	A row in a database table.
Report	Output of the database of specific information requested by the user.
Sort	Arranging data in a table based on one or more field.
Table	Contains information arranged in horizontal rows and vertical columns.

Goodheart-Willcox Publisher

Figure 10-1. Common terms related to databases and a brief explanation of each.

web-based live chat, direct mail, marketing materials, and social media. CRM systems can also give the staff detailed information on customers' personal information, purchase history, buying preferences, and concerns. With cloud-based CRM software, data are stored on an external, remote network that employees can access anytime and anywhere there is an Internet connection. Four popular vendors of CRM systems are Salesforce.com, Microsoft, SAP, and Oracle.

Tables

The foundation of a database is a table. A **table** contains information arranged in horizontal rows and vertical columns, as shown in Figure 10-2. A database table appears similar to a spreadsheet. Most databases contain more than one table. The tables are organized by topic.

Records

Rows in a database table are called records. **Records** contain all fields or units of information. This column is called ID by default, and the data in this column cannot be edited by the user. In most database programs, the software automatically generates the ID number. The column can be modified to make its name more meaningful, such as EMPLOYEE ID or INVENTORY NUM.

For example, if the table contains information about people who work at a particular company, each record would contain information about one person. This may include the employee's first and last names, date of hire, and Social Security number. There would be one record for each employee.

If the table contains all of the products available at a hardware store, each record would contain only data about one piece of inventory. For example, each record might contain the type of product, the name of the supplier, and the product's cost. Each product would have a separate record in the table.

GS5
Key Applications
4.3.2

Career Skills

Material-Moving Machine Operator

Material-moving machine operators work with robotic systems to load and unload high numbers of containers between large ocean-going vessels and transport vehicles in the port. Driven by a vast database and robotic movements, these systems move goods at a rapid rate. Some operators manage the systems via remote interface for a port far from their stations.

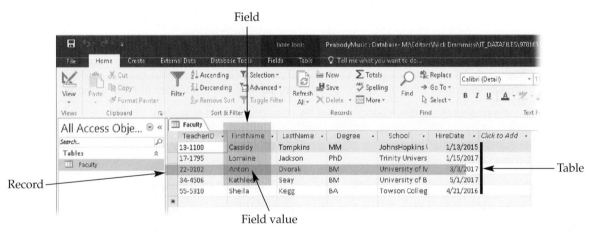

Figure 10-2. A table consists of records (rows) and fields (columns).

Fields

Columns in a database table are called fields. **Fields** contain units or items of information for each record. The names of the columns appear along the top of the table. For a table containing employee information, fields may be included for first name, last name, date of hire, and Social Security number. These labels will appear along the top of the table.

Microsoft Access

Microsoft Access is the database management software included in the Microsoft Office suite. Its best applications are for personal use or for small business management. All examples and discussions in this chapter are based on Microsoft Access. The parts of the Microsoft Access screen are identified in Figure 10-3.

Microsoft Access saves databases with the .accdb file extension. When a database file is saved, there will not be separate files in the folder for all of the tables, reports, forms, and queries created in the project. These items are all stored within the single database file.

As with all software, there are **Save** and **Save As** options in Microsoft Access. The **Save As** option allows the database to be saved under a different file name. The **Save** option saves the database under the current file name. However, if the file has not yet been saved, the **Save As** option will be activated.

GS5
Key Applications
4.3.1

Access
4.1.3

FYI

Microsoft Access is not included in all levels of the Microsoft Office suite, but can be purchased separately.

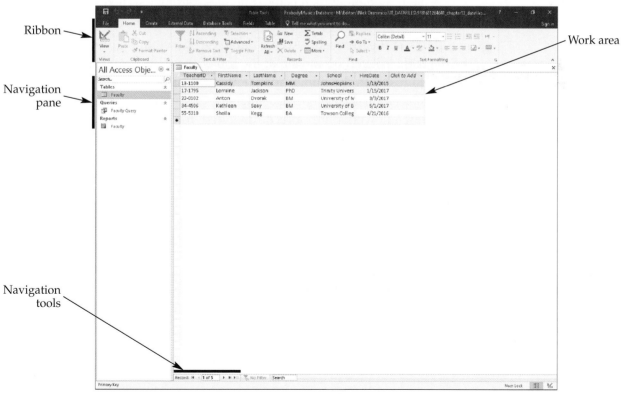

Goodheart-Willcox Publisher

Figure 10-3. The various parts of the Microsoft Access screen are identified here.

Microsoft Access is closed in the same manner as any Microsoft Office application. Click the standard close button (X) in the upper-right corner of the application window. You can also click **File>Close** in the ribbon. Whenever Microsoft Access is closed, the database file is automatically saved.

Examining a Database

The best way to learn about databases and a DBMS is to look at examples. First, you will examine an existing database. After that, you will look at how to create a database from scratch.

Consider the database created by the company Rizzo Landscapes. The owner is Troy Rizzo, who is a landscape architect, and his company provides a wide range of services, from site analyses and feasibility studies to drafting and administering construction documents for projects of various scales. He has set up three tables to track his data:

- customer information
- contract details
- invoices

This is the information that Troy tracks:

- contract number, which is a unique number assigned to each contract
- customer ID, which is a unique number assigned to each customer
- contract amount, which is the dollar amount for the full contract
- signing date, which is the date the customer signed the contract
- contract type, which is a brief description of the contract

Look at the Microsoft Access database shown in Figure 10-4. The title of the table is listed on the tab at the top of the table just below the ribbon. The field (column) headings appear along the top of the table. The fields are ContractNum, CustomerID, ContractAmt, SigningDate, and ContractType. Spaces are allowed, but not recommended, for inclusion in field names.

The records begin below the field headings. In this example, there are five records. Each row in the table represents a record and is related to the entry in the first field: ContractNum. For example, the fields in the record highlighted in blue in Figure 10-4 are all related to the same contract.

Ethics

Customer Information

A database may contain personal information about customers or employees. This information should be treated as confidential. It is unethical to share personal information about someone without his or her permission. Many people also consider the practice of selling customer data to other companies unethical. Companies often promote the fact that they do not sell customer data as a way to promote goodwill with customers.

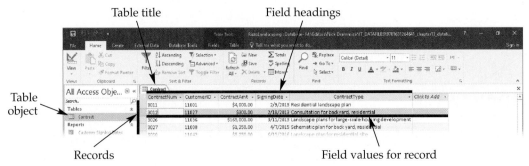

Table title   Field headings

Table object

Records   Field values for record

Goodheart-Willcox Publisher

Figure 10-4. Tables are the foundation of a database. The parts of a table are identified here.

HANDS-ON EXAMPLE 10.1.1 ✍

EXAMINING A DATABASE

A database consists of at least one table composed of rows and columns. The best way to learn about a database is to begin by looking at an existing database.

1. Insert your MS-OFFICE flash drive into the computer.
2. Applying what you have learned, create a folder on the flash drive named Chap10.
3. Navigate to the student companion website at www.g-wlearning.com, download the data files for this chapter, and save them in the Chap10 folder on your flash drive.
4. Launch Microsoft Access 2016.
5. On the startup screen, click **Open other files**>**Computer**>**Browse**.
6. Navigate to the Chap10 folder on your flash drive, and open the RizzoLandscaping.accdb database file.
7. If a security warning appears below the ribbon, click the **Enable Content** button.
8. Locate the navigation pane on the left, and make note of the objects that are part of the database. In this case, the database contains one object, which is a table named Contract. If the navigation pane is not visible, select **Home**>**Show**>**Navigation Pane**, or press the [F11] key on the keyboard.
9. Double-click the Contract table in the navigation pane to open the table.
10. Locate the table in the center of the screen. Notice the field labels along the top. The name of each record is determined by what appears in the first column, which in this case is the ContractNum field.
11. Right-click on the tab above the table that contains the table name, and click **Close** in the shortcut menu.
12. Click **File**>**Save As** in the ribbon, and then click **Save Database As** followed by the **Save As** button.
13. In the standard save as dialog box that is displayed, save the file as *LastName*RizzoLandscaping.accdb in the Chap12 folder on your flash drive.

Adding Data

As with spreadsheets, information will be added to a database after it is created. It is easy to add a new record to a table in a Microsoft Access database. Click in the first column for the new record, and enter the necessary data. Then, use the [Tab] key to move from left to right, entering data into each field as you go. Do not enter symbols, such as commas or dollar signs. The software will take care of that just as spreadsheet software does. Press the [Enter] or [Tab] key at the end of the record. Do not click the Click to Add column heading or a new field will be added to the table.

HANDS-ON EXAMPLE 10.1.2

ADDING DATA

1. Launch Microsoft Access, and open the *LastName*RizzoLandscaping.accdb file in the Chap10 folder on your flash drive, if it is not already open.
2. If a security warning appears below the ribbon, click the **Enable Content** button.
3. Double-click the Contract table in the navigation pane to open the table.

HANDS-ON EXAMPLE 10.1.2 (CONTINUED)

4. Click in the ContractNum field for the next available record. The next available record has an asterisk (*) to the left.
5. Enter 3015, and press the [Tab] key.
6. Continue adding the following data. Do not add the dollar signs or commas. Press the [Tab] key to advance through the database.

ContractNum	CustomerID	ContractAmt	SigningDate	ContractType
3015	11005	$1,500	3/1/2017	Schematic plan for backyard, residential
3022	11043	$22,000	4/14/2017	Landscape design for two entrances
3023	11071	$39,000	3/22/2017	Renovation of large multifamily housing open space

Editing Data

Access

2.3.1

Data that have already been entered into a database can be easily changed. Editing data in a database table is similar to editing data in a spreadsheet. Display the table that contains the record with the information to be edited. Then, click the cell to edit, and change the entry. Unlike a spreadsheet in Microsoft Excel, clicking the cell automatically activates it for editing, placing the insertion point within the cell. So, to completely replace the existing data requires erasing what is there and then entering the new data.

Deleting Data

Access

1.1.4, 2.3.3, 2.4.9

Incorrect data can be deleted. To delete data in a cell, click the cell in the table to activate it for editing. Then, use the [Delete] or [Backspace] key to remove the data.

Often, an entire record or field will need to be removed. This is a drastic move and should be well planned. In Microsoft Access, a deleted record or field cannot be restored using the **Undo** function. In the other Microsoft Office applications, the **Undo** function reverses the last changed. In Microsoft Access, the **Undo** function can reverse some, but not all, changes. Deleting a record or field is one of the changes that cannot be undone in Access.

To delete a record, move the cursor to the left of the record until it changes to a right-pointing arrow. Click to select the entire record or row. To select a field, move the cursor above the field until it changes to a downward-pointing arrow. With the record or field selected, press the [Delete] key. A warning appears asking to confirm the deletion and warning that the change cannot be undone, as shown in Figure 10-5. Click the **Yes** button to delete the record or field.

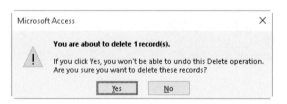

Goodheart-Willcox Publisher

Figure 10-5. When a record is deleted, the action cannot be undone.

HANDS-ON EXAMPLE 10.1.3

EDITING DATA

The data in a database will usually require updating. The ability to edit the data to update records is an important skill to master when working with databases.

1. Launch Microsoft Access, and open the *LastName*RizzoLandscaping.accdb file in the Chap10 folder on your flash drive, if it is not already open.
2. If a security warning appears below the ribbon, click the **Enable Content** button.
3. Double-click the Contract table in the navigation pane to open the table.
4. Click the cell in the 3015 record for the ContractAmt field. The cell is activated for editing, and the insertion point is within the cell.
5. Change the amount to 1750.
6. Move the cursor to the left of the record 3022 record until it changes to a right-pointing arrow, and click. The entire record is selected.
7. Press the [Delete] key.
8. Click the **Yes** button in the warning that appears. The record is permanently removed from the database.

Creating a Database Structure

Users can enjoy many benefits from a correctly designed database. In an educational or business setting, many people may want to use the data. If the organization is using a DBMS, it can improve its ability to share data. The organization can minimize inconsistencies among the different parts. As a result, the users will be able to make better decisions and be more productive.

Before a database is created, the purpose of the database must be determined. Then, how the information is to be organized into tables must be planned. First, decide exactly which information to track. These items will become the fields. Related fields will be in the same table. If necessary, additional tables can be created to group other related fields.

Data Types

Databases are particular about what type of data goes in each field. When the data types are correctly set up, the information is easier to retrieve. It also ensures that whoever is using the database is entering data in the proper manner. Deciding what type of data is going to go in a field also allows the system to establish how much room it needs to set aside. There are several different types of data that can be stored in the fields of a database, such as:

- text;
- numbers;
- currency;
- dates; and
- Boolean (yes/no).

Numbers are considered text if they are not going to be used for calculation.

Access
1.1.1

FYI

Users can choose database templates by clicking **File**>**New** and selecting the desired template.

Access
1.1.2

GS5
Key Applications
4.1

Fields can be sized to control the data entry. For example, a text field may need room for 50 characters for an address. A yes-no field only needs space for one character, a Y or an N, as shown in Figure 10-6.

In the Rizzo Landscaping example in the previous section, four data types were used. The contract number and the customer ID were numeric fields. The contract amount was a currency field. The signing date was a date field. The contract type was a text field.

Access
2.1.1

Creating a Table

The best way to learn how to create a database from scratch is to look at an example. In this example, a database will be created to help manage a music school. The director, Cassidy Tompkins, founded the Peabody Music School because of his popularity as a music teacher specializing in brass instruments. During the past two years, other qualified teachers have joined him to offer instruction in voice, piano, violin, cello, guitar, percussion, and other instruments. As the school continues to grow, he wants to keep track of information about students, teachers, and contracts. Mr. Tompkins wants to track this information about instructors:

- teacher ID
- first name
- last name
- degree
- school
- hire date

The database will contain fields to track this information. Once the database is set up, Mr. Tompkins will enter the data into these fields.

Defining Fields

When starting a database from scratch, begin by creating a table. When a blank database is started in Microsoft Access, a blank table is automatically created and displayed in the datasheet view. However, fields are defined in Microsoft Access in the design view. The **design view** is for developers of the database to set up fields, as shown in Figure 10-7.

FYI

To rename any table, right-click any table in the Navigation Pane and select **Rename** in the shortcut menu. The table may have to be closed for the name to be made editable.

Access
2.2.4

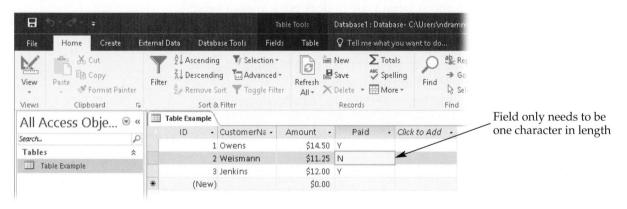

Goodheart-Willcox Publisher

Figure 10-6. The length of a text field can be set to limit entry. In this case, the length is one character to allow only an entry of Y or N.

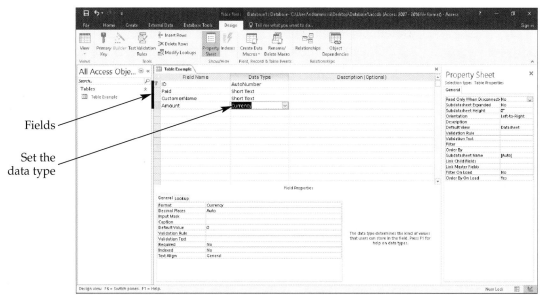

Fields

Set the
data type

Figure 10-7. The design view is where fields are set up. Ordinary users of the database will not see this view.

Ordinary users of the database will not see the design view. This prevents them from changing the fields or the data type.

To display the design view in Microsoft Access, click **Home>Views> View** in the ribbon. This button is a toggle between the datasheet view and the design view. The drop-down arrow below the button can also be clicked to display a drop-down menu. In some cases, there may be more views that can be displayed with this menu. When displaying a new table in the design view, it must first be named and saved.

The first field entered into a table is, by default, the primary key. The **primary key** is the field that will be used by the DBMS to keep track of records. In the design view of Microsoft Access, the row header for the primary key contains an icon of a key. There can be only one primary key in a table.

Each record must have a different value for the primary key. For example, when tracking people with a database, such as students or employees, the last name cannot be a primary key because there could be duplicates. Instead, a unique identification number should be used. Microsoft Access suggests the first field, which is the default primary key, be named ID. It also suggests the data type should be a number. These can be accepted or changed as needed.

Enter the name to use in the Field Name column or press the [Enter] or [Tab] key to accept the default value. To set the data type, click the drop-down arrow in the Data Type column, and then click the data type for the field. For example, if the field will be a date, click **Date/Time** in the drop-down list.

After fields have been defined, the user can further modify them to fit individual needs by making changes to the **Field Properties** section of the database, which is located beneath the design grid when in Design View. For example, the text that appears as a field caption can be changed by clicking into the text field and editing it, and field sizes can be changed by navigating to **General>Field Size** and entering a new size. Users can

FYI

Right-clicking on the tab name of the table displays a shortcut menu that can be used to switch views.

Access
1.2.2

FYI

To hide fields, right-clicking on a column or row header of a table and select **Hide Fields** from the shortcut menu.

Access
2.2.1, 3.2.4

Access
2.4.5

Access
2.4.3, 2.4.4

also change the data types of the fields by selecting a different type from **Datasheet**>**Data Type**.

Access
2.4.2

One of the more advanced customizations is the addition of validation rules. Validation rules restrict the data that can be entered into a database field. These rules can be added by selecting **Fields**>**Field Validation**>**Validation** in the ribbon. After making a selection, the user will be prompted to select a **Field Validation Rule**. Alternatively, users can add validation rules in the Validation Rule field of the **Field Properties** section of the database.

Access
2.4.7, 2.4.8

Consider establishing default values and input masks for your fields. Default values enable Access to automatically generate a value for specific new records. These can be established in Design View by navigating to **General**>**Default Value** and entering a value in the **Default Value** property box. The value entered will be dependent on the type of field. Input masks place data in correct locations and formats. For example, if a user is creating a field for a plus-four ZIP code, the format of the ZIP code will likely resemble 12345-1234. To ensure this format, the user can create an input mask that appears as _ _ _ _ _-_ _ _ _. When data is entered, it will be done so with proper formatting as dictated by the input mask. To establish input masks, select **General**>**Input Mask**>**Build (...)** to start the Input Mask Wizard.

Entering New Records

Once the table is set up in Microsoft Access, records are entered into the database using the datasheet view. Display the datasheet view by clicking **Home**>**Views**>**View** in the ribbon. Once the datasheet view is displayed, new records are created and data entered the same as previously discussed for an existing database.

HANDS-ON EXAMPLE 10.1.4

CREATING A DATABASE

When working with databases, sometimes you will have an existing database. However, many times you will need to create a database from scratch.

1. Launch Microsoft Access 2016.
2. On the startup screen, click **Blank desktop database**. A dialog box is displayed for naming the database and specifying its location.
3. Click in the **File Name** text box, and enter PeabodyMusic.
4. Click the **Browse** button (the folder icon), and navigate to the Chap10 folder on your flash drive.
5. Click the **Create** button. The database is created, and an empty table appears in the datasheet view.
6. Click **Home**>**Views**>**View** in the ribbon to display the design view. The **Save As** dialog box appears for naming the table.
7. Click in the **Table Name:** text box, enter Faculty, and click the **OK** button. The default for the first field, which is the primary key, is ID, and this value is active for editing.
8. Replace ID with TeacherID. Do not use spaces. This will be the field name for the primary key.
9. Press the [Tab] key to move to the Data Type column or click the cell in that column.
10. Click the drop-down arrow in the cell to view the different types. There are two types of text fields, short and long. This field will have only seven characters, which is considered short text.

HANDS-ON EXAMPLE 10.1.4 (CONTINUED)

11. Click **Short Text** in the drop-down list.
12. Press the [Tab] key to move to the Description column or click the cell in that column.
13. Enter Primary key in the cell, as shown. This is an optional field, but whatever is entered here will be displayed in the status bar in a form to help the user know what to enter.

Field name   Data type   Optional comment

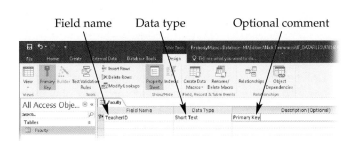

14. Press the [Tab] or [Enter] key to move to the next row.
15. Applying what you have learned, create the remaining fields shown below. If you need to make a change due to a typo or reconsideration, click the cell and correct the information.

Field Name	Data Type	Description
FirstName	Short Text	First name of teacher
LastName	Short Text	Last name of teacher
Degree	Short Text	Educational degree
School	Short Text	College or university attended
HireDate	Date/Time	Date hired

16. Right-click on the table name in the tab above the table, and click **Save** in the shortcut menu.

Data-sheet view

17. Click **Home**>**Views**>**Datasheet View** in the ribbon to display the datasheet view. If the table has unsaved changes, a message appears indicating the table must be saved before changing views.
18. Applying what you have learned, enter the records shown below to complete the table. In some cases, the data may extend beyond the width of the cell, which will not affect the data.

TeacherID	FirstName	LastName	Degree	School	HireDate
13-1100	Cassidy	Tompkins	MM	Johns Hopkins University	1/13/2015
17-1795	Lorraine	Jackson	PhD	Trinity University	1/15/2017
55-5310	Sheila	Kegg	BA	Towson College	4/21/2016
22-0102	Anton	Dvorak	BM	University of Maryland	3/3/2017
34-4506	Kathleen	Seay	BM	University of Baltimore	5/1/2017

FYI

Records and fields can be added to tables by selecting **Table Tools**> **Fields**>**Add & Delete**.

Access
2.2.2, 3.2.2

FYI

To add a description to a table, access Design View and select **Design**>**Show/ Hide**>**Property Sheet**. Click the **General** tab of the property sheet, and enter a description of the table in the Description field.

Access
2.2.3

HANDS-ON EXAMPLE 10.1.4 (CONTINUED)

Save

19. Click the **Save** button on the **Quick Access** toolbar to save the table.
20. Click the standard **Close** button (X) to close Microsoft Access.

TITANS OF TECHNOLOGY

Sergey Grin and Larry Page created Google while pursuing their PhDs at Stanford University. Google makes use of massive databases and has the most sophisticated search algorithms of any programs written. Its mission is "to organize the world's information and make it universally accessible and useful." Google runs more than one million servers in data centers around the world and processes over one billion search requests per day. Each data center is composed of high-performance computers that run all the time. Google maintains an index of websites, which is a large database. A Google search is a basic query on the index (database). According to Google, this database exceeds 95 petabytes in size, or nearly 100 million gigabytes. Google also can reach other databases of information that are not links, but can be accessed via queries.

10.1 | SECTION REVIEW

 CHECK YOUR UNDERSTANDING

1. What are the columns in a database table called?
2. Which part of a database is a row?
3. How do you undo the deletion of a record in Microsoft Access?
4. In which view are fields set up in Microsoft Access?
5. What is true about the value for each record in the field set as the primary key?

 BUILD YOUR VOCABULARY

As you progress through this course, develop a personal IT glossary. This will help you build your vocabulary and prepare you for a career. Write a definition for each of the following terms and add it to your IT glossary.

database	field
database management system (DBMS)	primary key
	record
design view	table

IMPORTING AND VIEWING DATA

auremar/Shutterstock.com

There are many ways to view the data once they have been entered. Users can see all of the data in the table view as they are entered. These data can be sorted and filtered to make specific records more obvious.

Tables containing many records can present a problem for the person entering or updating the data. It can be distracting to verify that data have been entered on the correct line. This difficulty can be overcome by showing only one record at a time in a form. Another way to view the data is through a report. This can be printed and formatted so the reader does not need to know how to use the DBMS to understand it.

TERMS

datasheet view
foreign key
form
one-to-many relationship
relational database
report

LEARNING GOALS

After completing this section, you will be able to:
- Explain how to import records into a database.
- Describe different ways in which to view data in a database.
- Explain the process of joining tables in a database.

Access
1.1.3, 2.1.2

FYI

Microsoft Access can import data from spreadsheets, text files, another Access database, and other databases and file formats.

FYI

To export data, click **External Data>Export** and select the appropriate file type.

Access
1.5.4

Access
1.4.2, 1.4.3, 1.4.4,
1.4.5

Importing Records into a Database

A database can be created from scratch. New fields and records can be added to a table. If needed, new tables can be created to group related data. Data can be entered directly into the database. However, sometimes the data already exist in some other form, such as in a spreadsheet.

If the data are located in a spreadsheet, instead of manually reentering the data into the database, the spreadsheet can be imported into the database. Importing existing data is much more efficient than reentering it, especially if the quantity of data is large. Data can be imported into a blank database or a database that already contains data.

In Microsoft Access, a wizard is used to import data from a spreadsheet, as shown in Figure 10-8. The columns in the spreadsheet should match the order of the fields in the database and the data types. Both the spreadsheet and the table in Access into which the data are being imported must be closed before starting the process. During the importing process, the user is given the opportunity to check the data before importing them.

Securing a Database

As with any computer-based project, backing up files is an important task. In the event of hard-drive failure or other loss of data, a backup can save time by not having to recreate a database from scratch. To create a database backup, select **File>Save As** in the backstage view. Select **Advanced>Back Up Database**, then click **Save As** to display a traditional **Save** dialog box.

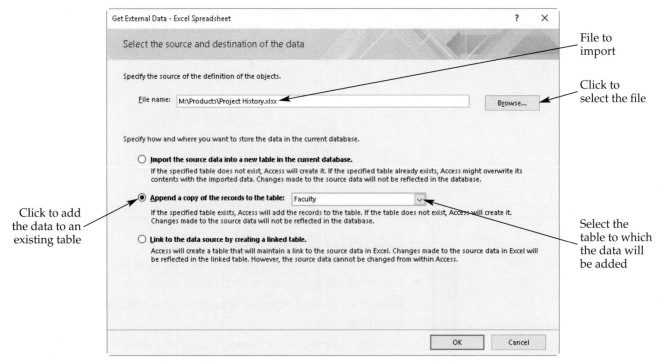

Goodheart-Willcox Publisher

Figure 10-8. Importing data from a spreadsheet into an existing table.

Splitting a database can improve its performance and lower the odds of data corruption, especially in databases that are shared across networks. To split a database, select **Database Tools>Move Data>Access Database**. When the Database Splitter Wizard opens, select **Split Database** and follow the on-screen instructions of the wizard.

To ensure only those with authorization are able to access a database, encrypt the database with a password. To encrypt a database in Microsoft Access, select **File>Open>Browse**. In the **Open** dialog box, browse to and select the desired file. Select the **Open** drop-down menu and click **Open Exclusive**. Once the file is opened, select **File>Info>Encrypt with Password**. The **Set Database Password** dialog box will appear. In the dialog box, enter the desired password in both the Password box and Verify box, then select **OK**.

HANDS-ON EXAMPLE 10.2.1

IMPORTING DATA

If data exist in a spreadsheet, they should be imported into the database instead of manually reentering them. This is done through use of a wizard.

1. Launch Microsoft Access, and open the *LastName*RizzoLandscaping.accdb file in the Chap10 folder on your flash drive, if it is not already open.
2. If a security warning appears below the ribbon, click the **Enable Content** button.
3. Double-click the Contract table in the navigation pane to open the table.
4. Applying what you have learned, display the design view. Make note of the field names.
5. Launch Microsoft Excel, and open the Troy1.xlsx file in the Chap10 folder on your flash drive. Note the first row contains the same field names used in the Rizzo Landscaping database and they are in the same order.
6. Close Excel, and return to Access.
7. Right-click on the tab above the table that contains the table name, and click **Close** in the shortcut menu.
8. Click **External Data>Import & Link>Import Excel Spreadsheet** in the ribbon. A wizard is launched to guide you through the process of importing data.

Import Excel Spreadsheet

9. Click the **Browse…** button on the first page of the wizard, navigate to the Chap10 folder on your flash drive, and open the Troy1.xlsx file.

> ## FYI
>
> Fields in a database, table, or query can be deleted by selecting the field and pressing the [Del] key on the keyboard.
>
> **Access**
> 2.4.9, 3.2.3

HANDS-ON EXAMPLE 10.2.1 (CONTINUED)

10. Click the **Append a copy of the records to the table:** radio button, as shown. This tells Access to add the data to an existing table. There is only one table in this database, so it is automatically listed in the corresponding drop-down list. If there were more than one table, the drop-down list is used to select to which table the data will be added.

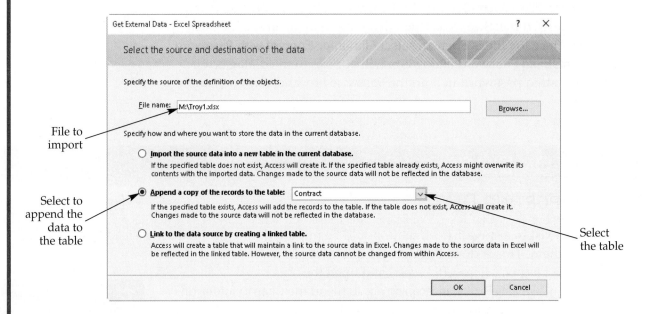

11. Click the **OK** button to display the next page of the wizard. This page shows the column headings in the spreadsheet as the field names for the database. The data will be imported as shown. If data are not correctly set up, click the **Cancel** button, fix the data in the spreadsheet, and start again.
12. Click the **Finish** button. The final page of the wizard is displayed, which offers the option to save the steps for importing the data.
13. Leave the **Save import steps** check box unchecked, and click the **Close** button.
14. Open the Contract table, and verify that the new records were imported.
15. Close the table.
16. Applying what you have learned, import the Troy2.xlsx spreadsheet file into the Contract table. Be sure to examine the spreadsheet file to verify the column names versus the field names in the database.

Access

1.3.1, 1.3.5

Viewing Data

The data in a database can be viewed in different ways. The basic way to view data is in table form. This is the datasheet view you have used so far. Another way to view data is in a form. Data can also be sorted, just as in a spreadsheet. To change the view of an object, simply select **Design>Views>View** from the ribbon.

Datasheet View

In Microsoft Access, the **datasheet view** displays data in table form. When a table is open, the navigation bar appears at the bottom of the

Access window, as shown in Figure 10-9. The text box indicates which record is currently selected and the total number of records.

The navigator bar contains options that allow you to move through the records in the table. If all of the records are visible on-screen, you can simply click a record to make it active. However, if there are more records than can fit on one screen, you must use the navigation options to see all of the records.

To move to the record above the current record, click the **Previous record** button. To move to the record below the current record, click the **Next record** button. To move to the first record in the table, click the **First record** button. To move to the final record in the table, click the **Last record** button. If the number of the record is known, the number can be entered directly in the text box.

Clicking the **New (blank) record** button in the navigation bar adds an empty record to the bottom of the table. You can then enter the data for the record.

Sorting and Filtering Data

Each record in a database contains related field data. The database can be sorted on one field and have all related information sorted with it. This is similar to sorting data in a spreadsheet. In Microsoft Access, the data are sorted by default on the first field entered in the table.

To sort the data by a field, click the drop-down arrow in the field header, as shown in Figure 10-10. This selects the entire field and displays a drop-down menu. Notice this drop-down menu is similar to the one used to sort data in Microsoft Excel. To sort the data in ascending order based on the selected field, click **Sort A to Z** or **Sort Smallest to Largest** in the drop-down menu. To sort the data in descending order, click **Sort Z to A** or **Sort Largest to Smallest** in the drop-down menu. These options are also available as **Home>Sort & Filter>Ascending** and **Descending** in the ribbon.

To filter the data, click the drop-down arrow in the field header or select the field and click **Home>Sort & Filter>Filter** in the ribbon. The same drop-down menu is displayed as when sorting data. Uncheck the **(Select All)** check box, and then check the check boxes for the values to include in the filtered data. Finally, click the **OK** button to filter the data.

Access
2.3.6, 2.3.7

Access
4.3.3

Green Tech

Database Energy Use
Many databases are in constant use, especially those driving websites. This means the database resides on a server that is always on and consuming power. One way to make these databases more green is to choose green energy suppliers for the servers running the databases. Green energy is generated from renewable sources, whereas traditional brown energy is generated from carbon-based sources, such as coal-fired plants.

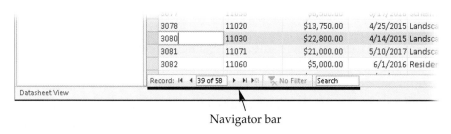

Navigator bar

Goodheart-Willcox Publisher

Figure 10-9. The navigator bar is located at the bottom of the datasheet view and contains tools for navigating the table.

Click to display
a drop-down menu

Select how
to sort

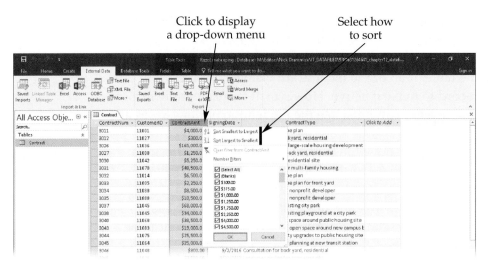

Figure 10-10. To sort a table by a field, click the drop-down arrow in the field heading, and then select how to sort.

HANDS-ON EXAMPLE 10.2.2

SORTING DATA

Data in a database can be sorted by fields. This allows the data to be viewed in the order most appropriate for the information that needs to be obtained.

1. Launch Microsoft Access, and open the *LastName*RizzoLandscaping.accdb file in the Chap10 folder on your flash drive, if it is not already open.
2. If a security warning appears below the ribbon, click the **Enable Content** button.
3. Applying what you have learned, open the Contract table.
4. Applying what you have learned, select the ContractAmt field.
5. Click **Home>Sort & Filter>Descending** in the ribbon. The data are sorted with the first record being contract number 3103 having a contract amount of $252,000.
6. Applying what you have learned, sort the SigningDate field in ascending order. After the sort, the first record should be contract number 3027 with a date of 4/7/2015.

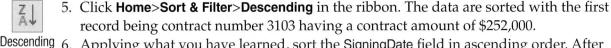

GS5
Key Applications
4.3.5

Access
1.3.2, 4.1.1

FYI

It is a good idea to include the name of the table with which a form is associated in the name of the form.

Form

Looking at the data in the table view can be difficult because the records are in narrow bands across the screen. It is easier for users and those entering data to see only one record at a time. Microsoft Access contains another object in addition to a table that makes this task simpler. A **form** is a database object used to display only certain data, one record at a time.

To create a form in Microsoft Access, click **Create>Forms>Form Wizard** in the ribbon. On the first page of the wizard, select which fields to include, as shown in Figure 10-11. To include a field, select it in the left-hand box, and click the single right-pointing chevron button (>). To include all fields, click the double right-pointing chevron button (>>). The fields listed in the right-hand box will be included in the form. To remove one of these fields, select it in the right-hand box, and click the single left-pointing chevron button (<). To remove all fields, click the double left-pointing chevron button (<<). On the second page of the wizard, select how the form will be arranged. The columnar layout is often the design selected. On the last page of the wizard, name the form and select whether to open the form or to modify its design. Once the form is created, it appears in the navigation pane along with the table on which it is based. If sub-forms are needed, they can be created by dragging one form onto another.

The navigation bar at the bottom of the Access window can be used to move through the form. Each page of the form displays one record. To close the form, right-click on the tab containing the form name, and click **Close** in the shortcut menu or click the standard close button (X) in the upper-right corner of the form. To open a form, double-click on it in the navigation pane.

Access

4.2.7

FYI

Themes can be applied to forms from the **Design** tab, and backgrounds can be inserted from the **File** tab.

Access

4.3.4, 4.3.6

FYI

To modify the order of the tabs on a form, right-click the form and select Design View from the shortcut menu. In Design View, select **Design>Tools>Tab Order** from the ribbon to open the Tab Order dialog box.

Access

4.3.1

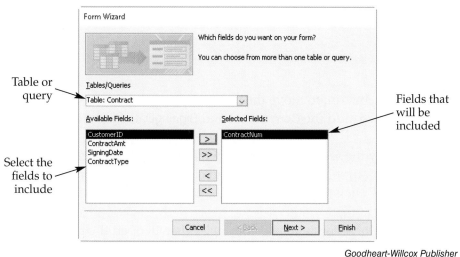

Goodheart-Willcox Publisher

Figure 10-11. A wizard is used in Microsoft Access to create a form.

HANDS-ON EXAMPLE 10.2.3

CREATING A FORM

A form can be created to display only certain data from records. This is an easy way to limit the data to only what needs to be seen.

Form Wizard

1. Launch Microsoft Access, and open the *LastName*RizzoLandscaping.accdb file in the Chap10 folder on your flash drive, if it is not already open.
2. If a security warning appears below the ribbon, click the **Enable Content** button.
3. Click **Create>Forms>Form Wizard** in the ribbon.

HANDS-ON EXAMPLE 10.2.3 (CONTINUED)

4. On the first page of the wizard, click the ContractNum field in the left-hand box to select it, as shown.

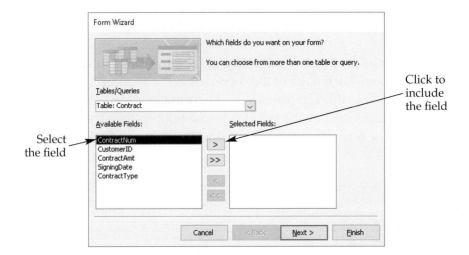

5. Click the single right-pointing chevron to move the field to the right-hand box.
6. Applying what you have learned, add the ContractAmt and SigningDate fields to the right-hand box.
7. Click the **Next** button to display the second page of the wizard.
8. Click the **Columnar** radio button to select that layout, and click the **Next** button.
9. On the next page of the wizard, click in the text box at the top of the page, and enter Contract Form. This is the name of the form.
10. Click the **Open the form to view or enter data** radio button. This will open the form as soon as it is created.
11. Click the **Finish** button. The form is created and opened. The first record of the database is displayed on the first page of the form. Notice that only data from the selected fields are displayed in the form.
12. Applying what you have learned, use the commands in the navigation bar to move to a new record.
13. Add the following information into the new record. Do not enter the dollar sign or comma. Press the [Enter] key after entering the last datum to save the new record.

ContractNum	3111
ContractAmt	$32,789
SigningDate	today's date

14. Applying what you have learned, open the Contract table and navigate to the record for contract number 3111. You may need to close and reopen the table to see the new record. Notice that several fields are empty. This is because they were not available in the form, so data could not be entered in these fields using the form.

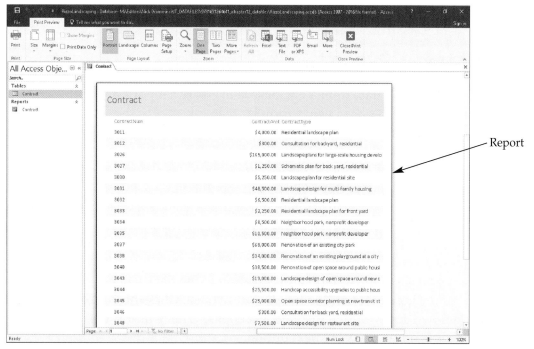

Report

Figure 10-12. A report is an output of data requested by the user.

Preparing a Report

Tables and forms deal with input. Another object in Microsoft Access contains output instead of input. A **report** is an output of the database of specific information requested by the user, as shown in Figure 10-12. A report is created in Microsoft Access in much the same way as a form is created. To create a report, click **Create>Reports>Report Wizard** in the ribbon. Then, follow the wizard to create the report. Access has preformatted designs for creating reports. A report can also be built from scratch in Design View by selecting **Create>Report>Report Design** from the ribbon.

In Microsoft Access, a report can be created that groups data by fields. For example, if the database contains sales data from four different regions, a report can be created that groups information by each region. Within these groups, the data can be further grouped by customer number or sales amount.

Once created, the report object is displayed in the navigation pane. To open a report after it has been closed, double-click on the report in the navigation pane. If a hard copy is needed, right-click on the report name tab, and click **Print Preview** in the shortcut menu. After viewing the print preview, if the user wants to save space, the report can be formatted into multiple columns like in Microsoft Word by choosing the desired number of columns from the **Page Layout>Page Setup>Columns**.

The print preview also allows other options. The report can be sent to a printer, e-mailed, exported as an Excel spreadsheet, or converted to a PDF file. The view of the report can be zoomed and reoriented if needed.

Access
1.5.1, 5.1.1, 5.1.2, 5.1.3

FYI

If the report does not appear in the navigation pane, try changing the view in the pane. Right-click on the pane, and click **Category>Tables and Related Views** in the shortcut menu. Then, right-click and click **Category>Object Type** to return to the previous view.

Access
5.3.1

HANDS-ON EXAMPLE 10.2.4

Access
5.3.1, 5.3.6, 5.3.7

CREATING A REPORT

One way of outputting data from a database is to create a report. A report is created in Microsoft Access in much the same way a form is created.

Report Wizard

1. Launch Microsoft Access, and open the *LastName*RizzoLandscaping.accdb file in the Chap10 folder on your flash drive, if it is not already open.
2. If a security warning appears below the ribbon, click the **Enable Content** button.
3. Click **Create>Reports>Report Wizard** in the ribbon.
4. Applying what you have learned, move the CustomerID, ContractAmt, and SigningDate fields into the right-hand box, and then click the **Next** button.
5. The next page of the wizard asks for grouping levels. Click the **Next** button to continue without creating any groups.
6. The next page of the wizard allows sorting of the data. Click the first drop-down arrow, and click **CustomerID** in the drop-down list. Click the button to the right of the drop-down arrow until it displays **Ascending**. This will sort the data by customer ID in ascending order. Click the **Next** button.
7. On the next page of the wizard, click the **Tabular** and **Portrait** radio buttons, and then click the **Next** button. This sets the layout of the report.
8. On the final page of the wizard, click in the text box, and enter Customer Signing Dates as the name of the report. This will be the title that appears on the report, so use spaces between words.
9. The header and footer of the report can be modified as needed. For example, text boxes can be added by choosing **Design>Control** in the ribbon. Once selected, the user simply clicks and drags the mouse to place the text box. An image can also be added to a report. To add an image, the user can select **Logo** from the **Header/Footer** group while in Layout View.
10. Click the **Preview the report** radio button, and click the **Finish** button. The report is generated and displayed, as shown. The **Print Preview** on-demand tab is displayed in the ribbon. Review the available commands.

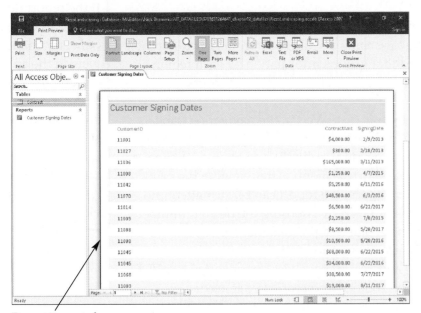

Report is created

FYI

Data sources can be modified at anytime by selecting **Tools>Convert Main Data Source**. This will launch the Data Connection Wizard, which will walk the user through the process of modifying data sources.

Access
4.2.3, 5.2.2

HANDS-ON EXAMPLE 10.2.4 (CONTINUED)

11. Right-click on the report name tab, and click **Close** in the shortcut menu.
12. Applying what you have learned, create a new report that includes the ContractNum and ContractType fields sorted in descending order by contract number. Name the report Contract Descriptions.

Joining Tables

Access

1.2.1, 1.2.5

Most databases contain more than one table. For example, the Rizzo Landscaping database includes a table of contract descriptions. However, it would more than likely include additional tables for the contact information of customers and payment of invoices.

However, it is not a good practice to put all data in one big table. As the amount of data increases, it would take a long time to load all of the data. This would slow down the retrieval process. To solve this problem, data are organized into separate categories that become individual tables. These tables can then be joined.

With a DBMS, data can be retrieved by joining tables that have a common field. Microsoft Access is a relational DBMS. A **relational database** is a collection of tables that have been joined. These relationships make it possible to see parts of the database instead of displaying entire tables.

To demonstrate how tables are joined, continue considering the Peabody Music School example from earlier in this chapter. Mr. Tompkins, the owner of the Peabody Music School, has been keeping track of student data in a text file, as shown in Figure 10-13. This text file is difficult to read. Each piece of data in the field contains a different number of characters. Importing the table into a database will allow better use and readability of the data.

To build a table to track the student information, analyze what is present in this file. Each of the fields is separated by commas. The text fields are enclosed within quotation marks. Numerical and date/time fields are not enclosed within quotation marks. Notice the date/time field includes the time as all zeroes for each record. These will be ignored when the data are imported into Microsoft Access. Also notice that there are no field names given in the file. The field names have to be determined by the person importing the table into the database.

Careful analysis of the text file shows that there are 10 fields in this table. The first field contains data for the primary key. Other fields are included for first name, last name, street address, city, state, ZIP code, phone number, date of birth, and student gender.

This text file has been imported into the Peabody Music School database as a table. The database is named PeabodyMusic2 in the Chap10 folder on your flash drive. There are three tables in the database. The original table is Faculty, and the two tables that have been added are Contract and Student. Notice how the text data in the Student table are arranged in the fields, as shown in Figure 10-14. The quotation marks present in the text file were not imported when the data were imported. Also notice that the time does not appear in the BirthDate field.

Student.txt - Notepad

File   Edit   Format   View   Help

```
"BOL7533","Eddie","Bolton","320 Main St","Gresham","MD","97236","410-760-5326",6/12/1994 0:00:00,"M"
"BRA7545","Lindsay","Brandenburg","78 Calaveras Ct","Beaverton","MD","97007","410-672-4409",8/20/1997 0:00:00,"F"
"BUR7500","Joshua","Burgess","11250 SW Walnut St","Baltimore","MD","97223","541-563-1135",1/12/1996 0:00:00,"M"
"BUR7559","Sara","Burmeister","279 Summer St","Cornelius","MD","97113","410-357-8410",9/24/1998 0:00:00,"F"
"CAR7534","Nicki","Carroll","1401 Lorraine Dr","Beaverton","MD","97229","410-617-3045",10/5/1996 0:00:00,"F"
"COR7531","Mary Beth","Corbett","205 Cedar St","Fairview","MD","97030","410-674-0838",7/26/1999 0:00:00,"F"
"ECK7542","Mark","Eckstein","12830 SW Trigger Dr","Beaverton","MD","97008","410-524-9610",3/27/1998 0:00:00,"M"
"FOR7548","Nicole","Forrest","19210 SE Division St","Baltimore","MD","97266","410-256-2368",10/24/2000 0:00:00,"F"
"GAR7553","Brett","Garver","17015 NW Holcomb Dr","Baltimore","MD","97229","410-690-8879",2/4/1999 0:00:00,"M"
"GIL7529","Aimee","Gilbertson","11763 SE Reedway St","Baltimore","MD","97266","410-762-3027",11/29/1995 0:00:00,"F"
"GRE7502","Melissa","Greco","1329 SE 135th Ave","Baltimore","MD","97233","410-256-4038",9/13/1998 0:00:00,"F"
"HAM7518","Akashi","Hamada","130 Maple Ave","Beaverton","MD","97229","410-617-7433",4/4/1997 0:00:00,"M"
"HAV7535","Laurie","Haverford","11286 SW Walnut St","Baltimore","MD","97223","541-563-7566",12/2/1998 0:00:00,"F"
"HIR7521","Erica","Hirsch","655 Langley Rd","Cornelius","MD","97123","410-547-2553",6/14/1997 0:00:00,"F"
"KAL7530","Ansis","Kalnajs","5504 SW 14th Ave","Baltimore","MD","97239","410-246-8864",4/23/1997 0:00:00,"M"
"LAM7537","Blake","Lamont","14305 SE Powell Blvd","Baltimore","MD","97236","410-761-1430",1/31/1999 0:00:00,"M"
"LIM7553","Youngho","Lim","14320 SW Barlow Rd","Beaverton","MD","97008","410-430-6218",3/15/2000 0:00:00,"M"
"MAK7556","Kim","Maki","15500 SW Allen St","Baltimore","MD","97223","541-563-6639",7/27/1999 0:00:00,"F"
"MCE7551","Danny","McElroy","1965 Alpine St","Cornelius","MD","97113","410-530-1269",12/13/1996 0:00:00,"M"
"MEH7551","Amrita","Mehta","18615 Yamhill Circle","Baltimore","MD","97233","410-491-0559",11/13/2000 0:00:00,"F"
"MEN7541","James","Mendoza","1347 Lancewood St","Beaverton","MD","97008","410-646-1155",4/18/1994 0:00:00,"M"
"MIL7512","Andy","Miller","6168 NE Rosebay Dr","Hillsboro","MD","97124","410-681-3379",2/16/1996 0:00:00,"M"
"PAP7524","Teddy","Pappas","78 Fairview Rd","Beaverton","MD","97007","410-672-6004",6/16/2000 0:00:00,"M"
"PEN7515","Dana","Pennimore","4015 SE 149th Ave","Baltimore","MD","97236","410-761-8155",11/20/1994 0:00:00,"F"
"RIV7511","John","Rivera","5436 NE Farmcrest St","Hillsboro","MD","97124","410-640-1517",5/22/1996 0:00:00,"M"
"ROC7545","Max","Roche","2385 Overlook Dr","Hillsboro","MD","97124","410-617-3717",3/23/1995 0:00:00,"M"
"SHA7522","Stacey","Shanahan","17440 Holcomb Dr","Baltimore","MD","97229","541-563-7998",8/22/1999 0:00:00,"F"
"SMI7538","Wilson","Smith","1634 Marian St","Gresham","MD","97233","410-258-4232",10/19/1995 0:00:00,"M"
"TAN7549","Kendra","Tang","2350 SE 157th Ave","Baltimore","MD","97233","410-761-7302",6/6/1999 0:00:00,"F"
"TEA7562","Jeff","Tealey","265 Elm St","Hillsboro","MD","97124","410-617-1027",10/14/2000 0:00:00,"M"
"THO7505","Maddie","Thorsten","60 Yearling Ct","Beaverton","MD","97008","410-524-2125",7/24/1996 0:00:00,"F"
"VAR7527","Kristin","Vargas","11084 SE 63rd St","Baltimore","MD","97222","410-762-5928",9/18/1995 0:00:00,"F"
"YAM7535","Angie","Yamamoto","8850 SW Burnham St","Baltimore","MD","97223","410-603-9451",9/30/1993 0:00:00,"F"
```

Figure 10-13. The data in a comma-delimited text file are hard to read, but can be imported into a database.

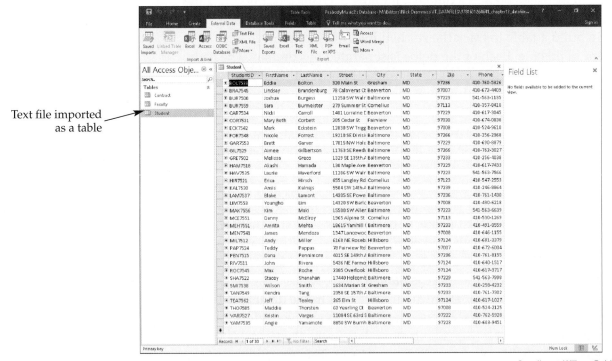

Text file imported as a table

Figure 10-14. When the comma-delimited text file is imported as a table, the data are automatically arranged in fields and records.

Table Relationships

For a DBMS to work when a database contains multiple tables, each table must be connected to at least one other table. This is necessary so that reports can be written using information from more than one table. For example, the school administrator may want to find the names of the students taking piano lessons. These data are found in separate tables. Or, the administrator may want to know the names of the students associated with a particular teacher, which are found in different tables.

To connect the tables, the relationships among the tables need to be understood. The best kind of relationship between two tables is one-to-many. A **one-to-many relationship** occurs when a single piece of data is related to several other pieces of data. Think of the Faculty, Student, and Contract tables. One teacher can have many contracts because he or she instructs many students in a variety of instruments. One student can have many contracts because he or she may be taking lessons on several instruments. These are one-to-many relationships. The fields in each table need to reflect these relationships. If two tables are to be related, the table on the "many" side of the relationship must have a copy of the "one" table's primary key in its list of fields.

The Contract table is used to track the contracts made between the students and the teachers. It contains information relevant to the individual music lessons. In the Design View, you can see how the table was built, as shown in Figure 10-15. Notice that it contains fields to hold the data from the primary keys of the other two tables. When tables are joined, the primary keys from other tables are called **foreign keys**. In the Contract table, the foreign keys are the StudentID and TeacherID fields, as indicated in the Description column for these fields.

Building Relationships

It is not enough to simply build tables with the extra fields in the "many" table. The DBMS does not know the tables are related until it

Foreign fields

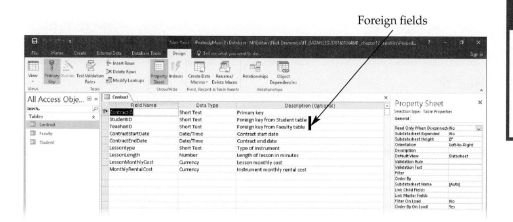

Goodheart-Willcox Publisher

Figure 10-15. The Contract table contains fields for foreign keys from the Student and Faculty tables. This is important when joining tables.

is told so. The DBMS must also be told the exact relationships between tables. Once the relationships are set, it is possible to write reports and ask the database to find specific data from more than one table.

In Microsoft Access, relationships are easily created using a visual representation of the tables, as shown in Figure 10-16. To create a relationship, click **Database Tools**>**Relationships**>**Relationships** in the ribbon. The tables are displayed in individual windows, which can be enlarged or moved using the mouse. Then, simply draw a line from the "one" table to the "many" table. Finally, specify the specific relationships.

To build a relationship through a template, select **Create**>**Template**>**Application Parts**. The drop-down menu from this button includes one section for templates and another for quick-start templates. From here, the user can select the desired type of template and follow the instructions in the ensuing wizard to build a table from a template with application parts.

Access

4.1.2

Relationships have been created

Goodheart-Willcox Publisher

Figure 10-16. Tables are joined by connecting visual representations of the tables with lines.

HANDS-ON EXAMPLE 10.2.5

JOINING TABLES

Most databases contain more than one table. To join the tables, they must be connected and the specific relationship between fields must be set.

1. Launch Microsoft Access, and open the PeabodyMusic2.accdb file in the Chap10 folder on your flash drive.
2. If a security warning appears below the ribbon, click the **Enable Content** button.
3. Click **Database Tools**>**Relationships**>**Relationships** in the ribbon. The three tables in the database are displayed as small windows within the view. Note: if a dialog box appears asking which of the three tables in the database should be included, one at a time select each table and click the **Add** button, then close the dialog box.

Relationships

HANDS-ON EXAMPLE 10.2.5 (CONTINUED)

4. Drag the Contract table to the middle of the view.
5. Click the TeacherID field in the Faculty table, drag it to the TeacherID field in the Contract table, and drop it. A dialog box appears asking the developer to create a relationship between the two, as shown.
6. Verify the TeacherID fields in the Faculty and Contract tables will be connected, and then click the **OK** button. A relationship is established between the fields. A line is drawn between the field in one table to the connected field in the other table.

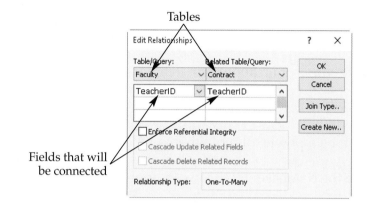

Tables

Fields that will be connected

7. Applying what you have learned, connect the StudentID field in the Student table to the StudentID field in the Contract table.

10.2 | SECTION REVIEW

CHECK YOUR UNDERSTANDING

1. What is used in Microsoft Access to step the user through importing data from a spreadsheet?
2. Which database object displays only one record at a time?
3. What is the basic difference between a form or table and a report?
4. When two tables within a database are joined, what does the database become?
5. What is the best kind of relationship between tables?

BUILD YOUR VOCABULARY

As you progress through this course, develop a personal IT glossary. This will help you build your vocabulary and prepare you for a career. Write a definition for each of the following terms and add it to your IT glossary.

datasheet view
foreign key
form

one-to-many relationship
relational database
report

QUERIES

Databases can be very large. The user never wants to see all data that is in it. Instead, the user wants to ask the DBMS to come up with a small piece of information. There are two basic ways of locating data in a database: searching and querying.

A database can be a powerful tool when a DBMS is used to manage the database. A DBMS can analyze all of the data in a database and generate results. Calculated fields can be included in the database to perform calculations on data. Statistical fields can be included to provide summary information on the data in a database.

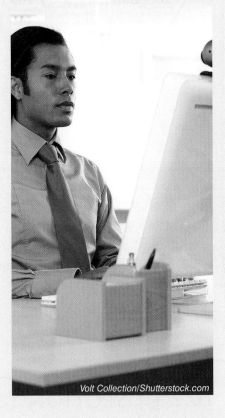

Volt Collection/Shutterstock.com

LEARNING GOALS

After completing this section, you will be able to:
- Describe ways in which data can be located in a database.
- Create a calculated field in a database.
- Explain the use of statistical fields in a database.

TERMS

action query

calculated field

criteria

crosstab query

multitable query

parameter query

query

searching

statistical field

Locating Data

Searching is defined as a method to find a particular value among a set of values. Another method used in finding information in a database is the query. A **query** includes not only searching, but also finding and organizing the related details of records that meet certain search conditions. A DBMS is very effective in quickly finding particular portions of information. When a user asks a DBMS to retrieve related pieces of information from a database, this is known as *querying* the database. Queries can pull information from one or more tables and then apply criteria to certain fields within those tables.

Queries are objects in a database, just as tables, reports, and forms are objects. Once a query is created, it becomes part of the database. In a Microsoft Access database, saved queries will be listed in the navigation pane.

Creating a Basic Query

The easiest way to create a basic query in Microsoft Access is to use the query wizard. It creates a query based on a single table or existing query. Click **Create>Queries>Query Wizard** in the ribbon. There is a choice of four basic queries that can be created with the wizard, as shown in Figure 10-17. A description of the selected query is displayed in the lower-left area of the dialog box. The simple query is the most basic query. Once the type of query is selected, the remaining pages of the wizard are similar to those found in the form or report wizards. The table on which to base the query must be specified, fields to include must be selected, and the query must be named.

When the **Finish** button is clicked in the wizard, the query is run and displayed (if you chose to display it). The query also appears as an object in the navigation pane. After the query is run, the user can make the results more meaningful by filtering the results for more specific information, if necessary. This is accomplished by selecting **Home>Sort & Filter**. To close the query, right-click on the query name tab, and click **Close** in the shortcut menu. To run the query again, double-click on the query in the navigation pane.

GS5
Key Applications
4.3.4

Access
3.1.1

Access
3.1.6

Access
3.3.2

FYI

If the query does not appear in the navigation pane, try changing the view in the pane. Right-click on the pane, and click **Category>Tables and Related Views** in the shortcut menu. Then, right-click and click **Category>Object Type** to return to the previous view.

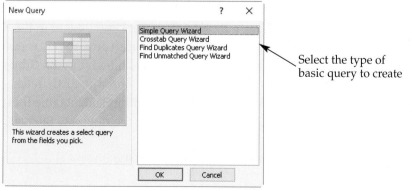

Select the type of basic query to create

Goodheart-Willcox Publisher

Figure 10-17. There are four types of basic queries that can be created using the query wizard.

HANDS-ON EXAMPLE 10.3.1

CREATING A SIMPLE QUERY

A query searches for and returns data that meet criteria specified by the user. For example, in the Peabody Music School database, a query can be used to list the first names and birth dates of students.

1. Launch Microsoft Access, and open the PeabodyMusic3.accdb file in the Chap10 folder on your flash drive.
2. If a security warning appears below the ribbon, click the **Enable Content** button.
3. Click **Create>Queries>Query Wizard** in the ribbon. The query wizard is opened.
4. On the first page of the wizard, click **Simple Query Wizard** in the list, and click the **OK** button.
5. On the second page of the wizard, click the **Tables/Query** drop-down arrow, and click **Table: Student** in the drop-down list, as shown. This specifies the query will be based on the Student table.

Query
Wizard

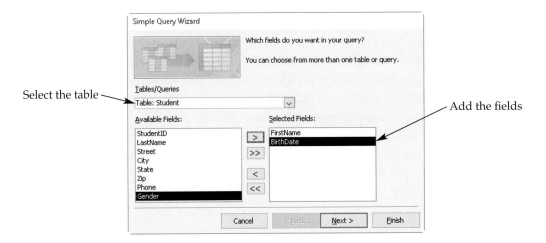

6. Applying what you have learned, move the FirstName and BirthDate fields to the right-hand box, and then click the **Next** button.
7. On the last page of the wizard, click in the text box, and enter the name StudentBirthDate.
8. Click the **Open the query to view information** radio button, and click the **Finish** button. The query is created and displayed. Only the first name of each student and his or her birth date appear in the query.
9. It is often helpful to manage query results so specific records can be found easily. Fields can be sorted by opening a query in Design View and select the drop-down menu in the **Sort** field of the desired record and clicking the **Run** command. Records can also be grouped by shared criteria through making a selection from the drop-down menu in the **Group By** field. Using what you have learned, sort the query in ascending order by birth dates.
10. Applying what you have learned, create a simple query using the Student table that returns the first name, last name, and city for each student. Save the query as StudentCity.

Creating an Advanced Query

The query wizard is a tool for quickly creating basic queries. On some occasions, an advanced query must be created using the query design view, as shown in Figure 10-18. To display the query design view, click **Create>Queries>Query Design** in the ribbon.

For example, consider the Peabody Music School database. The user wants to see first names of the students and the instrument that each student plays. In this case, the Student table contains the first names in the FirstName field and the Contract table contains the instruments in the LessonType field.

When the query design view is first displayed, you must select which tables and queries to show. See Figure 10-19. In the **Show Table** dialog box, click the **Table** tab, click a table to include, and click the **Add** button. Queries are listed in the **Queries** tab. Once all of the tables and queries are shown in the view, click the **Close** button to close the dialog box. Any relationships between the tables will be shown by lines, just as they are when joining tables.

> ## FYI
>
> Once a query is created and saved, the design view can be displayed in the same way it is for a table.

> ## FYI
>
> To reformat the fields within a query, a new data type must be selected by clicking **Datasheet>Data Type** and choosing the desired data type.
>
> **Access**
> ## 3.2.6

Tables containing the fields for the query

Query is constructed

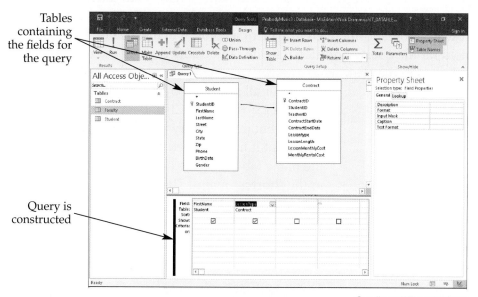

Goodheart-Willcox Publisher

Figure 10-18. An advanced query is created in the query design view.

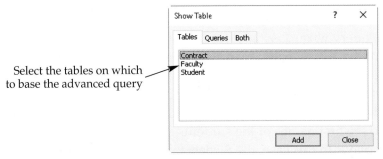

Figure 10-19. When creating an advanced query, you must first select which tables contain the fields that will be included in the query. Existing queries can also be used as the basis for the advanced query.

FYI

A field can be dragged from a table or query above the grid and dropped into a column in the grid as an easy way to specify the criteria for the query.

At the bottom of the query design view is a grid for creating the query. After the tables or queries on which to base the new query are displayed in the view, fields must be added to this grid. In the grid, click the **Field:** drop-down arrow in the first column, and select the field in the drop-down list. Notice that each field name begins with the name of the table in which it is located. Once a field is selected, the entry in the **Table:** row is automatically filled in. The first column in the grid defines one field for the query. Additional fields can be added using the remaining columns in the grid.

After all fields are chosen for the query, the query is ready to run. Click **Design>Results>Run** in the ribbon. The query is displayed, but at this point it has not been saved. Right-click on the name tab above the query, and click **Save** in the shortcut menu. The **Save As:** dialog box is displayed, as shown in Figure 10-20. Enter a name, and click the **OK** button. Once the query has been saved, it appears in the navigation pane.

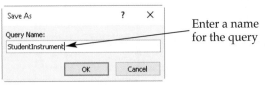

Enter a name for the query

Figure 10-20. After an advanced query is run, it must be saved.

HANDS-ON EXAMPLE 10.3.2

CREATING AN ADVANCED QUERY

A query can be based on more than one table or query. For example, using the Peabody Music School database, a query can be created based on both the Student and Contract tables.

1. Launch Microsoft Access, and open the PeabodyMusic3.accdb file in the Chap10 folder on your flash drive, if it is not already open.
2. If a security warning appears below the ribbon, click the **Enable Content** button.
3. Click **Create>Queries>Query Design** in the ribbon. The query design view is displayed, and the **Show Table** dialog box appears.

Query Design

4. Click **Student** in the list on the **Tables** tab of the dialog box, and click the **Add** button. Similarly, add the Contract table.

HANDS-ON EXAMPLE 10.3.2 (CONTINUED)

5. Click the **Close** button to close the **Show Table** dialog box. The two tables are displayed at the top of the query design view, and a grid for creating the query is displayed at the bottom of the view.

6. Click the FirstName field in the Student table, drag it to the first column in the grid, and drop it. The **Field:** and **Table:** rows are automatically completed in the first column. The **Show:** check box is also automatically checked.

7. Click the **Field:** drop-down arrow in the second column, and click **Contract:LessonType** in the drop-down list. The **Field:** and **Table:** rows are automatically completed in the second column, and the **Show:** check box is checked. Now the design is established, and the query is ready to run, as shown.

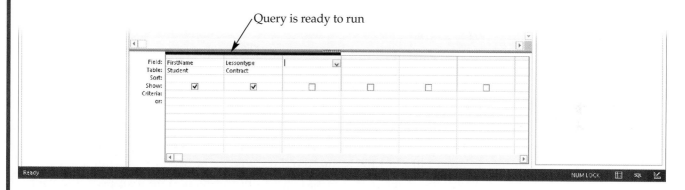

Query is ready to run

8. Click **Design>Results>Run** button in the ribbon. The query is created and displayed. Some student names appear more than once in the query. This means that the student has more than one contract for lessons.

Run

9. Right-click on the query name tab, and click **Save** in the shortcut menu.

10. In the **Save As:** dialog box, enter NamesInstruments as the name, and click the **OK** button. The query is named and appears in the navigation pane.

Crosstab Query

A **crosstab query** is one that displays desired information in rows with totals broken down in columns. For example, if a user wanted to know the subtotals for each month in a given time period, a crosstab query would list subtotals in rows with each month listed as a separate column. The easiest way to generate a crosstab query is to run the Crosstab Query Wizard by selecting **Create>Query>Query Wizard**.

Access
3.1.2

Parameter Query

A **parameter query** is one of the simplest advanced queries available in Access. It allows a user to create a query that can be easily updated with a given search term. When opened, a parameter query will prompt the user for a search term and will generate the results based on that search. To create a parameter query, remove the text in the Criteria field

Access
3.1.3

and replace with the desired search phrase in squared brackets. The brackets instruct the query to ask for input, and the text inside the brackets is what will be displayed in that prompt. For example, if the query should prompt the user for a customer ID, the phrase [Which Customer ID?] can be entered in the Criteria field. When run, the query will ask the user to input a customer ID and the results will appear based on the ID that is entered.

Access

3.1.4

Action Query

An **action query** is exactly what it sounds like—a query that performs an action when it is run. There are four types of action queries: append, delete, make-table, and update. Append queries retrieve data from one table and add them to another; delete queries delete data from tables based on input from the user; make-table queries create new tables from data stored in other tables; and update queries change the data on tables based on input from the user. These queries can be run by selecting the desired type from the ribbon by clicking **Design>Query Type**.

Access

3.1.5

Multitable Query

Multitable queries collect information from multiple tables. For example, if a user is attempting to retrieve two sets of data so they appear in one query but finds the two data sets are housed in separate tables, a multitable query can be used. To get both sets of data to appear, the user will have to include both tables in a query. The simplest way to do this is with the Query Wizard.

To use the wizard, select **Create>Other>Query Wizard>New Query**. Click **Simple Query Wizard**, then **OK**. In the **Tables/Queries** box, select the first table from which information is needed. Double-click on desired fields to move them to the Selected Fields list. Select a second table from the **Tables/Query** box, and select the desired fields from that table as well. After all desired fields are selected from all essential tables, select **Next**. A detail query is likely necessary for this type of information, since the user will need all fields from all records. Click **Detail (shows every field of every record)**, then select **Next** and **Finish**.

Entering Criteria

Sometimes, only certain records for a field need to be seen. Specific records can be requested by qualifying the query. The qualifiers on a query are called **criteria** in Microsoft Access. Criteria place limits or constraints on a query to fine-tune the requested information, as shown in Figure 10-21.

For example, using the Peabody Music School database, it is possible to query only the names of students who are taking flute lessons. The LessonType field contains the instruments, but a query that simply returns this field will list all instruments, not just flute. By entering criteria, the query can be qualified to return only those records that contain Flute in the LessonType field.

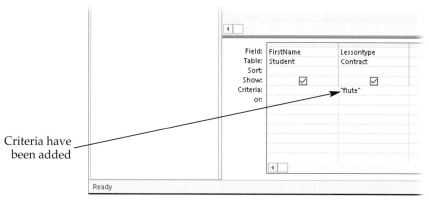

Figure 10-21. Criteria can be used to limit the information from a field.

HANDS-ON EXAMPLE 10.3.3

QUALIFYING A QUERY

A query can be qualified with criteria to limit the returned results. For example, a query can be created to return the monthly cost of students for one teacher, instead of for all teachers.

1. Launch Microsoft Access, and open the PeabodyMusic3.accdb file in the Chap10 folder on your flash drive, if it is not already open.
2. If a security warning appears below the ribbon, click the **Enable Content** button.
3. Double-click on the NamesInstruments query to open it.
4. Applying what you have learned, display the design view.
5. Click in the **Criteria:** text box in the second column (LessonType) in the grid at the bottom of the design view, and enter flute. If you move to a different cell in the grid, Access will automatically add quotation marks around the term.
6. Applying what you have learned, run the query. Only the students who have taken flute lessons are returned by this query.
7. Applying what you have learned, create a query that includes the LastName field from the Faculty table and LessonMonthlyCost from the Contract table with the criteria Maynard for the LastName field. Run the query, and save it as MaynardCost.

FYI

A query can be renamed at any time by right-clicking on a closed query and selecting **Rename** from the shortcut menu.

Access
3.2.1

Creating Calculated Fields

Access
3.3.1, 5.3.2

Sometimes a value needs to be known that is not found in the database, but can be calculated from the existing data. A **calculated field** is a field that performs a calculation based on data within the same table, as shown in Figure 10-22. This special field is also known as a "field on the fly."

For example, the Peabody Music School may want to know how much each lesson would cost if a certain amount is added to the existing monthly fee. This information is not in the database, but a calculated field can be built to show the new amount.

Calculated field

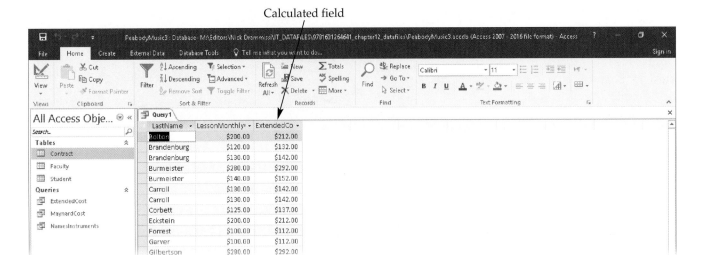

Figure 10-22. A calculated field can be used to generate a value based on data in the database. Here, $12 has been added to the monthly cost of each lesson with a calculated field.

HANDS-ON EXAMPLE 10.3.4

CREATING A CALCULATED FIELD

A calculated field can provide information not found in the database by performing a calculation on existing data. For example, a query can be created to display the result of adding $12 to the monthly fee for a faculty member.

1. Launch Microsoft Access, and open the PeabodyMusic3.accdb file in the Chap10 folder on your flash drive, if it is not already open.
2. If a security warning appears below the ribbon, click the **Enable Content** button.
3. Applying what you have learned, begin a new query based on the LastName field from the Faculty table and the LessonMonthlyCost field from the Contract table with the criteria "Kegg" for the LastName field. These two fields should be in the first two columns of the grid in the design view.
4. In the **Field:** row for the third column, add the following information: ExtendedCost: [LessonMonthlyCost] + 12. If necessary, you can widen the column by dragging the right-hand margin of the column.
5. Applying what you have learned, run the query. Extended Cost will appear in the query as the name of the calculated field. The values displayed in the ExtendedCost field are the values from the LessonMonthlyCost field with 12 added.
6. Applying what you have learned, save the query as ExtendedCost.

Creating Statistical Fields

Access
3.3.4, 3.3.5

A **statistical field** provides summary information related to other data within a table. It is a type of calculated field. Several built-in statistical calculations can be performed on a group of records. Some of the mathematical functions include **SUM**, **AVG** (average), **MAX** (maximum), and **MIN** (minimum). There are dozens of other built-in functions in Microsoft Access. Depending on what fields are included in the query, the statistical functions can give overall totals or totals divided by groups.

If the syntax of the function is known, the expression can be directly entered into the **Field:** row in the query design view, as shown in Figure 10-23. The expression builder in Microsoft Access can also be used to create an expression. To display the expression builder, click **Design>Query Setup>Builder** in the ribbon. The **Expression Builder** dialog box is displayed, as shown in Figure 10-24. The expression is constructed in the top box. The lower-left box contains the library of functions in a tree format. When an element is selected in the lower-left box, the items it contains are displayed in the lower-middle box. When an element is selected in the lower-middle box, the functions it contains are displayed in the lower-right box. Double-click a function in the lower-right box to add it to the expression being created in the top box.

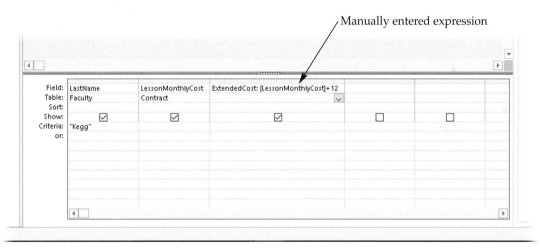

Manually entered expression

Goodheart-Willcox Publisher

Figure 10-23. Statistical field expressions can be entered directly into the Field: row in a query design view.

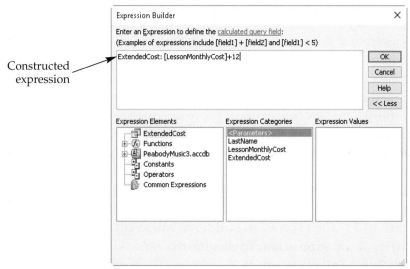

Constructed expression

Figure 10-24. The expression builder can be used to help construct a calculated field or a statistical field.

HANDS-ON EXAMPLE 10.3.5

CREATING A STATISTICAL FIELD

The **SUM** function can be used to add amounts, such as the monthly cost of music lessons. Microsoft Access has an automatic totals feature that can help in applying this function.

1. Launch Microsoft Access, and open the PeabodyMusic3.accdb file in the Chap10 folder on your flash drive, if it is not already open.
2. If a security warning appears below the ribbon, click the **Enable Content** button.
3. Applying what you have learned, begin a new query based on the LessonMonthlyCost field from the Contract table and the LastName field from the Faculty table.
4. Click the **Show/Hide Column Totals in Query Results** button in the **Show/Hide** group on the **Design** on-demand tab of the ribbon. A new row called **Total:** appears in the grid.

Σ

Show/Hide Column Totals in Query Results

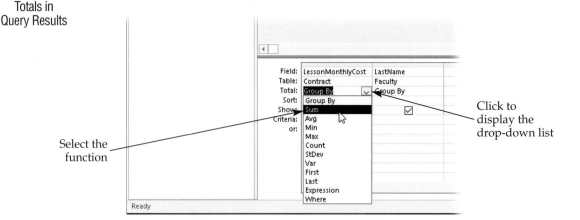

Select the function

Click to display the drop-down list

HANDS-ON EXAMPLE 10.3.5 (CONTINUED)

5. Click the cell in the first column (LessonMontlyCost) of the **Total:** row, click the drop-down arrow that appears, and click **Sum** in the drop-down list, as shown.
6. Applying what you have learned, run the query. The result displays one field that contains the total dollar amount of all lessons.
7. Applying what you have learned, save the query as LessonTotal.
8. Save the database file.

10.3 | SECTION REVIEW

 ### CHECK YOUR UNDERSTANDING

1. How does a query differ from a search?
2. What are the limits or constraints on a query?
3. Where can a user enter specific criteria to limit the information generated in a query?
4. What is the type of field that can generate a value not present in the database?
5. What is the purpose of a statistical field?

 ### BUILD YOUR VOCABULARY

As you progress through this course, develop a personal IT glossary. This will help you build your vocabulary and prepare you for a career. Write a definition for each of the following terms and add it to your IT glossary.

action query	parameter query
calculated field	query
criteria	searching
crosstab query	statistical field
multitable query	

Chapter Summary

Section 10.1
Introduction to Databases

- A database is a structured collection of related information organized for easily locating and retrieving the data. It consists of data arranged in tables, records, and fields.

- Data in a database can be added, edited, and deleted. The [Tab] key can be used to navigate through fields in a record.

- When creating a database structure, decide what information will be tracked. This information will become fields in a database table.

Section 10.2
Importing and Viewing Data

- Data from a spreadsheet can be imported into a database. The data can be appended to an existing database or added to a blank database.

- The datasheet view displays data in table form. Data can be searched and sorted in the table, and reports can be created to display data.

- A database may contain more than one table, which can be joined. Joining tables creates a relational database.

Section 10.3
Queries

- A query includes not only searching, but also finding and organizing the related details of records that meet certain search conditions. Queries can be created that are very simple or advanced with qualifiers called criteria.

- A calculated field is a field that performs a calculation based on data within the same table. It reports a value that is not found in the database, but can be created from data within the database.

- A statistical field is a type of calculated field that provides summary information related to other data within a table. Microsoft Access has several built-in statistical-calculation functions.

Now that you have finished this chapter, see what you know about computer applications by taking the chapter posttest. Access the posttest by visiting www.g-wlearning.com.

Chapter 10 Test

Multiple Choice
Select the best response.

1. Which of the following contains information about specific characteristics of the entry described in a record?
   A. table
   B. row
   C. report
   D. field

2. Which data type is used to store numbers that will be used for financial calculations?
   A. currency
   B. number
   C. general
   D. text

3. After a table has been created, which of the following options is used to add data from a spreadsheet to the table?
   A. addition
   B. navigation
   C. finish
   D. append

4. What feature or function includes searching, finding, and organizing the related details of records that meet certain search conditions?
   A. search
   B. find
   C. query
   D. locate

5. Which view is used to add new fields to a query?
   A. design
   B. datasheet
   C. text box
   D. navigation pane

Completion

Complete the following sentences with the correct word(s).

6. The foundation of a database is a(n) _____.

7. A row in a database contains related data and is called a(n) _____.

8. A column in a database, which contains the categories of data, is called a(n) _____.

9. A(n) _____ is a database object that illustrates only certain data one record at a time.

10. A(n) _____ performs a calculation based on data within a table.

Matching

Match the correct term with its definition.

A. DBMS
B. record
C. primary key
D. foreign key
E. statistical field

11. Type of calculated field that provides summary information related to other data within a table.

12. Handles the collection, storage, sorting, reporting, and organization of data.

13. Contains information related to the entry in the first column of the record.

14. Field in a related table with the same data as another table.

15. Unique identifier for a table.

Application and Extension of Knowledge

1. Before beginning these activities, navigate to the student companion website at www.g-wlearning.com, download the data files for this chapter, and save them in the Chap10 folder on your flash drive. Begin a new database titled Baltimore Art School, and save it in the Chap10 folder on your flash drive. Create a table, and save it as Sections. Change the name of the ID field to StudentID. Add the following fields, and save the table.

Name	Data Type
SectionID	Short text
StartingDate	Date/time
ClassName	Short text
Fee	Currency
CategoryID	Short text
Enrolled	Number

2. Open the Baltimore Art School database created in #1. Import the Microsoft Excel file Sections.xlsx from the Chap10 folder on your flash drive. Append the spreadsheet data to the Sections table. Open the Sections table. How many records were imported?

3. Open the Baltimore Art School database created in #2. Create a second table titled Category. Add the fields shown below to the table. Then, import the Microsoft Excel file Category.xlsx from the Chap10 folder on your flash drive. Append the data to the Category table. Create a relationship between the tables using the CategoryID fields. Consider the process for creating a relationship.

Name	Data Type
CategoryID	Short text
CategoryName	Short text
Description	Short text
Length	Short text

4. Open the Baltimore Art School database created in #3. Create a query that lists the CategoryName, StartingDate and Enrolled fields. Save it as EnrollmentByCategory. Create a second query that lists the ClassName, Fee, and Enrolled for the Beginning Watercolors class. Save it as WaterColor-Enrollment. How did the process of creating these two queries differ?

5. Open the Baltimore Art School database created in #4. Copy the WaterColorEnrollment query as a basis, and name the copy WaterColorRevenue. Create a new calculated field that computes the revenue from each section. The revenue is found by multiplying the fee by the number of students enrolled in the section. Name the calculated field Revenue. What is the formula you entered to create the calculated field? What is the revenue for each of the sections in the Beginning Watercolors class?

Online Activities

Complete the following activities, which will help you learn, practice, and expand your knowledge and skills.

 **Vocabulary.** Practice vocabulary for this chapter using the e-flash cards, matching activity, and vocabulary game until you are able to recognize their meanings.

Communication Skills

Listening. Engage in a conversation with someone you have not spoken with before. Actively listen to what that person is sharing. Next, summarize and retell what the person conveyed in conversation to you.

Reading. Figurative language is used to describe something by comparing it with something else. Locate an advertisement for mobile devices. Scan the information for figurative language about the product. Compare this with a description using literal language.

Writing. Make a list of actions a business can take to minimize risk to the environment from the technology it uses. Write a paragraph explaining your position.

Internet Research

Finding Credible Sources. Research the history of databases using various Internet resources. Describe each stage of database development. Write a short informal report on your findings.

Teamwork

Working with a partner, navigate to your school's website and find the faculty and staff directory. Using spreadsheet software, create a worksheet that lists each faculty or staff member's name, position, and other information, such as phone extension or room number. List as much information as you can.

Activity Files

Visit www.g-wlearning.com/informationtechnology/ to download the activity files for this chapter. These activities will expand your learning of the material presented in this chapter and allow you to practice what you have learned. Follow the instructions provided in each file to complete the activity.

Activity File 10-1 Auto Increment

Activity File 10-2 Compact and Repair

Activity File 10-3 Append Records

Activity File 10-4 Form Control

CAPSTONE PROJECT

The capstone project builds from one chapter to the next. It allows you to apply the skills you have learned to create a complete project in a desired career area. Read the instructions below for the career area you chose to work in for this course. Work in the same career area in each chapter.

Agriculture, Food, and Natural Resources

In this activity, you will assume the role of a database administrator for a large agribusiness in the agriculture, food, and natural resources industry. You will create and customize a database that will serve to track the employees. Access the *Introduction to Microsoft Office 2016* companion website (www.g-wlearning.com/informationtechnology/) to view the instructions for this chapter's Agriculture, Food, and Natural Resources capstone project.

Business, Management, and Administration

In this activity, you will create database structures for your capstone project company while maintaining your assumed role. These databases will be used to organize and report information to the owner of the company regarding reorganization. Access the *Introduction to Microsoft Office 2016* companion website (www.g-wlearning.com/informationtechnology/) to view the instructions for this chapter's Business, Management, and Administration capstone project.

Health Science

In this activity, you will assume the role of a database administrator for a large teaching hospital specializing in cardiac research. You will create and customize a database to track the patient volunteers and their medications. Access the *Introduction to Microsoft Office 2016* companion website (www.g-wlearning.com/informationtechnology/) to view the instructions for this chapter's Health Science capstone project.

Science, Technology, Engineering, and Mathematics

In this activity, you will continue working as a NASA communications team member to create database structures for the Near-Earth Object Project. You will use these databases to report to the public concerning near-earth objects. Access the *Introduction to Microsoft Office 2016* companion website (www.g-wlearning.com/informationtechnology/) to view the instructions for this chapter's Science, Technology, Engineering, and Mathematics capstone project.

GLOSSARY

A

absolute cell address. Indicates the formula will refer to the specified cell no matter where the formula is moved or copied. (8)

access key. Keyboard key or key combination used instead of the mouse to activate a command. Also called *keyboard shortcut.* (4)

action query. Query that performs an action. (10)

active cell. Currently selected cell, which is indicated by an outline around the cell. (8)

active window. Current window where any command that is entered will be applied. (4)

analytical report. Contains both information and analysis of the data. (6)

animating. Process of adding motion to an object. (7)

antipiracy technology. Technology that has been developed that makes it very difficult for someone to use pirated software. (6)

antivirus software. Cyber-defense software that removes malicious software from a computer. (1)

application software. Allows the user to perform specific activities, such as writing term papers, sending e-mail, paying taxes, editing photos, playing games, and taking online courses. (2)

argument. Value the function needs for the calculation. (9)

ascending order. When the lowest value is at the top of the list. Also called *A to Z order.* (4, 8)

attention grabber. Something to arouse the interest of the audience. (7)

B

background image. Overall image that appears behind all other elements on the slide. (7)

backstage view. View that is displayed when saving a file for the first time. (4)

backup. Copy of a file that can be safely retrieved if anything unfortunate happens to the most recent version of the file. (3)

bar chart. Best chart type for comparing individual values across categories. Also called a *column chart* in Microsoft Excel. (9)

block-style letter. Formatted so all lines are flush with the left-hand page margin. (6)

body. Message of a letter. (6)

Boolean operator. Defines the relationship between words in the search string. Also called *logical operator.* (1)

booting. Describes the use of a small program to get the computer running and the OS loaded. Also called *bootstrapping.* (2)

browser. Computer program that retrieves hypertext documents via the HTTP protocol and displays them on the computer monitor. (1)

bulleted list. Consists of separate lines of text with a small graphic, such as a dot, in front of the line. Also called an *unordered list.* (4)

C

calculated field. Field that performs a calculation based on data within the same table. (10)

CamelCase. Naming convention in which the beginning of each word in the name is capitalized. (3)

cell. Individual box where a row and column intersect. (4, 8)

censorship. Act of limiting access to information or removing information to prevent the information from being seen. (1)

central processing unit (CPU). Device that fetches coded instructions, decodes them, and then runs or executes them. Also called a *microprocessor* or *chip.* (1)

character style. Defines the text formatting for individual characters. (4)

chart. Illustrates data in a picture-like format. Also called a *graph.* (7, 9)

citation. Includes the author, publication date, source document, URL, and other relevant information for material that is referenced or paraphrased within the document. (6)

clincher. Statement to finish a presentation that will make an impact on the audience. (7)

closing. Removing a file or application from RAM. (4)

cloud computing. Involves storing and retrieving data from Internet-based spaces. (1)

collate. Arrange multiple copies of a document so all pages are in the correct order. (4)

column. Space between vertical grid lines. (8)

comma-separated values (CSV) file. Contains only the data from a spreadsheet with commas to denote the beginning and end of each datum in a row. (9)

common knowledge. Consists of notions and factual information that can be found in a variety of places. (6)

Note: The number in parentheses following each definition indicates the chapter in which the term can be found.

complimentary close. Sign-off for a letter. (6)

computer. Device that handles input, processes data, stores data, and produces usable output according to sets of stored instructions. (1)

conclusion. Writer's summary of what the audience should take away from the report. (6)

conditional formatting. Changes the appearance of a cell's value based on parameters set by the user. (9)

cookie. Small text file that websites put on the computer hard disk drive when a user visits the websites. (1)

copy. Exact duplicate of the original at the time the copy was made. (3, 4)

copy notation. Needed when others are being sent a copy of the letter. (6)

copyright. Ownership of a work and specifies that only the owner has the right to sell the work, use it, or give permission for someone else to sell or use it. (6)

Creative Commons (CC) license. Specialized copyright license that allows free distribution of copyrighted work. (6)

criteria. Qualifiers on a query. (10)

crop. Trim the outer portion of an image. (4)

crosstab query. Query that displays desired information in rows with totals broken down in columns. (10)

cut. Remove content from a document and place it on the system clipboard. (4)

D

data. Pieces of information gathered through research. (6)

database. Structured collection of related information organized for easily locating and retrieving the data. (10)

database management system (DBMS). Program that handles the collection, storage, sorting, reporting, and organization of data. (10)

datasheet view. Displays data in table form. (10)

data vandalism. Manipulation or destruction of data found in cyberspace. (1)

descending order. When the highest value is at the top of the list. Also called *Z to A order.* (4, 8)

design view. View that allows developers of the database to set up fields. (10)

desktop publishing (DTP). Process of using a computer to typeset text and place illustrations to create, edit, and publish documents. (5)

destination. Folder to where a file or folder is being transferred. (3)

dialog box launcher. Small arrow in the lower-right corner of groups on the ribbon. (4)

digital revolution. Ever-expanding progression of technical, economic, and cultural changes brought about by computers. (1)

document template. Document preformatted for a specific use and may contain placeholder text or images the user replaces with actual content. (4)

drag-and-drop. Procedure in which an item is selected in one location, moved with the mouse, and placed in another location. (3, 4)

E

editing. Make changes to the text, format, layout, or other aspects of the content. (4)

Electronic User's Bill of Rights. Details the rights and responsibilities of both individuals and institutions regarding the treatment of digital information. (6)

embedding. Form of copying and pasting. (9)

enclosure notation. Alerts the reader to materials that are included in the mailing along with the letter. (6)

encryption. Software process that encodes the file to make it unreadable unless the correct key is entered. (14)

endnote. Similar to footnote, but appears at the end of document. Also called the *bibliography.* (6)

end user license agreement (EULA). Contract outlining the set of rules that every user must agree to before using the software. (2)

external audience. Audience that will probably need more background information about your topic. (7)

extracting. Term given by Windows to the process of taking a file out of a ZIP file. (3)

F

fair use doctrine. Allows individuals to use copyrighted works without permission in limited situations under very strict guidelines. (6)

field. Contains units or items of information for each record. (10)

file association. Process in which Windows links a file name extension to a software program. (3)

file attribute. Characteristic of a file about the display, archiving, and save status of the file. (3)

file compression. Process of compacting the data in a file or group of files to reduce the overall size. (3)

file format. Indicates the manner in which the data a file contains are stored on the disk. (2)

file management. Working with files on the hard disk or other storage medium. (3)

file name. Label that identifies a unique file on a computer system. (3)

file name extension. Tells the Windows operating system which software to use to open the file. (3)

file path. Drive and folder location of a file plus its file name. (3)

file properties. All information about the file, but not the data contained within the file. (3)

file tree. List of available drives and folders shown in the navigation pane; can be expanded to display subfolders and the files contained within them. (3)

filtering. Allows some data to be hidden from view. (8)

firmware. Circuitry and software that hold instructions for initializing the hardware and loading the main OS. (2)

folder. Container in which files are stored. (3)

folder name. Label that identifies a unique folder on a computer system. (3)

folio. Page number placed outside of the body copy. (6)

font. Set of characters of a typeface in one specific style and size. (5)

footnote. Numbered annotation that appears once at the bottom of a page. (6)

foreign key. Primary key from another table. (10)

form. Database object used to display only certain data one record at a time. (10)

format painter. Copies the formatting applied to selected text and then applies that formatting to a second text selection. (4)

formatting. Changing the appearance of characters. (4)

formula. Equation in Microsoft Excel. (8)

fraction. Number of parts of a whole. (8)

function. Preprogrammed formula in spreadsheet software. (9)

G

graphic. Illustration, photograph, and drawing shape. (7)

H

hacking. Activity by computer programmers to break into the e-mails, websites, computer systems, and files of other computer users. (1)

handles. Used to change the size of the image. (4)

handout. Printed material that is distributed to an audience. Also called a *leave-behind*. (7)

hard disk drive. Sealed unit that contains a stack of individual disks, or platters, which are magnetic media that rotate at a very high speed. Also called a *hard drive*. (1)

hardware. Physical components of the computer. (1)

heading. Words and phrases that introduce a section of text. (6)

help. Resource to assist the user in learning how to use a feature of the program. (3)

hyperlink. Electronic link between a marked place in a document to another place in the document or to another document, file, or web page. (7)

hypertext markup language (HTML). Language used to create documents that tell browsers how to assemble text, images, and other content to display as a web page. (1)

I

informational report. Contains facts, data, or other types of information. (6)

input. Function that translates data from the human world into computer data. (1)

inserting. Adding a media file to a document. Also called *attaching*. (4)

insertion point. Location where text or images will be placed within the document. (4)

inside address. Name, title, and address of the recipient. (6)

intellectual property. Something that comes from a person's mind. (6)

internal audience. Has a specific background and experience. (7)

introduction. Discusses the purpose of a report and the benefits of the ideas or recommendations one is presenting. (6)

J

justification. Technical term for paragraph alignment. (5)

K

kerning. Amount of space between two letters. (5)

key tip badge. Little box that appears over each command in the **Quick Access** toolbar and the ribbon tabs. (4)

killer app. Software application so compelling that people buy a computer just to be able to use it. (8)

L

landscape. Layout or orientation is when the long edge is on the top and bottom. (4)

leading. Technical term for vertical spacing between lines of text and paragraphs. (5)

letterhead. Information about an organization. (6)

library. Collection of similar files and folders that are displayed together, but that may be stored in different locations. (3)

licensing agreement. Contract that gives one party permission to market, produce, or use the product or service owned by another party. (6)

line chart. Used to display trends over time. (9)

line spacing. Amount of space between lines of text. (5)

linking. Similar to embedding, but a connection is maintained between the copy and the original source. (9)

logical function. Function that tests for true or false. (9)

M

mainframe computer. Provides centralized storage, processing, and overall management of large amounts of data. (1)

malware. Software that intentionally performs actions to disrupt the operation of a computer system, collect private information, or otherwise harm the computer or user. Short for *malicious software*. (1)

margins. Points at the top, bottom, left, and right of the page beyond which text is not placed. (5)

master page. Defines the page size, recurring areas for type and graphics, and placement of recurring element. Also called the *master*. (5)

maximized. Describes a window that fills the entire screen. (4)

merge. Combine multiple cells into a single cell. (8)

metadata. Details about a file that describe or identify it. (4)

minimized. Describes a window that is still running, but hidden from view except for the button on the taskbar corresponding to the application. (4)

mixed punctuation. Style in which a colon is placed after the salutation and a comma after the complimentary close. (6)

modified-block-style letter. Places the date, complimentary close, and signature to the right of the center point of the letter. (6)

motherboard. Connects all of the hardware in the computer. (1)

move. Remove content from a source location and place it in a destination location. (3, 4)

multitable query. Collects information from multiple tables. (10)

N

naming convention. Pattern that is followed whenever a file name is created. (3)

nested. Describes a subfolder within the parent folder. (3)

numbered list. Consists of separate lines of text with numbers in sequential order in front of the text. Also called an *ordered list*. (4)

numbers. Floating point number data type. (8)

O

on-demand tab. Tab that is displayed depending on what is selected in the program document. (4)

one-to-many relationship. Occurs when a single piece of data is related to several other pieces of data. (10)

opening. Placing a file's content into RAM so the content can be used. (4)

open punctuation. Style in which there is no punctuation after the salutation or complimentary close. (6)

open source. Applies to software that has had its source code made available to the public at no charge and with no restrictions on use or modification. (6)

open-source software. Software that has no licensing restrictions. (2)

operating system (OS). Software that manages all of the devices, as well as locates and provides instructions to the CPU. (2)

orphan. First line of a paragraph that falls immediately *before* a page break. (5)

output. Data provided to the user. (1)

P

packet. Small file fragments on which the routing mechanism is based. (1)

page break. Where the document changes from one page to another. (5)

page layout. Refers to how the type is placed on the page. (5)

paragraph style. Defines the formatting for a paragraph. (4)

parameter query. Allows a user to create a query that can be easily updated with a given search term. (10)

paraphrasing. Expressing an idea using different words. (6)

paste. Occurs when content from the system clipboard is added to the document at the insertion point. (4)

patent. Gives a person or company the right to be the sole producer of a product for a defined period of time. (6)

percentage. Fraction of 100. (8)

peripheral device. Attached device that is not critical to computer operation. Also called *peripheral*. (1)

personal computer. Processing device designed to meet the needs of an individual user, whether in the home, a business, or a school. (1)

phishing. Attempt to get sensitive information by appearing as a harmless request. (1)

pie chart. Chart that displays the relative size of each fractional part of a whole. (9)

piracy. Unethical and illegal copying or downloading of software, files, or other protected material. (6)

plagiarism. Claiming another person's material as your own. (6)

podcasting. Distribution of audio files over the Internet via automated or subscribed downloads. (2)

port. Point of interface between the motherboard and external devices. (1)

portrait. Layout or orientation is when the long edge of the paper is on the sides. (4)

postscript. Information included after the signature. (6)

presentation. Contains individual slides used to communicate information to an audience. (4)

presentation. Speech, address, or demonstration given to a group. (7)

presentation notes. Notes used to keep the speaker on topic. Also called *speaker notes*. (7)

primary key. Field that will be used by the DBMS to keep track of records. (10)

primary research. First-hand research conducted by the writer in preparation for writing a report. (6)

principal. Amount of a loan. (9)

printing. Outputting the content of a file. (4)

print preview. Shows the document exactly how it will look when printed. (4)

processing. Transformation of input data and acting on those data. (1)

productivity software. Type of application software that supports the completion of tasks. (2)

proofing. Process of checking the document for errors. (5)

proposal. Typically contains an idea and attempts to persuade the reader to take a certain course of action. (6)

proprietary software. Owned by the creator and cannot be sold, copied, or modified by the user without permission from the creator. Also called *closed software*. (2)

protected view. View in which most or all of the editing functions have been locked. (4)

public domain. Refers to material that is not owned by anybody and can be used without permission. (6)

Q

qualitative data. Information that provides insight into how people think about a particular topic. (6)

quantitative data. Facts and figures from which conclusions can be drawn. (6)

query. Includes not only searching, but also finding and organizing the related details of records that meet certain search conditions. (10)

quotation. Exact repeat of a passage of another author's work. (6)

R

random-access memory (RAM). Memory that can be changed. (1)

range. Selection of more than one cell. (8)

ransomware. Software that encrypts files or blocks the user's access to programs until the user pays to unlock them. (1)

readability. Measure of how easy it is for the reader to understand and locate information within a document. (5)

read-only. Means the file can be opened and viewed, but cannot be changed. (4)

read-only memory (ROM). Memory that cannot be changed. (1)

recommendation. Action the writer believes the reader should take. (6)

record. Contains all fields or units of information. (10)

recycle bin. Special folder used as a collection point for all files and folders that have been deleted. (3)

reference initials. Indicate the person who keyed the letter. (6)

relational database. Collection of tables that have been joined. (10)

relative cell address. Specified as the number of rows and columns that the second cell is from the first cell. (8)

report. Output of the database of specific information requested by the user. (10)

reserved symbols. Characters that Windows uses for special meaning. (3)

restoring. Displaying a minimized window. (4)

ribbon. Main command interface for the Microsoft Office suite of software. (4)

root. Top folder in a folder hierarchy. (3)

row. Space between horizontal grid lines. (8)

S

salutation. Greeting in a letter and always begins with *Dear.* (6)

scope. Guideline of how much information will be included. (7)

search engine. Software program that looks through massive databases of links and information to try to identify the best matches for the search request. (1)

searching. Method to find a particular value among a set of values. (10)

secondary research. Data and information already assembled and recorded by someone else. (6)

serif. Small mark that extends from the end strokes of a character. (5)

server. Stores data and responds when requested by other computers in the network. (1)

service mark. Similar to a trademark, but it identifies a service rather than a product. (6)

shortcut menu. Point-of-use menu displayed by right-clicking. (3)

signature block. Writer's name and title. Also called the *signature.* (6)

slide master. Predefined slide on which the position and formatting of text boxes and graphics is specified. (7)

sorting. Arranging a list in either ascending or descending order. (3, 4, 8)

source. Folder where the file or folder being transferred is originally located. (3)

spreadsheet. Special type of document in which data are organized in columns and rows. (4, 8)

spyware. Software that secretly collects a user's data and behavior. (1)

statistical field. Provides summary information related to other data within a table. (10)

style. Group of formatting settings that can be applied in one step. (4)

style sheet. Desktop publishing file that saves the attributes of every font that will be used in a project. (5)

subfolder. Folder contained within another folder. (3)

subject line. Helps the reader know the content of the message before reading. (6)

supercomputer. Has processing power that can handle complex jobs beyond the scope of other computer systems. (1)

system clipboard. Virtual container for storing data. (4)

system image. Backup that is an exact duplicate of all data on the drive, including the drives required for Windows to run, your system settings, programs, and document files. (3)

system requirements. Specifications for the processor speed, RAM, hard drive space, and any additional hardware or software needed to run the software. (2)

system software. Includes four types of software: the operating system, utility programs, device drivers, and programs. (2)

T

table. Contains information arranged in horizontal rows and vertical columns. (10)

table of contents. Lists the major sections and subsections within a report with page numbers. (6)

tabs. Preset horizontal locations across the page in a document. (5)

task manager. Analyzes what is going on in the system and reports the results. (3)

template. Formatting and organizational suggestions that can help the user create a professional-looking document. (2)

term. How many periods it will take to repay a loan. (9)

text. String data type. (8)

theme. Set of specified colors, fonts, and effects. (7)

touch system. When user does not look at the keyboard when entering information, rather has memorized the location of keys based on hand position. (5)

track changes. Feature for logging markups. (5).

trademark. Protects taglines, slogans, names, symbols, or any unique method to identify a product or company. (6)

transition. Method of shifting from one slide to the next. (7)

troubleshooting. Systematically analyzing a problem to find a solution. (3)

typeface. Design of characters. (4, 5)

U

utility program. Assists in managing and optimizing a computer's performance. (2)

V

virtual printer. Outputs a file instead of a physical hard copy. (4)

visual design. Arrangement of the visual and artistic elements used to accomplish a goal or communicate an idea. (5)

volume label. Name of the device itself. Also known as the *volume name.* (1)

W

what-if analysis. When a parameter in a data model is changed to see how the outcome will be altered. (8)

widow. Last line of a paragraph that falls immediately *after* a page break. (5)

wildcard. Used in the search box to represent an unknown character. (3)

windowed. Window that is visible, but does not fill the entire screen. (4)

workbook. Excel file. (8)

worksheet. Grid of vertical and horizontal lines where work is done in a spreadsheet. (8)

wrap text. Allows a new line within the cell to be automatically started when the length of the text exceeds the width of the cell. (8)

Z

zooming. Changing the magnification of the view. (4)

APPENDIX A
MATH SKILLS REVIEW

Table of Contents

Getting Started

Math skills are needed in everyday life. You will need to be able to estimate your purchases at a grocery store, calculate sales tax, or divide a recipe in half. This section is designed to help develop your math proficiency for better understanding of the concepts presented in the textbook. Using the information presented in the Math Skills Handbook will help you understand basic math concepts and their application to the real world.

Using a Calculator

There are many different types of calculators. Some are simple and only perform basic math operations. Become familiar with the keys and operating instructions of your calculator so calculations can be made quickly and correctly.

The following is a scientific calculator that comes with the Windows operating system. In Windows 10, launch the calculator by clicking the **Start** button followed by **All apps** and then **Calculator**. In Windows 8, launch the desktop calculator by clicking the **Apps** button and then **Calculator** in **Windows Accessories** group. Do not use the calculator app located in the **Apps** group. It has limited features. In Windows 7, launch the calculator by clicking the **Start** button followed by **Accessories** and then **Calculator**. To display the scientific view, click the button in the upper-left corner of the calculator, and then click **Scientific** in the drop-down menu. In Windows 8 and Windows 7, click the **View** pull-down menu, and click **Scientific** in the menu.

Solving Word Problems

Word problems are exercises in which the problem is set up in text, rather than presented in mathematical notation. Many word problems tell a story. You must identify the elements of the math problem and solve it.

Strategy	How to Apply
List or table	Identify information in the problem and organize it into a table to identify patterns.
Work backward	When an end result is provided, work backward from that to find the requested information.
Guess, check, revise	Start with a reasonable guess at the answer, check to see if it is correct, and revise the guess as needed until the solution is found.
Substitute simpler information	Use different numbers to simplify the problem and solve it, then solve the problem using the provided numbers.

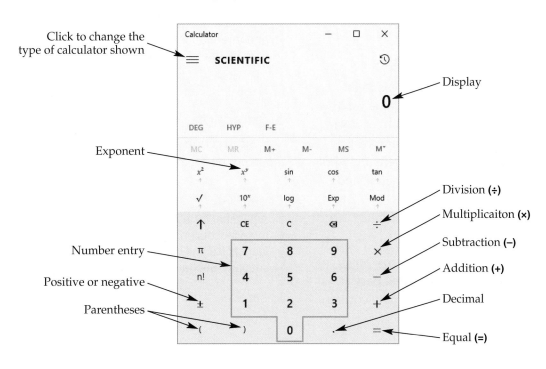

Click to change the type of calculator shown

Display

Exponent

Division (÷)

Multiplicaiton (×)

Subtraction (−)

Number entry

Addition (+)

Positive or negative

Decimal

Parentheses

Equal (=)

There are many strategies for solving word problems. Some common strategies include making a list or table; working backward; guessing, checking, and revising; and substituting simpler numbers to solve the problem.

Number Sense

Number sense is an ability to use and understand numbers to make judgments and solve problems. Someone with good number sense also understands when his or her computations are reasonable in the context of a problem.

Example
Suppose you want to add three basketball scores: 35, 21, and 18.
- First, add 30 + 20 + 10 = 60.
- Then, add 5 + 1 + 8 = 14.
- Finally, combine these two sums to find the answer: 60 + 14 = 74.

Example
Suppose your brother is 72 inches tall and you want to convert this measurement from inches to feet. Suppose you use a calculator to divide 72 by 12 (number of inches in a foot) and the answer is displayed as 864. You recognize immediately that your brother cannot be 864 feet tall and realize you must have miscalculated. In this case, you incorrectly entered a multiplication operation instead of a division operation. The correct answer is 6.

Numbers and Quantity

Numbers are more than just items in a series. Each number has a distinct value relative to all other numbers. They are used to perform mathematical operations from the simplest addition to finding square roots. There are whole numbers, fractions, decimals, exponents, and square roots.

Whole Numbers

A whole number, or integer, is any positive number or zero that has no fractional part. It can be a single digit from 0 to 9, or may contain multiple digits, such as 38.

Place Value

A digit's position in a number determines its *place value*. The digit, or numeral, in the place farthest to the right before the decimal point is in the *ones position*. The next digit to the left is in the *tens position*, followed by the next digit in the *hundreds position*. As you continue to move left, the place values increase by multiples of 10 to thousands, ten thousands, and so forth.

Example
Suppose you win the lottery and receive a check for $23,152,679. Your total prize would be *twenty-three million, one hundred fifty-two thousand, six hundred seventy-nine dollars.*

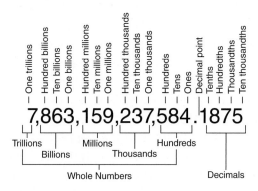

Addition

Addition is the process of combining two or more numbers. The result is called the *sum.*

Example
A plumber installs six faucets on his first job and three faucets on his second job. How many faucets does he install in total?

6 + 3 = 9

Subtraction

Subtraction is the process of finding the *difference* between two numbers.

Example
A plumber installs six faucets on her first job and three faucets on her second job. How many more faucets did she install on the first job than the second? Subtract 3 from 6 to find the answer.

6 − 3 = 3

Multiplication

Multiplication is a method of adding a number to itself a given number of times. The multiplied numbers are called *factors,* and the result is called the *product.*

> ### Example
> Suppose you are installing computers and need to purchase four adaptors. If the adaptors are $6 each, what is the total cost of the adaptors? The answer can be found by adding $6 four times:
>
> $$\$6 + \$6 + \$6 + \$6 = \$24$$
>
> However, the same answer is found more quickly by multiplying $6 times 4.
>
> $$\$6 \times 4 = \$24$$

Division

Division is the process of determining how many times one number, called the *divisor,* goes into another number, called the *dividend.* The result is called the *quotient.*

> ### Example
> Suppose you are installing computers and buy a box of adaptors for $24. There are four adaptors in the box. What is the cost of each adaptor? The answer is found by dividing $24 by 4:
>
> $$\$24 \div 4 = \$6$$

Decimals

A decimal is a kind of fraction with a denominator that is either ten, one hundred, one thousand, or some power of ten. Every decimal has three parts: a whole number (sometimes zero), followed by a decimal point, and one or more whole numbers.

Place Value

The numbers to the right of the decimal point indicate the amount of the fraction. The first place to the right of a decimal point is the tenths place. The second place to the right of the decimal point is the hundredths place. As you continue to the right, the place values move to the thousandths place, the ten thousandths place, and so on.

> ### Example
> A machinist is required to produce an airplane part to a very precise measurement of 36.876 inches. This measurement is *thirty-six and eight hundred seventy-six thousandths* inches.
>
> 36.876

Addition

To add decimals, place each number in a vertical list and align the decimal points. Then add the numbers in each column starting with the column on the right and working to the left. The decimal point in the answer drops down into the same location.

> ### Example
> A landscaper spreads 4.3 pounds of fertilizer in the front yard of a house and 1.2 pounds in the backyard. How many pounds of fertilizer did the landscaper spread in total?
>
> $$\begin{array}{r} 4.3 \\ +\ 1.2 \\ \hline 5.5 \end{array}$$

Subtraction

To subtract decimals, place each number in a vertical list and align the decimal points. Then subtract the numbers in each column, starting with the column on the right and working to the left. The decimal point in the answer drops down into the same location.

> ### Example
> A landscaper spreads 4.3 pounds of fertilizer in the front yard of a house and 1.2 pounds in the backyard. How many more pounds were spread in the front yard than in the backyard?
>
> $$\begin{array}{r} 4.3 \\ -\ 1.2 \\ \hline 3.1 \end{array}$$

Multiplication

To multiply decimals, place the numbers in a vertical list. Then multiply each digit of the top number by the right-hand bottom number. Multiply each digit of the top number by the bottom number in the tens position. Place the result on a second line and add a zero to the end of the number. Add the total number of decimal places in both numbers you are multiplying. This will be the number of decimal places in your answer.

> **Example**
> An artist orders 13 brushes priced at $3.20 each. What is the total cost of the order? The answer can be found by multiplying $3.20 by 13.
>
> ```
>      $3.20
>   ×     13
>   --------
>        960
>   +   3200
>   --------
>     $41.60
> ```

Division

To divide decimals, the dividend is placed under the division symbol, the divisor is placed to the left of the division symbol, and the quotient is placed above the division symbol. Start from the *left* of the dividend and determine how many times the divisor goes into the first number. Continue this until the quotient is found. Add the dollar sign to the final answer.

```
   3.20
3)9.60
  9↓    Product of 3 × 3
  06    Bring down the 6
   6↓   Product of 2 × 3
   0    No remainder
```

> **Example**
> An artist buys a package of three brushes for $9.60. What is the cost of each brush? The quotient is found by dividing $9.60 by 3.
>
> ```
>    3.20
> 3)9.60
>   -9↓
>    06↓
>    00
> ```

Rounding

When a number is rounded, some of the digits are changed, removed, or made zero so the number is easier to work with. Rounding is often used when precise calculations or measurements are not needed. For example, if you are calculating millions of dollars, it might not be important to know the amount down to the dollar or cent. Instead, you might *round* the amount to the nearest ten thousand or even hundred thousand dollars. Also, when working with decimals, the final answer might have several more decimal places than needed.

To round a number, follow these steps. First, underline the digit in the place to which you are rounding. Second, if the digit to the *right* of this place is 5 or greater, add 1 to the underlined digit. If the digit to the right is less than 5, do not change the underlined digit. Third, change all the digits to the right of the underlined digit to zero. In the case of decimals, the digits to the right of the underlined digit are removed.

> **Example**
> A company's utility expense last year was $32,678.53. The owner of the company is preparing a budget for next year and wants to round this amount to the nearest 1,000.
>
> **Step 1:** Underline the digit in the 1,000 place.
>
> $3**2**,678
>
> **Step 2:** The digit to the right of 2 is greater than 5, so add 1.
>
> 2 + 1 = 3
>
> **Step 3:** Change the digits to the right of the underlined digit to zero.
>
> $33,000

Fractions

A fraction is a part of a whole. It is made up by a numerator that is divided by a denominator.

$$\frac{\text{numerator}}{\text{denominator}}$$

The *numerator* specifies the number of these equal parts that are in the fraction. The *denominator* shows how many equal parts make up the whole.

Proper

In a *proper fraction*, the numerator is less than the denominator.

Example

A lumberyard worker cuts a sheet of plywood into four equal pieces and sells three of them to a carpenter. The carpenter now has 3/4 of the original sheet. The lumberyard has 1/4 of the sheet remaining.

Improper

An *improper fraction* is a fraction where the numerator is equal to or greater than the denominator.

Example

A chef uses a chili recipe which calls for 1/2 cup of chili sauce. However, the chef makes an extra-large batch that will serve three times as many people and uses three of the 1/2 cup measures. The improper fraction in this example is 3/2 cups of chili sauce.

Mixed

A mixed number contains a whole number and a fraction. It is another way of writing an improper fraction.

Example

A chef uses a chili recipe that calls for 1/2 cup of chili sauce. However, the chef makes an extra-large batch that will serve three times as many people and uses three of the 1/2 cup measures. The improper fraction in this example is 3/2 cups of chili sauce. This can be converted to a mixed number by dividing the numerator by the denominator with any remainder appearing above the original denominator:

The remainder is 1, which is 1 over 2. So, the mixed number is 1 1/2 cups.

$$2\overline{)3} \quad \begin{array}{r} 1 \\ \underline{-2} \\ 1 \end{array}$$

Reducing

Fractions are reduced to make them easier to work with. Reducing a fraction means writing it with smaller numbers, in *lowest terms*. Reducing a fraction does not change its value.

To find the lowest terms, determine the largest number that *evenly* divides both the numerator and denominator so there is no remainder. Then use this number to divide both the numerator and denominator.

Example

The owner of a hair salon asks 10 customers if they were satisfied with the service they recently received. Eight customers said they were satisfied, so the fraction of satisfied customers is 8/10. The largest number that evenly divides both the numerator and denominator is 2. The fraction is reduced to its lowest terms as follows.

$$\frac{8}{10} = \frac{8 \div 2}{10 \div 2} = \frac{4}{5}$$

Addition

To add fractions, the numerators are combined and the denominator stays the same. However, fractions can only be added when they have a *common denominator*. The *least common denominator* is the smallest number to which each denominator can be converted.

Example

A snack food company makes a bag of trail mix by combining 3/8 pound of nuts with 1/8 pound of dried fruit. What is the total weight of each bag? The fractions have common denominators, so the total weight is determined by adding the fractions.

$$\frac{3}{8} + \frac{1}{8} = \frac{4}{8}$$

This answer can be reduced from 4/8 to 1/2.

Example

Suppose the company combines 1/4 pound of nuts with 1/8 cup of dried fruit. To add these fractions, the denominators must be made equal. In this case, the least common denominator is 8 because $4 \times 2 = 8$. Convert 1/4 to its equivalent of 2/8 by multiplying both numerator and denominator by 2. Then the fractions can be added as follows.

$$\frac{2}{8} + \frac{1}{8} = \frac{3}{8}$$

This answer cannot be reduced because 3 and 8 have no common factors.

Subtraction

To subtract fractions, the second numerator is subtracted from the first numerator. The denominators stay the same. However, fractions can only be subtracted when they have a *common denominator*.

Example

A snack food company makes a bag of trail mix by combining 3/8 pound of nuts with 1/8 pound of dried fruit. How much more do the nuts weigh than the dried fruit? The fractions have common denominators, so the difference can be determined by subtracting the fractions.

$$\frac{3}{8} - \frac{1}{8} = \frac{2}{8}$$

This answer can be reduced from 2/8 to 1/4.

Example

Suppose the company combines 1/4 pound of nuts with 1/8 cup of dried fruit. How much more do the nuts weigh than the dried fruit? To subtract these fractions, the denominators must be made equal. The least common denominator is 8, so convert 1/4 to its equivalent of 2/8. Then the fractions can be subtracted as follows.

$$\frac{2}{8} - \frac{1}{8} = \frac{1}{8}$$

This answer cannot be reduced.

Multiplication

Common denominators are not necessary to multiply fractions. Multiply all of the numerators and multiply all of the denominators. Reduce the resulting fraction as needed.

Example

A lab technician makes a saline solution by mixing 3/4 cup of salt with one gallon of water. How much salt should the technician mix if only 1/2 gallon of water is used? Multiply 3/4 by 1/2:

$$\frac{3}{4} \times \frac{1}{2} = \frac{3}{8}$$

Division

To divide one fraction by a second fraction, multiply the first fraction by the reciprocal of the second fraction. The *reciprocal* of a fraction is created by switching the numerator and denominator.

Example

A cabinetmaker has 3/4 gallon of wood stain. Each cabinet requires 1/8 gallon of stain to finish. How many cabinets can be finished? To find the answer, divide 3/4 by 1/8, which means multiplying 3/4 by the reciprocal of 1/8.

$$\frac{3}{4} \div \frac{1}{8} = \frac{3}{4} \times \frac{8}{1} = \frac{24}{4} = 6$$

Negative Numbers

Negative numbers are those less than zero. They are written with a minus sign in front of the number.

Example

The number −34,687,295 is read as *negative thirty-four million, six hundred eighty-seven thousand, two hundred ninety-five.*

Addition

Adding a negative number is the same as subtracting a positive number.

Example

A football player gains nine yards on his first running play (+9) and loses four yards (−4) on his second play. The two plays combined result in a five yard gain.

$$9 + (-4) = 9 - 4 = 5$$

Suppose this player loses five yards on his first running play (−5) and loses four yards (−4) on his second play. The two plays combined result in a nine yard loss.

$$-5 + (-4) = -5 - 4 = -9$$

Subtraction

Subtracting a negative number is the same as adding a positive number.

Example

Suppose you receive a $100 traffic ticket. This will result in a −$100 change to your cash balance. However, you explain the circumstance to a traffic court judge, and she reduces the fine by $60. The effect is to subtract −$60 from −$100 change to your cash balance. The final result is a −$40 change.

$$-\$100 - (-\$60) = -\$100 + \$60 = -\$40$$

Multiplication

Multiplication of an odd number of negative numbers results in a *negative* product. Multiplication of an even number of negative numbers results in a *positive* product.

Example

If you lose two pounds per week, this will result in a –2 pound weekly change in your weight. After five weeks, there will be a –10 pound change to your weight.

$$5 \times (-2) = -10$$

Suppose you have been losing two pounds per week. Five weeks ago (–5) your weight was 10 pounds higher.

$$(-5) \times (-2) = 10$$

Division

Division of an odd number of negative numbers results in a *negative* quotient. Division of an even number of negative numbers results in a *positive* quotient.

Example

Suppose you lost 10 pounds, which is a –10 pound change in your weight. How many pounds on average did you lose each week if it took five weeks to lose the weight? Divide –10 by 5 to find the answer.

$$-10 \div 5 = -2$$

Suppose you lost 10 pounds. How many weeks did this take if you lost two pounds each week? Divide –10 by –2 to find the answer.

$$-10 \div -2 = 5$$

Percentages

A percentage (%) means a part of 100. It is the same as a fraction or decimal.

Representing Percentages as Decimals

To change a percentage to a decimal, move the decimal point two places to the left. For example, 1% is the same as 1/100 or 0.01; 10% is the same as 10/100 or 0.10; and 100% is the same as 100/100 or 1.0.

Example

A high school cafeteria estimates that 30% of the students prefer sesame seeds on hamburger buns. To convert this percentage to a decimal, move the decimal point two places to the left.

$$30\% = 0.30$$

Representing Fractions as Percentages

To change a fraction to a percentage, first convert the fraction to a decimal by dividing the numerator by the denominator. Then convert the decimal to a percentage by moving the decimal point two places to the right.

Example

A high school cafeteria conducts a survey and finds that three of every 10 students prefer sesame seeds on hamburger buns. To change this fraction to a percentage, divide 3 by 10, and move the decimal two places to the right.

$$3 \div 10 = 0.30 = 30\%$$

Calculating a Percentage

To calculate the percentage of a number, change the percentage to a decimal and multiply by the number.

Example

A car dealer sold 10 cars last week, of which 70% were sold to women. How many cars did women buy? Change 70% to a decimal by dividing 70 by 100, which equals 0.70. Then multiply by the total number (10).

$$0.70 \times 10 = 7$$

To determine what percentage one number is of another, divide the first number by the second. Then convert the quotient into a percentage by moving the decimal point two places to the right.

Example

A car dealer sold 10 cars last week, of which seven were sold to women. What percentage of the cars were purchased by women? Divide 7 by 10 and then convert to a percentage.

$$7 \div 10 = 0.70$$

$$0.70 = 70\%$$

Ratio

A ratio compares two numbers through division. Ratios are often expressed as a fraction, but can also be written with a colon (:) or the word *to*.

Example

A drugstore's cost for a bottle of vitamins is $2.00, which it sells for $3.00. The ratio of the selling price to the cost can be expressed as follows.

$$\frac{\$3.00}{\$2.00} = \frac{3}{2}$$

$3.00:\$2.00 = 3:2$

$3.00 to $2.00 = 3 to 2

Measurement

The official system of measurement in the United States for length, volume, and weight is the US Customary system of measurement. The metric system of measurement is used by most other countries.

US Customary Measurement

The following are the most commonly used units of length in the US Customary system of measurement.

- 1 inch
- 1 foot = 12 inches
- 1 yard = 3 feet
- 1 mile = 5,280 feet

Example

An interior designer measures the length and width of a room when ordering new floor tiles. The length is measured at 12 feet 4 inches (12' 4"). The width is measured at 8 feet 7 inches (8' 7").

Example

Taxi cab fares are usually determined by measuring distance in miles. A recent cab rate in Chicago was $3.25 for the first 1/9 mile or less, and $0.20 for each additional 1/9 mile.

Metric Conversion

The metric system of measurement is convenient to use because units can be converted by multiplying or dividing by multiples of 10. The following are the commonly used units of length in the metric system of measurement.

- 1 millimeter
- 1 centimeter = 10 millimeters
- 1 meter = 100 centimeters
- 1 kilometer = 1,000 meters

The following are conversions from the US Customary system to the metric system.

- 1 inch = 25.4 millimeters = 2.54 centimeters
- 1 foot = 30.48 centimeters = 0.3048 meters
- 1 yard = 0.9144 meters
- 1 mile = 1.6093 kilometers

Example

A salesperson from the United States is traveling abroad and needs to drive 100 kilometers to meet a customer. How many miles is this trip? Divide 100 kilometers by 1.6093 and round to the hundredth place.

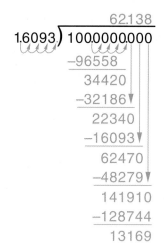

Estimating

Estimating is finding an *approximate* answer and often involves using rounded numbers. It is often quicker to add rounded numbers, for example, than it is to add the precise numbers.

Example

Estimate the total miles a delivery truck will travel along the following three segments of a route.

- Detroit to Chicago: 278 miles
- Chicago to St. Louis: 297 miles
- St. Louis to Wichita: 436 miles

The mileage can be estimated by rounding each segment to the nearest 100 miles.

- Detroit to Chicago: 300 miles
- Chicago to St. Louis: 300 miles
- St. Louis to Wichita: 400 miles

Add the rounded segments to estimate the total miles.

$$300 + 300 + 400 = 1{,}000 \text{ miles}$$

Accuracy and Precision

Accuracy and precision mean slightly different things. *Accuracy* is the closeness of a measured value to its actual or true value. *Precision* is how close measured values are to each other.

Example

A machine is designed to fill jars with 16 ounces of peanut butter. The machine is considered accurate if the actual amount of peanut butter in a jar is within 0.05 ounces of the target, which is a range of 15.95 to 16.05 ounces. A machine operator tests a jar and measures the weight to be 16.01 ounces. The machine is accurate.

Suppose a machine operator tests 10 jars of peanut butter and finds the weight of each jar to be 15.4 ounces. The machine is considered precise because it fills every jar with exactly the same amount. However, it is not accurate because the amount differs too much from the target.

Algebra

An *equation* is a mathematical statement that has an equal sign (=). An *algebraic* equation is an equation that includes at least one variable. A *variable* is an unknown quantity.

Solving Equations with Variables

Solving an algebraic equation means finding the value of the variable that will make the equation a true statement. To solve a simple equation, perform inverse operations on both sides and isolate the variable.

Example

A computer consultant has sales of $1,000. After deducting $600 in expenses, her profit equals $400. This is expressed with the following equation.

$$\text{sales} - \text{expenses} = \text{profit}$$
$$\$1{,}000 - \$600 = \$400$$

Example

A computer consultant has expenses of $600 and $400 in profit. What are her sales? An equation can be written in which sales are the unknown quantity, or variable.

$$\text{sales} - \text{expenses} = \text{profit}$$
$$\text{sales} - \$600 = \$400$$

Example

To find the value for sales, perform inverse operations on both sides and isolate the variable.

sales	−	$600	=	$400
	+	$600	+	$600
sales			=	$1,000

Order of Operations

The order of operations is a set of rules stating which operations in an equation are performed first. The order of operations is often stated using the acronym *PEMDAS*. PEMDAS stands for parentheses, exponents, multiplication and division, and addition and subtraction. This means anything inside parentheses is computed first. Exponents are computed next. Then, any multiplication and division operations are computed. Finally, any addition and subtraction operations are computed to find the final answer to the problem. The equation is solved from left to right by applying PEMDAS.

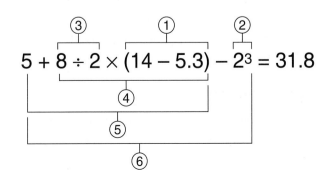

$$5 + 8 \div 2 \times (14 - 5.3) - 2^3 = 31.8$$

Recursive Formulas

A *recursive formula* is used to determine the next term of a sequence, using one or more of the preceding terms. The terms of a sequence are often expressed with a variable and subscript. For example, a sequence might be written as a_1, a_2, a_3, a_4, a_5, and so on. The subscript is essentially the place in line for each term. A recursive formula has two parts. The first is a starting point or seed value (a_1). The second is an equation for another number in the sequence (a_n). The second part of the formula is a function of the prior term (a_{n-1}).

Example

Suppose you buy a car for $10,000. Assume the car declines in value 10% each year. In the second year, the car will be worth 90% of $10,000, which is $9,000. The following year it will be worth 90% of $9,000, which is $8,100. What will the car be worth in the fifth year? Use the following recursive equation to find the answer.

$$a_n = a_{n-1} \times 0.90$$

where $a_1 = \$10,000$

a_n = value of car in the nth year

Year	Value of Car
n = 1	$a_1 = \$10,000$
n = 2	$a_2 = a_{2-1} \times 0.90 = a_1 \times 0.90 = \$10,000 \times 0.90 = \$9,000$
n = 3	$a_3 = a_{3-1} \times 0.90 = a_2 \times 0.90 = \$9,000 \times 0.90 = \$8,100$
n = 4	$a_4 = a_{4-1} \times 0.90 = a_3 \times 0.90 = \$8,100 \times 0.90 = \$7,290$
n = 5	$a_5 = a_{5-1} \times 0.90 = a_4 \times 0.90 = \$7,290 \times 0.90 = \$6,561$

Geometry

Geometry is a field of mathematics that deals with shapes, such as circles and polygons. A *polygon* is any shape whose sides are straight. Every polygon has three or more sides.

Parallelograms

A *parallelogram* is a four-sided figure with two pairs of parallel sides. A *rectangle* is a type of parallelogram with four right angles. A *square* is a special type of parallelogram with four right angles (90 degrees) and four equal sides.

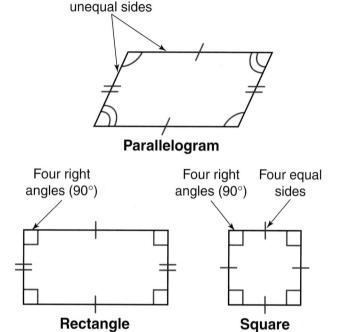

Two pairs of unequal sides

Parallelogram

Four right angles (90°)

Rectangle

Four right angles (90°)   Four equal sides

Square

Example

Real-life examples of squares include ceramic floor and wall tiles, and each side of a die. Real-life examples of a rectangle include a football field, pool table, and most doors.

Circles and Half Circles

A *circle* is a figure in which every point is the same distance from the center. The distance from the center to a point on the circle is called the *radius*. The distance across the circle through the center is the *diameter*. A half circle is formed by dividing a whole circle along the diameter.

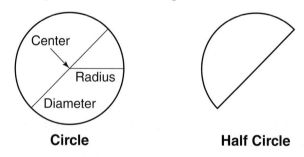

Center

Radius

Diameter

Circle   **Half Circle**

Example

Real-life examples of circles include wheels of all sizes.

Triangles

A three-sided polygon is called a *triangle*. The following are four types of triangles, which are classified according to their sides and angles.

- *Equilateral:* Three equal sides and three equal angles.
- *Isosceles:* Two equal sides and two equal angles.
- *Scalene:* Three unequal sides and three unequal angles.
- *Right:* One right angle; may be isosceles or scalene.

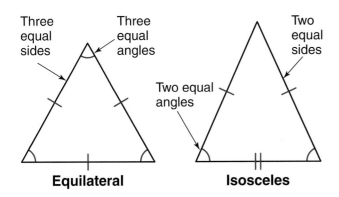

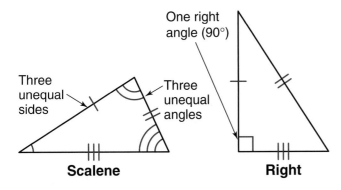

> **Example**
> Real-life examples of equilateral triangles are the sides of a classical Egyptian pyramid.

Perimeter

A *perimeter* is a measure of length around a figure. Add the length of each side to measure the perimeter of any figure whose sides are all line segments, such as a parallelogram or triangle. The perimeter of a circle is called the *circumference*. To measure the perimeter, multiply the diameter by pi (π). Pi is approximately equal to 3.14. The following formulas can be used to calculate the perimeters of various figures.

Figure	Perimeter
parallelogram	2 × width + 2 × length
square	4 × side
rectangle	2 × width + 2 × length
triangle	side + side + side
circle	π × diameter

> **Example**
> A professional basketball court is a rectangle 94 feet long and 50 feet wide. The perimeter of the court is calculated as follows.
>
> 2 × 94 feet + 2 × 50 feet = 288 feet

> **Example**
> A tractor tire has a 43-inch diameter. The circumference of the tire is calculated as follows.
>
> 43 inches × 3.14 = 135 inches

Area

Area is a measure of the amount of surface within the perimeter of a flat figure. Area is measured in square units, such as square inches, square feet, or square miles. The areas of the following figures are calculated using the corresponding formulas.

Figure	Area
parallelogram	base × height
square	side × side
rectangle	length × width
triangle	1/2 × base × height
circle	π × radius^2 = π × radius × radius

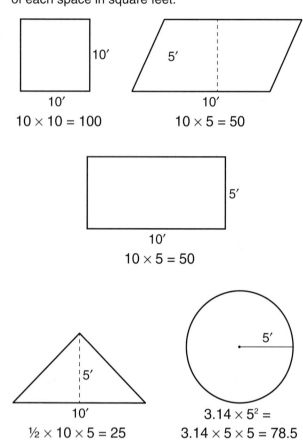

Example
An interior designer needs to order decorative tiles to fill the following spaces. Measure the area of each space in square feet.

10′
10′
$10 \times 10 = 100$

5′
10′
$10 \times 5 = 50$

5′
10′
$10 \times 5 = 50$

5′
10′
$\frac{1}{2} \times 10 \times 5 = 25$

5′
$3.14 \times 5^2 =$
$3.14 \times 5 \times 5 = 78.5$

Surface Area

Surface area is the total area of the surface of a figure occupying three-dimensional space, such as a cube or prism. A *cube* is a solid figure that has six identical square faces. A *prism* has bases or ends which have the same size and shape and are parallel to each other, and each of whose sides is a parallelogram. The following are the formulas to find the surface area of a cube and a prism.

Object	Surface Area
cube	$6 \times side \times side$
prism	$2 \times [(length \times width) + (width \times height) + (length \times height)]$

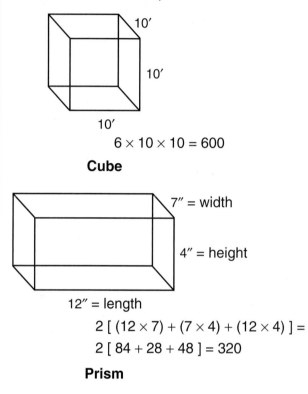

Example
A manufacturer of cardboard boxes wants to determine how much cardboard is needed to make the following size boxes. Calculate the surface area of each in square inches.

10′
10′
10′
$6 \times 10 \times 10 = 600$
Cube

7″ = width
4″ = height
12″ = length
$2 [(12 \times 7) + (7 \times 4) + (12 \times 4)] =$
$2 [84 + 28 + 48] = 320$
Prism

Volume

Volume is the three-dimensional space occupied by a figure and is measured in cubic units, such as cubic inches or cubic feet. The volumes of the following figures are calculated using the corresponding formulas.

Solid Figure	Volume
cube	$side^3 = side \times side \times side$
prism	$length \times width \times height$
cylinder	$\pi \times radius^2 \times height = \pi \times radius \times radius \times height$
sphere	$4/3 \times \pi \times radius^3 = 4/3 \times \pi \times radius \times radius \times radius$

Find the volume of packing material needed to fill the following boxes. Measure the volume of each in cubic inches.

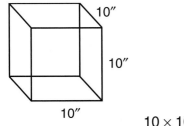

10″
10″
10″

$$10 \times 10 \times 10 = 1000$$

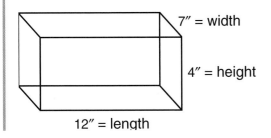

7″ = width

4″ = height

12″ = length

Example
Find the volume of grain that will fill the following cylindrical silo. Measure the volume in cubic feet.

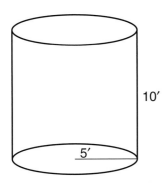

10′

5′

$$3.14 \times 5 \times 5 \times 10 = 785$$

Example
A manufacturer of pool toys wants to stuff soft material into a ball with a 3-inch radius. Find the cubic inches of material that will fit into the ball.

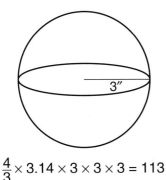

3″

$$\frac{4}{3} \times 3.14 \times 3 \times 3 \times 3 = 113$$

Data Analysis and Statistics

Graphs are used to illustrate data in a picture-like format. It is often easier to understand data when they are shown in a graphical form instead of a numerical form in a table. Common types of graphs are bar graphs, line graphs, and circle graphs.

A *bar graph* organizes information along a vertical axis and horizontal axis. The vertical axis runs up and down one side; the horizontal axis runs along the bottom.

A *line graph* also organizes information on vertical and horizontal axes; however, data are graphed as a continuous line rather than a set of bars. Line graphs are often used to show trends over a period of time.

A *circle graph* looks like a divided circle and shows how a whole object is cut up into parts. Circle graphs are also called *pie charts* and are often used to illustrate percentages.

Example
A business shows the following balances in its cash account for the months of March through July. These data are illustrated below in bar and line graphs.

Month	Account Balance	Month	Account Balance
March	$400	June	$800
April	$600	July	$900
May	$500		

Account Balance

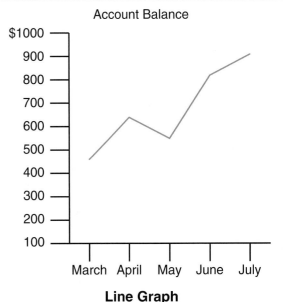

Line Graph

Example
A business lists the percentage of its expenses in the following categories. These data are displayed in the following circle graph.

Expenses	Percentage
Cost of goods	25
Salaries	25
Rent	21
Utilities	17
Advertising	12

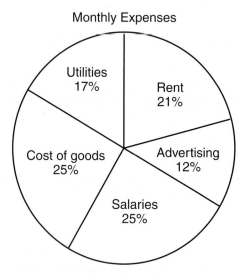

Monthly Expenses

Circle Graph

Math Models for Business and Retail

Math skills used in business and retail are the same math skills required in everyday life. The ability to add, subtract, multiply, and divide different types of numbers is very important. However, this type of math is often focused on prices, taxes, profits, and losses.

Markup

Markup is a retailing term for the amount by which price exceeds the cost. One way to express markup is in dollars. Another way to express markup is percentage. The *markup percentage* is the amount of the markup as a percentage of the cost.

Example
A retailer pays $4 for a pair of athletic socks and prices them for sale at $7. The dollar markup is $3.

selling price − cost = dollar markup

$7 − $4 = $3

Example
A pair of athletic socks, which cost $4, is priced at $7. The dollar markup is $3 . To find the markup percentage, divide $3 by $4. The markup percentage is 75%.

markup dollars ÷ cost = markup percentage

$3 ÷ $4 = 0.75 = 75%

Percentage Markup to Determine Selling Price

The selling price of an item can be determined if you know the markup percentage and the cost. First, convert the markup percentage to a decimal. Next multiply the cost by the decimal. Then, add the markup dollars to the cost to determine the selling price. Another way to find the selling price is to convert the markup percentage to a decimal and add 1.0. Then multiply this amount by the cost.

Example
A pair of athletic socks costs $4, which the retailer marks up by 75%. Find the selling price.
1. Convert the markup percentage to a decimal.

75% = 0.75
2. Multiply the cost by the markup.

cost × markup = dollar markup

$4 × 0.75 = $3
3. Add the $3 markup to the $4 cost to find the selling price. The selling price is $7.

$4 + $3 = $7

A pair of athletic socks costs $4, which the retailer marks up by 75%. Find the selling price.

1. Convert the 75% markup percentage to 0.75 and add 1.0.

$$0.75 + 1.0 = 1.75$$

2. Multiply 1.75 by the $4 cost to find the selling price.

$$\$4 \times 1.75 = \$7$$

Markdown

A *markdown* is the amount by which the selling price of an item is reduced. Sometimes a markdown is also called a *discount*. To find the amount of a markdown, subtract the new or discounted price from the original price. A markdown can also be expressed as a percentage of the original price. Sometimes this is called a *percentage discount*.

A package of meat at a supermarket is originally priced at $10. However, the meat has not sold and is nearing its expiration date. The supermarket wants to sell it quickly, so it reduces the price to $6. This is a markdown of $4.

selling price – discounted price = dollar markdown

$$\$10 - \$6 = \$4$$

A package of meat at a supermarket is originally priced at $10. However, the meat has not sold and is nearing its expiration date. The supermarket wants to sell it quickly, so it marks down the price by $4. The markdown percentage is determined by dividing the $4 markdown by the original $10 price.

markdown ÷ selling price = markdown percentage

$$\$4 \div \$10 = 40\%$$

Gross Profit

Gross profit is a company's net sales minus the cost of goods sold. *Gross margin* is often expressed as a percentage of revenue.

A wristband manufacturer generated net sales of $100,000 last year. The cost of goods sold for the wristbands was $30,000. The net sales of $100,000 minus the $30,000 cost of goods sold leaves a gross profit of $70,000.

net sales – cost of goods sold = gross profit

$$\$100,000 - \$30,000 = \$70,000$$

The gross profit of $70,000 divided by the net sales of $100,000 is 0.70, or 70%.

gross profit ÷ net sales = gross margin percentage

$$\$70,000 \div \$100,000 = 0.70 = 70\%$$

Net Income or Loss

Net income or loss is a company's revenue after total expenses are deducted from gross profit. Total expenses include marketing, administration, interest, and taxes. A company earns a *net income* when gross profit exceeds expenses. A *net loss* is incurred when expenses exceed gross profit.

A wristband manufacturer had a gross profit of $70,000. In addition, expenses for marketing, administration, interest, and taxes were $50,000. Net profit is calculated by subtracting the total expenses of $50,000 from the gross profit of $70,000. The net profit was $20,000.

gross profit on sales – total expenses = net income or loss

$$\$70,000 - \$50,000 = \$20,000$$

Break-Even Point

A *break-even point* is the number of units a company must sell to cover its costs and expenses and earn a zero profit. Use the following formula to find a company's break-even point.

total costs ÷ selling price = break-even point

Sales Tax

Sales tax is a tax collected on the selling price of a good or service. The sales tax rate is usually expressed as a percentage of the selling price. Sales tax is calculated by multiplying the sale price by the tax rate.

Example

Suppose you buy a T-shirt for $10.00. How much is the sales tax if the tax rate is 5%? Convert 5% to a decimal (.05) and multiply it by the sale price.

sale price × sales tax rate percentage = sales tax

$$\$10 \times 0.05 = \$0.50$$

Return on Investment

Return on investment (ROI) is a calculation of a company's net profit as a percentage of the owner's investment. One way to determine ROI is to divide net profit by the owner's investment.

Example

Suppose you start a dry-cleaning business with a $100,000 investment, and you earn a $20,000 net profit during the first year. Divide $20,000 by $100,000, which equals a 20% return on your investment.

net income ÷ owner's investment = return on investment (ROI)

$$\$20,000 \div \$100,000 = 0.20 = 20\%$$

APPENDIX B
PUNCTUATION, CAPITALIZATION, AND NUMBER EXPRESSION

Terminal Punctuation

In writing, **punctuation** consists of marks used to show the structure of sentences. Punctuation marks used at the end of a sentence are called *terminal punctuation*. Terminal punctuation marks include periods, question marks, and exclamation points.

Periods

A **period** is a punctuation mark used at the end of a declarative sentence. A *declarative sentence* is one that makes a statement. A period signals to the reader that the expressed thought has ended.

The final exam will be on May 26.

Alma traveled to Lexington to visit her friend.

A period can be used within a quotation. A period should be placed inside a quotation that completes a statement. If a sentence contains a quotation that does not complete the thought, the period should be placed at the end of the sentence, not the end of the quote.

Jacobi said, "The project is on schedule."

She told me, "Do not let anyone through this door," and she meant it.

Question Marks

A **question mark** is punctuation used at the end of an interrogative sentence. An *interrogative sentence* is one that asks a question. A question mark can be used after a word or sentence that expresses strong emotion, such as shock or doubt.

Will the plane arrive on time?

What? Are you serious?

A question mark can be part of a sentence that contains a quotation. Place the question mark inside the quotation marks when the quote asks a question. Place the question mark outside the quotation marks if the entire sentence asks a question.

Teresa asked, "Will the work be finished soon?"

Did he say, "The sale will end on Friday"?

Exclamation Points

An **exclamation point** is a punctuation mark used to express strong emotion. Exclamation points are used at the end of a sentence or after an interjection that stands alone. An exclamation point can be used at the end of a question rather than a question mark, if the writer wishes to show strong emotion.

Ouch! Stop hurting me!

Will you ever grow up!

As with other terminal punctuation, an exclamation point can be part of a sentence that contains a quotation. Place the exclamation point inside the quotation marks when the quote expresses the strong emotion. Place the exclamation point outside the quotation marks if the entire sentence expresses the strong emotion.

All of the students shouted, "Hooray!"

She said, "You are disqualified"!

Internal Punctuation

Punctuation marks used within a sentence are called **internal punctuation**. These marks include commas, dashes, parentheses, semicolons, colons, apostrophes, hyphens, and quotation marks.

Commas

A **comma** is a punctuation mark used to separate elements in a sentence. Commas are used to separate items in a series.

Apple, pears, or grapes will be on the menu.

A comma is used before a coordinating conjunction that joins two independent clauses.

The sun rose, and the birds began to sing.

Commas are used to separate a nonrestrictive explanatory word or phrase from the rest of the sentence.

Gloria's husband, Jorge, drove the car.

Yes, I will attend the meeting.

A comma is placed before and after an adverb, such as *however* or *indeed*, when it comes in the middle of a sentence.

Preparing a delicious meal, however, requires using fresh ingredients.

When an adjective phrase contains coordinate adjectives, use commas to separate the coordinate adjectives. The comma takes the place of the word *and*.

The long, hot summer was finally over.

Commas are used to separate words used in direct address. The words can be proper nouns, the pronoun *you*, or common nouns.

Quon, please answer the next question.

Everyone, please sit down.

Commas are used to separate elements in dates and addresses. When a date is expressed in the month-day-year format, commas are used to separate the year.

On December 7, 1941, Japan attacked Pearl Harbor.

When only the month and year or a holiday and year are used, a comma is not needed.

In January 2010 she retired from her job.

A comma is used after the street address and after the city when an address or location appears in general text.

Mail the item to 123 Maple Drive, Columbus, OH 43085.

A comma is used to introduce a quotation.

The speaker attempted to energize the workers by saying, "The only limits are those we put on ourselves."

Dashes and Parentheses

A **dash** is a punctuation mark that separates elements in a sentence or signals an abrupt change in thought. There are two types of dashes: *em dash* and *en dash*. The em dash can be used to replace commas or parentheses to emphasize or set off text. To give emphasis to a break in thought, use an em dash.

My history teacher—an avid reader—visits the library every week.

The en dash is used as a span or range of numbers, dates, or time.

We won the baseball game 6–3.

Barack Obama served as President of the United States from 2009–2017.

Parentheses are punctuation marks used to enclose words or phrases that clarify meaning or give added information. Place a period that comes at the end of a sentence inside the parentheses only when the entire sentence is enclosed in parentheses.

Deliver the materials to the meeting site (the Polluck Building).

Use parentheses to enclose numbers or letters in a list that is part of a sentence.

Revise the sentences to correct errors in (1) spelling, (2) punctuation, and (3) capitalization.

Semicolons, Colons, and Apostrophes

A **semicolon** is an internal punctuation mark used to separate independent clauses that are similar in thought. A semicolon can also be used to separate items in a series. Typically, items in a series are separated with commas, but if the serial items include commas, a semicolon should be used to avoid confusion.

Twelve students took the test; two students passed.

We mailed packages to Anchorage, AK; Houston, TX; and Bangor, ME.

A **colon** is an internal punctuation mark that introduces an element in a sentence or paragraph.

The bag contains three items: a book, a pencil, and an apple.

A colon is also used after a phrase, clause, or sentence that introduces a vertical list.

> Follow these steps:

An **apostrophe** is a punctuation mark used to form possessive words. It is most commonly used in conjunction with the letter *s* to show possession. Position of the apostrophe depends on whether the noun is singular or plural. If singular, place the apostrophe between the noun and the *s*. If plural, place the apostrophe after the *s*.

> Akeno's dress was red.
>
> The students' books were to be put away before the exam.

A **contraction** is a shortened form of a word or term. It is formed by omitting letters from one or more words and replacing them with an apostrophe to create one word—the contraction. An example of a contraction is *it's* for *it is*.

Apostrophes can also be used to indicate that numbers or letters are omitted from words for brevity or writing style.

> Leisure suits were in style in the '60s. (1960s)
>
> The candidates will meet to discuss activities of the gov't. (government)

Hyphens

A **hyphen** is a punctuation mark used to separate parts of compound words, numbers, or ranges. Compound words that always have a hyphen are called **permanent compounds**.

Some adverbs, such as *on-the-job*, always have hyphens.

> The close-up was blurry.
>
> My mother-in-law made dinner.
>
> Their orientation includes on-the-job training.

Compound adjectives have hyphens when they come before the words they modify, but not when they come after them.

> The well-done pot roast was delicious.
>
> The delicious pot roast was well done.
>
> These out-of-date books should be thrown away.
>
> Throw away the books that are out of date.

In some words that have prefixes, a hyphen is used between the prefix and the rest of the word.

> My ex-wife has custody of our children.

When a word is divided at the end of a line of text, a hyphen is used between parts of the word.

> Carter ran down the hall-
> way to answer the door.

Quotation Marks

Quotation marks are used to enclose short, direct quotations and titles of some artistic or written works.

> "Which color do you want," he asked.
>
> "The Raven" is a poem written by Edgar Allan Poe.

A quotation need not be a complete sentence; it can be a word or a phrase as spoken or written by someone. See the examples that follow.

> When the mayor refers to "charitable giving," does that include gifts to all nonprofit organizations?

When writing dialogue, the words of each speaker are enclosed in quotation marks with the appropriate punctuation mark.

> Anna arrived at the office and greeted her coworker, Joan. "Good morning. You're getting an early start today."

Chapter or section titles within complete books, movies, or other artistic work are typically shown in quotation marks. The full title of the work is typically italicized.

> "Books and Journals" is the first chapter in The Chicago Manual of Style.

Quotation marks are used to enclose words that are meant to show irony.

> Although Connie had the afternoon off, she was too "busy" to help me.
>
> In a survey of small businesses, one in five managers said their companies are "sinking ships."

Capitalization

Capitalization is writing a letter in uppercase (B) rather than lowercase (b). Capital letters signal the beginning of a new sentence and identify important words in titles and headings. Capital letters are also used for proper nouns, for some abbreviations, in personal and professional titles, and for parts of business letters.

A sentence begins with a capital letter. Numbers that begin a sentence should be spelled as words, and the first word should be capitalized.

> Thirty-three students took part in the graduation ceremony.

Capitalize the first, last, and all important words in a heading or title.

> *Gone with the Wind*
>
> *The Adventure of the Hansom Cabs*

For numbers with hyphens in a heading or title, capitalize both words.

> *Twenty-One Candles*

Do not capitalize articles or prepositions within a heading or title unless it is the first word in the title.

> *The Finest Story in the World*

When a title and subtitle are written together, only the first word of the subtitle is capitalized regardless of the part of speech.

> *Presidential Priorities: College's 10th president outlines three campus goals*

Do not capitalize coordinating conjunctions (*yet*, *and*, *but*, *for*, *or*, and *nor*) in a heading or title.

> *Pride and Prejudice*
>
> *Never Marry but for Love*

Do not capitalize parts of names that normally appear in lowercase (Ludwig van Beethoven).

> His favorite composer is Ludwig van Beethoven.

Capitalize the first word in the salutation for a letter.

> Dear Mrs. Stockton:

Capitalize the first word in the complimentary close for a letter.

> Sincerely yours,

Proper nouns begin with a capital letter. Recall that a proper noun is a word that identifies a specific person, place, or thing.

> Joe Wong is the principal of George Rogers Clark High School.

Capitalize initials used in place of names.

> UCLA won the football game.

Capitalize abbreviations that are made up of the first letters of words.

> HTML stands for hypertext markup language.

Months and days, as well as their abbreviations, should be capitalized.

> Mon. is the abbreviation for Monday.

Abbreviations for names of states and countries should be capitalized.

> The price is given in US dollars.

Capitalize abbreviations for directional terms and location terms in street addresses.

> She lives at 123 NW Cedar Ave.

Capitalize call letters of a broadcasting company.

> My favorite television show is on CBS.

Abbreviations that note an era in time should be in capital letters.

> The article included a map of Europe for the year 1200 CE.

Capitalize titles that come before personal names and seniority titles after names.

> Sen. Carl Rogers called Mr. Juarez and Dr. Wang.
>
> Mr. Thomas O'Malley, Jr., spoke at the ceremony.

Capitalize abbreviations for academic degrees and other professional designations that follow names.

> Jane Patel, LPN, was on duty at the hospital.

Number Expression

Numbers can be expressed as figures or as words. In some cases, as in legal documents and on bank checks, numbers are written in both figures and words. When the two expressions of a number do not agree, readers are alerted to ask for clarification.

Number expression guidelines are not as widely agreed upon as rules for punctuation and capitalization. Follow the guidelines in this section for general writing. If you are writing a research report or an article for a particular group or publication, ask whether there are number expression guidelines you should follow for that item.

Numbers Expressed as Words

In general writing, use words for numbers one through nine.

One dog and three cats sat on the porch.

Use figures for numbers 10 and greater. (See other style guides for exceptions to this guideline.)

She placed an order for 125 blue ink pens.

When some numbers in a sentence are 9 or less and some are 10 or greater, write all the numbers as figures.

The box contains 5 books, 10 folders, and 15 pads of paper.

Use words for numbers that are indefinite or approximate amounts.

About fifty people signed the petition.

Use words for numbers one through nine followed by *million*, *billion,* and so forth. For numbers 10 or greater followed by *million*, *billion,* and so forth, use a figure and the word.

Two million people live in this region.
By 2016, the population of the United States had grown to over 300 million.

When a number begins a sentence, use words instead of figures. If the number is long when written as words, consider revising the sentence so it does not begin with a number.

Twenty copies of the report were prepared.

When two numbers come together in a sentence, use words for one of the numbers.

On the bus, there were 15 ten-year-olds.

Use words for numbers with *o'clock* to express time.

Come to my house for lunch at eleven o'clock.

Use figures with *a.m.* and *p.m.* to express time.
The assembly will begin at 9:30 a.m.

To express amounts of money, use figures with a currency sign.

The total amount is $18,395.40.

Do not use a decimal and two zeros when all dollar amounts in a sentence are whole amounts.

The charges were $5, $312, and $89.

For an isolated amount less than $1, use figures and the word *cents*.

Buy a cup of lemonade for 75 cents.

When an amount less than $1 appears with other amounts greater than $1, use figures and dollar signs for all of the numbers.

The prices were $12.50, $0.89, and $12.45.

For a large, even dollar amount, use the dollar sign, a figure, and a word, such as *million* or *billion*.

The profits for last year were $5 million.

Days and years in dates should be identified with figures.

On February 19, 2015, the court was not in session.

Use words for fractions. Note that a hyphen is placed between the words.

Place one-half of the mixture in the pan.

Use figures for mixed numbers (a whole number and a fraction).

I bought 3 1/2 yards of red fabric.

When writing a number with decimals, use figures.

The measurements are 1.358 and 0.878.

Use figures in measurements, such as distance, weight, and percentages.

We drove 258 miles today.
The winning pumpkin weighs 50 pounds.
Sales have increased 20 percent in the last year.

Pages, chapters, figures, or parts in a book should be referenced with figures.

Open your book to chapter 3, page 125.
Refer to figure 6 on page 72 for an example.

INDEX